Modernism's Metronome

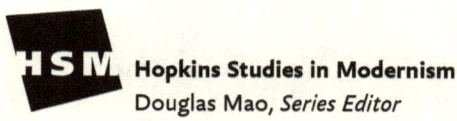

Hopkins Studies in Modernism
Douglas Mao, *Series Editor*

Modernism's Metronome

Meter and Twentieth-Century Poetics

Ben Glaser

Johns Hopkins University Press
Baltimore

© 2020 Johns Hopkins University Press
All rights reserved. Published 2020
Printed in the United States of America on acid-free paper
9 8 7 6 5 4 3 2 1

Johns Hopkins University Press
2715 North Charles Street
Baltimore, Maryland 21218-4363
www.press.jhu.edu

Library of Congress Cataloging-in-Publication Data

Names: Glaser, Ben, author.
Title: Modernism's metronome : meter and twentieth-century poetics / Ben Glaser.
Description: Baltimore : Johns Hopkins University Press, 2020. | Series: Hopkins studies in modernism | Includes bibliographical references and index.
Identifiers: LCCN 2020011217 | ISBN 9781421439518 (hardcover ; acid-free paper) | ISBN 9781421439525 (paperback ; acid-free paper) | ISBN 9781421439532 (ebook)
Subjects: LCSH: Modernism (Literature)—United States. | American poetry—20th century—History and criticism. | Modernism (Literature)—Great Britain. | English poetry—20th century—History and criticism. | Poetics—History—20th century. | English language—Versification. | Rhythm in literature.
Classification: LCC PS310.M57 G57 2020 | DDC 811/.509112—dc23
LC record available at https://lccn.loc.gov/2020011217

A catalog record for this book is available from the British Library.

Special discounts are available for bulk purchases of this book. For more information, please contact Special Sales at specialsales@press.jhu.edu.

Johns Hopkins University Press uses environmentally friendly book materials, including recycled text paper that is composed of at least 30 percent post-consumer waste, whenever possible.

Contents

Acknowledgments vii

Introduction 1
The "Metronome" 6
Meter and Modern Aurality 14
Meter as Vestige 21

1 **Modernist Scansion: Robert Frost's Distorted Vernacular** 30
Frost's Theory of Meter and Practice of Scansion 33
The "Hen Dekker Syllables" of "For Once, Then, Something" 44
The Late Meter of "Directive" 53

2 **Penty Ladies: T. S. Eliot, Satire, and the Gender of Modern Meter** 56
"Too Penty" Ladies 60
Meter after Satire: *The Waste Land* 67
Formal Sensibility for a Post-metrical Culture 75

3 **"No Feet to Walk On": Pound's Late Victorian Prosody** 81
Late Victorian Pound 82
"Anima" Meter: Bare-Foot and Stub-Toed 87
The Riposte against Meter 92
Pan, Syrinx, and Sappho: Pound's Editorial Control and H.D.'s *HERmione* 98

**4 Metristes: Formal Feeling in Sara Teasdale,
    Georgia Douglas Johnson, and Louise Bogan** 107
  Sara Teasdale and the Labor of the Line 111
  Georgia Douglas Johnson's Metrical Bars 114
  Louise Bogan's Precise Pentagon 123

**5 The Prosody of Passing: Jean Toomer and
    James Weldon Johnson** 135
  Spirituals after the Victrola 138
  Cane as Collection 144
  Kabnis's Unheard Blues 152
  James Weldon Johnson: Re-scanning the
    Anglo-American Tradition 156
  Rhythmic Exegesis 167

**6 Folk Iambics: Sterling Brown's *Outline for the Study
    of the Poetry of American Negroes*** 181
  "Black" Rhythm's Double Audience 182
  Brown's *Outline* and Johnson's *Book of American Negro
    Poetry* 188
  "When de Saints Go Ma'ching Home" 192

Conclusion. Prosody after Form 207

Appendix. Scansion and Metrical Notation 219
Notes 225
Works Cited 259
Index 281

Acknowledgments

This project began in graduate school at Cornell University, a decidedly encouraging place to pursue my interests in meter, poetics, and theories of genre. For my sense of the linguistic richness of poetry and the value of generative approaches, I am indebted to John Bowers. Debra Fried's unparalleled feeling for prosodic form and poetics across many periods was always humbling and provocative. Roger Gilbert helped me map out twentieth-century poetry, and Jeremy Braddock introduced me to modernist studies and its diverse perspectives on poetry and its institutions. Jonathan Culler, my chair, has been a steadfast supporter for fifteen years, sharing work, coediting an essay collection, and honing my style and argumentation.

I owe my sense of academia at its best to an exceptional graduate community. For our ongoing conversations about life and work, my thanks to Alexis Briley, Becky Colesworthy, Bradley Depew, Sean Franzel, Adam Grener, John Hicks, Aaron Hodges, Rob Lehman, Alex Papanicolopoulos, Seth Perlow, Sarah Pickle, Danielle St. Hilaire, Sarah Senk, Robin Sowards, Cecily Swanson, and Audrey Wasser. My thinking about poetry is filled with the memory of Alan Young-Bryant, one of my first and best friends at Cornell. I treasure our time together.

This book began and finished with the wonderful hospitality of Sarah and Justin Harlan-Haughey. It progressed during my time at Skidmore College thanks to my generous chair, Mason Stokes, and with the excellent company of Steven Millhauser, Steve Stern, Rachael Nichols, and Scott Enderle.

Yale has afforded me the necessary time, collegial environment, and financial assistance for this project. I want to first thank my junior colleagues for their consistent geniality: Tasha Eccles, Marta Figlerowicz, Alanna Hickey, Cajetan Iheka, Priyasha Mukhopadhyay, Joe North, Jill Richards, and Sunny Xiang. The Poetics Working Group—with past and present members including Michael Abraham, Greg Ellerman, Clay Greene, Tim Kreiner, Chelsie Malyszek, Jessie Modi, Lukas Moe, Tessie Prakas, Justin Sider, and my current co-organizers, Naomi Levine and Lacey Jones—has been my favorite place to think alongside colleagues and graduate students. I've learned a tremendous amount from reading brilliant dissertations on poetics by Edgar Garcia, Rebecca Rush, Josh Stanley, and Eric Weiskott. My thanks to Jordan Brower and Paul Franz for ongoing conversations about our discipline and poetry, and to Kassidi Jones for fact checking my work on Georgia Douglas Johnson. The amazing participants in my graduate seminars on historical poetics and modernism provided me the opportunity to test and refine my theories of modern poetics and contemporary methods. I have benefitted immensely from the formal and informal mentorship of Ardis Butterfield, Langdon Hammer, and my current chair, Jessica Brantley. For long conversations about poetic form, I thank my former Yale colleagues Ian Cornelius and Anthony Reed. I relish both past and future opportunities to think with Leslie Brisman, David Bromwich, Paul Fry, Jacqueline Goldsby, David Kastan, R. John Williams, Stefanie Markovits, Stephanie Newell, Cathy Nicholson, John Durham Peters, Emily Thornbury, and Caleb Smith. Outside the English Department, I have been glad for discussions of family and work with Marijeta Bojovic, Robyn Creswell, Robin Dembroff, Dan Greco, Pauline LeVen, Meghan O'Rourke, Dixa Ramirez, and Anna Zaruznaya.

The individual chapters of this book developed in diverse colloquia, panels, and conferences. I thank Jason David Hall and the organizers of "Metre Matters," a fantastic 2008 conference at Exeter (UK) for showing me early on how rich the field of prosody could be. My gratitude to Dorothy Wang for an invitation to speak at Williams College about my Frost materials and to share my ideas about Sterling Brown with students; to Lauren Kimball, Meredith McGill, Nick Gaskill, and the Rutgers poetics group for discussing a very early version of chapter 4; to Brian Kane, J. D. Connor, and the Sound Studies Working Group at Yale for an invitations to share work in progress; to the same and Yale's Whitney Humanities Center for joining me in co-organizing a multiday interdisciplinary symposium on techniques of listening; to Natalie Gerber, David Nowell Smith, Ewan Jones, Tom Cable, and Peter Elbow for having me join a discussion of rhythm and intonation at UMass Amherst; to Carmel Raz, Rick Cohn, and Roger Grant for inviting me to present a workshop at the Max Planck Institute for Empirical Aesthetics in Frankfurt; and to the many panel organizers, coparticipants, and visitors of Yale's poetics working group, including Max Cavitch, Harris Feinsod,

Acknowledgments

Ryan Heuser, Walt Hunter, Erin Kappeler, Noelle Morrissette, and Justin Tackett, who have sustained a growing conversation about modern poetics and prosody.

I received crucial financial and research assistance from Yale's Morse Fellowship, the Whitney Humanities Center's Griswold Research and Hilles Publication Funds, and the dean of the Faculty of Arts and Sciences for funding a colloquium to develop my manuscript. I am grateful to the research librarians and staff at the Huntington Library, the Harry Ransom Center at the University of Texas at Austin, Yale's Beinecke and Sterling Libraries, and the University of Chicago's Special Collections Research Center, which also granted me a Robert L. Platzman Fellowship. I feel a special obligation to T. V. F. Brogan for his lifelong work producing an annotated bibliography of *thousands* of prosodic documents, and to the Princeton Prosody Archive for extending that work and giving it a beautiful online presence.

My scholarly life and work began in Jennie Jackson's undergraduate courses in popular poetry and lyric theory, grew with her guidance of a sprawling honors thesis on James Merrill's *Changing Light at Sandover*, and continue thanks to more than a decade and a half of her support and intellectual provocations. She inspires me to reimagine the field not just in my writing but in my own teaching and mentorship. In graduate school I read Yopie Prins's work, then met her, and have benefited from her generosity and brilliance ever since. Neither my career nor this book would be possible without Meredith Martin's investments in historical prosody and in me; the breadth of her knowledge, sense of method, and drive are constant inspirations.

Many readers directed the development of the manuscript, especially James Longenbach, Aldon Nielsen, my generous and thorough press reviewers, and my incredibly supportive series editor Doug Mao. My editor, Catherine Goldstead, is a model of responsiveness and clarity. My copy editor, Carrie Watterson, dealt magisterially with varying systems of scansion and my varying prose tendencies. The marketing team and cover designer let me see the book from the outside, finally, after so many years inside its covers. Thanks also to my indexer, Alexa Selph. I am deeply appreciative of the entire team at the press for substantially developing and improving this book with me.

I hope the rhythmic babbling and rhyming my research encouraged is some compensation to my little songsters, Margaret and Alan. They delight me with their hard poets' work of building language. Their caring teachers at Mishkan Israel Nursery School made it possible to finish this book. My parents, Simeon and Barbara Glaser, are responsible for my love of literature and poetic form, from their earliest rhyming and storytelling. I share that gift with my wonderful and supportive siblings Lou and Hannah. My endlessly caring in-laws, Wiley and Andrea Winders, have welcomed me into their family. The book itself is dedicated to Melissa, who has shared in every moment of its long struggle to take shape and who inspires me with her intense twin love of literature and family.

I gratefully acknowledge permission to use excerpts from the following work:

An early version of chapter 1 appeared in *ELH* 83, no. 2 (Summer 2016): 603-31. Copyright © Johns Hopkins University Press. Published with permission.

A portion of chapter 5 appeared in *New Perspectives on James Weldon Johnson's "The Autobiography of an Ex-Colored Man,"* edited by Noelle Morrissette. Copyright © 2017 University of Georgia Press. Published with permission.

An early version of chapter 6 appeared in *PMLA* 129, no. 3 (2014): 417-34, 608. Used by permission of the copyright owner, The Modern Language Association of America.

"When de Saints Go Ma'ching Home" from *The Collected Poems of Sterling A. Brown*, edited by Michael S. Harper. Copyright © 1980 by Sterling A. Brown. Reprinted by permission of Jacqueline M. Combs. First excerpt appears on page 195.

Modernism's Metronome

Introduction

> Is there another passage in literature that can number among the protagonists in its drama the meter itself?
>
> —Hugh Kenner on Ezra Pound's Canto 81 ("To break the pentameter, that was the first heave"), "Blood for the Ghosts"

Meter's afterlife in twentieth-century poetics is both unstable and inescapable. It channels a range of aesthetic pleasure, taxonomic impulses, literary-historical imaginaries, and literary-critical beliefs. For many modern poets and critics, and in the dominant story bequeathed by them, meter appears increasingly as acoustical debris clung to by sinking poets and conservative readers. Iambics in particular were reconceived as the too-easily mechanically heard and reproduced verse substrate that Pound (following F. S. Flint) famously rejected as the "sequence of a metronome" in favor of "the musical phrase."[1] This book diagnoses the disavowal of meter as a cover for modern poetry's nostalgia for earlier metrical culture, anxiety about its marginality and limited readership, and dependence on literary criticism. Meter's uncanny and ambivalent persistence make it a constant "protagonist," or tragic hero, whose charge is to critique those forms, dogmas, and institutions that would transcend a flawed metrical poetics and culture. It is what Raymond Williams calls an "actively residual (alternative or oppositional)" form, straining against the hegemonic vision of poetry and poetic tradition instilled by and on behalf of modernism.[2] I name the form of meter's persistence the metrical "vestige," a self-conscious poetics through which poets mark the limits of modern and indeed twentieth-century poetics, metrical and otherwise.

In pursuing a historical account of modern prosodic culture, this book follows studies of modernism that have increasingly questioned high modernism's "fundamental and recurrent principle [of] the self-sufficiency of the artist" and of the aesthetic object's autonomy.[3] Propping up the apparent sufficiency of Pound's "musical phrase" is the "aggressive modernist fiction [of music's] fenced-off autonomy" that requires, Josh Epstein argues, "willful deafness to the crescendoing hum of modern life."[4] Modernism's "music," usually in the form of "rhythm" and "cadence," is a late and defensive consolidation.[5] This project also builds on scholarship that finds continuity between modernists and "non-modernists" like Thomas Hardy or E. A. Robinson—poets who explore the gaps and limits of poetic expression through traditional forms.[6] Others have noted how even studies that seek to expand the canon of modernism tend to hunt for proto- or alt-modernists as part of a continued narrative of progress.[7]

Yet while modernist studies no longer treats modern poetry as a coherent set of experimental poetic practices, the decline of meter and advent of rhythm and free verse remains foremost among those addictive narratives that keep us from "know[ing] the history of the poetry of the first half of this century."[8] Observing the legacy of modernism—our long and influential association of "experimental prosody and political history" and resulting hunt for "metrical iconoclasm"—Max Cavitch has pointed criticism toward meter's encoding of a "somatic experience of lasting estrangement."[9] Cavitch rereads eighteenth- and nineteenth-century American poetry against this association, laying out a prehistory for this study: "Poetry's liberation from the shackles of meter is one of the most important non-events in late nineteenth-century literary history." His case study of Stephen Crane marks the "conventional" device of refrain as an "immanent critique of free verse as a manifestation of identity or personal freedom."[10] In this study, that critique emerges in the metrical practices and theories of poets writing at the threshold of what lyric theory has revealed to be poetry's disciplinary reimagination as autonomous lyric.[11] Offering a sustained reappraisal of one of lyric reading's most decisive formal narratives, this book exposes twentieth-century ideologies of form and genre to redefine what we think of as the modern relationship between "poetry" and "form."

The "non-event" of meter's breaking sprawls across modernism and its aftermath. It deafens us to the work of meter, to how modern poets engage meter to mark an estrangement from genre and the reading public. Where recent work in American and Victorian historical poetics, building especially on Yopie Prins's landmark *Victorian Sappho* (1999) and "Victorian Meters"

(2000) and more recently Meredith Martin's *Rise and Fall of Meter* (2012), has understood the discourse of meter as central to poetry and poetics, no full-length study of modernism has explored the persistent significance of meter in the epoch of its perceived obsolescence. Martin's work, particularly her juxtaposition of Pound's misconstrual of historical forms to Robert Bridges's anxious attempt to reestablish prosodic competency, is a rare exception to the path usually taken by modern poetry studies with respect to versification. Indeed, meter appears so rarely in recent studies of modern poetry and poetics that it is hard to know how scholars feel about it.[12]

Much of the work on meter after the emergence of free verse has occurred in a neo-formalist vein by poet-critics invested in recovering metrical techniques for use and appreciation. In *Missing Measures: Modern Poetry and the Revolt against Meter* (1990), Timothy Steele traces the modernist disdain for meter and helps mark the contingency of the rise of free verse. Recognizing that disdain for meter did not preclude its covert presence, Annie Finch's *Ghost of Meter* assiduously discovers meter "lurking behind the arras" of free verse (alluding to T. S. Eliot's famous formulation).[13] Both Steele and Finch are important touchstones, but neither theorizes meter's broad cultural presence or iconic value in assessing poetry's reception and circulation. Alan Holder rightly finds that meter's "statutes" are, for Steele, represented as "few and clear" to avoid the "whole history of confusion and controversy."[14] The latter constitutes modern poetry's substrate, not a hurdle for contemporary prosodic analysis. Before Steele and Finch, Harvey Gross surveyed the style of metrical poets in the early twentieth century, largely to show the richness of the "traditional metrical system" and how poets like Yeats happily avoided the "metronomic metrical pulse."[15] Yet recognizing the aesthetic significance of meter demands a greater sense of its horizons. At the time of Gross's writing in the 1960s, "poets compose metered verse with the faint sense that they are betraying the *Zeitgeist*."[16] This late and uncertain desire for meter is reflected in Gross's conception of the English verse tradition: "In English verse syllable-stress meters establish the normative convention. Against this convention, or against the memory of it, poets achieve distinctive prosodies."[17] We know too much about breaking convention and its distinctive results—that could mean anything from Frost's loosened iambics to Mina Loy's neo-Skeltonics or Marianne Moore's syllabics. But rebelling against the "memory" of convention is an awkward dance, as in William Meredith's "About Poetry, II: Iambic Feet Considered as Honorable Scars" (1963). Meredith allegorizes meter as a protective response to a running battle between free verse and "My wife/—the principle of order everywhere—."[18] This echoes Chris Beyers's sense that prosody forms "a battleground for competing ideologies, a constant struggle to re-allegorize the 'meaning' of form";[19] but to engage metrical convention as a scar caused by others' battles undermines prosody's "distinctiveness" in the twentieth century.

The studies cited here have the virtue of reaching—as poets did—for continuity between twentieth-century prosody and that of earlier periods. They struggle within the dominant narrative of meter's "breaking" as the achievement of a new prosody and a new life for poetry as a genre. What one finds more often is some extension of the modernist invention I adumbrate below under the sign of the "metronome": an alignment of meter, artifice, unconscious borrowing, mass culture and the commodity form, sterile femininity, a failure to inhabit the spirit of American newness, deafness to spoken (usually American rather than poetic) language, and the lack of individualized form or rhythm. For Edwin Fussell, most nineteenth- and early twentieth-century American verse, including Robert Frost's, "smack[s] of the foreign and the old."[20] Donald Davie and later Marjorie Perloff maintained that Wallace Stevens's metricality signaled a conservative lineage to the Romantic lyric.[21] Even Gross's careful defense of Stevens's prosody, attentive to its valedictory strains and "motionless sound," waits for "feelings of the heart" in "less obviously 'artificial' rhythms."[22] Efforts to hold onto deeper continuities with the metrical past show strain as well. Martin Duffell argues that modern prosody remains an "extension of individual choice that characterized Western society in the period," despite how "poetry-reading habits changed significantly" as public and private audition ceded ground to primarily visual reading.[23] It may be true that some modern poets "knew successful examples of stress-syllabic metrics, dolniks, and free verse, and felt at liberty to follow their individual preferences"—but this book suggests that "preference" or "active choice" fails to resolve a hotly debated and uncertain prosodic field.[24] Skipping over the period of meter's highest contention—roughly 1880-1920, as Martin and others have argued, allows scholars to pretend that modernists transcend the messy politics of meter.

The idea that poets "choose" their verse form or develop signature rhythms is the outcome of modern ideologies of form dovetailing with practices of lyric reading. There is little doubt, for example, among Pound scholars that he could create and we can discern a "metrical signature" from Greek patterns (a language he had limited knowledge of) or that he and Eliot "adopt natural speech rhythms."[25] Formalisms of rupture, freedom, and natural speech do not match the restrictions, entanglements, and opportunities modern poets encountered with every decision about verse form. Modern poets (including Pound and Eliot) wrote in meter out of necessity, not simple choice, to engage with and combat the literary-historical exclusions built into the reading public's prosodic expectations. Here I take inspiration from Marcellus Blount's assessment of the sonnet's political history as a "zone of entrapment and liberation": "These forms necessarily involve the Afro-American writer's participation in the larger cultural discourses that have represented race and gender as terms of 'otherness' within a battle zone for repeating and revising forms of cultural oppression." Blount builds his analysis of the sonnet from black feminist recognition of, in Mary Helen Washington's terms, "the little spaces men have allotted women."[26] As Debra Fried has shown of Edna St. Vincent Millay's sonnets, and as I discuss in chapter 4, women poets found it "necessary" to map and engage this same metrical battleground. The intervention Blount and Fried find in the sonnet tradition, which is perhaps the most recognizable vestige of the broader Anglo-American metrical tradition, is not a modernist byway—and to sideline it again is to reproduce an erasure of minority poetics.

The study of twentieth-century poetry from the perspective of its historical prosody manifests the surprising frequency and intensity with which poets reevaluated the legacies of poetic culture and poetry as cultural capital by returning to the medium of meter and diagnosing its modern function. Meter turns out to be neither "missing" nor a "ghost" but the phantom limb of a genre uncertain about its mediation and purpose in a fragmented literary and auditory culture. Meter's mercurial ability to transfer sound through existing regimes of scansion, education, and elocution haunts efforts to escape into alternate prosodies, particularly those putatively based in speech rhythm and intonation. As a 1934 survey of modern prosodic theory frames the problem, even "the most exhaustive knowledge of [English's] colloquial or prose use is not a sufficient guide to the best rendering of an English poem."[27] In 1938 C. S. Lewis diagnosed "widespread metrical ignorance" and the rise of vers libre as a "symptom [. . .] of some revolution in our whole sense of rhythm [. . .] reaching deep down into the unconscious."[28] These are late but not unusual manifestations of a still-prominent and always anxious modern prosodic criticism that culminates in what Martin describes as the Edwardian "Prosody Wars." This account, read alongside

the breadth of the Princeton Prosody Archive (1570-1923) (https://prosody
.princeton.edu/), evidences meter's central place in poetic discourse, from
philological inquiry to appearances in basic grammars and newspaper editorials well past the fin de siècle.

Although metrical practice and prosodic science often seemed, even to more "formal" or traditional poets, like a crutch or atavism, its nostalgic, ironic, and above all stubborn and widespread persistence reminds us of the uncertain pathways of poetry as it searches for phenomenal and recognizable form. Meter recalls that only willfully *less* "exhaustive knowledges" (i.e., of African American music or indigenous poetries) could convince readers they were tuned into something new and exciting or into a "poetry" now understood as a space of constant prosodic revolution. In the present study, I turn from this modern concept of poetic form and the ahistorical theorization of poetry—a confused modernist version of the (still-Romantic) "lyric"—that it sustains. I look instead to early twentieth-century metrical forms for their rich sense of political legacy, contested history, and disciplinary formation.

The "Metronome"

Although the assault on meter is not so pervasive or conclusive as has been understood, it nevertheless forms a critical pivot in the history of poetry and poetic form in the early twentieth century. It should be understood as a manufactured crisis, insofar as fluent metrical verse was still being written and experiments remained possible at least through the 1910s, but also a true crisis, insofar as the same verse might be heard or performed as metronomic. This is not a study of the popular culture of versification, though such widespread practices and theories, like the mass-cultural poetics studied by Mike Chasar, represent a healthy "surprise to poets and literary critics today who have long imagined poetry to have occupied at best a marginal place in the twentieth-century United States."[29] Nor can it recapitulate Martin's full study of the nineteenth- and early twentieth-century's "rich heritage of experiment, debate, and contested metrical discourse"; what matters most here is her charge that we read against Pound's and other modernists' "obfuscation," "misreading," and "collapse" of that heritage—a false unity built in response to the aggressive nationalizing unity of George Saintsbury's foot-based prosody and belief in the "English ear." "Between 1904 and the First World War," Martin observes, "schools promoted an increasingly abstract model for English meter and the modernist avant-garde arose to protest the metronome of similar sounding poetry that they wrongly associated with Victorian metrics."[30] Modern poets and critics orient themselves around this radical reconception of traditional metrics in which meter as such, rather than certain metronomic practices, is an atavism in need of breaking and replacing by "rhythm," free verse, and experiments in non-accentual-syllabic meters (as if these had no history).

The tendency to thump alternating syllables and to recognize verse only in that rhythm had in fact been a long-standing concern of elocutionists, one that peaked not coincidentally with the rise of Anglo-American modernism in the 1910s. Likewise, prosodists had long understood how the limits of training kept experimental meters from gaining cultural value. A generation after Longfellow wrote the hexameters of *Evangeline* (1847) and the Scandinavian-inspired *Song of Hiawatha* (1855) and Tennyson wrote his "Experiments: In Quantity" (*Enoch Arden*, 1864), prosodic criticism had come to see Victorian games of translation as, in Frost's terms, "the wrong track or at any rate on a short track."[31] The prehistory of modern experiments in quantitative meters or syllabics points at once to modernism's dangerous proximity to its Victorian other and to its dangerous distance from niche yet nevertheless public techniques of metrical play.

Throughout the individual readings in my chapters, the idea of meter as fundamentally "metronomic" is most significant as a modernist foil. It is a foundational invention of modernity in and as poetic form, one of many such doomed anti-historical efforts—a doomed and "self-destroying attitude" because, as James Longenbach puts it, "any rejection of the past turns out to be a repetition of a rejection that has already been made."[32] It served to epitomize those "mechanical tendencies" that drove Pound and others toward (among other things) primitive and orientalist concepts of "rhythmic vitality,"[33] but its rejection is as mechanical as its supposed form. Liberation from meter and Victorian prosody subtends free verse's claim, especially in America by way of Walt Whitman, to a democratic convergence of "individual, unstereotyped," and "organic rhythms."[34] Pound's command "don't chop your stuff into separate iambs" evokes the antithetical action of scansion, newly (and still) understood as either a prescription for automated versifying, pedantic finger counting, or simply a description of what is best grasped intuitively.[35] Yet the threat of "chopped" language would never belong to meter alone. *Poetry Magazine* editor Harriet Monroe writes a fairly exasperated letter to Eliot in 1934 doubting the *Cantos'* "qualities as poetry [. . .] all about Martin Van Buren and in my opinion merely choppy prose."[36]

Monroe was not Pound's ideal reader, but her judgment shows how the early attack on meter and scansion as "metronomic" would be essential as a unifying position. What begins primarily as a critique of elocution becomes the most legible response available to a deep anxiety about whether and how well readers could recognize prosodic form and, in extremis, poetry as a distinct and valuable genre.

Pound's oft-cited mantra from Canto 81, "To break the pentameter, that was the first heave," has suggested an early and decisive "break" with meter as such. Although it sounds as if Pound refers to his own efforts, or perhaps Imagism, he likely has in mind the longer tradition of Browning, Swinburne, Yeats, and diverse departures into alternate meters or challenging iambics by lesser-known figures like Charles Doughty. The development of *The Cantos* and even this particular line suggest that "pivoting the pentameter" would be a more appropriate if less catchy description. Beneath his manifesto assertion lies a metrical puzzle: the rhythm after the caesura, /xx//, is defiantly un-metronomic, hinting to the right ears at an accentual version of the Adonic pattern (long-short-short-long-long) that ends the Sapphic stanza. Ironically, quite a few critics have misremembered the dictum in order to make it more iambic. Moreover, many have treated pentameter itself as responsible for a metronomic "heave":

```
x    /    x    /    x  x    x  / x x
To break the heave of the pentameter
W    S    W    S    W  S    W  S W S
```

In my brief appendix I explain this two-layered approach to scansion, used throughout the book to indicate divergences between abstract template—W(eak) and S(trong) positions—and possible performance (the common *x* and / symbols). Perhaps critics iambicize or metrify Pound's famous phrase because they sense, correctly, how legible metrical parody was for Pound and many of his peers. Parody, Carolyn Williams has shown, is decisive in establishing modern literary genres.[37] Metrical parody is the baseline of F. S. Flint and Pound's shared Imagist dictum: "As regarding rhythm: to compose in the sequence of the musical phrase, not in sequence of a metronome."[38] The dropped article in the second clause renders it iambic in rhythm, giving readers a familiar taste alongside the contrasting triple rhythm "of the músical phráse." As I discuss in chapters 2 and 3, Eliot's and Pound's iambic parody grounds their early metrical and anti-metrical poetry.

Eliot eventually swerved toward a different vision if not practice of meter, but Pound sustained his obsessive mockery for decades.

Ford Madox Ford shared in the parody, aligning the potential for mechanical exercises of meter with the danger posed to poetry by industrial modernity. Where John Masefield and other contemporaries approved of Yeats's hypnotic reading style—"he stressed the rhythm until it almost became a chant"[39]—Ford found the hieratic style oppressive. Reflecting on his childhood experience of hearing Browning, Tennyson, and the Rossettis read, Ford writes, "They held their heads at unnatural angles and appeared to be suffering the tortures of agonizing souls. It was their voices that did that. [. . .] And it went on and on—and on! A long, rolling stream, of words no-one would ever use, to endless monotonous, polysyllabic, unchanging rhythms, in which rhymes went unmeaningly by like the telegraph posts, every fifty yards, of a railway journey."[40] "And it went on and on—and on!" mocks the iambic rhythm of metrical performance while likening it to a more general mechanization of communications and experience. Prins notes how Tennyson's mode of recitation intentionally performs "a meticulous reinscription of the meter."[41] This performance element helps explain Virginia Woolf's now-unconventional opinion that "blank verse has proved itself the most remorseless enemy of living speech."[42] The more common canard has it facilitating speaking subjects and natural language, a transhistorical defense reacting, perhaps, to celebrations of free verse and its claim to "living speech." Defenses of free verse took special effort to distinguish new prosodies from meter's metronome: Amy Lowell worried that the metronome's "inexorable tick" lingered dangerously even in performances of nonsyllabic, musically "cadenced" verse.[43] William Carlos Williams spends more than half of his introduction to a 1971 illustrated edition of Whitman's poetry attacking "The Establishment" of "Standard English Verse" from the Elizabethans on but gives only a negative example ("Lilacs") of Whitman's struggle to "outstrip the mathematicians" by adopting a term Williams explicitly "invented": "the variable foot."[44] Here, more than a half century after Pound's dictums about Imagism, the metronomic or "mathematical" idea still leverages the new prosody that readers will have to find themselves.

The problem facing defenders of a post-metrical modern poetics is that *they* had to invent meter's sequel; they too did so largely through negation. Writing in 1919, Monroe argued that limited metrical competence concealed a general incompetence in matters of verse aesthetics: "'To have read

Hiawatha in the eighth grade' [. . .] does not make a competent connoisseur, and one may not turn down the imagists because one can't scan them in finger-counted iambics."⁴⁵ Hugh Kenner, in a midcentury defense of Pound's "metric," finds it necessary to "guard [the reader] from the supposition that the essence of metric is a mechanical pattern from which dramatic deviations take place, and hence that *vers libre* is inherently lacking in leverage."⁴⁶ In this desire to adapt the sort of "leverage" detectable by binary scansion— felt as well in Kenner's adoption of "metric," the term Eliot used in 1917 to explain Pound's prosody precisely in terms of its relation to metrical patterning—we sense how scansion remained the troubled desideratum of free verse. Denis Donoghue is even less patient with scansion in juxtaposing "form," which is not "unproblematically given" and thus requires (renewed) formalist attention, to the straightforward "counting of syllables in an iambic pentameter." This is part of his broader contention about the evident inadequacy of "common forms" to the most "exacting poets," but that story about formal inadequacy boils down to frustration with formal education— an ancient concern now remedied, it seems, by narrowing and repudiating historical verse reception.⁴⁷

Leaving aside the fact that the scansion as well as performance of accentual syllabic verse is rarely an exercise in counting, even the idea that counting is "unproblematic" would strike historians of musical meter, historical prosodists, as well as linguists as a serious elision.⁴⁸ It is a substantial cognitive task, a matter of both historical and present debates that are less relevant here than critics' desires to transcend them. As Martin shows, counting was essential to but also a concern for poets like Williams and Bridges who worked in and theorized syllabics at this moment.⁴⁹ The dismissal of counting is an excellent example of how even reasonable worries about meter are simultaneously an effort to leave behind prosodic study in favor of a (new) formalism and an extension of centuries of irritation about the state of prosody as a discipline. Ironically, modernism's early and sustained critique of meter as "metronome" is a late but certainly not final moment in a long and mostly doomed history of prosodic reformation. Modernism's meta-metrical games, insults to prosodic theory, and discoveries of new feet or cadences are eighteenth- and nineteenth-century tics identifiable across the Princeton Prosody Archive. The Edwardian period's "lacerating phase of anxiety, disillusionment, and seeming futility" was already suffused by a fear of metrical devolution.⁵⁰ Larzer Ziff's study of the 1890s argues that neither the advance of prosodic science nor disdain for the "tea-pot" poets of the 1870s and

1880s led to improvements in metrical form.[51] The first extended history of English prosodic theory, T. S. Omond's *English Metrists* (1903), begins with a lament that both metrists and many poets failed to distinguish between rhythm and meter precisely because they forced iambic meter to obey a strict alternating rhythm. He sees the metronomic bias or "mechanical view of meter" inaugurated very early, among Shakespeare's contemporaries.[52] Although Omond tries to locate the death knell of the mechanical view of prosody well prior to the first publication of his *English Metrists*, he expresses concern that "similar mistakes [are] made even now."[53] Indeed, as late as 1886 (and 1901 in reprint) Joseph Mayor recommended that boys and girls be taught to "observ[e] how the mechanical pendulum swing of scansion is developed."[54]

Pedagogical projects like Mayor's point to the more significant threat of the metronome: as a regime of training the attention and listening of future poetry readers. A stark example of such training is R. F. Brewer's infelicitously titled *Orthometry: The Art of Versification and the Technicalities of Poetry* (1893, reprint 1908, 1912, 1918). *Orthometry* hopes to save the young poet from himself by "in<u>duc</u>ing <u>him</u> to <u>try</u> his '<u>pren</u>tice <u>hand</u> / U<u>pon</u> a <u>ba</u>llad, <u>say</u>, a <u>ron</u>deau, <u>or</u> a <u>son</u>net."[55] I've lineated and underlined to show how the prose is metricized in a probably unconscious show and tell. In an early essay manuscript, Harriet Monroe worries about such young poets "playing charming tricks with rhymes and cadences. They are mouthing their words and trying experiments with sounds, imitating old-time rhymes with ballade and rondel, or assuming an Elizabethan simplicity which they can not wear with Elizabethan grace."[56] Monroe, who to Pound's ongoing frustration accepted and encouraged a wide range of verse, nevertheless aligns with him in defense of "rhythm" and against the newly codified prosodic theories of Saintsbury as promulgated in manuals like *The Art of Versification* (1913) that offered training in "technical expression."[57] Monroe's specific corrective lay in a return to Sidney Lanier's 1880 *Science of English Verse* and what she takes to be its Copernican revolution from accentual-syllabic to temporal scansion. Yet Monroe conspicuously ignores the regular citation of Lanier throughout *Art of Versification* as well as the latter's shared investments in abstract ideas of rhythm.[58] Monroe's selective reading sustains the otherwise weak or inaudible distinction between finger tapping and musical scansion by insisting on the distinction between metrical technique and a metaphysics (or physics) of poetic sound.

Monroe's critique turns out to be one of difference without distinction:

an institutional gesture positioning one not-so-new mainstream vehicle for poetry (the magazine, the editor) against another (the manual). T. S. Eliot performs a parallel gesture, orienting modernism toward rhythm and against versification as technique, in response to Robert Bridges's *Milton's Prosody* (1893). Bridges's study was originally aimed at correcting students' tendency toward metronomic readings of Milton. In the revised 1921 edition, Bridges recalls the unusual uproar that followed the first publication: it "converted some of the younger poets, who 'nimbly began dancing'; they introduced Miltonic inversions so freely into their blank verse that champions of the prevailing orthodoxy raised an indignant protest in the newspapers."[59] Bridges depicts a culture in which a good sense of how and when to adapt older models has given way to faddishness and then knee-jerk prosodic conservatism. Yet for T. S. Eliot this proves the failings of technical study as such. He sidelines Bridges's "catalogue [of] systematic irregularities" as "interesting" but no means to "gain an appreciation of the peculiar rhythm of a poet."[60] In chapter 2 I show the lengths Eliot went to over three decades of poetry and essays to make that rhythmic "appreciation" stick; it began, crucially, with a salvo against prosodic scholarship.

My individual chapters elaborate a sense of modernity's disciplinary crisis of prosody and of poets' formal response to that crisis. It may help here to focus the sprawl of modern metrical anxiety by giving one example of a "bad" but also self-conscious "metronomic" practice drifting into the twentieth century: the prosodic and stylistic nadir evident in a fondness for inserting the adjective "little" wherever another metrical foot and a bit of nostalgia were called for. It is common to hear, in Pound's cutting phrase, "words shoveled in to fill [the] metric pattern."[61] E. A. Robinson's "Oh, for a Poet" (1896) complains of "little sonnet-men" while quietly recording in its meter the sins of the "shrewd mechanic way."[62] Later, Robinson uses iambs to build a character unable to escape his present want of cash through nostalgic fantasy: "Miniver thought, and thought, and thought,/and thought about it." Almost defined by typographic inscription as a series of minims, Miniver Cheevy's awkward need for the past is doubly indicated by his entrapment in bluntly enjambed foot-thoughts and in his name's skewed dactyl (Míniver), which disturbs the iambic motion with a sad hint of lost grandeur. In "The Watch" (1915), Frances Cornford's "little watch" conveys "in every tick:/I am so sick, so sick, so sick."[63] The literally little village poet, Petit, of Edgar Lee Masters's *Spoon River Anthology* (1915) is, against his Romantic will, another Miniver or "little sonnet man"; his metronomic verses go "Tick, tick,

tick, what little iambics,/While Homer and Whitman roared in the pines."[64] One is almost tempted to say "íambícs," in keeping with the line's assonance, to aid the contrast with the flexible feet of the next and final line. Would-be "Georgian Poets" faced Roy Campbell's withering questions: "Can you write in rhyme and meter?" and "Are you easily exalted by natural objects?"[65] But Rupert Brooke, nominally a Georgian Poet, beat Campbell to the punch with the faux nostalgia of "The Old Vicarage, Grantchester" (1912) and its "little room," "little kindly winds," and (in English's most forbidden rhyme, which Frost plays on as well) "breeze/Sobbing in the little trees." As Martin notes, Brooke is one of many under-acknowledged poets who ambivalently mourned "a soon-to-be-lost audience for metrical poetry."[66] Brooke binds his metronomic meter directly to both nostalgia and artificial time in the self-delusion (and artificial poetical inversion) of the final couplet: "Stands the Church clock at ten to three?/And is there honey still for tea?"[67] *The Waste Land* drafts describe a poetess, Fresca, with "tresses fanned by little flutt'ring Loves"[68]—a mimetically paltry version of Popian pentameter. This parody of "little" fin-de-siècle versification really should have been recognizable to Pound, yet he thought it either a poor imitation or misdirected parody of Pope. Eliot's misogynistic association of rigid meter and women's verse appears an insufficient marker of intent and authority as his bad meter sucks the air out of the line and undermines the poem's knowing relation to a declining Western tradition. Rhetorical bathos, in other words, cannot resolve the ambivalent desire to be both in and against the metronome.

In these examples of stagnancy by design, we begin to see how meter, when operating as a reflexively vestigial form or sound, sustains an effort to better understand the feelings of modernity's lost or mechanized subjects. Through meter and its subjugation of diction these poets mark time as sick, stuck, or otherwise out of joint, albeit with a measure of parodic distance. These pre- or non-modernist negotiations of mechanicity begin well before canonical modernist poets launch their attacks and their own satires in and of meter. What they gain from their simultaneous attention to and practice of mechanical form is a recollection of the dueling pleasure and strain of repetition, and of its wide-ranging symbolic and social values.

Several recent reevaluations of early twentieth-century poetics emphasize the need for new recognition of the forms and stakes of repetition and mechanicity. Nadia Nurhussein reveals the seemingly paradoxical "mechanical complexity" of laborious forms like dialect orthography, like metrics a prominent component of fin-de-siècle reading practice very much at risk of being lost after modernism. The mechanical repetition of "little" hints at a parallel between meter and poetic diction, whose formulaic badness is the subject of Daniel Tiffany's recent work on modern poetry and kitsch. Tiffany argues that poetic diction's kitschiness reveals how all aesthetic beauty relies on "replication" and "seriality" (here following Elaine Scarry). He could be describing the fear of metronomic meter in diction's troubling "'contagion of imitation' [. . .] a basic structural affinity between beauty and the reproducibility of mass culture." The modernist discourse of meter, as of diction, exposes how modern ideologies of poetic form rely on fictive authenticity always verging on self-parody or be-"little"-ment. To return to canned diction or mechanical meter is, in Tiffany's terms, to recognize the general "distress" we feel in "a historical echo chamber of borrowed language."[69]

These studies of poetics and mechanicity reassert what Cavitch calls the "disruptive power of the conventional" against "the fiction of the unique voice."[70] Nurhussein explicitly positions her revisionary study of dialect poetry as a practice of literacy against lyric reading: to read dialect or to scan (however "mechanically") is to listen for "constructedness, as opposed to the ethereal and mysterious inspiration" of lyric. Work in modernist sound studies points in the same direction, toward Joyce's "authenticity [. . .] served by (quasi-) automaticity" and Beckett's "repetition" that at once "empties words of meaning" and "generates its own internal effect and meaning."[71] Such reevaluations suggest that we listen to meter within the broader modern soundscape and without the fear of contagious artifice and repetition generated by the past century's expressivist investments in rhythm.

Meter and Modern Aurality

The modern soundscape is littered with metrical artifacts, little loops of orthographically recorded and notated sound. Like poetic diction and dialect, meter reminds modernism of a perennially unfinished aesthetic task, here that of formalizing sound and reproducing it on literature's own terms. Meter's conception as "metronome" aims to cordon off the limits of poetics, a vestigial "withered stump[] of time" (*TWL*, I.124); but meter inevitably confirms the uncertain status of poetic sound as an object and phenomenological experience. The instability of sound and the proliferation of efforts to secure it for disciplined hearing has been widely acknowledged in sound studies scholarship. "Sound objects," to take the speculative title of a recent collection, do not present themselves to a given aurality; they demand the kind of alternative apprehension that modern poetry itself calls out for as a response to the pressures of modernity. The "extraordinarily generative fascination with the object" and ambivalent appeal of the commodity form, which for Doug Mao maps out modernist aesthetics, becomes even more frantic when faced by sound and its time objects, especially meter.[72] Sound studies of modern literature have emphasized "the formal difficulties of mediating voice and sound," though the absence of prosody is felt when they seek "more systematic analyses of modernist forms in terms of their capacities to mediate rhythms, sonic textures and vocal derangements."[73] Seeking to analyze "modernist form" begs the question, as "form" mediates not through transformation (as in Eliot's famous catalytic reaction) but by setting aside the media and historical practices of prosodic inscription (rather than "rhythm") and vocal arrangements (i.e., dialect). This study of meter benefits from sound studies' historical and theoretical interrogations of sonic cultures, while recalling how modernist theories of form are frequently poised against the media- and genre-literate practices of metrical theory and practice.

The contrast between modern concepts of form and Victorian theories of prosody is instructive here. Yopie Prins has shown how the polymetrical long nineteenth century was simultaneously obsessed with the "metrical mediation of voice" and the "materialization" of that voice in orthography as well as performance.[74] From Jason Rudy's work we learn that the inverse is also true, that prosody was rooted in material sciences and became a way of conceptualizing physiology.[75] Jason Hall has recently unearthed the continued investment, into the twentieth century, in "materialist metrics" driven by laboratory investigations and recording techniques. His analysis of laboratory prosodist Ada Snell is particularly important, as she sought to move from the abstraction of meter toward a "mechanized scansion" but also recognized that this did not produce an "objective rhythmical 'record.'"[76] Empirical studies like Snell's, or statistical linguistic analyses like Adelaide Crapsey's, materialize meter in ways that can look rote or alien to "how poets really write" and to close reading but ultimately reflect passionate investments in linguistic, sonic, and graphic media. By contrast, modernist "forms" seem less to be mediating voice and sound than to be fleeing medium—as reflected in the ideals of medium specificity or objectivity.

What meter and technical scansion question in this context is the freedom of sound and voice from orthography, print, and later recorded media: a freedom but also exile from what Lisa Gitelman calls a "ground upon which literate English speakers negotiated their own identity" despite "glimpsing everywhere the potential failure of textual representation to recuperate aural experience."[77] The critique of the metronome is, from this perspective, a fatalistic acceptance that aurality is non-recuperable and that literary (rather than literate) identity requires the advent of a new ground. For example, when T. S. Eliot reads the jumble of Englishes and historical prosodies in *Ulysses*'s "Oxen of the Sun" chapter, he predictably confirms "the futility of all the English styles."[78] As I show in chapter 2, the negative achievement of "futility" allows Eliot-as-critic to juxtapose modern poetic culture to the putatively secure metrical cultures of Dante or the Elizabethan court. With less nostalgia, Joyce juxtaposes the modern literary-linguistic soundscape to the idealized organic metrical culture of Anglo-Saxon alliterative verse.

Ulysses, however, gives meter and practices of scansion a more dynamic role in the modern soundscape, configuring such specialized listening as at once ecstatic and absurd. In the "Aeolus" chapter, for example, Professor MacHugh excitedly pronounces that the word "Ohio" is a "perfect cretic," "long, short, and long."[79] What reader of prose cohabits MacHugh's world enough to hear this quantitative metrical pattern at work in an alien language? This moment brings forward the contingency of the hunt for formalized sound amid the raucous newspaper and faculty offices of modernity. That contingency is decisive, this book argues, not only for the history and theory of prosodic practice but for the tradition of poetics and formalism that emerges in the wake of modernism.

Ulysses develops a more complex relation between meter, poetry, and history than the quick satire of MacHugh's metrification. It values the aesthetic sensibility operating in the precarious moment when a vestigial metrical practice—here classical scansion—ecstatically plucks out a sound. Earlier Stephen Dedalus half-jokes, "I am, a stride at a time," tramping i-am-bically along a strand of prose and sand: "Stephen closed his eyes to hear his boots crush crackling wrack and shells" (3:10-11). More generatively than MacHugh, whose half-cocked philology depends on a parodic version of "O Tannenbaum,"[80] Stephen's hearing actively transforms a song about "Madeline the mare" into "deline the mare," precisely his walk on the beach (3:24). But the "ineluctable modality of the visible" (3:1) swiftly takes back over when Stephen reopens his eyes. As with MacHugh, the aural falls short of intersubjectivity: "Rhythm begins, you see. I hear" (3:21).[81] We see rhythm, and perhaps scan it as metrical, but do we hear it collectively? What if poetry's "ethereal" music or rhythm gets recognized only through what Leopold Bloom calls "musemathematics," or "symmetry under a cemetery wall" (11:834-35)? MacHugh's "Ohio" and Stephen's "I am"-bics are caught, as was Joyce, between individual rhythm and metrical training, between the aesthetic pleasure of rhythm and the obsessive mode of its taxonomies. Not only modernism but twentieth-century criticism requires an effort to escape the distasteful problem of technical training without losing such training's ultimate dedication to aesthetic attention.

The recurrent modernist travesties of meter as a metronome cast modern auditory culture as the technocratic ruin of a genuine metrical culture and prosodic study as fundamentally a matter of mere technicity that delimits the listening and performing public's engagement with poetry. One way to understand the wide but specialized franchise of meter as understood by modernists is as a practice of what Jonathan Sterne has called "audile technique." Sterne uses the term to define bourgeois culture's increasingly technicized and regimented practices of listening, as exemplified by the intense documentation and training surrounding stethoscope use. Audile technique's primary characteristics are the "separation and idealization of technicized hearing," "construction of a private acoustic space," and "commodification and collectivization of individuated listening."[82] The "singing-masters" Yeats seeks in Byzantium might be read as a defense against the Marconi School of Wireless's "competent, socially superior observer [who] ensures the solemnity of the situation and guides the ears of those in training."[83] There is a parallel threat in the phonograph, which in Friedrich Kittler's description dissolves the "feedback loops of consciousness, hearing oneself speak, seeing oneself write."[84] Its mindless combination of "writing and reading, storing and scanning, recording and replaying" sounds a lot like elocution, now become an entire media environment against which modernism recoiled. As the editors of *Sounding Modernism* note, the gramophone in *Ulysses* ("kraahraark," 6:963-65) speaks with "a marked difficulty that can only register as the ribald and satirical laughter of a symbolic medium at the limits of an analogue recording medium."[85]

The threat of meter-as-audile-technique is that poetry seems to have so little control over how hearing gets "technicized," such that reading becomes a commodity that consumes commodities. Given that the long and diverse prosodic elaboration of poetry across the preceding two centuries was now cast as the oppressively regimented "metronome," fantasies of a return to prosody as craft or performance had to be projected well into the medieval or Renaissance past—or onto nonwhite practices, as I discuss in my final two chapters. Pound, who sought his first master in Yeats (and then wished to be his sole colleague), and others in the metrical cultures of Italy and the more distant past could not "trust the reader to read [Cavalcanti's Italian] for the music after he has read the English for the sense."[86] In his treatise on Pound's "metric," T. S. Eliot wonders whether modern poetry can establish the new "training" needed to escape both meter and the false escape from it: "Any verse is called 'free' by people whose ears are not accustomed to it"; "what the poems do require is a trained ear, or at least the willingness to be trained."[87] In wondering about the "willingness to be trained" without explicitly naming the trainer (school, poet, critic, or perhaps ideally the poem?), Eliot reveals a career-long ambivalence about the role of criticism in modern prosody. Exiled from even the unkempt authority of metrical education, he cannot foreclose charges—Yvor Winters's for example—of mannerism and appealing only to the "half-trained."[88] As Langdon Hammer notes, the flip side of modernism's claim to formal innovation is the increasing and paradoxical necessity of criticism as a supplement to the supposedly autonomous textual object. If criticism constitutes a "curtailment of poetry's traditional scope, a limitation of a fundamental kind," it is troubling not only for its necessity but for its inefficacy in prosodic matters.[89] Prosodic "training" seemed corrupt and embarrassing, a betrayal of art's elite status. But that culture of active and actual listening remains modern poetry's object of desire and loss, papered over by the condemnation of meter and embrace of rhythm.

We can hear that desire in T. S. Eliot's feeling that "scansion tells us very little" about vers libre. Originally a conservative gesture, it can easily read as a defense of non-metrical verse's triumph over merely technical or philological responses to poetry. Likewise, Winters's sardonic sense that forming any grounds for judging "experimental" prosodies would "require a very thorough knowledge of all the best poems employing the medium in the second and third decades of our century, a sensitive and conscientious study of several years in duration, the immersion of the student in a particular way of feeling, the acquisition of a new and difficult set of habits of hearing and of audible reading."[90] A range of descriptive efforts from the 1910s through 1930s attempted to develop such a "way of feeling." These include the laboratory assessments of rhythm and cadence studied by Jason David Hall, the "'field' of rhythm studies" surveyed by Michael Golston through which poetics becomes a pseudoscience of racialized bodies, and of course the many theorizations of free verse.[91]

Following critics like Charles O. Hartman and Stephen Cushman, who have explored free verse's anxious rhetoricity and unstable terminology, this study is less interested in the things we might call analyses of rhythm than in the insecurity caused by the invention of a supposedly post-metrical, or post-metronomic prosody.[92] The modern distrust of prosodic training and other modes of audile technique continues an older unease with print mediation and its publics. Bartholomew Brinkman has explored poetic modernism's struggle to ground genre by "formally mediat[ing]" the material conditions of book production and collection in mass print culture.[93] In his study of the "valedictory" mode in Swinburne and other Victorian poets, Justin Sider shows how the period's many figurations of "silent song" reflect "the paradox of the poet's cultural authority in an era of multiplying publics and print capitalism"; in Prins's direct formulation, meter is a "print medium," and its conspicuous lack of fluency constitutes a "caesura of the modern."[94] Modernism remains elegiac and anxious about the poet's noisy reception, and its valedictions are necessarily extreme. W. E. B. Du Bois concludes *The Souls of Black Folk* (1903), a text in doubtful search of tremendously literate listeners, with a striking envoi: *"Hear my cry, O God the Reader; vouchsafe that this my book fall not still-born into the wilderness.[. . . L]et the ears of a guilty people tingle with truth."*[95] This call to rebuild silent reading *sub specie æternitatis* marks untrained ears as the precondition for silencing African American expression. Others blame mass media for deficient ears: in 1909 Florence Farr, a colleague of Yeats, develops a fairly elaborate system for setting poems to subdued melodies as a defense against "newspaper readers [. . .] inclined to resent the idea that the sound in words, or the relation of words to each other, is of any account."[96] Written in a very different disciplinary setting, I. A. Richards's *Practical Criticism* (1929) worries that modern print culture requires "stereotyping and standardizing both our utterances and our interpretations"—one version of this being "the notion that verses must conform to metrical patterns," which "leads to mechanical reading" and "to bitter complaints against irregularity and a refusal to enter into poems which do not accord smoothly with the chosen pattern." Like Farr, Richards fears that the "public neither understands the kind of importance that attached to the movement of words in verse, nor has any just ideas of how to seize this movement or judge it."[97] He imagines that poor performances of poetry forever circulating on gramophone records will alienate young readers now deprived of the chance to encounter (with the right critical mediation) written poetry and written meter. Across *Practical Criticism*, mechanicity cross-pollinates with industrialism, print culture, poetic form, phonography, and reading in general.

Rather predictably, scansion or notational systems were not the corrective sought by now-major modernist figures like Richards, Eliot, W. C. Williams, or even Amy Lowell, despite her laboratory graphs of rhythm. Pound comments about the need for advanced notation and invested in such practices for music, but he never develops his own prosodic systems and prefers to talk about Greek feet rather than scan them. As I show in chapter 1, Frost's scansions are important evidence for his poetics but are largely restricted to his notebooks; what deliberate and public efforts I do find occur in the African American tradition and are related to explicit pedagogical efforts. Few poets, it seems, wanted to be prosodic or phonetic reformers on the scale of George Saintsbury, Robert Bridges, or Henry Higgins of George Bernard Shaw's *Pygmalion* (1913). As Jennifer Buckley shows, Shaw himself struggled to implement a phonographic script as part of his "desire for a quasi-musical theater notation capable of capturing the acoustics of a sound-centered theater on the page."[98] His lament that very few performers or readers would actually know his script foregrounds the problem of mediation and legibility that such scripts were meant to mitigate. Shaw's effort brings the aesthetic aspirations of the poet-as-language reformer too close to stenographic training. It calls up the dehumanized typist in *The Waste Land*, who "smoothes her hair with automatic hand / And puts a record on the gramophone" in strict pentameter (*TWL*, ll. 255-56).

The typist helps Eliot anathematize phonographic and metronomic poetics, yet as I argue in chapter 2, there is no sound insulation between her, her enclosing meter, and Eliot's versification. What alternative is there to instrumentalized and mechanical sound as a means of recording language and making it available to readers? One lay in the rebuilt phenomenology of Pierre Schaeffer's "reduced listening" and composition of concrete music, but as Brian Kane has observed, Schaefferian formalism obsesses over technique to overcome the obscurity and fault of untrained or under-experienced listeners.[99] Julie Beth Napolin has described the fantastic preservation of sound in what she terms "the fact of resonance": disembodied, atmospheric sound unperturbed but also unredeemed by recording technologies. This is the song of Ariel in *The Tempest*, which mysteriously emanates from the typist's gramophone for the reader but not for her (gramophones cannot listen to themselves). Ariel's song moves "upon the waters," like the presence of God, and belongs to both "air" and "earth." To hear such magical song in modernity requires an "atmospheric listening [. . .] a historical and diffusive mode of attentiveness" that tends, Napolin shows in her study of Faulkner, to haunt characters and "the written word" alike.[100] As I discuss in my first chapter, Robert Frost likewise dreamed of a universal sensitivity to the kinds of murmurs that pass through doors stripped of speaker, semantics, and lexis but not the pitch contours and rhythms of "sentence sounds." Yet he knew this only works when you've already heard and recognize the sentence sound. In my reading of Frost, "sentence sound" is a trap for critics and readers, as Frost's meter strenuously and even cruelly counters his reader's generic expectations for remediated regional voice. The behaviorist B. F. Skinner heard something more troubling than ur-sentences in the ambient sound of his humming lab equipment: "a rhythmic pulse: di-*dah*-di-di-*dah*—di-*dah*-di-di-*dah*. Suddenly I heard myself saying 'You'll never get out; you'll never get out.' An imitative response had joined forces with some latent behavior." Here rhythm leads to pure projection. Skinner subsequently developed an "audile projective test," akin to a Rorschach, using phonography.[101] This is an extreme example of how the dream of pure audition unencumbered by expectation, semantics, or visual representation gives way to incarcerated and mechanized consciousnesses. This fear of automated yet idiosyncratic responses to prosody, both metrical and not, suffuses modern poetry.

The mechanization of sound in Skinner is a function of automated hearing, not metrical pattern. Indeed, the problem is that "di-*dah*-di-di-*dah*" is not a meter, not a space in which poets might exercise their will rather than succumbing to deterministic projections. What I find in modern poets' metrical practices and investments is an effort to listen to poetry's symbolic medium on the rocks, and to position themselves against the false freedom that comes with free verse or sound recording—evidently not freedom in Skinner's laboratory, where all sound is warped by the mediating human mind if nothing else. To write in meter is to stay with a historical medium and interrogate literary and technological progress, albeit at the constant risk of descending into nostalgia and embarrassment. This produces the self-referential, dissonant, often tense, resigned form of the "metrical vestige."

Meter as Vestige

For the poets studied here, meter does not merely participate in audile technique. It is at most a synecdoche for this broader media ecology, which is why it remains so iconic yet unsatisfying a foil. Its presence in twentieth-century poetics is that of a vestige, in the biological sense of organs that no longer fulfill their evolutionary function yet remain present and can come to serve new functions. Even when virtually useless, as in the muscles that once moved our ears, their lingering signals can be observed and interpreted (to evidence attention, in the case of ear muscles). The term is inspired by Sterling Brown's "Vestiges," the final section of his first book of poems (*Southern Road*, 1932). Written in a range of meters and fixed forms, especially sonnets, "Vestiges" looks at a distance like juvenilia or some lingering coda to the blues- and vernacular-inspired poetry for which Brown is rightly famous. These "Vestiges" have been repurposed by Brown to signal something else. As I argue in my final chapter, they are not nostalgic or atavistic but instead capture the logic of an anachronism that must be studied for complex synchrony, not filed away through racialized visions of literary and prosodic history.

The dynamic temporality of the Brownian "vestige" resonates across the deployments of meter studied in this book. Some modern poets, Yeats in particular, stand outside this study because their practice of meter evokes relative continuity and comfort with a longer metrical tradition. The end of "An Irish Airman Foresees His Death" (1919), for instance, at once embodies and recognizes in its meter a stoicism become, as David Bromwich puts it, "a satisfying aesthetic image":

> I balanced all, brought all to mind,
> The years to come seemed waste of breath,
> A waste of breath the years behind
> In balance with this life, this death.

Bromwich hears in these lines the "pretense of restraint,"[102] which suggests the Wordsworthian logic of a pleasant metrical constraint freely entered into by the poet. But what becomes, in modern meter, of the Romantic desire that Simon Jarvis locates in his study of Wordsworth—the "felt need to give utterance to non-replicable singular experience in the collectively and historically cognitive form of verse."[103] For the poets studied here, the pretense of historical and metrical stoicism comes apart in the face of the felt *non*-"collectivity" of verse cognition.

I want to give two shorter examples of reflexively vestigial meter in two divergently modern poets, Thomas Hardy and Hart Crane, each of whom might have received extended treatment in this study. Hardy, like Jude hunting for the fleeting resonance of church bells ("faint and musical, calling to

Introduction 23

him, 'We are happy here!' "),[104] seems always out of step with his time and represents that distance in his listening practice. His poem "In a Museum" (1917) tries to liberate aestheticized sound through a risky act of poetic will that depends on prosody:

I
Here's the mould of a musical bird long passed from light,
Which over the earth before man came was winging;
There's a contralto voice I heard last night,
That lodges with me still in its sweet singing.

II
Such a dream is Time that the coo of this ancient bird
Has perished not, but is blent, or will be blending
Mid visionless wilds of space with the voice that I heard,
In the full-fugued song of the universe unending.[105]

The poem invents a fossilized "coo" out of a mere "mould" and figures private listening as having the same extreme temporal structure. Yet the poem hesitates over the fantastical blending, in "dream" Time, of personal and abstract geological memory. It wants to traverse "here" and "there" within one mind and one rhyme, relying on the richness of the speaker's fancy and the resources of the poetic stanza. But stanza, speaker, diction, and above all meter are themselves fossils, demanding our fancy to make them "coo." The polyptoton "blent, or will be blending" is a strange rhetorical blend of obsolete and living diction, rendering us uncertain how to blend the odd poem "here" in front of us with the "there" of obsolescing conventions of song and speaker. This is the structure of the vestige: outdated forms that will not stop echoing and that demand new listening, like the fossil sound that awkwardly figures our close listening to this poem.

Hardy's proliferation of stanza and metrical forms, some historical, some invented, but all anachronistic, requires that his readers bootstrap a sense of his form. Readers almost universally failed, and Hardy felt "paralyzed" that his intentional forms were "set down to blundering, lack of information, pedantry."[106] Dennis Taylor's survey of Hardy's stanzas produces a "metrical appendix" to nineteenth- and twentieth-century prosody as much as to his own book. Once critics recognized the intent behind Hardy's meter, Taylor observes, they complained of the arbitrary-seeming "choice of metre" and absence of "expressive form." That struggle to listen to meter's formal vestiges is figured in Hardy's extraordinary recovery of fossilized sound. Fled is that music, not deeper into the forest but into the depths of time. How do we get to the poem's loose pentameter—Is it in duple or triple meter? Rising or falling?—without an act of sheer will? And once we have it, how can we value it as something other than mere "choice"?

The difficulty of scanning, performing, and interpreting meter in a poem like this defines the metrical vestige. As Taylor observes, centuries of prosodic study struggled toward suitable theories of meter, and I agree that it is only in the late Victorian period that theorists reached an adequately "abstract" sense of meter. It is a cruel twist for poets like Hardy, so invested not only in meter but in its theorization, that the peak of his poetic career coincides with the modernist riposte against meter as metronome. The metronome undoes the abstract understanding of meter by concretizing a specific rhythm. Poems like "In a Museum" have no prosodic horizon that can "blend" past and present—only syntax, will, and a faint affinity for cosmological theories of rhythm. Its meter exceeds what Kristin Hanson, in her study of Milton's "L'Allegro," calls the "mental work to arrive at and remain committed to [an iambic] understanding of the form." This work was a "way of life" for Milton's poem, but only a vestige of that hearing ear awaits the modern meter of poets like Hardy, Frost, or as Natalie Gerber has shown, Wallace Stevens.[107]

In contrast to Hardy, Hart Crane only rarely writes in meter, no doubt arriving too late for metrical experiment to feel inevitable even as it became necessary to his poetics. In Allen Tate's early evaluation, Hart Crane is one of a new "race of poets" emerging between 1920 and 1925 who were drawn back to meter even as they "could not accept limitation; possibly they saw no valid limitations they could work with."[108] Through Tate's critical judo, to knowingly accept the arbitrary limitations of meter restores poetry's formal coherence as the poet's suffering and unease. Crane's dialectical negation of meter becomes less the poet's achievement than the critic's triumphant confirmation of ideas about poetic genre. Although Tate is sensitive that late modern meter proceeds under suppression, he ignores the feeling of impossible desire channeled by meter. Crane can revel only briefly in metrical plenitude as an ecstatic escape from history:

There, beyond the dykes

I heard wind flaking sapphire, like this summer,
And willows could not hold more steady sound.

These lines end the ars poetical pilgrimage "Repose of Rivers" (1926) with just half of the iambic pentameter quatrain that elsewhere serves as Crane's "metrical signature."[109] Their temporality is inhuman, as befits a speaker who is a river, suggesting that the fragment of epic meter requires a transcendental state of listening and being not evidenced in modern aurality.

In Allen Grossman's precise account, Crane "refus[ed] to devise a structure that dissimulated the resistance of reality to desire." This produces the metrical vestige: a residue of lyricism that will be "resisted." Grossman also points to the threat Crane, Hardy, and all of the poets studied below perceived from the myth of post-metrical prosody; they could not make the "modernist concession to the weak mystification of open-form speculation toward merely secular infinities." The modernist reconstruction of the prosodic field toward such "infinities," and corresponding foreclosure of what Grossman calls the "historicity [. . .] of forms and styles," underlies Crane's feeling of homelessness. As a poet of the metrical vestige, he faced historical styles as "an array of undisqualified possibilities" that were constantly getting disqualified by the present's prosodic ideologies and in particular by the ironization and repudiation of meter.[110] This is the metrical vestige: simultaneously "undisqualified" and inadequate, but therefore resistant to ideals of poetry's transcendence of historical limits as rhythmic lyric.

At once elegiac and liberatory, the metrical vestige turns poets from formal ideologies that permit an abstract generic coherence for poetry and toward efforts to feel out the fate and function of poetry in modernity. This is the bitter medicine prescribed by modernism's most famous metronome, Man Ray's 1923 *Objet à détruire*. Originally a working metronome set to cadence brush strokes, with a cut-out eye representing a looming audience, Man Ray literalized the destruction in a revolt against his own artificial program. He broke the metronome but then changed tack, rebuilding the readymade using a picture of a former lover's eye. In 1932 he published an ink drawing of this version, more ambiguously called *Object of Destruction*, with new instructions: "Cut out the eye from a photograph of one who has been loved but is seen no more. Attach the eye to the pendulum of a metronome and regulate the weight to suit the tempo desired. Keep going to the limit of endurance. With a hammer well-aimed, try to destroy the whole at a single blow."[111]

What had been a means of composition and the thrill of rupture becomes a project of memory; to break the timekeeper is to fail and fall back into the illusion of freedom from nostalgia. The poets I study here "endure":

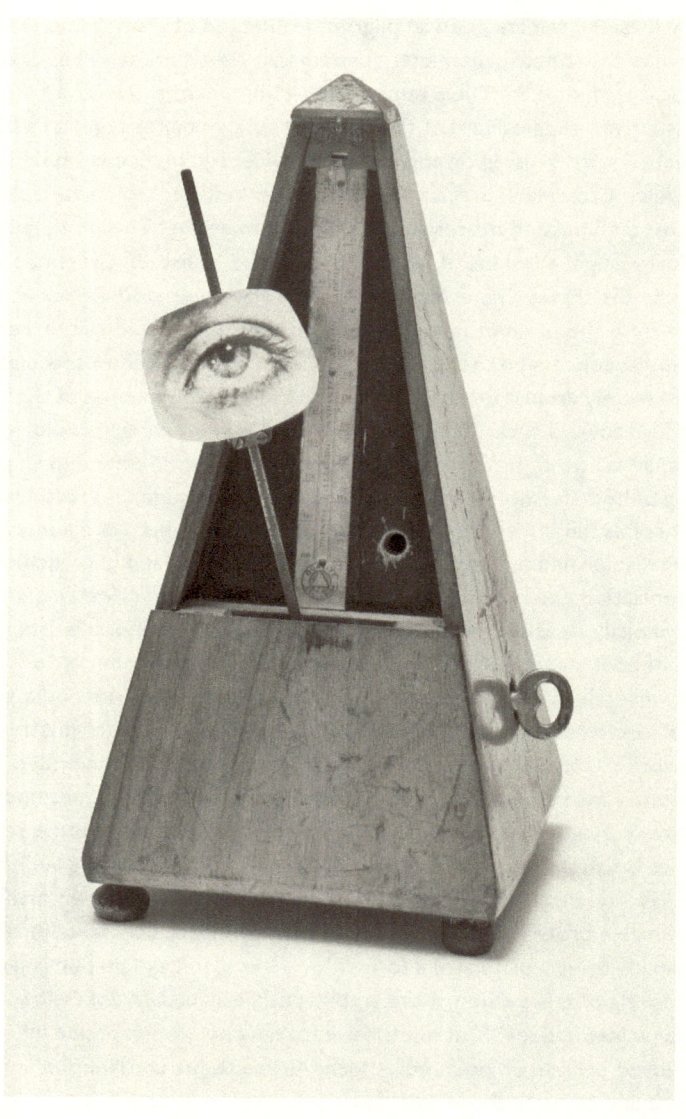

Indestructible Object (or Object to Be Destroyed). Man Ray, 1964 (replica of 1923 original). Metronome with cutout photograph of eye on pendulum. James Thrall Soby Fund, The Museum of Modern Art, New York, NY. © The Museum of Modern Art/Licensed by SCALA/Art Resource, NY.

writing in meter is not for them a conservative gesture but a fundamental questioning of the historical force of the "single blow," "break," or "heave" offered peremptorily by free verse and manifesto modernism. The metrical sonnet was precisely the right form for Edna St. Vincent Millay to follow biology's model and "struggle on without a break" against romantic and sexual roles. The metrical vestige is suffused with a sense of having lost its simple materiality or generic potency, yet that sense of absence insulates the poet from the fetish versions of rhythm and above all its patriarchal and racialized form. The subject of the final two chapters of this book, rhythm's harboring of racial ideologies constrains modern black poetics but also carves out a critical and often parodic role for meter. For example, in "Mill Mountain," the final poem of Brown's "Vestiges," a blank verse pastoral monologue binds metrical and generic uncertainty to the speaker's marginal position. A vagrant camping outside town, his address to his sleeping child reflects on his literary as much as social condition: "strange pastoral for poor city dwellers, child." The mournfulness cannot conceal a rising sense of anger at dispossession and contingency that lives in the monologue through the subdued and slow pentameter.

Such moments remind us that the illusion of poetic freedom—whether in the urbanity of traditional pastoral or the visual appearance of free verse—depends upon implicit whiteness, and that the seemingly free forms developed by black poets (i.e., jazz) are also "fixed" by white audiences and tastemakers. Poised against false freedom and organicity, the metrical vestige insists upon the artifice of all poetic forms and genres. It recognizes that readers will perform all manner of potentially errant tasks: scansion, allusion tracing, canon building, performances that concretize or ignore the abstract meter, misremembering, assumptions about the speaker and poet's race and gender, and more. Every chapter that follows touches in some way on poets who recoil from readerships—whether for their technical limitations, mass-cultural affinities, or assumptions about race and gender—while seeking to engage and transform them by composing through vestigial meters.

The metrical vestige does not have a single meaning or function. It would look very different amid the new institutional contexts of the midcentury, for example, in poets like Gwendolyn Brooks, Robert Lowell, John Berryman, and James Merrill; at different points in W. H. Auden's long career; or in a primarily English context. Focused on the period before World War II, and largely on American poets, my readings show metrical poetry variously oriented around metrical experiment, satire, affective attachment, recovery, and revisions of literary history. Chapter 1 reads meter's function in Frost against the dominant critical belief in his vernacular precision, showing how meter consistently distorts expectations of regional voice. It is a vestige of poetry as a fundamentally written medium rather than a conduit for rhythmic speech. In chapters 2 and 3 I explore Eliot's and Pound's experience of meter as form gone wrong and in need of redemption through either satire or idiosyncratic investments in alternate formal lineages. As a vestige of a once-adequate socio-aesthetic order, meter haunts their potential escape from a culture they cast as effete, enervating, and metronomic in order to shore up their own poetics. In chapter 4 I show how modern women poets respond to prosody's male oversight in their practices of meter. Following the lead of H.D., who contends with Pound's poetic authority in a specifically prosodic domain, I focus on the formal feeling for meter as a vestige in Sara Teasdale, Georgia Douglas Johnson, and in particular Louise Bogan. Despite their differences, these poets each reevaluate sentimental, poetess, and lyric traditions through both metrical invention and extensive metaprosodic reference.

The final two chapters of the book study the racialization of rhythm and the importance of the metrical vestige to New Negro Renaissance poets seeking to determine their own formal traditions rather than accept uncritical vernacularity or musicality. They write against what Kofi Agawu has called our "rhythm bias," the musicological (and broadly Western) invention of "black" or "African" rhythm as a fantastically "complex" other to Western music.[112] As Tsitsi Jaji notes, early twentieth-century writers anticipate Paul Gilroy's "lament over the instrumentalization of music as 'a cipher for racial authenticity'"; metrical technique was a primary means to decode and refuse that cipher.[113] Chapter 5 builds a conversation between prosody and passing, showing the ambivalent relationship between African American poets and both a "usable" vernacular rhythmic past and a free verse rhythmic future in which they would be accused of imitation or passing. I argue that Jean Toomer struggles to conceive prosody as a space in which everyone might pass, including black poets in black musical forms and white poets in traditional meters. Where Toomer considers the limits of racialized listening, James Weldon Johnson more directly challenges meter's implicit whiteness by appropriating, satirizing, and developing a critical pedagogy for the Anglo-American tradition. Chapter 6 explores Sterling Brown's kindred pedagogical, critical, and poetic attention to the formal framing of race. It centers on a reading of the polymetrical masterpiece "When de Saints

Go Ma'ching Home" as it builds its vernacular poetics around the metrical vestige.

In my conclusion I ask how the rise of rhythm and demotion of meter as one form among many transform practices of reading and theories of genre in the New Criticism and subsequent formalist methodology. By turning to the unread and misread life of meter within both high modernism and in the space-clearing operations of black and women poets, I argue for the broader importance of studying historical prosody as part of ongoing critical efforts to renovate the canons of twentieth- and twenty-first-century poetry. Against a criticism still straining to express coherence within new dogmas of post-metrical form, my studies of versification and its reception show a diverse poetic culture returning again and again to the limited vestige of a generic foundation offered by meter. The complexity of these returns shows why it is a mistake to understand modernism's widespread investments in meter as conservative; they do not signify a desire to return to the past values or functions of poetry but the will to understand what happened to its public form.

1 Modernist Scansion
Robert Frost's Distorted Vernacular

> Now those of my readers who have never *heard* ["Pease Porridge Hot"] pronounced according to the nursery conventionality, will find its rhythm as obscure as an explanatory note; while those who *have* heard it, will [. . .] wonder how there can be any doubt about it. [. . .] The chief thing in the way of this species of rhythm, is the necessity which it imposes upon the poet of travelling in constant company with his compositions, so as to be ready at a moment's notice, to avail himself of a well understood poetical license—that of reading aloud one's own doggerel.
>
> —Poe, "The Rationale of Verse"

This chapter explores Robert Frost's attempts to engage the historical, technical, and broadly public practice of scansion as it existed up to and through the early twentieth century. He writes against the modernist antipathy toward and subordination of meter laid out in my introduction. Despite his obvious prominence in canons of American poetry, Frost fits poorly into the formal narrative that embraced "rhythm" as the privileged concept of versification while reinventing meter as the production of "metronomic" iambic rhythms. This chapter reveals the complexity of Frost's metrical experiment— and our struggle to read and hear it—to theorize modern meter as a practice of testing and reforming how poetry's readers listen, scan, and perform. Partly this aligns Frost with the elitism of moderns who distance themselves from prosodic technique, but I also find in Frost's meter and metrical theories a critique of that distancing act and its reliance on illusions of abstract rhythm and voice.

By the time Frost began his publishing career in London in 1912, encouraged (or harassed) by Pound, scansion had already been cast as an outdated analytic tool: a prop for simplified aural appreciation, elocutionary recitation, and the writing of doggerel. It certainly seemed unhelpful to the composition or reception of free verse. Frost's horizon, however, was composed of the dual threat of the metronome: both the inadequacies of metrical training and the call to transcend scansion as such. My goal here is not to celebrate traditional meter, or Frost's achievement in it, but to emphasize instead the unease Frost felt with the shift from existing prosodic training toward the more abstract concepts of prosody amenable to free verse. Whereas Whitman famously proffers a free verse "tally" of the hidden thrush's song in "When Lilacs Last in the Dooryard Bloom'd" (1865), Frost insists in poems like "The Oven Bird" (1916) that only songs like that of the "loud" ovenbird, which "everyone has heard," reverberate in modernity's "diminished" acoustical field.[1] He accordingly charted a now-eccentric course toward new habits for the production, scansion, and performance of iambic meters.

I trace that effort at length because Frost was one of the last major American poets to write almost exclusively in meter and perhaps the last to design and promulgate a new accentual-syllabic meter, his "loose iambics." Many other poets have developed flexible uses of meter, and many others have tried to create new ones (Robert Bridges's or Adelaide Crapsey's syllabics, for instance),[2] but no other poet since Hopkins plays so fundamentally with existing historical practices of scansion. To Derek Walcott's ear, Frost "dislocates the pivot of traditional scansion."[3] Most important to this study is his explicit investment, both in his prose and poetry, in contemporary discourses of prosody and scansion. He writes in light of the historical disjunction between modern versification and scansion. His practice of the metrical vestige stems less from a feeling or desire for meter, as in Hardy or Crane, than from his unpleasant awareness of the struggling metrical contract underpinning poetry's circulation. His antipathy toward free verse, discussed below, has partly to do with a critique of its limited tonal range and partly to do with a general conservatism, but it stems primarily from his sense that free verse forecloses an essential incitement of readers' techniques of listening.

Frost's prosody is not only a matter of varying and renewing iambic meters. Many of the most important poets of the twentieth century composed metrical verse without falling into mechanicity. Iambic pentameter permits many "different individual rhythms" over a normative base, and the dramatic potency it had from Shakespeare and Marlowe to Tennyson and Browning can be found in twentieth-century poetry.[4] Rather, I am interested in Frost's experiment, at the level of scansion, within the decision-making algorithms of early twentieth-century readers of metrical poetry. Where Harriet Monroe mocked the "connoisseurship" of those who "finger-counted iambs," Frost ensures that finger counting will get it wrong (and then hopefully improve). I make this argument at greater length, and with support from generative metrics, in a separate essay on Frost's "loose iambics."[5] While I defer that technical study here, I hope to preserve the logic of scansion as an intentionally difficult and therefore meaningful exercise.

The problem, for both Frost and our study of prosody, is one of historical ear training. In response to the changing status of meter in modernity and, more broadly, to the changing mediation of sound and the speaking voice in modern poetry, Frost demands a refined practice of scansion. The twentieth century did not respond well to that demand, at least outside the pragmatist criticism of Reuben Brower and Richard Poirier (discussed below) and generative metrics. Natalie Gerber argues eloquently that Frost's theories of prosody and sound have not fared well compared to those of other modernists because they demand awareness of higher levels of the phonological hierarchy, specifically intonational contours. The necessary attentiveness to aspects like pitch runs up against the incapacity of historical scansion to provide readers with needed guidance in "explicit prosody." Gerber notes "well-known accounts of the failure of readers to interpret Frost's poems right until they heard him read" and his "displeasure" at this.[6] Sensing this errancy, Frost developed and tested the vestigial form of meter as a way of thinking through poetry's awkward modern aurality.

The history of Frost's reception is a long effort to sideline prosodic difficulty in favor of claims about efficacious voicing or performance. Already in the 1910s many of Frost's peers in London thought he may as well have discarded meter altogether or was in the process of doing so. Amy Lowell heard Frost's movement away from "set iambic" but assumed this meant coming close to free verse.[7] Richard Aldington echoed the sentiment but was less accepting of Frost's "rather stumbling blank verse" (it is interesting that he notes the stumbling).[8] Ford Madox Ford could not understand why Frost did not just write in free verse.[9] Pound stresses his having "the good sense to speak naturally."[10] Against this modernist backdrop we can read

Frost's technical innovation as refusing not only the existing metrical contract but also the assumption that free verse offered less mediated acoustical relations and a more secure ground for poetry as a genre of the speaking voice. By forcing us back to the mediating role of scansion, Frost gives us instead a series of uncanny voices channeled through the vestiges of meter. To hear those metrical voices, we need to roll back the abstractions of voice, rhythm, and form, and follow instead Frost's historical practices of scansion.

Frost's Theory of Meter and Practice of Scansion

Although Frost was a pioneering poet-performer, his criticism suggests he was primarily interested in the "hearing" and "imagining ear" responding to the medium of the written page.[11] Writing (inaccurately) as "the only person going who works on any but a worn out theory (principle I had better say) of versification," he speaks vibrantly of "sentence sounds" at once "definitely and unmistakably indicated by the context" and "summoned by the audile imagination."[12] This looks like evidence of Frost's vernacularity and orientation toward speech, yet his notebooks resist faith in a phenomenology of voice fluidly heard across the meter. He most emphatically evokes that doubt in describing a synesthetic "image of intonation that fades as you try to bring it to the lips."[13] The "fading" of intonation haunts the practice of reading for sentence sounds. Such sounds derive less from spoken language practice than from the complex phenomenology of "voices behind a door that cuts off the words" and wordless "cries of nature."[14] Frost seems almost to regret having to reword his sentences for the sake of a poem. Yet those words are our only cue to prosodic structure, suggesting that readers must suddenly practice scansion via syntax and "context" (a nebulous concept then as now, but Frost has partly in mind higher-order syntax), rather than through mere "grammatical clusters of words."[15] The implicit proposition is that readers must develop and perform a mode of scansion dislocated from historical norms that emphasized the linear sequence of syllables and words. No reader would have been trained, and few readers would have understood what it meant to scan "the vital sentence" from "context," as Frost urges in a letter to Sidney Cox, especially when faced by books of poems like *A Boy's Will* (1913) that are so metrical (mostly strict iambic) on the whole.[16] Even in 1939, when Frost writes "The Figure a Poem Makes" as a preface to the revised *Collected Poems*, he must urge readers that meter alone cannot produce diverse poetic sounds, because "we need the help of context-meaning-subject matter."[17] So, when Frost does characterize meter as necessary to "sentence sound"—he writes of the "strained relation" between "speaking intonation" and "regular preestablished accent and measure"— we should focus on the phenomenological potency of "strain" rather than a benign tension between accentual rhythm and metrical norm.[18] How might that "strain" punch through local divergences to reader's half-conscious efforts to scan?

Frost describes the vestigial practice of scansion as an "Age of accent on 'and.'"[19] He means by this that the average performer ignores syntax, and would stress the word "and" in lines like "The heartache, *and* the thousand natural shocks" (*Hamlet*, 3.1.63, my emphasis). The "age of accent on 'and'" indicates more than the limits of contemporary performance. It suggests a flattening of language by a weight equally distributed to prepositions and, ironically here, away from "ache." The same would occur in a flawed recitation of Keats, "My heart aches, and a drowsy numbness pains/My sense," lines that rupture the clichéd "heartache" through unexpected consecutive monosyllables and the caesura between verb phrases after the third syllable.

To write in an "age of accent on 'and'" required of Frost not a choice between meter and free verse but an effort to jar the reader from a sense of prosody as a cordoned-off zone of counting or elocutionary performance. He had to break not meter but traditional scansion. Such emphatic focus on breaking and reforming scansion conceives poetry not as a unique medium for the human voice to perform identity or the ear to exercise Eliot's "audile imagination" but as a space of writing and reading. In practices of scansion we discover the difficult, modern core of Frost's poetics, where the desire for an experience of universal sound meets the reality of an untrusted mass readership with variably trained hearing.

The formidable technical attention to meter through the fin-de-siècle and early 1910s echoes across Frost's notebooks, letters, and poetry. In the letter to John Bartlett where Frost invokes the powers of the "audile imagination" to summon "sentence sound," he gives as an example the following:

One-two-three—go!
No good! Come back—come back.
Haslam go down there and make those kids get out of the track.[20]

It would be a challenge to notate the intonational contour of this vignette because there are no conventions with which to do so. The description would be so elaborate that we would be better off just reciting it to each

Modernist Scansion

other, if we happen to be in the same place. But if we concatenate lines 1 and 2, we get something very near the rhyming, pentameter-(loose) alexandrine sequence a reader might recognize as ending the Spenserian stanza, for which there are conventions for notation. Two of the three examples given in the letter rhyme, hinting that Frost is intentionally bending genres. Indeed, a contemporaneous notebook shows that the decasyllabic count of the first lines enticed Frost to try his hand at a scansion:

```
    /     /     /     /    /    ˘              /     ˘      /     ˘
One-two-three-go! No Good             Come back, come back.
  ˘    /   ˘   /    ˘   /              ˘    /    ˘     /

  ˘    ˘    ˘    ˘     ˘    /   ˘      ˘    /    /
Let me not to the marriage             of true minds
  ˘   /   ˘   /   ˘    /    ˘          /    ˘    /            21
```

The first line is Frost's attempt to scan the rough accentual rhythm of the ten syllables, but he could not have expected it to be a good description, much less a helpful analysis. The counted numbers seem to deserve not a tenth of a line but, to change units, a quarter note each, as in "One-two-three-four / I declare a thumb war." What really matters to this performance must be pitch, or pacing, or some other element not indicated by the crude markings. This seems to be just Frost's point; he is at once showing the flexibility of meter by juxtaposing his vignette to Shakespeare (scanned in the fourth and sixth line above) and exposing the shortcomings of scansion. In the final line of the scansion, Frost marks the abstract pattern tracking both lines, proving himself something of a generative metrist avant la lettre.[22] In this same notebook, he mocks the musical scansion advocated by Harriet Monroe:

> On Seeing Shakespeare's Rhythm Done in Musical Notation by Harriet.—
> all I can say is it's a damn poor tune.[23]

Frost is referencing Monroe's adoption of a tradition of musical notation, best known through Sidney Lanier though also attempted by the eighteenth-century prosodist Joshua Steele. For Frost this is, in effect, free verse scansion of metrical poetry. There is a prosodic joke in Frost's entry, in that the second line, "all I can say is it's a damn poor tune," is one of his typically monosyllabic and vernacular lines of iambic pentameter. Frost's implication is that Shakespeare's vernacular requires a sense of the historical meter and

> No long-er mourn for me when I am dead
> Then you shall hear the sur-ly sul-len bell

Harriet Monroe's musical scansion of Shakespeare. Monroe, "Editorial Comment," 65.

its flexibility, not fanciful scansions aimed at precise timing. His resistance to non-metrical or free verse scansion is not only a matter of taste or his own form but a keen feeling for the irony of granting free verse the sort of continuity and adaptability of "tradition" through a practice, scansion, that it fundamentally dismisses. This moment and others show a broader antagonism toward contemporary scansion and promise extreme attention to how readers will carry themselves forward from word to word.

Frost's mockeries of free verse, his many notebook scansions, and his early work in several meters (largely strict) leave us with the question of how Frost intended us to scan his verse. We are told to listen for intonation, though Frost worried that "the words of a sentence cant communicate an intonation to one who hasn't previously heard it."[24] There is to my knowledge only one instance in the notebooks or letters where Frost attempts to notate the relative stress of an entire line, perhaps following Otto Jespersen, "Tense2 thy2 strings2 and1 break4 the1 third 2½." To mark "third" with "2½" feels satirical, an excessively quantitative approach he could not have given much credence to.[25]

If the circulation of sound is so historically contingent that it depends on variably trained or accustomed ears that may lack the necessary prior experience of "sentence sounds," and for whom typographic notation is at best a half measure, what is the value of Frost's disruptive innovations? Setting aside loose iambic meter's effort at a transformative engagement with the higher phonological order of intonation, I focus here on how Frost flexed "strict" iambic pentameter throughout his career to highlight problems of intonation, voicing, audition, and ultimately the coherence of reader and speaker alike.

In the simplest terms, strict iambic pentameter is a decasyllabic line, with or without elision ("flower" counted as one syllable) and resolution ("in a" counted as one syllable), sometimes with feminine ending, and tending toward alternating stress. In Frost's notation:

˘   ´   ˘   ´   ˘   ´   ˘   ´   ˘   ´

This pattern is visible in line 6 of Frost's notebook scansion: he has suggested the underlying norm, or iterating pattern, that subtends both Shakespeare and his own vernacular example. There are two essential tendencies for this line as practiced from the sixteenth century through the early twentieth century:[26]

1. The fixed "lexical" stress in polysyllabic words does not occur in odd positions (except after caesurae).
2. Monosyllabic words have no fixed stress and can therefore go anywhere (though this can lead to a lot of difficulty scanning and performing lines).

The first is prescriptive, often strictly and even explicitly so in prosodic history. In his review of *A Boy's Will*, Pound commends Frost for not "gunning about for the circumplexious polysyllable."[27] This points to Frost's penchant for monosyllables while critiquing the Edwardian tendency to flesh out metrical lines by adding convenient polysyllabic words with stresses in even positions. Number (2) is a corollary to (1) and critical to almost all writing, performance, and scansion of English meter. One consequence of these rules is that lines become radically simple to scan when there are automatic stresses "circumplexing" (wrapping around) the line (Donne's "Before, behind, between, above, below") and radically difficult to scan when there are none. Frost rarely violates rule (1) about lexical stress. In "Birches" (*Mountain Interval*, 1920, *CPPP*, 117) the trouble is audible (mismatches in bold):

```
Some boy too far from town to learn baseball.
 W   S   W   S   W   S   W   S   W   S
```

We know to stress the first syllable of the compound, as in "báseball gàme" or "báseball plàyer," and not basebáll, as in "it's called base*ball*, not base*puck*." (Perhaps the boy also grew up "too far from town" to learn the pronunciation.) The line is metrical because Frost, like most poets, treats compound words as pairs of monosyllables—but the result is awkward. "Birches" also has several lines with feminine endings unusually composed of compounds ("cóbwèbs," "snów-crùst," "íce-stòrm"). These effect a rare instability of line ending that, together with enjambment, metrically models the grown speaker's yearning to become again a "swinger of birches." Even that phrase requires a very unusual elision of "swing'r" or resolution of "swin<u>ger of</u>." Taking advantage of monosyllables' metrical properties, as well as loosened rules for elision and resolution, Frost's strict iambic poetry divests readers of their inherited metrical contract and associated performance techniques.

This struggle is a subplot across "Home Burial" (*North of Boston*, 1915, *CPPP*, 55-58), a poem justly lauded for pushing readers into subtle and studied performances of tone in part through its skillful blank verse. Reuben Brower emphasizes the achievement of "breathlessness" and "hurrying" in the poem and the role of Frost's blank verse in such pacing.[28] Although he celebrates "subtle shadings of stress and of phrasing almost certainly traceable to the dramatic role which the poet imposes on the reader," he nowhere finds a way to include such "qualitative" elements in scansion itself.[29] Robert Pinsky finds that the poem "makes its voice or voices present to our imagination" partly through its blank verse, which is "more than a vehicle; it is a physical presence: as corporeal as the infant's corpse."[30] Can a necrotic or undead voice be "present" to us? Tone is too tidily united here with style and meter, as if the performer's syntax and sense of context feel no critical obstruction from the (dead?) body of the versification. To say that Frost was so skilled at meter as to find no impediment to natural speech or "voice" is to miss a desired and marked mediation. Rather, the dramatic dialogue must work to free itself from the intractable prosody of its script and into the fluid air of utterance; it gains the certainty of genre only if we obscure the poem's seemingly lower-order resistance to becoming a series of speech acts. Yet meter behaves too poorly to be overlooked; as with free verse, called "free," Eliot reminds us, only "by people whose ears are not accustomed to it,"[31] Frost's verse can be freed from the ambivalence of meter only by modern critical ears overly accustomed to the idea of poem as speech or speaking subject(s):

> He said twice over before he knew himself:
> "Can't a man speak of his own child he's lost?"
>
> "Not you!—Oh, where's my hat? Oh, I don't need it!
> I must get out of here. I must get air.—
> I don't know rightly whether any man can" (ll. 33-37)
>
> [. . .] And it's come to this,
> A man can't speak of his own child that's dead."
>
> "You can't because you don't know how to speak." (ll. 72-74)

That these passages would be far simpler to perform with italics betrays Frost's casual cruelty toward his prospective readers: we too "don't know how to speak." The cruelty is bound to the failure of meter to guide intonation with some regularity by either matching and promoting stress in even positions or limiting divergence to known exceptions (initial and post-caesural trochaic inversions, elisions). Earlier I described such lines as difficult to scan, but this is not quite accurate. It is very easy to count off from left to right, see ten syllables, to note that the rule against lexical stress in odd positions holds, and to call it blank verse. But that scansion does nothing to help us perform the line, and scansion in turn demands no information from dramatic performance. This emptying out of scansion occurs because Frost abuses the central flexibility of English meter discussed above: monosyllables have historically been permitted to have or lack stress in any position, yet even poets as metrically audacious as Hopkins, Browning, and Stevens rarely adopt this license.[32]

Meter's regulatory function in this poem lies not in facilitating or enhancing speech but in quantitatively meting it out. For instance, the woman's search for hat and air—"Not you! Oh, where's my hat? Oh, I don't need it!/I must get out of here, I must get air" (ll. 38-39)—breaks into two-, four-, and six-syllable chunks of monosyllabic words; dialogue tends to break into ten-syllable lines as if by arithmetical concatenation. Even split lines follow the arcane law: "But the child's mound—"/"Don't, don't don't, don't," she cried" (ll. 31-32). The time of the emotive dash is compressed to zero, to the silent visual space within the broken shared line, as the poem embodies foreclosed life in a procrustean meter that lops off feet, or parts of feet, leaving masses of "don't" and other word-matter.[33] Sometimes these chunks break into iambic feet, but the low frequency of polysyllabic words, especially within the dialogue, repeatedly disturbs metrical entrainment. Frost's "don'ts," like the "one-two-three-go" of his notebooks, constitute an amorphous syllabic mess that both encourages and debilitates our mechanisms of metrical counting. Consider the lines

```
But the world's evil. I won't have grief so
 W   S   W     S W | S   W    S    W  S
If I can change it. (ll. 106-7)
```

The enjambment, like the dash between the split lines, only adds to the sense of speech sound circumscribed by arithmetical accretion (here three sets of five syllables with only one dodgy polysyllable). The poem's scattered feminine endings and syllabic resolutions are not an escape but reminders that outside meter's control there is only "spillage, a profligacy of language."[34]

Where modernism rejects meter for being metronomic, Frost makes modernity's readers feel the absence of its guide like a phantom limb. His lines approximate the abstract grids that Rosalind Krauss describes as "autonomous" but inhospitable to the autonomous self, the "flattened, geometricized, ordered [. . .] antinatural, antimimetic, antireal" structure central to modernist visual art.[35] A few years after Frost publishes *North of Boston*, in the late 1910s, T. S. Eliot and Ezra Pound return to Gautier and the satirical potency of the tetrameter quatrain, with its clipped resistance to speech's freedom, yet eventually the quatrains (and satire) would fall away; in Frost we see prosodic form already achieving an expansive, impersonal presence. The rhetorical question "can't a man speak?" for instance, asks whether humanity has a voice in the face of tragedy in part by opening a prosodic mismatch between our multiple performative options and the man's presumably singular identity. Should we stress "man" here? Perhaps, but the husband is not yet stressing gender at this stage of the drama. He has not yet entrenched himself in the right to specifically male grief. The wife, by contrast, emphasizes gender when she echoes the husband: "I don't know rightly whether any man can." This line lines up stress on "man" as its tenth syllable, following polysyllabic stress on the previous three even syllables. Following this addition of stress to "man" and away from "can," the husband lines up "man" with metrical expectation: "A man must partly give up being a man/ With womenfolk"; "A man can't speak [. . .] " (ll. 52–53). Meter renders the intonational contour certain only after the husband has become thoughtlessly certain in his utterances. In contrast, the man's first hint at gender is almost accidental: "He said twice over before he knew himself/ 'Can't a man speak of his own child he's lost?'" Randall Jarrell teases out the logic of these lines to show how poorly composed the man is, how he regresses into repeated, unconscious repetitions in moments of strain. Rather than claim "I have a right to speak," the man "cites the acknowledged fact that any member of the class *man* has the acknowledged right to mention [. . .] that member of the class of his belongings, *his own child*."[36] The "magnificently dissonant, abject, aggrieved querulousness" of the man's subconscious legalese reveals how little he himself belongs to this category, "man," and how little he "owns" this belonging, the child.[37]

Modernist Scansion 41

That the alternating-stress meter promotes neither "man" nor "owns" suggests not only this "dissonant" identity but the dissonance of trying to perform that identity. How important is the "twice over" here? Should one repeat the utterance in performance, and if so, should one dramatize a shift in stress or insist upon uncritical repetition? The choice is between

1. Can't a màn spéak (no contrastive stress); and
2. Can't a mán spèak (contextual, contrastive stress).[38]

It is hard if not impossible to know whether the contrastive stress of (2) is mandated, because part of interpreting the poem is sorting out how and when the couple interprets the conflict as one of gender. The question is pointedly unresolvable at this moment, unlike the later moment when Frost resolves it for us through the meter's expected alternating stress: "a *man* can't *speak* [. . .]" (my emphases). When meter returns it is thanks to the character's new syntax, which avoids the interrogative reversal of subject and auxiliary verb (can't a man → a man can't) that previously thrust the subject up against the main verb (can't a man *speak*) without the intercession of the normally unstressed auxiliary (a *man* can't *speak*). In other words, the act of questioning inhibits, through the relation of interrogative syntax and metrical scheme, our performance of the line. How different (though hypermetrical) the line would be as "Can't a <u>father</u> <u>speak</u>." Subtleties of intonation might still be up for interpretation, but meter would stably affirm our dramatic choice to stress gender. In Poirier's terms, our performance of "Home Burial" has been actively and meaningfully dis-"entitled"; we do well then to turn our attention not to voice or dramatic expression but to "the fantastic and baffling variability of sounds in any sentence or phrase, and of how this precludes . . . arriving at any sure sense of meaning. The meaning of a piece of writing for [the practiced reader] is in the perceived difficulty of securing one."[39] Meter's failure to guide performance is not just the poem's meta-prosodic meaning but an experience of frustration tailored specifically to ear training and scansion circa 1910. The end of the poem leaves us, like the man, grasping for order:

```
  /   /   /     x   x  / x   x   x   /     / x
"If—you—do!" She was opening the door wider.
  W   S   W     S   W  S   W   S   W     S x
"Where do you mean to go? First tell me that.
I'll follow and bring you back by force. I will!—"
```

The scansion of "If—you—do . . . " is intended, like Frost's dashes, to visualize awkwardness. The polysyllable "opening" installs stress but also requires elision, while "wider" clashes with "door." The scansion indexes an extreme condition of speech, specifically the denaturing, due to distorted cadence, of the alternating stress that makes English amenable to iambics in the first place. In the final line Frost forces an atypical resolution of "<u>follow and</u>," further indexing the incommensurability of speech rhythm and meter. The final prosodic hysteria of italics mocks the orthographic representation of complex voicing. Italics are rare in Frost because the reader is meant, under normal conditions, to intuit stress and tone. The exclamation mark should suffice, as there is no way for "will" not to carry full stress. The only other italics in the poem ("You *couldn't* care!") actively relocate stress. The supplemented "will" turns us away from "sentence sound" and metrical guidance to the brute fact of formatted print and the left-to-right accretion of syllables. Just as the woman closes the door on further talk, the poem closes the door on lived sound and dramatic genre in favor of the mediated murmurs of the audile imagination. It is the poem's final lesson in the dissociation of both character and reader from speech, and of the poet from anything but vestigial meter.

Generative approaches to scansion have suggested that Frost's loose iambic poems bring higher-order syntactic and phonological elements—what Frost calls "context"—back into our too-rote modes of parsing the line. But as Frost knew, phonological acuity is, like listening sensitively to an angry spouse, a limited resource. As Stefanie Markovits has argued, the Victorian verse novel subtly models and drives the slow burn of marriage through the persistent appeal of metrical law.[40] The diminished vestige of the latter is perfectly matched to the withered intersubjectivity of "Home Burial."

Such equations of prosodic and communicative crises pervade Frost's corpus. Early work like the variably rhyming, loose iambic sonnet "Mowing" stands out for its sustained pastoral, its faith in a new genre Frost called "talk-song," and a hard-won metrical freedom juxtaposed to virtually all of the surrounding poems in *A Boy's Will*. It explicitly concerns the evanescence, hyper-particularity, and limitations of sound and hearing, translating the task of modern listening into a pivot from the strict iambic contract. My aforementioned article on Frost's "loose iambics" elaborates this technical achievement; here it suffices to observe Frost's transformative echo, in "Mowing," of the sententious and metrically rigid "Tuft of Flowers." The ellipsis indicates uncertainty:

Modernist Scansion 43

```
And hear his long scythe whispering to the ground
("Tuft")
 W    S    W    S    W        S    W    S    W        S
And that was my long scythe whispering to the ground
("Mowing")
.............................  S        W    S    W        S
```

Little is left to chance in "Tuft," despite the modest flexibility of metrical mismatches ("scythe," "to"). Strict scansion can proceed in "Mowing" only if we already know that "long" is in a strong position, which is of course possible, but this is the product of labor. As "Mowing" puts it, "The fact is the sweetest dream that labor knows." What happens when the labor of listening—of poetic scansion—gives way to the "easy gold" of free verse instead of phonological fact? Or when ear training undergoes the kind of devolution and decay that Frost surveys across the New England land- and soundscape?

This theorization of prosody as "labor" forms an inflection point very early in Frost's career. In most of *A Boy's Will*, grammar dovetails with prosody, as taught by historical handbooks of rhetoric and grammar, and lines scan with schoolroom order even as they profess independence. Scansion becomes less an analytic aid than a mild proof of the poem's form and the reader's abilities. That Frost was nearly forty in 1913 when he produced this first volume with London publisher David Nutt hints that some of the poems must look archly at those representing earlier stages of aesthetic and social development.[41] Subsequent volumes provoke the labor promised in "Mowing" yet with little sense of its efficaciousness. In one of his darkest poems, "To Earthward" (1923, *CPPP*, 210), Frost finds himself in a state of unsought leisure, joy that paradoxically "lacks salt." The poem shifts from the celebration of labor's strain to masochism. Relieving a sore hand, the speaker discovers

> The hurt is not enough:
> I long for weight and strength
> To feel the earth as rough
> To all my length.

Instead of labor and listening, the feeling of anesthesis necessitates violence—here couched in terms belonging to meter: weight, strength, length, and roughness. Frost's effort to give new weight to the length of the line, pressing down on the whole body rather than just the feet, proceeds through pain and endurance. "To Earthward" hints that after the early development of loose iambics, listening and scansion cease to be a process of subjective reflection or dramatic voicing. Versification becomes sound, and sound is ambiguously linguistic or even human.

Later poems like "Design" (1936, *CPPP*, 275) emphasize the world's general illegibility and bind that theme to the poem's own indeterminate and multiple scansions. As James Murphy has shown, "Design" idiosyncratically and ironically positions its titular word with respect to meter.[42] Asking half-heartedly what providential order there is in a white moth caught by a white spider on a white flower, the poem concludes:

```
What but design of darkness to appall,
 W      S       W         S
If design govern in a thing so small.
 W   S W              S
```

We are left wondering whether "design" breaks or redefines the design of meter. Frost repeatedly pairs themes of uncertain listening with ambiguous formal design. For example, there is the wildly rhyming sonnet "Hyla Brook" (1916, *CPPP*, 115) with its wandering, ephemeral river-song; the bluntly rhyming "The Aim Was Song" (1923, *CPPP*, 207), where human music helps a personified wind "see" "the wind the wind had meant to be"; or the variably rhyming "Oven Bird" (*CPPP*, 116) with its wordless, unsung song.[43] Together such works suggest a broader effort to figure and perform the unstable grounds of human knowledge and desire through prosody's quasi-legible, vestigial forms.

The "Hen Dekker Syllables" of "For Once, Then, Something"

Like "Mowing," Frost's poem "For Once, Then, Something" (1923, *CPPP*, 208), takes the conflict between particularity and legibility as the basis of its drama and parses that conflict through a surprising prosodic strategy. The poem is written in the highly formulaic hendecasyllabic meter most associated with Catullus, a choice interesting not merely for its eccentricity and orientation toward a potentially limited audience, but because Frost explicitly wrote his "Hen Dekker syllables" to "tease the metrists."[44] As such it is the poem in which Frost most explicitly foregrounds critical and prosodic reception (or criticism's poor reception of prosody circa 1923). Even this awareness is a trope repeated from Tennyson's "Hendecasyllabics"

Modernist Scansion 45

(1864) an "experiment in quantity" that jokes about itself as a "metrification."[45] Here I largely leave aside the question of how Frost attempts to sound Catullian, focusing rather on how the poem conspicuously diverges from Tennyson's parodic effort. Ultimately, Frost's singular experiment in a classical, quantitative, translated meter becomes all the more idiosyncratic because of its divergence from a nineteenth-century model for adapting the meter. After choosing a decisively non-iambic rhythmic form, Frost proceeds to destabilize his own chosen rhythmic contour by retaining ambiguous intonational contours. He does this in spite of the seeming requirement, in Tennyson, of emphatically evoking a specific repeated rhythm.[46] The poem therefore parallels Frost's general movement away from rhythm toward abstract meter, again with implications for legibility that the poem thematizes explicitly. Prosody recreates a skewed vision of the world (synesthetically pairing sight with hearing) in which both the speaker and his critical "others" participate.

> Others taunt me with having knelt at well-curbs
> Always wrong to the light, so never seeing
> Deeper down in the well than where the water
> Gives me back in a shining surface picture
> Me myself in the summer heaven godlike
> Looking out of a wreath of fern and cloud puffs.
> Once, when trying with chin against a well-curb,
> I discerned, as I thought, beyond the picture,
> Through the picture, a something white, uncertain,
> Something more of the depths—and then I lost it.
> Water came to rebuke the too clear water.
> One drop fell from a fern, and lo, a ripple
> Shook whatever it was lay there at bottom,
> Blurred it, blotted it out. What was that whiteness?
> Truth? A pebble of quartz? For once, then, something.

The poem generally scans according to the following template of weak and strong positions, though this pattern does not orient the poem's rhythm as might be expected:

S W S W W S W S W S W

Nineteenth-century hendecasyllabics use this rubric less as a metrical template for experimentation than as a guide to rhythm, transforming the longs and shorts of the Latin into stress and unstress.⁴⁷ The Latin meter allows for certain variations, schematized here by translator Peter Green:

```
   /       /      /     /     /
– –| – ~  ~ –  | ~ – | ~ – | –
– ~|   –       |     |     | ~
~ –|
```

Green notes the translator's dilemma when faced with a system containing both quantitative (— = long and ~ = short) and accentual (/ = stress) schemes:

> Latin and Greek vowels possess fixed quantities, long or short . . . and this creates a metrical schema independent of, and indeed contrapuntal to, accentual stress and ictus. In English . . . which has no fixed vowel quantities, and thus *only* accentual stress to work with, any attempt to reproduce classical metres is bound to suffer from two serious drawbacks: (a) the sole guide to both accentual stress and metrical schema will be the translator's ingenuity in shaping the line so that the reader instinctively emphasizes the right words; and (b) since this means that more often than not schema and stress pattern will be made to coincide, the contrapuntal effect that forms so attractive a feature of Latin or Greek verse is always in danger of being lost.⁴⁸

The limitations on translating classical meter did not prevent Victorian poets like Tennyson from finding in the alternate *accentual* schema a resource for diverging from set iambic rhythms.⁴⁹ This displacement of iambic expectations is certainly one key effect of turning "iambic into hendecasyllabics" and creating "Hen Dekker syllables." To scan these lines using the familiar strict alternating-stress scansion we need to drop one syllable (indicated by Δ), creating syncopation at the level of scansion as well as performance:⁵⁰

```
    Once, when trying with chin against a well-curb,
    W  S    W   S   Δ   W    S    W S   W  S  (W)
       I discerned, as I thought, beyond the picture,
    W  S  W    S       Δ  W    S      W   S    W    S (W)
```

These lines are not far from headless iambic pentameter or trochaics, given that both "trying" and "as I" could occupy single metrical positions. The scansion shows the shadow iambics, five feet with an opening mono-foot and exactly one midline unfooted element. This suggests that the primary technical difference (which creates the perceived rhythmical differences) between "Hen Dekker syllables" and loosened iambic verse could be that in loose verse unfooted syllables can appear anywhere in the line but in hendecasyllabics must appear between the second and third feet.

This scansion begins to show how Frost is not only participating in a tradition of translated classical meters but writing against that tradition and back toward an iambic horizon. To thoroughly commit itself to the hendecasyllabic meter, the poem might have placed a lexically stressed syllable (that is, the primary stress of a polysyllabic word) consistently in the third position, as does Tennyson:

> O you Chórus of indolent reviewers,
> Irrespónsible, indolent reviewers,
> Look, I cóme to the test: a tiny poem
> All compósed in a metre of Catullus,
> All in quántity, careful of my motion. (ll. 1-5, my accents)[51]

Of note is Tennyson's Catullian placement of rigidly stressed stock phrases like "Indolent reviewers" and conspicuously awkward words like "metrification" to satisfy and emphasize the meter. In both Catullus and Tennyson, the unusual stress patterns at the opening and close of the line consistently become containers for critical, comical messages. Tennyson repeats the epithet-noun phrase "indolent reviewers" no fewer than five times, always in the second half of the line. Polysyllabic words like "metrification," which could only be used line initially in strict iambic verse (because of trochaic inversions), are given a conspicuous midline position ("This metrification of Catullus"), while words like "horticultural" and "Irresponsible," which cannot easily begin an iambic line, do just that. Further aiding the appearance of a hendecasyllabic rhythm are the largely end-stopped lines, which emphasize the feminine endings. This aids familiarity even though more complex line endings like Frost's compound "well-curbs" would be acceptable accentual versions of Catullus. Tennyson also prefers to put syllables in the consecutive weak positions that do not elide into a single position ("to the" and "in a" would resolve, if Tennyson allowed resolution, but one struggles to count "chorus'f" or "litt'l" as single positions). While the Catullian pattern permits one long syllable in that place, the accentual effect would completely lose the choriamb and sound far too trochaic.

Tennyson's emphasis on the non-iambic stress rhythm suggested by the

Latin meter does not entirely transfer to Frost's experiment. His copy of Catullus shows he knew, like Tennyson, about the Latin line's accentual structure:

```
  ́     ́   ̆  ̆  ́        ́      ́
Cui dono lepidum novum libellum⁵²
```

The scansion seems to be focused primarily on stress, because at least for this poem he omits the symbol for a quantitative long syllable. Or perhaps the scansion was done by or for Frost's daughter Lesley, for whom Frost devised a contest to write English poems based on Catullus's meter. Lesley would likely have gone about the task by following an accentual pattern roughly equivalent to the Latin, slotting in stress contours much as a Latin schoolchild would obey quantity with the help of a *Gradus ad Parnassum*. Perhaps then the double off-stresses in the copy of Catullus were markers that Lesley could most easily follow.

Frost took the contest elsewhere with his "Hen Dekker syllable" poem. Its aim is less to echo Catullus, or even to diverge from iambics along what Frost considered the "short" track of the nineteenth century's invented meters,[53] than to mark the transformation of the metrical form when brought into contact with New England intonation. Frost's witty renaming signals his effort to convert Latin meter, with its quantities, to New England accents. Though he spoke of it as a "strict performance" in which he turned "iambic into hendecasyllabics,"[54] it is equally an effort to adapt the flexibility of iambic meter to the rigid rhythm of English hendecasyllabics.

Frost's flexibility takes two forms. Foremost is the tendency to downplay stressed positions by avoiding lexical stress in favor of monosyllables. Just under 40 percent (29 of 75) of stressed positions (1, 3, 6, 8, 10) contain lexical stress. Though a higher percentage than found in Frost's iambic verse, this is low compared to Tennyson (over 60 percent, 65 of 105 positions lexically stressed, including secondary stress). Many of Frost's lines have only one position thus locked down, and none have more than three. These are lines in Tennyson that pull viciously against the accentual mapping of long = stressed, short = unstressed because they can be easily parsed by the very different iambic metrical contract ("O blatant Magazines, regard me rather"). One can imagine particularly "blatant" prosodists objecting to such teasing lines while more subtle ears would hear the joke. Another line places "is" in a strong position to mock its own "dainty meter":

```
So fantastical is the dainty meter  (14)
 S  W  S  W W  S   W   S W    S W
```

But most of Tennyson's poem preserves the hendecasyllabic rhythm through the choriambic SWWS coming after the opening trochee.

These few challenges to the accentual classical meter become Frost's entire project: not only his disruption of hendecasyllabic scansion but a reflection of his strict meter generally. By contrast, Frost's loose iambics demand that the reader recognize the syntactic and semantic value of words and structure the meter accordingly, almost like free verse but with an identifiable relationship to iterative accentual-syllabic meters. In his hendecasyllabics we see instead the model for a particularly difficult strict verse with rigidly aligned but ambivalently satisfied positions. It is tempting to think of such tricky iambics as similar to Milton's or Hopkins's counterpointing: efforts, not unlike loose iambics, to perturb or dislocate traditional strict meter with a clear hope that the ear will recover and grow. In "For Once," however, the experiment is not merely one of dislocation but of active "teasing" to the point of perversity. Frost adopts and then dissolves a form whose presence should be as stately as well-formed strict iambics and just as successful in guiding intonation.

Given the poem's occasion as a metrical exercise, John Talbot observes "the matter of the poem came out of its meter." Yet the "meter" is not a fixed or iconic entity but rather a complex and disfiguring realization. Talbot suggests that Frost, like Catullus and Tennyson, uses the meter as a medium for riposte against those who would see him as a bumpkin-poet. Frost may indeed be "wielding hendecasyllabics"[55] in this manner, but his "teasing" of the metrists goes beyond merely showing his chops in a classical pattern. The deeper "teasing" stems from Frost's strangely muted or "blurred" realization of the meter; "Hen Dekker syllables" are akin to those specific sentence sounds that according to Frost must already be known to the reader to be heard, failing to belong to a set of universally legible formulae or even formulae known to metrists and classicists. The effect of this particularity is, as in the case with Frost's loose iambics, the decisive absence of clear guides to performance.

The poem's varying affinity for its chosen metrical pattern is crucial to its larger meditation on what the "something" is that the poet has seen and how he is to tell the "others" about it. Frost's synesthetic joke, perhaps at the expense of Imagism or Pound's "phanopoeia," is that the speaker's extreme absorption in visuality must be mediated, in a poem, by a metricized speech that defies our powers of interpretive listening. Where strict meter and its traditional scansion allow a reader to see and hear how the poet has manipulated the expectations set up by a recognizable underlying pattern, and where loose meter rejects a priori metrical form for one that registers syntax and meaning, Frost's hendecasyllabics are a meter without strong precedent for variation in English (unlike Catullus's hendecasyllabics, which permitted certain variations in both quantity and stress contour). Frost asks us to look for the interplay of rhythm with the abstract pattern when that pattern has virtually no precedent other than the foreign one given by Catullus.[56] The task appears monumental when one considers that the irregular development and redevelopment of iambic verse, from Chaucer's borrowing from the French to later Elizabethan efforts, took centuries (Dryden refused to believe that Chaucer had "ten syllables in a verse where we find but nine").[57] In the poem's interplay of phrasing and meter, the reader discovers not mutual support (i.e., the phrasal rhythms help define the meter, and the meter guides performance) but rather an indeterminacy of presentation.

I discuss the poem's idiosyncratic meter at such length because the poem, to a greater extent than any of Frost's other works save perhaps "Mowing," takes as its subject the uncertain phenomenology of experience specifically as communicated in poetry. In "Mowing" we are invited to listen carefully to the labor of the poet just as the mower (or mower-poet) listens to his world. "For Once" offers no such invitation to experience our reading as mimetic of the speaker's experience. It decrypts and dramatizes Frost's synesthetic "image of intonation that fades as you try to bring it to the lips": the speaker's attempt to see a fixed object through a mess of distractions becomes the reader's attempt to get down to the poem's ambiguous, equally nebulous sound.

In the second half of the poem, the speaker staring down the well at his reflection comes close to seeing something "beyond the picture,/Through the picture" (ll. 8-9). Poirier comments that this scene participates in a common literary topos in which an "individual identity gets elevated above its own reflected image so that it may then gaze down on itself as if it were, absurdly, looking into the source of life's mystery."[58] Frost enhances the absurdity of the moment by having the speaker behave as if the droplet of water came and eradicated the *one* possibility for perception. The speaker all but invites the skeptical "Others" to ask why he does not wait for the ripples to clear and then look again. And if that added absurdity is insufficient, what are we to make of the near personification of the ferns ringing the well-curb, whose missive droplet "came to rebuke the too clear water"?

These absurdities seem to mock the speaker's hope that his personal way of looking will produce a well-defined experience of "something." His subjective vision is bound up with an impressionistic projection of agency and with too much investment in a singular spot of time. Katherine Kearns has noted in this regard the poem's "apprehension" about "lyric self-reflexiveness."[59] Yet neither does the skepticism of the "Others" seem any less absurd in the belief that there is a correct or literally *right* angle at which to look down wells and to avoid the interference of reflection.

The poem converts its unanswerable epistemological question about how to look at the world into a question of tone:

> One drop fell from a fern, and lo, a ripple
> Shook whatever it was lay there at bottom,
> Blurred it, blotted it out. What was that whiteness?
> Truth? A pebble of quartz? For once, then, something. (ll. 12-15)

The question of how to interpret the tone and meaning of the last two lines is largely a question of how to stress them. Do we hear in "what was that whiteness?" an echo of the intense listening of "Mowing's" "what was it it whispered?" That "whispering" is evanescent yet also realized in the poem's meter and diction. Its seriousness as a poetic object relies upon the reader finding her own evanescent sounds in the prosodic form of the poem. Nowhere in that poem are we told "lo, a whisper," and we are warned *not* to look for things like personified ferns. If the speaker's experience of "whiteness" is as serious as the labor in "Mowing," that seriousness must lie not in the speaker's experience but in its ineffability. We cannot elevate "was" into "*was*"—into a sign of retrospection, despite the hendecasyllabic meter's determination to stress it. We learn to stress the experience of the past in "Mowing"—"what was it it whispered?"—through our experience of the meter's whispering. The hendecasyllabic meter instead vaguely tells us to stress "was" in consecutive lines, pulling us into an "age of accent on 'was'" where grammatical function words rise ambivalently to metrical prominence. Do we stress "was" because the pattern tells us to, or do we freely stress it and incidentally shore up the pattern? Do we have a reason to defy the pattern and try out "*what* was that whiteness?" That might stress the object's qualities over subjective experience. The problem is that either choice begs the poem's question of how experience and its objects determine each other.

These final lines epitomize Frost's pervasive metrical ambiguity: a complexity in poetry stemming not from imagery or syntax but from the reader's effort to replicate a poem's speech acts. They confirm Poirier's sense that "vocalizing" makes readers sensitive not to intonation as such but to its "baffling variability."[60] In the very last line "there are enticements to significance," writes Poirier:

> There are, however, no entitlements. It is by that particular phrase ["for once, then, something"] . . . that one is held to so strict an accounting. The phrase refuses to surrender its vagueness to any one of a variety of competing emphases, which can fall on the word "once" or on the word "something" or, by different prolongations of the voice, on "then."[61]

The haze of stress contours conjured by the monosyllabic phrases of the final lines form a specialized kind of ambiguity, a set of "intonational possibilities" as well as interpretations that constellate without settling. That ambiguity is particularly jarring given the traditional allure of classical and foreign meters as providing new rhythmic contours or more physically imposing sonic efforts (as in Longfellow's trochaic *Hiawatha* [1855] or Pound's alliterative strong-stress "Seafarer" [1911]).

From the heights of the gazer's "shining surface picture," wreathed in ferns, against the "summer heaven godlike" (both rhythmically fixed phrases, as in Tennyson), the poem concludes with parallel visual and metrical ambiguity. Unlike "Mowing" there is no resting place, no moment where speaker and reader can "[leave] the hay to make" in perfect iambs and inhuman, grammatical intransitivity. In "For Once" our prosodic labor continues to the very end, matching but not resolving the final ambiguity of whether the speaker has found "something" or not and whether that is decisive or underwhelming. The poem teases not only the metrists and epistemologists but the modernists who envisioned poetic language stripped of adjectives and descriptive flourishes, Pound's "direct treatment of the thing." Modernism's desire for the "rich phenomenality" of the material object descends here from a mode of "truth" to another precarious sentimental attachment.[62]

The vestigiality of "Hen Dekker syllables" forecloses the would-be soundscape of free verse, but this turn against modernist "others" is less significant, I believe, than the metrical vestige's simple feeling of inadequacy. Frost's poem turns above all against the metrical vernacularity he evokes in his "talk-songs." "For Once" is a dark poem, a Catullian riposte to his own faith in versification and the benefits of prosodic mastery. We would need something beyond the meter, a grace note, to solve the ambiguities of form and tone that emerge in spite of the normally rigid meter—or to spite it. The very late Victorianism of Frost's translated meter speaks, finally, to meter's inability to sustain dramatic performance.

The Late Meter of "Directive"

In his late masterpiece "Directive" (*Steeple Bush*, 1947, *CPPP*, 341) Frost creates a dispossessed landscape suited to the metrical confusion without recovery we see in "For Once, Then, Something." It is a poem about a guide who promises to neglect us, to get us lost so that we can parabolically "find ourselves." If we are lost, it is because we wish to (or must get) "Back out of all this now too much for us." There may be a dozen ways of performing this line, a "too muchness" created by the monosyllabic prosody that both mimics and creates the line's content. It echoes the very similar metrical "too muchness" and lost iambicity of Wordsworth's "The World Is Too Much with Us" (1807). Wordsworth's poem may have taught Frost how to strategically lay waste to meter not by abandoning it (it too is "too much" with us) but by registering its vestigiality. Frost's opening line asks not only whether we can situate ourselves without a guide, but whether we can hear a poem's language when meter provides virtually no hint for performance (and may, like the speaker-guide, "only have at heart our getting lost"). It is only when we are returned to "a time made simple by the loss/of detail, burned, dissolved, and broken off/Like graveyard marble sculpture in the weather" (ll. 2-4) that the iambic rhythm of the past emerges. This false history, "made simple by the loss of detail," is the temporality revealed by the metrical vestige.

How much freedom we have to read the first line of "Directive" is never resolved: iambs could never really save us. Later we're told to "make yourself up a cheering song of how/Someone's road home from work this once was," suggesting that the aestheticized soundscape depends on self-delusion. Sonic self-preservation may also depend on escaping the nursery rhyme cadence haunting the only short-footed line in the poem, "Sómeone's road hóme from wórk this once wás." The final line, "Drink and be whole again beyond confusion," is commonly misread as optimism, as if aesthetic power could direct us *past* confusion any more than nostalgia performs the work of mourning. Phillip Booth notes that much of the poem trades in stock images from Frost's earlier work, a shattered return to "his poetry's wellspring."[63] Its retreat to the rustic is cold pastoral. Aren't we merely "again beyond confusion"? Even the "whole" might be a "hole," given the pervasiveness of holes in the poem. There is the "cellar hole / Now slowly closing like a dent in dough"; the strange, repetitive acoustics of the "serial ordeal / Of being watched from forty cellar holes / As if by eye pairs out of forty firkins"; even the "pecker fretted apple trees," the glacier's "chisel-work," and the field now "no bigger than a harness gall" are holes of a sort, worse holes in being the product of nature's slow, anthropomorphized, perhaps sexual violence.[64]

"Directive" proves and extends William Empson's observation that meter is at the core of poetic ambiguity and that we should take this ambiguity not as mere intrigue or productive paradox but as a centrifugal force upon language and meaning:

> The reason that ambiguity is more elaborate in poetry than in prose, other than the fact that the reader is trained to expect it, seems to be that the presence of metre and rhyme, admittedly irrelevant to the straightforward process of conveying a statement, makes it seem sensible to diverge from the colloquial order of statement, and so imply several colloquial orders from which the statement has diverged.[65]

For Empson this is a liberation from the "order" of mimesis into the polyvocality of language in all its rich ambiguity. In Veronica Forrest-Thomson's terms, prosody forces us out of "bad naturalization" and back to artifice by "fictionalizing" the empirical as such.[66] Frost registers that this "divergence" from the natural order produced by lyric reading is also oppressive. Meter may free the poet from merely setting down, gramophonically, his or her speech, but it also insists that in poetry there is never a single sonic order to recognize and reproduce. Frost's modernist meter constitutes a core rejection of the dramatic and communicative imperatives that drove the rejection of meter in the first place.

Just as the past in "Directive" can be only an object of nostalgia, the metrical vestige can no longer fix poetic genres or performance. Modern poetry seems to have decided this early, largely because it could not trust a popular association of versification, genre, and literary merit. Neither could Frost and the poets studied across this book—many of them canonically "modern"—but they responded by feeling and enduring the vestigiality of meter, rejecting a theory of expressive rhythm no less indebted to Romanticism and the nineteenth century than accentual-syllabic meter. The abandonment of meter for free verse rhythm came with the attendant hope that new meters would create new genres that could be perceived and embraced by new generations of readers. Frost met this hope with a devout skepticism, suggesting that newness must mean uncertainty about experience, that poetry must register that uncertainty, and that it can (and for Frost must) do so by strategically echoing a vestigial prosody still felt and desired though offering no resolution and only small compensation.

2 Penty Ladies
T. S. Eliot, Satire, and the Gender of Modern Meter

> Strolling through those colleges [. . .] the body seemed contained in a miraculous glass cabinet through which no sound could penetrate. [. . . A] kindly gentleman [. . .] regretted in a low voice that ladies are only admitted to the library if accompanied by a Fellow.
>
> —Virginia Woolf, *A Room of One's Own*

Frost was famously skeptical about free verse. Pound and Eliot famously became skeptical, returning to metrical quatrains in the late 1910s in what is often read as "an essentially restorative gesture, as a traditionalist's attempt to smooth over the cracks in cultural history that had been spreading since the second half of the nineteenth century."[1] Rather than charting a turn from and then back to meter, from rejection of tradition to a recalibrated, critical embrace of tradition, in this chapter and the following I trace Eliot's and then Pound's long-standing ambivalence toward modern prosodic culture and meter's vestiges within it. Eliot's core response to meter's apparent etiolation is to treat its flaws as effeminacies and then recover, by negation, a masculine metrical practice. This is part and parcel with his and Pound's well-known and oft-critiqued critical and editorial misogyny. The narratives of modernism as a revolt against effeminacy and against the metronome are mutually sustaining—though neither, I try to show, gets their author very far.

The formal redemption narrative might make sense for a quatrain poem like Eliot's "Whispers of Immortality," but its literary historiography depends on a misogynistic twist of modernism's "program of obsessive cultural hygiene":[2]

Penty Ladies 57

> Grishkin is nice: her Russian eye
> Is underlined for emphasis;
> Uncorseted, her friendly bust
> Gives promise of pneumatic bliss.
>
> The couched Brazilian jaguar
> Compels the scampering marmoset
> With subtle effluence of cat;
> Grishkin has a maisonette;[3]

These stanzas follow a modernist impulse to attack a "feminized realm of aesthetic beauty" as "the end game of a culture in racial decline, the sterile product of too much cultivation."[4] Against cultural decline Eliot wields, for the brief postwar moment between *Prufrock and Other Observations* (1917) and *The Waste Land* (1922), the quatrain and strict iambics as a male poet's prerogative. In the second stanza Grishkin is shunted by the semicolon into headless iambic tetrameter. Her quatrains contrast with the rhythmic freedom the poem first affords Donne and Webster, who wrote in famously flexible meter. They did not write in these quatrains, which serve rather to mimic and master Grishkin's "pneumatic bliss."[5] Eliot here masquerades in distressed forms with an ironic feeling of superiority over occupants like Grishkin or lyric poetesses. This gendered masquerade is a negative version of what Michael North calls the "racial masquerade": the belief that white poets can safely adopt nonwhite personae or styles for an infusion of energy.[6]

In his study of Picasso's *Ma jolie*, T. J. Clark describes how "painting itself" becomes "a form of doleful violence against the nude." Yet no "empirical quiddity" results from this steady process of gendered negation in which "every vestige of integrity or sensual presence is done to death—every vestige but that of 'paint itself,' put on with such delicate, sober virtuosity—in the belief, apparently, that only there would some genuine grasp of the body be possible." The similarly gendered rejection of meter in favor of rhythm "itself" follows this belief, sacrificing the vestige in the hope of a new aesthetic body for poetry. Yet Eliot's fraught odalisques, like Picasso's nudes, never cease to wonder whether "any other ground for representation had been secured."[7]

In her biography of Eliot, rightly scathing in its reproach of his anti-Semitism and sexism, Lyndall Gordon finds the "distortion of women [. . .]

inexplicable in a man of questioning intelligence."[8] Some of that intelligence asserts itself, I argue, as Eliot recognizes the inadequacy of gendering meter and satirizing women poets as a means of securing a response to the complexities of literary history and the history of form. A range of critics has discussed how Eliot, Pound, and other "Men of 1914" established literary authority by developing socio-aesthetic foils from the art and sensibility of the Victorian, Edwardian, and Georgian periods.[9] The progressive women's movement, for example, "provided a maternal object against which the modernists might launch an explosive revolt."[10] Modernist poems strategically contain female figures like the "older, cultured woman" associated with "empty social ritual and repetition."[11] Gail McDonald finds that the feminine could be "something to be envied, a symbol and source of powerful vitality [. . .] though in need of harnessing"; the latter was made possible by an ironic posture modeled on "the sophisticated and knowing presences of Laforgue's poetry."[12] She adds that Eliot's and Pound's worry about cultural authority and their resulting effort to assume for poetry the "orderly rigours of science" demanded "dissociation from the presumed chaotic ease of the feminine."[13]

Pound's and Eliot's early poetries contain obsessive references to overly sentimental, often hysterical or melodramatic women mired in an outdated culture. They create distance from their gendered objects—usually objects of satire, unless sufficiently wan and maidenly—with the formal control of meter. This is an old proposition, mastered in Pope's satire or Browning's dramatic irony. Eliot seeks further authority by isolating an antithetically feminine prosody belonging to poetess figures like Fresca from *The Waste Land* drafts. Rigid meter and abject femininity may be strange bedfellows, especially when one recalls the male gendering of blank verse in the nineteenth century. Oliver Wendell Holmes contrasts the easy performance of pentameters by "an individual of ample chest and quiet temperament" to struggles with "the octosyllables of Scott or Tennyson or Longfellow" by "a person of narrower frame and more nervous habit."[14] Yet as early as 1893 Harriet Monroe identifies the "feminine grace" of accentual-syllabic forms inherited from French and with a muddy philological imaginary later discovers an alternative in the "rugged cadences" of Whitman's "strong Hebraic music."[15]

The gendering of form and genre has a much broader basis in modern literature, though it often returns to specific prosodic forms. In Joyce's *Portrait of the Artist*, Stephen Dedalus advances synchronously through literary forms and stages of life. The motor of the bildungsroman is in part the way he "dissolve[s] the maternal bond in order to accomplish a full differentiation of self and world."[16] In his pre-"differentiated" days Stephen is too sentimental, which fittingly leads him to compose in the fin-de-siècle light verse form of the villanelle.[17] Perhaps not coincidentally, Pound denatures the form in "Villanelle: The Psychological Hour" (1915) just as he finishes serially publishing Joyce's *Portrait*. Virginia Woolf's Orlando carries with them a juvenile poem, "The Oak Tree," which they successfully off-load only in the Victorian era (while biologically female). The reader is under no illusion that either the poem or Orlando's Victorian moment are laudable—Orlando publishes the poem, marries, starts a family, and in some sense surrenders independence to survive.[18] The bad form of the aesthetic object here is written in women's meter, serving a female (or worse, feminizing) subjectivity. Eliot's impersonal meter rejects the feminine not only by policing sentimentality but also by positing versification as an object, liberated from female subjectivity. This is an example of what Doug Mao calls modernism's "test of production," an effort to believe in the literary-aesthetic object's "extra-subjective integrity" despite the dual threats of commodification and the imperial (here female) subject.[19] Meter as vestige lacks that object-like integrity; only a strong dose of masculine irony and chauvinism could make meter an impersonal or "hard" form.

The "rejection of the feminine" was, in McDonald's account, "double-edged": "The female was something to be feared, linked as it was to amateurism, flaccidity, and emotionality. On the other hand, to accept this definition of femininity was to accede to the system of values that had, in the first place, 'feminized' and disempowered the poets."[20] In keeping with this dynamic, to reject meter as feminine atavism was to commit, ironically, to a neo-Victorianism—one all the more troubling given Pound and Eliot's actual appreciation for Victorian metrics. To what extent, then, do their portraits of women reflect upon if not reject the "illusion of some absolute otherness" through which the male poet reaffirms a valued place of seclusion and alienation?[21] I agree with Enikő Bollobás's suggestion that the insulation provided by irony and critical judgment fails because the "alienation and ennui" of Eliot's women are not essences so much as the effects of the "male script" that denies them "a self outside the heterosexual context"[22] Accordingly, Pound's and Eliot's gendering of meter as an atavism naively taken up by Victorian poetry reveals not a masculine alternative but the limits of modern poetry's formal autonomy and generic self-concept. The gendering and then control of meter appears as a central condition for satire as a "textual machine or mechanism for producing difference" and for preserving a privileged subject position within modern poetry, but meter's gendering also reveals satire's "anxiety about proximity."[23] The underlying desire for meter that drives modern poetry's deployment of metrical vestiges cannot be resolved by a chauvinistic rhetoric of difference. The chapter accordingly closes with a study of how Eliot must reinvent the history of meter and metrical poetry as an object for formalist criticism.

"Too Penty" Ladies

My focus here is limited to Eliot's early association of meter with decadent or effeminate culture, up to *The Waste Land*, where I argue he turns against the too-convenient investment in gendered form. I leave aside his later investment in figures of female grace—the paradoxical "lady of silences [. . .] torn and most whole" of *Ash Wednesday* (1930) or Marina, "more distant than stars and nearer than the eye." I chart this path through *The Waste Land* to better understand the force of Eliot's desire, albeit sexist, for the vestiges of meter and thus his unwillingness to permanently ground it in fragile dichotomies.

Meter cadences the satire of "The Love Song of J. Alfred Prufrock" (1915, *CPTSE*, 3) through its differential framing of two kinds of women. When, at the end of his monologue, Prufrock dreams of returning to the ocean and its singing mermaids (in one draft "sea-girls" was "sea-maids"), the totalized and mythic space of the ocean is recalled in a relatively flexible iambic meter:

> I have seen them riding seaward on the waves
> Combing the white hair of the waves blown back
> When the wind blows the water white and black.
>
> We have lingered in the chambers of the sea
> By sea-girls wreathed with seaweed red and brown
> Till human voices wake us, and we drown. (ll. 126-31)

This is not merely a passage of iambic pentameter but a lesson in metrical flexibility absent from the rest of the poem. Only the final line winds the metronome. Before this line moments of contiguous stress, paired with assonance, sustain unusually vivid imagery—the "white hair of the waves blown back" and the "sea-girls wreathed with sea-weed." The accomplishment of the rhythm and alliteration embody the hope for escape into inhuman otherness up to the point where we "wake" into despair and strict iambic rhythms.

The "waking" iambic rhythm parallels Prufrock's famous synecdochic substitution for himself, which carefully performs a pleasantly mindless rhythmic and alliterative scuttling: "I should have been a pair of ragged claws / Scuttling across the floors of silent seas" (ll. 73-74). The alliteration exactly matches stress, avoiding any tension with meter beyond the initial trochaic inversion. Prufrock and his metrical rhythm can neither ride "seaward on the waves" nor linger in the ocean bottom's realm of unconscious repetition. That mindlessness echoes another rhythmic scuttle, belonging to the poem's chatty women, sticking in the ear of Prufrock and reader alike. Their crass refrain, "In the róom the wómen cóme and gó / Tálking of Míchelángeló" (ll. 13-14 and 35-36, my emphasis), overrides "talk" with metrification into simple tetrameter. The rhyme and refrain pull both lines away from speech into alternating stress not proper to the Italian name "Michelangelo." The poem, as Prufrock's "song," measures out women's taste as a metronomic "come and go" in which the artifice of rhyme and meter overwhelms language.

The metronomic form of the chatting women insinuates itself into Prufrock's repetitive language and rhythm. His words are full of iambic, metricized phrases, frequently formed around a rhetorically fruitless "and," which tend to double or triple themselves: "a toast and tea," "tea and cakes and ices," "visions and revisions," "decisions and revisions," "works and days," "days and ways." These sterile doublings rhetorically and prosodically express Prufrock's emasculation. Metrical rhythm physically enacts the formulation by (presumably) female eyes tormenting Prufrock: "And I have known the eyes already, known them all— / The eyes that fix you in a formulated phrase" (ll. 55-56). These eyes, which "fix" and "formulate" Michelangelo acoustically, transfix Prufrock's cadences.

This reading of Prufrock's "fixing" into alien rhythm reveals a modern psyche overwritten by feminine surroundings. The original title was "Prufrock among the Women." Just as Prufrock is circumscribed by his feminized rhythms, so is the poem by its repeated prosodic and thematic echoes from French symbolist poetry and other sources. According to Peter Nicholls, the poem's "moments of dramatic self-interrogation," moments where we might glimpse a dramatic figure battling his surroundings, are consistently "revealed as literary allusion."[24] Whether this really troubles the poet's autonomy from Prufrock depends upon his comfort with a reception defined by skilled echo tracing. Edmund Wilson easily tracks down in Eliot the cadences of Laforgue and Corbière, suggesting not only that the debt was an open secret but also that for a certain group the echoes would have been precisely the point of the poem.[25] Pound's annotations to Eliot's drafts show striking intimacy with his idiom and style. For example, his annotations on the manuscript of "The Death of the Duchess" include "Pruf" and then "cadence reproduction from Pr or Por." Pound's second comment annotates a line clearly indebted to Prufrock's rhythms: "And if I said 'I love you' should we breathe/[...] as before?" (Both "Portrait of a Lady" (1915) and "Prufrock" have many lines beginning with "and" and containing "should": "And should I then presume"; "and should I have the right to smile"). Pound's ear is so attuned to intonations of hesitancy in Eliot's earlier work that he suggests a strange inversion of this line: "And if I said I love you *we should* breathe/ . . . as before?" The intonation shifts to an appropriately meek, pathetic worry about what might happen, about what one's lover "should say," and this is precisely the transformation Prufrock undergoes and which defines the Duchess.[26] This male sociality of the rhythmic echo, in which Pound helps Eliot echo and modify his own intonational contours, may preserve the male poet as one who can knowingly constitute and revise himself via prosodic formulae. From this perspective Prufrock's isolated song can escape from effeminate culture into rhythmic form so long as poetry can find a way to more happily "talk to a coterie or to soliloquize" than Eliot thought possible in his criticism.[27]

"Portrait of a Lady" (*CPTSE*, 8) polices that coterie by lampooning Eliot's undergraduate teas with Adelaide Moffatt.[28] The poem is a triptych of scenes taking place in December, April, and October. As the seasons revolve, the woman becomes increasingly worried by her relation to the speaker; first she speaks abstractly of friendship, then of the man as a friend who has not yet reached his hand "across the gulf," and finally she asks "why we have not developed into friends." The male speaker resembles Prufrock, climbing stairs and observing women speaking about art. The poem is more explicit than "Prufrock" in contrasting the man's mobility and autonomy with the lady's stasis. At various points in the poem the man invites his (presumably male) auditor with "Let us take the air"; he is seen ascending her stairs; he takes his hat to leave, plans to go abroad for an extended trip. The lady remains in the smaller spaces of drawing and concert rooms. After hearing a concert of Chopin, she regrets the music's exposure; the man by contrast reimagines the music "transmitted," as if by radio (another "latest Pole"):

> We have been, let us say, to hear the latest Pole
> Transmit the Preludes, through his hair and finger-tips.
> "So intimate, this Chopin, that I think his soul
> Should be resurrected only among friends
> Some two or three, who will not touch the bloom
> That is rubbed and questioned in the concert room." (ll. 1:8-13)

Her refrain, contrasting with the man's invitation to a walk and closer to "In the room the women come and go," is "I shall sit here, serving tea to friends." She lives in the Prufrockian realm of "velleities" (small wills) and "carefully caught regrets" that reflect how she herself is "carefully caught" by the circumstances of gender.

The man, conscious of the tight physical and emotional spaces in which he finds himself, reacts strongly to their first conversation:

> Among the windings of the violins
> And the ariettes
> Of cracked cornets
> Inside my brain a dull tom-tom begins
> Absurdly hammering a prelude of its own,
> Capricious monotone
> That is at least one definite "false note."
> —Let us take the air, in a tobacco trance,
> Admire the monuments,
> Discuss the late events.
> Correct our watches by the public clocks.
> Then sit for half an hour and drink our bocks. (ll. 1:29-40)

To prepare his escape into the masculine public sphere, the man differentiates himself and his discourse by insinuating that the lady's conversation is responsible for setting the "dull tom-tom" going. His distaste associates her words with "the ariettes/of cracked cornets." The "capricious monotone" and "dull tom-tom" render the contrast between gendered minds and spaces as a matter of rhythm.[29] To consider meter an impoverished experience because of the absence of pitch (a monotone, or a muted "false note") is, as Frost recognized, to ask of meter something it has never provided, in English or other accentual-syllabic poetries, and that Eliot and his masked representative cannot remedy.

The poem cannot alter the relation between phonology and poetics, so it differentiates the man's mobility, enacted in his curtailed lines and framing rhymes, from the woman's stasis, embodied through her generally pentameter iambic rhythms and limited rhyme repertoire. The rhymes of "ariette"/"cracked cornet" and "monuments"/"late events" each abandon the longer line; this blunt catalexis reflects the man's prerogative. Across the poem he arrogates to himself the right to shorten or lengthen the meter whenever a rhyme might cordon off the lady. Prosody permits the role of spectator: "Now that lilacs are in bloom/She has a bowl of lilacs in her room/And twists one in her fingers while she talks." "Talks" rhymes back three lines to "clocks"/"bocks" and forward three lines to a parenthetical, which cuts off the lady's talk: "(Slowly twisting the lilac stalks)." The play of expanded rhyme and catalexis extends to anagram: the "monotone" she effects turns into a "false note." The lady, by contrast, cannot control rhyme and variable line length as framing devices. She shortens her lines only twice without creating the same kind of ironic distance. The second instance, for example, creates the poem's lone triplet: three end-stopped four-beat headless lines at odds with the man's more fluid, variable line lengths.

> We must leave it now to fate.
> You will write, at any rate.
> Perhaps it is not too late. (ll. 3:22–24)

The strict alternating stresses of the first two lines and the rhyme make us expect the third line to follow suit, but it is as rhythmically depressed as the sentiment it expresses. If there is any freedom from the rigors of the "dull tom-tom," it does not serve the lady well. The same will be true, with the added crisis of caesurae, of the hysterical wife figure in *The Waste Land*. Such lines perform Eliot's metrical theory, setting up a norm to enable variation, but the result is a poetics in which iambic rhythms not only sound normative but "signal metricality."[30] When Eliot signals metricality he positions the male speaker as one who must create meaningful variation.

The man makes it explicit that engaging with and then portraying the lady demands his heightened plasticity:

> And I must borrow every changing shape
> To find expression . . . dance, dance

> Like a dancing bear,
> Cry like a parrot, chatter like an ape. (ll. 3:26-29)

The history of forms, however much it is a bestiary, remains his to adapt for expression. He may feel, like Eliot himself, that he must "ape" older forms to gain momentum, but his Promethean "dance," "cry," and "chatter" is no doubt preferable to iambic ennui. Better to be "Apeneck" Sweeney than Grishkin. The lady, like Fresca of *The Waste Land* drafts and the wife figure in "A Game of Chess," is surrounded by metonymic accoutrements; she accumulates rather than reinvents past forms.

The lady's ineffectual relation to culture and its history marks a gendered limit on the right to "borrow" for expressivity in the manner of satire. That the male speaker can flippantly occupy or even compose a rigidly metrical heroic couplet rhyming "clocks" and "bocks" immediately after complaining about the "dull tom-tom" monotone shows his predilection, if not quite facility, for turning cultural detritus into poetry. Yet so long as that cultural detritus is produced by, surrounds, or is identified with the lady, she cannot similarly rewrite her life in heroic couplets: Pope's Flavia is no "wit."[31] "Portrait of a Lady" is therefore not only a poem focused through a misogynistic persona but also a poem about who can satirically manage tradition. It determines who can rise, through hardened metrical satire, from effeminate culture to a position of shared and cultivated understanding, but it has little ability to preserve the necessary distinction between the male subject and female object. Just as Prufrock is no Hamlet, this speaker reveals himself to be no Augustan satirist. He is, instead, a figure of failing irony and self-consuming bathos:

> I feel like one who smiles, and turning shall remark
> Suddenly, his expression in a glass.
> My self-possession gutters; we are really in the dark. (ll. 3:16-18)

Where the smiling satirist darkly holds up a mirror to the world (as when the speaker connects the woman's voice with the "cracked cornets" her hearing produces), the speaker in this moment has turned the mirror in the wrong direction. He is like the speaker of "Hysteria," "involved" in a woman's laughter and "lost finally in the dark caverns of her throat."[32] In the poem's final line the speaker imagines the lady's death and asks himself, "And should I have the right to smile?" (l. 3:41). What will happen if he smiles? It was the lady who took the fall when the man found, in conversation with her, that his "smile falls heavily among the bric-à-brac" (l. 3:9). When she is dead and he smiles, there may be only the frightening specter of his own rigid expression. The strict tetrameter of this final line, associated thus far with the feminized refrains of this poem and of "Prufrock," finalizes the collapse of ironic distance. This phrase is pure echo, a formalized loss of "self-possession" unmitigated by gendered foils. The prospect of vers libre as metered, rhyming lines with variable length or catalexis remains a male fantasy.

Eliot tries, abortively, to find muse figures to gaze upon and positively authenticate his forms. "La Figlia che Piange" (1916, *CPTSE*, 26) sculpts a young girl in the moment a man takes his leave of her. Discarding the masks of "Prufrock" and "Portrait," Eliot constructs an idealized man in this moment of flight from mere body:

> So I would have had him leave,
> So I would have had her stand and grieve,
> So he would have left
> As the soul leaves the body torn and bruised,
> As the mind deserts the body it has used. (ll. 8-12)

The third-person pronouns "he" and "him" provide only the most meager insulation; across the poem "I" slips into "he" and memory into portraiture. Failing the test of impersonality, the poem ends with another kind of control: the sudden onset of near-regular-length iambic pentameter. The control comes with a cost, however, as the refrain of "weave, weave the sunlight in your hair" withers into Prufrockian neurasthenia:

> And I wonder how they should have been together!
> I should have lost a gesture and a pose.
> Sometimes these cogitations still amaze
> The troubled midnight and the noon's repose. (ll. 21-24)

A fading echo of Yeats's dream of Innisfree, "where midnight's all a-glimmer and noon a purple glow," the speaker's overwrought metrical "cogitations" interrupt meditative "repose."

This metricized state of self-consuming observation ends *Prufrock and Other Observations* and may explain the sudden need for the more calculated metrical turn of the satires of 1918-1920—and to Sweeney's antithetical id. Pound advertises his like-minded *Hugh Selwyn Mauberly* (1920) as a correction of the excesses of free verse, but I think Eliot's pivot has more to do with finding a role for meter that cordons off vestigial desires and personal regrets. A biographical reading, centered on the unhappy marriage to Vivienne, may be in order—"La Figlia" is probably about Emily Hale, his lost Boston Brahmin match[33]—but that is less important than a new understanding of Eliot's literary-historical vision and the role of meter in it. The viscerally misogynistic (and often anti-Semitic) quatrains of his late 1910s poems "Whispers of Immortality," "Burbank with a Baedecker," "Sweeney Erect," and "Sweeney among the Nightingales" double down on the metronome's uniquely modern potential as a torture wheel for decrepit civilization. But the alignment of meter, satire, and misogyny does more: it redeems Eliot's nostalgic attachments to metrical culture. The angry redemption proves fleeting, as it does for the speaker of "Portrait." In *The Waste Land* we can hear its energies failing and find Eliot reaching toward a less composed and artificial treatment of prosodic history.

Meter after Satire: *The Waste Land*

"When satire enters Eliot's writings in the early drafts of *The Waste Land*," Rob Lehman writes, "it [. . .] does so as a means of managing a dangerous proximity. Once again, the threat comes from the denigrated products of a fallen culture and from the possibility that the distinction between the high and the low might prove undecidable."[34] There are some notable remnants of metrical satire in the final version:

> When lovely woman stoops to folly and
> Paces about her room again, alone,
> She smoothes her hair with automatic hand,
> And puts a record on the gramophone. (ll. 253-56)

Eliot likens the woman's gesture to the automated movement of the gramophone, which passes automated music to her ears. Her pacing is metrical, mimicked by isolated adverbs—"again" and "alone"—that seem packed in to fill out the strict meter and rhyme. This is how she, and music, merely fill out their spots in what Stanley Cavell calls modernity's "phonographic culture" of instrumentalized sound.[35]

Yet gendered metrical satire falters as just another mechanized mode, another of literary history's ruins, as Eliot compresses the process of initiating and undermining satire begun in "Portrait of a Lady." The figure of "Mrs. Equitone" stands out: both her name and the message she is to receive— "Tell her I bring the horoscope myself:/One must be so careful these days" (ll. 58-59)—mark her status as a denigrated, female product. The name, like "a brand of audio equipment," "suggests a stay-at-home upper-middle-class woman so neutral that her voice never rises or sinks—the mechanical voice of one of the lost."[36] Arriving at the end of a list of ambiguously serious tarot cards, she reveals the bathos latent not only in the tarot reading but in many (if not all) of the poem's allegorical and mythic elements. Her bad leveling, like the metronome's, captures "Madame Sosostris, famous clairvoyante" (a cross-dresser from Aldous Huxley's *Crome Yellow*) well below the level of double-gendered Tiresias's pedigreed clairvoyance. The tarot reading moves between upper- and lowercase, separating women into two poles: the high tone of "Belladonna, Lady of the Rocks" (l. 49) and the vagaries of the uncapitalized grammatical apposition "the lady of situations" (l. 50). While the poem may try to distance itself from its audio equipment (as from the empty "O O O O" of the "Shakespeherian rag" [l. 128]), it also insinuates into itself the more serious "fall from archetype to mere type, to wholly impure contingency" modeled by the transition from "Lady" to "lady."[37] The broad continuum between the poem's speakers and Mrs. Equitone reflects the larger struggle to interpret culture and to interpret the (faux) vatic proclamations of the poem itself. What *The Waste Land* recognizes across its lingering metrical masquerade is the impossibility of sustaining a masculine ideal of modern poetics through satirical distance from feminized meter.

The drafts of *The Waste Land* are far more obviously indebted to satire and metrical masquerade than is the final version. Before Pound got to it, "The Fire Sermon" began with a sequence of heroic couplets clearly indebted to Augustan satirical works and particularly Swift's "Lady's Dressing Room" and Belinda's toilette episode in Pope's *Rape of the Lock*. The allusions to Pope and Swift are fairly direct, as when the dubiously named heroine Fresca dreams of "pleasant rapes," has her "tresses fanned by little flutt'ring Loves," and applies perfume to "Disguise the good old hearty female stench."[38] With this last line and its "good old hearty" adjectives, Eliot brings the mockery forward in time to the present, yoking stylistic parody to obvious misogyny. What the speaker now parodies, alongside womankind, is a perceived tendency among certain poets of the previous (Edwardian and then Georgian) decades to add adjectives to fill out a line that has no good reason (emotional or descriptive) for being as long as it is. Fresca the poetess is an automaton uncritically engaged with tradition (if she is in fact modeled on Nancy Cunard, that engagement would produce anthologies as well).[39] She might write verse similar to that of the Georgian Poets, a movement associated by modernists with the aesthetic fault of mechanically creating metrical lines and thus flailing for diction.[40]

Eliot's satire here continues the gendering of meter in his early poems. Though Pound seems to have edited as if the Fresca passages represents Eliot's sincere effort to echo Pope, the meter is too bad to be his and must reflect some other principle. His composition process strongly supports this reading, as massively over-adjectival lines like "Disguise the good old hearty female stench" (60 percent adjective) began as the only modestly excessive "disguise the good old female stench."[41] The added "hearty" smacks of the worst excesses of meter, of diction, and of an artificial process of composition. Pound curtails pentameter in almost every instance. For instance, Tiresias's pentameter quatrains about the typist and clerk in "The Fire Sermon" received censure because the "verse [was] not interesting enough as verse to warrant so much of it." The only extended section of iambic pentameter in *The Waste Land* that Pound did not try to cut is the second verse paragraph of "The Fire Sermon," "A rat crept softly," admitted perhaps because Pound appreciated the sharp juxtapositions to *The Tempest* and to Andrew Marvell's "To His Coy Mistress" in "But at my back from time to time I hear / The sound of horns and motors, which shall bring / Sweeney to Mrs. Porter in the spring" (196–98).[42] Pound nevertheless complains about the superfluous "shall" that helps Eliot preserve the precise meter in a much blunter form than the heroic couplet it echoes from John Day's *Parliament of Bees*.[43] Eliot appears most unwilling to accept Pound's de-metrification of the beginning of "A Game of Chess," in which a hysterical woman sits framed by her toilette and furniture and tries to engage a speaker (perhaps her husband) in dialogue. Pound calls the first three lines "too tum-pum at a stretch" and marks a later line as "too penty."[44] Eliot makes some changes but far fewer than in the Fresca and Tiresias sections. I believe that Eliot, though willing to reconstruct Tiresias's stanzas and eliminate the Fresca couplets outright, was unwilling to revise the beginning of "A Game of Chess" because he wanted one last test of meter's framing power: setting the metronome, so as not to be set by it. Pentameter is demanded, moreover, by the broadly synthetic and accretive tendency that Hannah Sullivan thinks Pound "misunderstood" because of his cutting aesthetic.[45] Yet what Eliot discovers is, predictably, not a space for self-preservation but the necessity of meter's vestigiality: the wife figure and her corresponding iambics express the suspended progress of prosodic technique that no one—male speaker, Tiresias, poem, poet—transcends. Pound cuts into versification that seemed to embody the hysterical woman it purported to contain. Indeed, Wayne Koestenbaum describes the draft as "a female hysteric" seeking a return to precise, masculine language (i.e., to be handed to Pound).[46] What happens, Eliot had to know and Pound could only repress for him, when meter is both under the skin yet belongs to the hysterical female other?

Unlike Mrs. Equitone, Madame Sosostris, the typist, or the bar patrons, the woman described in "A Game of Chess" lives in an elevated situation that brings her closest to Fresca, the world of the literary salon, and "talk of Michelangelo." Her furniture and jewelry mark her as a consumer with aesthetic taste, separate from the women in the bar and from the typist, each consumed by kinds of reproduction. She refuses to sit as a benign object of observation. The description "under the firelight, under the brush, her hair / Spread out in fiery points" links her to Pre-Raphaelite figures of aesthetic potency—D. G. Rossetti's poems and paintings in particular—which resonated for Pound, H.D., Mina Loy, and Eliot himself in "Figlia."[47] But such figures now conjure feelings of enclosure, of aestheticism as a further bourgeois entrapment. The severe beauty of Jenny or paintings such as *Lady Lilith*, which struck Loy as revealing an "egoless purity," remain contained within a tight domestic space (in Rossetti's "Jenny" this is embodied in the symbol of her "cage sparrow"). In Eliot that enclosure forces the "egoless purity" of the Pre-Raphaelite female figure into an uninspiring hysteria, a tedious failure to communicate that ultimately indicts male desire and its poetic manifestations.

In the drafts, Eliot wishes Fresca had never written, that she had been content to be (like Jenny) "more sinned against than sinning."[48] Banishing Fresca-the-poetess in favor of the upper-class female aesthete avoids much of the awkwardness of writing satirical couplets that belong at once to Fresca, Pope, and Eliot. Eliot himself notes "the writer to-day who was genuinely influenced by Pope would hardly want to use that couplet at all."[49] Yet "A Game of Chess" confirms that the poem has not found a new relation to the forms it still invests in: the metrical style is cathected without the control or understanding that develop much later in the Anglican mysticism of *Murder in the Cathedral* and *Four Quartets*. What control there is comes from Pound's aggressive obstetrics. Eliot's ambivalence toward both the woman and her formal enclosure is embodied by the figure of the nightingale in the "sylvan scene" displayed on the mantel. The nightingale no longer plots out mythic history as it did in "Sweeney among the Nightingales," whose impersonal narrator shifts ecstatically from identifying birds with society women to literal nightingales to mythic singers "in the bloody wood / When Agamemnon cried aloud." In *The Waste Land* the nightingale hovers awkwardly between the mythical past and the historical present, between Ovid lodged in a drawing room and the lady forced into the unfortunate myth:

> Above the antique mantel was displayed
> As though a window gave upon the sylvan scene
> The change of Philomel, by the barbarous king
> So rudely forced; yet there the nightingale
> Filled all the desert with inviolable voice
> And still she cried, and still the world pursues,
> "Jug Jug" to dirty ears. (ll. 97–103)

The juxtaposition of "sylvan scene" and drawing room lacks irony, despite the conjunction "yet." The drafts tried to sustain dramatic irony by having the woman reflect on the painting's composition, "displayed / In pigment, but so lively, you had thought / A window gave upon a sylvan scene."⁵⁰ The draft, once called "In the Cage," also held onto the Browning-like metrical caging of Eliot's earlier dramatic monologues. Pound's edits now begin to operate as a means of self-scarring. In my reading of "Portrait of a Lady," catalexis could still stand as a male prerogative, an intentional trimming of a vestigial and feminine tradition. In "A Game of Chess" each shortened line proves the result of lopping off whichever syllables or phrasing Pound derided. Nor was this systematic. There is certainly filler (mostly adjectives) that Pound rightfully dismissed, sometimes with explicit strikethrough: "where the ~~swinging~~ glass," "~~and~~ flung their smoke," "~~upon the hearth,~~" "you had thought," "into the dirty ear of death," "and other tales," "~~where~~ staring forms," "spread out in ~~little~~ fiery points ~~of will~~." The last is especially egregious given the known badness of "little" and Eliot's subtler use of "velleities" to approximate "little wills" back in "Portrait." Other adjectives, fitting or not, continue supporting the weakened pentameter. These include "burnished," "fruited," "golden" (cut from one line and slapped onto "Cupidon" in the next), a redundantly "rich" profusion of "satin cases," perfumes both "strange" and "synthetic," "coffered" ceiling, "coloured" stone, "carved" dolphin with extra unstressed syllable (-èd), and the "antique" mantel. Why does Eliot so haphazardly abandon the earlier pretense of masculinist metrical framing and then, with Pound's help or imposition, scarify his versification?

The verse paragraph is pulled in two directions not by warring meters but by irreconcilable attitudes toward metrical composition. There are occasional lines of dynamic blank verse rhythm here, as in the lurching hendecasyllabics of "unguent, powdered, or liquid—troubled, confused" or choriambic symmetries of "leaned out, leaning, hushing the room enclosed" and "under the firelight, under the brush, her hair." But the acceptance of Pound's edits erases that possibility for meter. A decade letter Pound believed only "Eliot or I may have enough technique to get one more last wheeze out of the ole pentameter"; his reasoning involved technical skill, but that wheeze also requires the coterie process of policing and scarring the line.

As it circulated, *The Waste Land* lacks this specialized key for reassembling local practice as living form. What "The Game of Chess" proves is that the pentameter is neither a secret preserve, an "inviolable voice" for the male poet to return to, nor a clear target for metrical satire. Cal Bedient characterizes the passage as a struggle between a speaker's "airless, nauseated description of the room" and the woman's Philomela-like attempts to escape.[51] This aptly describes both aspects of Eliot's effort to escape meter's vestigiality, with Pound forcing a violent metamorphosis. The choice at the end of the passage is between hysteria and psychosis; when the woman tries to leave her room—her potentially endless stanza of penty rhythms and ornate diction—the result is only more confinement inside a broken but nonetheless assertive pentameter:

> "My nerves are bad to-night. Yes, bad. Stay with me.
> "Speak to me. Why do you never speak? Speak.
> "What are you thinking of? What thinking? What?
> "I never know what you are thinking. Think." (ll. 111-14)

These lines, more broken than free, are neither strictly metronomic like Prufrock's society women and scuttling claws nor flexible like his mermaids. The first line jars at "stay," and the second divides up its ten (mostly mono-) syllables so that scansion never finds its feet. The third and fourth lines manage decasyllabics through the blunt insertion of monosyllabic words ("What," "Think"). In the metrical style of "Portrait of a Lady" the lines might have read, "My nérves are bád to-níght. Yes, bád. Please stáy./Spéak to me. Whý do yòu so rárely spéak?" The lines' "withdrawal" from or approach to iambic pentameter is now just one of the poem's many thematized "dead sounds."[52] Bedient describes how

> something like the ragtime paradigm "O O O O" rules her rhythm so that everything she utters snaps without buoyancy, is spasmic. A dactylic clutching and rasping motif [. . .] recurs like an uncontrollable tic. Then, too, she does haggish things with iambs, leaving them hardly distinguishable from the twitches of nervous prose.[53]

The heaviness, "spasms," and dactyls reflect how the lady's escape from the "airless" pentameter results only in a further entrapment in vestigial meter. The "O O O O" pulls the man/speaker/poem's lines into another haggishness, and the syncopation of ragtime could only liberate rhythm with the more sustained efforts at rhythmical and dialectal blackface one glimpses in Eliot's awful "Columbiad" letters.[54]

The wife figure and her broken decasyllabics symbolize something satire can't fix: a culture of "dirty ears" that Eliot no longer believed could be trained or escaped. How does one scan "jug jug," "twit twit," or "drip drop drip drop drop drop drop" without winding the metronome? These are limitations of form to which Eliot, despite Pound's protestations, submits himself. Meter's vestigial presence expresses the (unchanged, inviolable) social restrictions on poetry and poetics that Eliot and other modernists had previously isolated as an effect of the feminine or sentimental, and that now appear as the ineluctable descent of culture from aristocratic endeavor to middle-class commodity.

The blasted pentameter of this passage returns in Tiresias's quasi-quatrains in "The Fire Sermon." Dual gendered, Tiresias might seem to transcend the cultural decay manifest in the typist's sexual misadventure with the clerk:

> I Tiresias, though blind, throbbing between two lives,
> Old man with wrinkled female breasts, can see
> At the violet hour, the evening hour that strives
> Homeward, and brings the sailor home from sea,
> The typist home at teatime, clears her breakfast, lights
> Her stove, and lays out food in tins. (ll. 218-23)

When Tiresias describes the epic possibilities of the hour—the return of Odysseus—he inhabits a flexible and enjambed Miltonic meter. The enjambments of "see" and "strives" would be at home in the invocation to book 3 of *Paradise Lost*. The enjambment of "lights/ Her stove" does not participate in that tradition. It is typographic: the extra beat of "lights" belongs in the next line, which is missing a beat. This prosodic juxtaposition of structural enjambment to arbitrary distortion is, again, not Eliot's invention but Pound's accident. The draft lines obeyed a meter and rhyme scheme identical to both the preceding lines and several subsequent ABAB quatrains:

> The typist home at teatime, who begins
> To clear away her broken breakfast, lights
> Her stove, and lays out squalid food in tins,
> Prepares the room and sets the room to rights.[55]

It is unsurprising to find Pound objecting to the melodramatic adjectives "broken" (but not "squalid," though Eliot takes it out as well), the prepositional phrase "in tins" (which Eliot leaves in), the plainly redundant phrasing of the fourth line, and the overall subordination of diction to rhyme and meter.[56] More surprising is Eliot's divestment from the iambic quatrain, which becomes two lines of free or unmetrical verse through uncritical subtraction. As in earlier passages, Pound is not mandating the final form, only what should be left out. Eliot takes this as an opportunity to abdicate formal authority, to be left with fragments rather than ruins of form.

Tiresias might have performed a more complex metrical system than Fresca or the original metrical "cage" of "A Game of Chess." His hexameters and shorter lines, also present in "Portrait of a Lady," might signify the "freedom within form" Eliot eventually discovered in Milton. But just as Tiresias aims to bring the clerk and typist "under the lash of the style," so too is he subordinated to the revision.[57] He is not a vers librist dwelling with meter's ghost but another reactionary poet rushing back to Hulmean "classicism." The young man's breaking of pentameter lines in "Portrait of a Lady" brought the threatening lady under style's lash; across *The Waste Land* the wielder of the lash is more directly the recipient of its violence. No one, including the would-be satirist or aloof observer, avoids metrical satire's universal stroke.

Eliot's openness to metrical disfiguring by revision is one of *The Waste Land*'s most important generic gestures. It is the form of the "noisy extremes" that serve, Josh Epstein argues, to limit Eliot's otherwise violent and "totalizing drumbeats."[58] The scarred meter is the local and embodied form of Eliot's macro-level abandonment of any effort to transform meter's historical disruption into a new metrical structure. The famous first lines hint at the latter through their calculated thematic and formal inversion of the *Canterbury Tales*:

> April is the cruelest month, breeding
> Lilacs out of the dead land, mixing
> Memory and desire, stirring
> Dull roots with spring rain. (ll. 1-4)

The motifs drawn from Chaucer—the coming of spring, the beginning of a pilgrimage—are rebuffed in parallel with his prosody, which gives way to trochaic and sharply enjambed verse. He is well on his way to the curtailed lines of "The Hollow Men" (1925), which in Hannah Sullivan's terms "seem determined to chasten the ear."[59] Nigel Fabb and Morris Halle's creative effort to scan *The Waste Land*'s opening as a "loose iambic meter that we have not encountered elsewhere in English poetry" or Martin Duffell's claim that the reader "has only to disregard the last word in a line or combine it with the opening of the line that follows" tells us more about the strain of sample size and the phenomenology of reading than metrical structure itself.[60] Eliot cannot sustain this dream of a generative meter and such capable readers. He relies instead upon a repertoire of rhythmic phrases and other echoes shared with Pound and select others. That supplement, alongside the repudiation of the metronome, redeemed meter from promiscuous and reified sound at the cost of accepting its vestigial presence, its fading dream of order and authority.

Formal Sensibility for a Post-metrical Culture

In his many critical reflections on meter and its historical development, Eliot reinvents his desire for the metrical vestige as a conscientious objection to audile technique and, ultimately, a new formalist dogma. Some of Eliot's first writings on meter come in his 1917 treatise *Ezra Pound: His Metric and Poetry*. The choice of "metric" suggests both meter as the measure of the line and the mathematical notion of a measure that a priori defines a space. On one hand, Eliot focuses on Pound as a metrical poet, differentiating his living, modulating verse from "what is called the 'music' of Shelley or Swinburnian, a music often nearer to rhetoric." He is emphatic about "the great variety of rhythm which Pound manages to introduce into the ordinary iambic pentameter."[61] Yet as I observed in my introduction, Eliot worries about audiences' "training" and whether his own treatise can overcome their uncertain "willingness to be trained."

Either because of this uncertainty or out of a desire to preserve Pound's autonomy, the treatise resists its own act of critical mediation. The complete lack of scansions or formal descriptions of Pound's "metric," while surprising for a treatise defending against claims of formal dissoluteness, reflects Eliot's agreement with critics he cites that technical "self-consciousness" would be a bad thing. He resists one critic's accusation of Pound's "hieratic formalization," but neither does he accept that critic's celebration of other poets' "simple untaught muse." Eliot recognizes the latter ideal as intuitionist dogmatism linked to a desire for "simple metre," but he also knows that to scan a more complex meter would be to confirm a view of modernism as "cultivated by a guild of adepts [in] austere laboratories."[62] His way out of this trap is to invoke an ideal of formal "mastery" and to construe it as an outcome of reading Pound rather than as mere dogma. Looking closer, however, Eliot's idea of mastery derives from Pound's critical rather than poetic writing. Eliot states (and who would now say otherwise?) that "there are not [. . .] two kinds of verse, the strict and the free; there is only a mastery which comes of being so well trained that form is an instinct and can be adapted to the particular purpose in hand."[63] The basis for this now-common idea is not a poem but Pound's contemporary essays on the musician and instrument maker Arnold Dolmetsch. In these essays Pound juxtaposes "major form" to "minutiae" and gives as evidence not the history of poetry but the history of music.[64]

As for Pound's ideas, the technicalities of education, composition, and improvisation within large-scale artistic "structure" are deferred in turn to a treatise by Dolmetsch on seventeenth- and eighteenth-century music. Poetry is aspiring to music, we might note, not for melody and harmony but for music theory's potent formalism. Behind this shifting sequence of authority and critical sensibility is a rejection of the "detail" that has a great deal to do with Victorian and post-Victorian metrical education. When Pound complains that contemporary music training "lays stress on having a memory like a phonograph" and forces years of "tum, tum, tum, tum tum" scales, he reveals how Eliot's abstract ideals of formal "mastery" are ultimately rooted in Imagism's ur-critique of the "metronome."[65]

Eliot avoids Pound's blunt stigmatization of meter, which alongside his early tendency toward iambics has allowed criticism to see him as a traditionalist counterpoint to Pound or Williams. But Eliot's criticism from its beginnings makes a more radical claim to aesthetic sensibility as a formalist rather than prosodic critical achievement. A decade after his early celebration, Eliot returns to the "isolated superiority" of Pound's 1926 collection *Personae* to repeat his claim that "a man who devises new rhythms is a man who extends and refines our sensibility; and that is not merely a matter of technique."[66] Eliot's formalist and rhythmic sensibility retains prosody as unmediated sound through what he famously calls the "auditory imagination": "the feeling for syllable and rhythm, penetrating far below the conscious levels of thought and feeling [. . .] sinking to the most primitive and forgotten."[67] An early articulation of this unconscious "feeling" can be heard in "Reflections on Vers Libre," where Eliot dreams of a different society's ability, in the realm of prosody and beyond, to achieve the "ideal state" in which "the good New grow[s] naturally out of the good Old." The fate of meter, whether in Swinburne or Fresca's "little" iambics, is a plain example of "tradition [. . .] lapsing into superstition" and then requiring "the violent stimulus of novelty. [. . .] This is bad for the artist and his school, who may become circumscribed by their theory and narrowed by their polemic."[68] Eliot's own attempt to avoid that circumscription leads to paradox, as he recommends that readers recognize "the unperceived evasion of monotony" in vers libre's ghostly meters.[69] To escape the paradox of metrical sprezzatura that works only when its labor is perceived, Eliot can only remark the present's distance from more organic metrical cultures in which his own essay would be superfluous.

Those cultures cease with a failure of the "auditory imagination" that Eliot locates above all in Milton. His two essays on Milton mark his foremost effort to reconstruct a usable history of prosody after the fall of meter into superstition and polemic; yet as in *His Metric*, Eliot manages a new prosodic history only by fundamentally shifting the ground of judgment from prosody to form and formal "mastery." In his 1936 "Milton I," Eliot describes feeling lost in "mazes of sound" produced by Milton's "hypertrophy of the auditory imagination." Milton's "dislocated" metrical sensibility, proven by Eliot's own hearing, is defined by a subordination of syntax and diction to "musical value." This forms the basis for Eliot's now-infamous "dissociation of sensibility": meter's baroque hypertrophy makes it "necessary to read [*Paradise Lost* . . .] first solely for the sound, and second for the sense."[70] The alienation of Eliot's own auditory imagination is the saving grace in a narrative of generic decay wherein poets and readers forcibly recombine sound and sense. The same mode of listening and prosodic historiography condemns Tennyson's *In Memoriam* (1850) as a misbegotten epic whose "technical power" persists without spirit.[71] In Eliot's ear the pronounced metrical techniques of Milton and Tennyson (and most everyone between) echo only as vestiges of a lost aurality, a metrical culture of subtle and unremarked innovation. Ironically, *In Memoriam* already thematized the "sad mechanic exercise" of meter but also, crucially, a psychological "use in measured language." Citing these lines, Jahan Ramazani notes a Victorian "immersion" in melancholic loss that characterizes the modern elegy; in Eliot, criticism becomes the elegiac genre par excellence, and much of its melancholic condition derives from the loss of Tennyson's already ambivalent metrical culture.[72]

Eliot ends "Milton I" with a shrug, explaining that he has "measured" Milton from an "outside perspective"—though he implies that all post-Restoration poetics are defined by that alienation. Returning to the scene of abject modern sensibility in his 1947 "Milton II," Eliot redeems that very dislocation—his alienation from Milton's meter—as an immanent effect of Milton's greatness:

> Our sense of sight must be blurred, so that our *hearing* may become more acute. *Paradise Lost* [. . .] makes this peculiar demand for a readjustment of the reader's mode of apprehension. The emphasis is on the sound, not the vision, upon the word, not the idea; and in the end it is the unique versification that is the most certain sign of Milton's intellectual mastership.[73]

This is a remarkable change of fortune for "versification" under the new title of *sound*. Metrical effects that once bifurcated reading may enchant and stimulate our apprehension. As proof of meter's spiritual return from vestige to sound, Eliot concludes the essay with a blunt readjustment of his own prior prosodic judgment: "In studying *Paradise Lost* we come to perceive that the verse is continuously animated by the departure from, and return to, the regular measure."[74] Nearly verbatim from 1917's "Reflections" and *Ezra Pound: His Metric*, this comment seems to reinvest in the metrical contract. But by 1947 Eliot has set up new terms for the reader's investment in meter. "Milton II" polices the critical engagement with versification, disdaining Robert Bridges's "catalogue [of] systematic irregularities which give perpetual variety to Milton's verse" as "interesting" but not a means to "gain an appreciation of the peculiar rhythm of a poet." In other words, Bridges contributes to the metrical culture of minutiae and ornament that misled Eliot in "Milton I." Retrained in "rhythm," Eliot reevaluates his "peculiar feelings" as the result of larger form: the "wave-length" of Milton's periods and paragraphs, which correspond nicely to the "horizontal chord" Pound heard in "Provençal canzos."[75] Condemning *specialized* ears" from Bridges back across the eighteenth and nineteenth centuries to Samuel Johnson while holding onto his own 1900s and 1910s metrical training, Eliot wants to transcend meter and metrical discourse through rhythmic sensibility.[76]

Once Eliot is on the terrain of rhythm, he can make the even bigger leap to form. However brilliant and influential, Milton's prosody ultimately serves Eliot as a principle of formal iconoclasm rather than technique. He is "the greatest master in our language of freedom within form." By the 1940s this statement has lost its metrical origins. As a figure of abstract formal freedom, Milton can reorient and revise literary history away from the metrical tradition's evolving contract: "His work illustrates no principles of good writing; the only principles that it illustrates are such as are valid only for Milton himself to observe."[77] Liberated from his own embeddedness in metrical culture and training, Eliot can now search for the "great poet [. . .] who can profit from the study of Milton." Yet as I have been suggesting, it is the great formalist critic who profits most. He profits at the expense of the metrist and those poets for whom scansion and technical innovation drive the experience of the poem—whether Victorians like Hopkins and Hardy or modern women and African American poets working dialectically with the English metrical tradition.

Eliot's two Milton essays reflect modernism's overall abstraction of prosody from historical forms and metrical debates toward idealized "rhythm." That subject is taken up in this book's conclusion. Here, Eliot's essays show his dependence on transforming nostalgia for non-vestigial meters into a post-metrical or "auditory" critical sensibility. John Guillory has shown how Eliot's anxieties about the "situation of his coterie within [literary] culture" led to his distinctive literary historiography. Specifically, Eliot's embrace of a tradition of "minor" Elizabethan poetry, flourishing in the refined atmosphere of manuscript circulation and fundamentally distinct from Romantic and Victorian canons of taste, allowed him to imagine his own coterie within modern literary culture traversing the infamous "'dissociation of sensibility' [. . .] in the other direction."[78] The Milton essays show how that crossing required more than a poetic coterie or Pound's midwifery; it required a new critical vocabulary carefully poised against long-standing currents of metrical scholarship and training. To reclaim Milton from his precarious position in literary history, falling toward Augustan technicity, it was necessary to form not only a new literary judgment (as in "Milton I") but an entirely new formalist framework for what constitutes such judgment.

The critical certainties of 1947 include a post-metrical sensibility not yet available a quarter century before. Eliot's early essays and poetry feel doubly dissociated: not only from a culture where poetry expresses "the mind of a whole people" but from the aristocratic culture that succeeded it. He associates the latter with Dryden and other Restoration dramatists who wrote in "a form the acceptance of which had [. . .] to come by diffusion through a small society." Absent this "intellectual aristocracy" it falls to literary criticism to save the poet from having to speak "to a coterie or to soliloquize."[79] He may have had in mind John Stuart Mill's definition of lyric as soliloquy—as utterance overheard by an audience of which the poet-speaker was happily unaware—in which case Eliot may appear resistant to lyricization. Yet that is merely the irony of modern lyric reading: even as Eliot seemingly rejects lyric for its association with sentimental, metronomic verse, his imagining of all poetic reception as "Prufrock among the women" authorizes lyric reading's more significant abstraction of poetry from reception and thus genre.[80] Identifying and rejecting a metrical soundscape of mechanically reproduced chatter promises freedom from the vicissitudes of mass taste, as does Eliot and Pound's repertoire of rhythmical allusions, but these hardly count as an escape from the contingencies of modern audile technique back to an organic culture of metrical composition. The critique of the metronome had to evolve into something less vulnerable than the coterie: literary criticism's post-metrical, lyric theory of poetry.

3 "No Feet to Walk On"
Pound's Late Victorian Prosody

> Pound: An architect who, in the middle of the construction of his ideal design, falls in love with the scaffolding, decides this is what he wanted, this is what he'll keep.
>
> —Christian Wiman, *Ambition and Survival*

The previous two chapters elaborated two different practices of the metrical vestige. Frost's technical experimentation turned quickly from faith in his own powers to metrical ripostes against modern listening. Like Thomas Hardy, Frost saw himself as a theorist of meter, but the horizon of both his meter and theory could not be Hardy's (already obsolescing) Victorian public. The most pernicious form of modern audile technique for him lay in the pseudo-democratic ideals and flat tone of free verse. By contrast, T. S. Eliot wanted meter to be less dogmatic, representing a sensibility rather than a technical prescription. His unfulfilled desire to write in historical meter—as part of a historical metrical culture and its sensibility—depended on a succession of supports: first gender and irony, then Pound's mediations, and finally his reconfiguration of poetry as genre defined by formal innovation and dependent on formalist judgment.

Ezra Pound was modernism's prosodic impresario, now generally read as the avant-garde figure who articulated and epitomized the break from nineteenth-century poetics. Yet he too composed metered verse in response to the vestigiality of meter; his legacy of disruption began with more than a decade of metrical games, played as much with his own oeuvre as with others'. Pound continued to fuss about bad metrical technique from his first critique of the "metronome" in the 1910s well into the 1930s—and his critical defenders have never stopped. Revisiting Pound's early poetics and practice of the metrical vestige helps us understand the inaccuracy of the anti-metrical history he bequeathed. Meredith Martin is right that Pound in the 1920s "engages with metrical discourse at the same time as he rejects it so that he can position himself as the arbiter and authority," yet I find he had an inconveniently richer sense of and desire for the recent metrical past and argue that his early poetry betrays the bad faith behind his poetic authority.[1] His angsty debt to Victorian meter belies the narrative produced by poetry's retheorization as a "rhythmic" phenomenon. As with Eliot, discomfort with this debt and distrust of modern audile technique leads initially to a sexist formation. In Eliot's case this was mostly limited to poems that anathematize and control feminized culture. Pound's version of this dynamic was primarily to seek out "anima" figures, female muses that occupied and authenticated verse forms that might otherwise languish as Swinburnian mush. As critics have noted, however, these Neoplatonic "divine intermediaries" are a limited part of his "multifarious" relationship to women, paralleling his effort to place strong female literary figures in "amorous subject positions."[2] He sought to install real anima figures in his literary orbit: Mina Loy, Marianne Moore, Alice Corbin Henderson (coeditor of *Poetry*), and above all Hilda Doolittle (H.D.). Pound's long editorial reach turns his fictions of formal control into literal disciplining of women poets' prosody, circumscribing their metrical self-determination. I explore his editorial and personal guidance of H.D. and Henderson, and argue that H.D.'s roman à clef *HERmione* (written 1927, published 1981) responds to that control by pointing out Pound's own metrical pretensions. The broader effect of such control over women poets writing in meter is the subject of chapter 4.

Late Victorian Pound

In his unpublished "Swinburne: A Critique" Pound delights in the aesthete poet's "Wondrous pattern leading nowhere,/Music without a name." The struggle to "lead nowhere" is Pound's early struggle for poetry itself: the desire to achieve an aestheticist refusal of function within a genre. For poetry, this entails the insubordination of prosody to the demands of narrative, diction, and representation. Pound's ambivalence is obvious, of course, in the "critique" of Swinburne and Paterian aestheticism more generally, shared with Eliot, Frost, and many other moderns.[3] To "lead nowhere" is not only to dissent from cultural norms but also to drop out of literary history. Pound's apparent animus for late Victorian meter can make sense only with the caveat that the actual metrics of Swinburne and Browning were the object of desire and continued enthusiasm. Eliot's "Prufrock," which Pound championed, is typical in its desperate effort to admire Browning by including lines that "parody the style and assumptions of Tennyson."[4] Teaching such distinctions was necessary for recovering a non-vestigial meter and then renewing poetic genres like the modern dramatic monologue.

Pound's poetry and criticism, like Eliot's, never musters faith in such subtle distinctions and parodic exercises. Poetic music "leads nowhere" because of the bad or absent training of all prospective audiences. Eliot is quick to differentiate Pound's "music" from "what is called the 'music' of Shelley or Swinburne, a music often nearer to rhetoric (or the art of the orator) than to the instrument."[5] Across three decades of criticism, Pound repeatedly attacks metronomic tendencies. His 1934 "Treatise on Meter" still echoes with the "bump" of meter as a kind of "gadget" that cranks out "ti tum ti tum ti tum ti tum ti tum" and converts Romance syllabics into accents "merely strung along with a swat on syllables two, four, six, eight, ten of each line."[6] He resents "thick-eared 'modern' philologists" incapable of the lengthy patterning and echoes of medieval Provençal verse. He describes the latter's elaborate rhyme patterns as a "horizontal chord" placing extreme demands on the "auditory memory."[7] This cognitive or technical component of Eliot's "auditory imagination" has been attenuated by the prosthetic memory of audio recording and simplified metrical training.

Like Frost, Pound believed that his writing was oriented toward higher-order intonation rather than accent, but his desire to guide the reader through alternate notation remained speculative: "All typographic disposition, placings of words on the page, is intended to facilitate the reader's intonation, whether he be reading silently to self or aloud to friends. Given time and technique I might even put down the musical notation of passages or 'breaks into song.'"[8] Although some scholars, like Harriet Monroe, attempted musical notations of poetry, Pound did not, to my knowledge, find "time and technique" despite efforts to innovate in the notation of music. His notational fantasy parallels several other audile imaginaries, including his early and abortive dissemination of Greek's "storehouse of wonderful rhythms"[9] as well as troubadour stanzas. The development of the "image," "which presents an intellectual and emotional complex in an instant of time," into the abstract energy of the "vortex" and the visual simultaneity of the Chinese ideogram, is another leap away from Western temporal notation and faith in sound as such.[10] The advent of "absolute rhythm," in which every "emotion" has a "rhythm-phrase to express it"[11] epitomizes the desire for notational accuracy without actual notation. All modern theories of rhythm involve the negation or transcendence of notational and typographic practices, even and especially when they produce scientific measurements (though Pound did not value those). In Daniel Albright's account, the affective and phenomenal claims of absolute rhythm remain "a largely untested hypothesis":

> Pound used absolute rhythm to mean two different, indeed contradictory, things: first, as a principle of a kind of science of affect, according to which a specific emotion naturally must terminate in a specific rhythm; second, as a principle in the graphology of style, according to which a writer's rhythms are a direct reflex of his unique sensibility, as valid a mode of identification as a fingerprint on a manuscript.[12]

In his early poetry Pound tries to reconcile the opposing demands of universal affect and private style by publicizing his private relationship to the vestiges of meter. The latter, centered on his suffering of metronomic iambics, could be counted upon to provoke dissatisfaction while sustaining the ear's attention. The poems that most emphatically demarcate the history of poetic style also reproduce metrical suffering. An unpublished poem entitled "Fodder" (1914), sent to Harriet Monroe for *Poetry* but labeled "optional" and later "canceled," shows Pound's struggle to build an ecstatic voice around negation:

> O Bacchus!
> O all my black panthers,
> [. . .
>   . . .] especially chew up Walter de la Mare
> And Ralph Hodgson,
>   and all the pretty, pretty poets
> Who sing in timpty-tumpty metres.[13]

Presumably "fodder" refers to the sacrificial "pretty poets," but it can also refer to this poem, served up to *Poetry* with little faith that the non-iambic meters of the opening lines would have any value or provoke recognition (despite the reference to Bacchus/bacchius foot). The iambic form of the curse—"all the pretty pretty poets"—tries to leverage the entropic decay of metrical culture into a universal modern "sensibility." Similarly, *Hugh Selwyn Mauberly* attempts to contain "'bad' poems attributable to Mauberly" alongside Pound's own "critique of aestheticism."[14] Where some readings distinguish Mauberly's impoverished "Medallion" from the lovely "Envoi" that precedes it, Gail McDonald hears knowing failure: "All that Pound can manage—and it seems to me that Pound damns this failing—is the carved woman of 'Medallion,' not the singing woman of 'Envoi.'"[15] From "Fodder" through to *Mauberly*, Pound struggles to generate a new metrical form outside of satire. What might appear like a broad societal failing still felt, to Pound, like his own formal inadequacy. To condemn metronomic or penty meter is to condemn his own ear and pen, a prosodic impasse that drives his first decade of substantial production and experiment.

The initial development of *The Cantos* reproduces this structure in which suffering the Victorians becomes Pound's suffering of his own Victorian anachronism. Like Eliot's scarred meter in *The Waste Land*, Pound's suffering within the metrical vestige emerges in his process of drafting and publication. In the three "Ur-Cantos" published in *Poetry* in 1917, Pound begins by citing one of the most famously difficult of long poems, Robert Browning's *Sordello* (1840), whose metricality was clear to Pound but not therefore easily scannable. This is true as well of Pound's opening line: "Hang it all, there can be but one Sordello." Such decasyllabic lines with feminine endings recur throughout the Ur-Cantos, almost always iambic, yet the challenging monosyllables, alongside the frequent changes in line length, obscure the meter. The reference to Browning helps, however, to encourage an iambic scansion and from there we might note divergences that exceed even Browning's irregular iambics. Yet Pound's multiple inverted feet ("Your Sordello, and that the modern world [. . .]"), changing line length, foreign words, and monosyllables make scansion of meter in terms of irregular departures a largely futile approach. The departures turn not so much within meter but into and against scansion itself, teasing rather than rewarding the sharpest ears. Take, for example, Pound's critique of Wordsworth's prosody, which builds on the earlier critique of Browning's "opprobrious rhymes":

> "The lyre should animate but not mislead the pen"—
> That's Wordsworth, Mr. Browning. (What a phrase!—
> That lyre, that pen, that bleating sheep, Will Wordsworth!)
> That should have taught you avoid speech figurative
> And set out your matter
> As I do, in straight simple phrases[16]

The first line scans as a perfectly balanced alexandrine and makes Wordsworth appear guilty of just the kind of overly sonorous equation his original sonnet avoids through enjambment and modest metrical complexity ("And taught her faithful servants how the lyre/Should animate, but not mislead, the pen"). After two lines in pentameter, the fourth line serves as a suddenly rough hinge, Pound's proof of prosodic flexibility:

```
That should have taught you avoid speech figurative
 W    S      W      S          . . .
```

The line's awkward idiom (one expects the more iambic "taught you to avoid") lets Pound revel in his prescriptivism with rough adjacent stresses and a hidden phrase boundary: "Thát should have táught you: avóid spéech fígurative!" This playful twist depends on meter as both form and content. Here, a half decade after the Imagist manifesto instructed poets to write "in the musical phrase, not in sequence of the metronome," the early *Cantos* re-perform that juxtaposition as an act of interventionist prosodic historiography. Conspicuously absent is "free verse," which Pound and Eliot had shuffled off the scene years earlier: "Some mean merely 'spontaneous writing.' some mean ditto and hope that it corresponds to an emotion. Vid. Guido Cavalcanti, by me. Some mean a very complicated system of combining rhythmic units. God save all our souls."[17]

In short, there is nothing simple about the "simple phrase" because it requires (still in 1917) the elaborate setup of meter and the metrical tradition. The Ur-Cantos, in both their metrical and unmetrical sequences, require a mutated but still iambic scansion, depending not only upon a metrical contract but on a sense that metrical raggedness must henceforth be the condition of meter's vestigial persistence. The meter asks, here, what the canto itself asks of Sordello: "say I take your whole bag of tricks, / Let in your quirks and tweeks, and say the thing's an art-form." In the 1910s Pound was left holding this bag, which meant forcibly claiming metrical "things" as art.

In *A Draft of XVI Cantos* (1925) Pound tries to move on, jettisoning Wordsworth, pushing Browning to the second canto and surrounding him with the new soundscape of the onomatopoetic sea spirit "So-shu" and blind Homer's "ear, ear for the sea-surge." In his reference to Browning the ghost of iambics has gone, along with the larger public audience of *Poetry* (*Draft* was published in an illuminated Three Mountains Press edition of one hundred):

Hang it all, Robert Browning,
there can be but the one "Sordello" (ll. 1-2)

The 1930 edition finishes the privatization of literary history, adding "But Sordello, and my Sordello?" without the scare quotes, sending both reader and poet back to the medieval Italian source.

This slowly dissipating Victorian afterlife shows the persistence of Pound's negation of Victorian meter. Indeed, even in the 1930s Pound continues to attack scholarly attention to prosody. Writing to a University of Chicago English professor in 1932, he forbids both meter and free verse to young poets and in doing so effectively precludes any pedagogy of prosodic form:

> Highly doubtful/in fak damn unlikely that any infant is goin to lisp anything immortal in whispers of ten syllables to the line.
>
> Eliot or I may have enough technique to get one more last wheeze out of the ole pentameter, but I very much doubt whether anybody who is ass enough to START now 1932 on that hobby horse will get to the winnin post AT all.
>   kerump kerump kerump kerummpah bunp
> sez another of yr/   fledglings.
>
> I spose any ole thing will do as exercise// and vers libre too dangerous fer them that can construct. . . .
>   still no use floppin back to pre 1910.
>
> IF they are too lazy to look up a verse form, they are too lazy to live.[18]

We hear again Pound's hobbyhorse, the "kerumping" of iambic rhythm, as if the metronome was the fate of all but those with "enough technique"—here Eliot and himself. By 1932 the sense of the "danger" of free verse is itself a holdover from earlier debates. In its place Pound leaves his interlocutors with a set of ellipses. What could a teacher or student take from what follows the ellipses, a proscription of meter ("no use flopping back to pre-1910") that is itself a kind of "flopping back" to post-1910? Nor is it clear where Pound would have the students "look up" verse forms. Pound's ellipses point only to his own long development, his slow rejection and reformation and ironic investments in meter, free verse, and historical and foreign sources like troubadour or Chinese poetry. Pound is effectively arguing, here and in *The Cantos*, that his long serial poem is the best modern encyclopedia of and guide to versification. Its famous effort to "contain history" began in turn with the containment and rewriting of the history of prosody.

"Anima" Meter: Bare-Foot and Stub-Toed

In and before the early version of *The Cantos*, and up through *Hugh Selwyn Mauberly* and Pound's abandonment of London, that containment required an elaborate and uneasy deployment of the metrical vestige. Pound invokes a range of muse-figures to motivate his metrical vestiges, from H.D. in *Hilda's Book* (1905) through to the "carved" women of Mauberly's medallions—the latter a final condemnation of how his earlier partial female figures failed to authorize his prosodic sensibility. With his *Canzoni* (1911), Pound starts to feel out the attitudes to urban modernity that will more thoroughly occupy *Ripostes* (1912) and also begins to test the limits of inherited forms. In "Au Salon," the penultimate poem in the sequence "Und Drang," he damns a culture of polite tea but nonetheless seeks to take it with "some circle of not more than three." Inside this select coterie, juxtaposed to the "whole aegrum vulgus" (diseased rabble), a few "verities" return, including "Some certain accustomed forms,/the absolute unimportant." This ends a sequence of loose trimeter, starkly different from the satirical curtailed iambics of Eliot's "Portrait of a Lady." It seems that circa 1911, the salon is not yet threatened by the kinds of women chastened in both Eliot's and Pound's portraits of ladies. The metrical form of these lines embodies and preserves Pound against the monotonous rhythm of "days and hours" (soon to become Prufrock's "works and days" and "days and ways") mimicked in rigid iambic verse.

Canzoni is dedicated to Olivia and Dorothy Shakespear, women who might form the coterie circle of three. Pound's returns to meter demand not just faith in a coterie—later to be developed with Eliot as the primary interlocutor—but the presence of potent female figures like the fiery-haired Pre-Raphaelite enchantress of "The House of Splendour" (a section of "Und Drang"):

Her gold is spread, above, around, inwoven,
Strange ways and walls are fashioned out of it.

And I have seen my Lady in the sun,
Her hair was spread about, a sheaf of wings,
And red the sunlight was, behind it all.
[...]
Here am I come perforce my love of her
Behold mine adoration
Maketh me clear, and there are powers in this
Which, played on by the virtues of her soul,
Break down the four-square walls of standing time. (ll. 4-8, 17-21)

Playing on the meaning of "stanza" as room, the speaker liberates himself by reimagining it as a woman's body. Adoration splits the four "walls" of blank verse's "standing time." The meter can be willfully inhabited once made modestly flexible and associated with the more immediately thrilling repetitions of physical contact.

Edwin Fussell reads Pound's metrical lines as proof of a continued, unconscious entrapment in European meter. That might be true of his earliest work in *Hilda's Book*, yet Pound's early poetry remains a highly conscious and affectively charged dance with meter. As Hugh Kenner puts it, albeit too optimistically, Pound's explicit references to meter foreground an effort to renovate "the entire history of English versification from Chaucer to 1945."[19] The poems Pound removed from *Canzoni* show his struggle with that renovation; these counterpoint the Pre-Raphaelite formal exercise of "The House of Splendour" and adjacent poems powered by female objects. I suspect he removed the poems "Leviora" and "Redondillas: Or Something of That Sort" precisely to avoid indicting the vestiges of a metrical tradition he still believed he could inhabit.

"Leviora" is a sequence of two sonnets, the first titled "Against Form."[20] It ticks off complaints against the "well-groomed sonnet" and its "bardlets and bardkins." It can remain a sonnet because the Lady it addresses prefers the sonnet to honest, "unrimed speech." She is not a figure for form, as in "House of Splendour," but of taste: "let all be taste, and bid the heart be dumb," sardonically ends the poem. The poem cannot turn "against form" because of the Lady's interceding judgment; it can turn only against her as a figure of form's mediation. It ceases to develop after its octet, which ends "Let us be all things so we're not absurd / Dabble with forms and damn the verity" (ll. 7-8). In "Und Drang" Pound held onto "a few verities" *in* "accustomed form." The difference driving the irony is that the female addressee has become an arbiter of his style.

In "Redondillas, or Something of That Sort" (c. 1910), Pound couples deliberately "hobbledy," "stub"-toed, non-rhyming dactylic hexameters with an explicit investment in rhyme: "I love the subtle accord / of rimes wound over and over."[21] The cylinder-like image of winding sounds signals the acoustical power of a traditional device even as the coarse echoes of Virgil testify to the impossibility of epic meter. The random and scattered rhymes ("for," "love," "accord," "over") cannot "wind" like a sonnet, bob and wheel, Skeltonic leash, or Spenserian stanza. The poem seems uncertain about what it wants to be: originally titled "Locksley Hall 40 Years After," it in no way resembles Tennyson's famous rhyming trochaic octameter. (Its roughness may approximate that of Tennyson's sequel, "Locksley Hall Sixty Years After" [1886]) It is more clearly an echo of Whitman (Pound: "I sing the gaudy to-day and cosmopolite civilization") that drifts toward Virgilian dactylics after a space of broken iambic pentameter. The "subtle accords" of rhyme and meter, of musical verse more generally, are desired impossibilities: "I would sing to the tune of *'Mi Platz'* / were it not for the trouble of riming." What song offers to poetics with one hand (steady rhythm, tonality) it removes with another (rigid stanzas, rhyme). Pound cues up these forms only long enough to evaluate their purchase, their ability to "sing the American people" or "mirror my age," before either discarding them or roughing them up enough not to cloy. This heavily meta-prosodic poem does not indict specific forms—indeed it shows great affection for them—but doubts efforts to adapt, perform, or hear them: "We ever live in the now/it is better to live in than sing of"; "not six men believe me/when I sing in a beautiful measure." A decade before *The Waste Land*, Pound sets up at the table of Western forms, tuning one after another, and ultimately subjects not only the forms but himself to withering irony ("behold how I copy my age,/Dismissing great men with a quibble"). His final charge to "behold then the the the that I am," with "the" a jarring condensation of himself as Whitmanian lover of "all delicate sounds," asks us to accept a poem in which all poetic sounds are vestigial "the"s. Clearly if such a poem rejects meter, it does so carefully and nostalgically, scanning every line and asking us repeatedly to do the same.

When Pound does publish his nostalgia for the alienated beauty of meter, he places figures of female beauty in metrical forms so that they might share his antipathy toward modern soundscapes. In "A Virginal" (1912, *PTEP* 243), for instance, Pound plays with meter to juxtapose a negative experience of the world to a positive experience of the titular woman (perhaps playing the instrument). The world threatens to obscure the speaker's memory of the woman and makes his accents unruly ("No, no! Go from me. I have left her lately" and "No, no! Go from me. I have still the flavor."). The description of the woman, by contrast, is highly formulaic, composed of multiple similes and almost continuous alternating stress. As one of Pound's anima figures, she evokes "an atmosphere in which [. . .] emotions can have some human meaning" and "enables [the poet] to make beautiful forms."[22] These muse-like figures demarcate Pound's blank verse and other iambic stanzas from more immediate filiation with Victorian modernity.

The prominence and necessity of the anima figure for Pound's early writing reflects how modernism more generally "wrote itself out on [. . .] the body of a textuality that was already gendered."[23] Beginning with the unpublished *Hilda's Book* (1905-1907), written for H.D., Pound literalizes that male inscription in his impositions on both female figures and actual women writers. *Hilda's Book* is remarkable less for its pseudo-Elizabethan or troubadour style than as a material object. In both manuscript and typescript form it is too small, approximately 4 × 6 inches, for its pentameter lines. Lines break after six or seven syllables, wherever a word ends. Like Wordsworth embracing the enclosure of the sonnet in "Nuns Fret Not," Pound enjoys and explicitly thematizes masculine restraint. In "L'Envoi" he aspires, with questionable humility and painful bluntness, to becoming "Right subtle tongued in complex verse restraint" (*PTEP*, 15).[24] In "Thus Ides Till" (*PTEP*, 15) he performs that restraint by strategically overrunning his lines: "To run thy prayse I ne hold [margin break] not my feet" breaks mimetically mid-foot, pretending to subordinate his pentameter to his muse's shapeliness.

An anima/muse figure also energizes masculine form in "Apparuit" (1912, *PTEP*, 231), an experiment in quantitative Sapphics in which Pound works, according to Stephen Adams, "not by rule but aural intuition." The adaptation of Greek meter is fairly complex, not merely a substitution of stress for quantity, and includes several lines that seem to violate the metrical pattern: "Scansion and pronunciation require some practice."[25] This would have to be based on repeated phrasal contours: for example, the accentual choriambs (/ x x /) and Adonics (/ x x / x) that occur in a structured manner in "Apparuit" occur more variably in "The Return," also from *Ripostes*, and across *The Cantos*—if one is inclined to join certain critics.[26] This readership is anything but secure: from e. e. cummings's classically trained perspective, Pound's quantitative experiments are "studied obscurity."[27]

"Apparuit" must therefore be at once a lesson in accessing the prosodic potency of anima figures and a lesson in reading larger rhythmic structures. We might think of the muse-like figures of these poems as not only permitting authorship but pushing the reader to train and study to gain access to the works. Their presence assists the male speakers of Pound's other portraits of women in maintaining ownership and affinity with the chosen prosodic form: the speaker of "A Virginal" has his "feet planted [. . .] firmly on the ground."[28] Although "A Virginal" does develop a somewhat complex rhythmic figure by contrasting the stark openings of octave and sestet with subsequent lines, it is female grace that temporarily redeems its iambicized form: "slight are her arms, yet they have bound me straightly." There seems in any case to be enough distance between the imaginary "virginal" woman and fin-de-siècle meter to keep Pound from worrying about irony. The virginal muse figures a different hearing and training that the reader must also achieve.

The Riposte against Meter

In *Ripostes'* treatments of contemporary topics, when Pound removes his archaic masks and female statuary, rigid meter changes its role to that of critical emblem of modernity and modern audition. "Phasellus Ille," a thinly veiled attack on contemporary magazine culture, deliberately targets its own blank verse as part of a literary culture that refuses to "shake up the stagnant pool of its convictions":

> Nay, should the deathless voice of all the world
> Speak once again for its sole stimulation,
> 'Twould not move it one jot from left to right. (*PTEP*, 235)

The mild pun on printing or linear movement ("jot" comes from "iota," the smallest letter in Greek) suggests a possible failure of performance, and the monosyllables and plosive *t*s seem calculated to limit rhythmic appeal. A pun on feet in the final lines again worries about modern anesthesis:

> Come beauty barefoot from the Cyclades,
> She'd find a model for St. Anthony
> In this thing's sure *decorum* and behavior.

"Beauty," here, goes unshod. As Carolyn Burke notes, there was an expectation among modernist poets and audiences that the "emancipated female poet" would "like Isadora Duncan [. . .] naturally express herself in 'free-footed verse.'"[29] A Greek muse or Sappho figure could be represented in meter, but not one with this "decorum" and rhyme. Pound envisions a more classical decorum for "Beauty," antithetical to his culture's procrustean "behavior." T. H. Jackson finds that "Phasellus Ille" is "knowingly mannered."[30] It shares this with the two poems that follow: "An Object," whose iambic "thing, that hath a code and not a core," and "Quies," which rues the absence of a lady and picks up on the typographic themes of mere "thingness": "the day / Hath lacked a something since this lady passed; / Hath lacked a something. 'Twas but marginal."

"Portrait d'une Femme" (1912, *PTEP*, 233) is Pound's most ambitious effort to modernize his anima figures, situating them in contemporary London and framing them in a suitably complex meter. Like "A Virginal" and "Apparuit," which Jackson sees as "buttressed with stylistic bric-a-brac," "Portrait d'une Femme" turns to highly formulaic phrasing and meter to embody its subject.[31] The poem's female addressee differs markedly from Pound's anima figures. The "femme" is in part Florence Emery Farr, a theorist and performer of musical voicing (*The Music of Speech*, 1909) who worked with Yeats in the late 1900s. Pound admired Farr, and even considered working with her on psaltery settings of poetry, but resisted her approach to performance and would undoubtedly have been pleased at the ascent of his own prosodic theory in Yeats's estimation.[32] In Rachel Blau DuPlessis's account, the poem manages Farr's cultural potency by figuring her as a muse to negate her real agency and historical existence.[33] My concern here is with how Pound manages the formal mechanism of meter to separate his cultural work from Farr's.

Like "Phasellus Ille," "Portrait" mirrors cultural stagnation with the rigid "left to right" movement of the metrical line:

> Your mind and you are our Sargasso Sea,
> London has swept about you this score years
> And bright ships left you this or that in fee:
> Ideas, old gossip, oddments of all things,
> Strange spars of knowledge and dimmed wares of price.　　　5
> Great minds have sought you—lacking someone else.
> You have been second always. Tragical?
> No. You preferred it to the usual thing:
> One dull man, dulling and uxorious,
> One average mind—with one thought less, each year.　　　10
> Oh, you are patient, I have seen you sit
> Hours, where something might have floated up.
> And now you pay one. Yes, you richly pay.
> You are a person of some interest, one comes to you
> And takes strange gain away:　　　15
> Trophies fished up; some curious suggestion;
> Fact that leads nowhere; and a tale for two,
> Pregnant with mandrakes, or with something else
> That might prove useful and yet never proves,
> That never fits a corner or shows use,　　　20
> Or finds its hour upon the loom of days:

> The tarnished, gaudy, wonderful old work;
> Idols and ambergris and rare inlays,
> These are your riches, your great store; and yet
> For all this sea-hoard of deciduous things,   25
> Strange woods half sodden, and new brighter stuff:
> In the slow float of differing light and deep,
> No! there is nothing! In the whole and all,
> Nothing that's quite your own.
>   Yet this is you.   30

With the first line we join a prosodic masquerade into stagnant meter and unattractive sound. The mass of diphthongs and long, low syllables ("your," "you," "are," "our," later "you are a") anticipates the poem's general awkwardness of diction and tendency toward unnecessary phrases and superfluous adjectives—"bright ships left you this or that in fee." Both Robert Frost and an editor at the *North American Review* disparaged the poem's style.[34] Frost annotated his personal copy with a series of marginal notes pertaining to poetics and, in several instances, prosody. Frost's critique seems to be aimed at problematic uses of imagery or derivative stylistics but also at meter. This may have been revenge for Pound's attempt, during Frost's years in England, to perform some Imagist fat-cutting on an unnamed piece: Pound cut two words out of fifty, but Frost thought this "spoiled my metre, my idiom and idea."[35] Frost's annotations, unearthed by Josephine Grieder,[36] show just how careful the balance must be for these three aspects to work together:

	style:	
	You are a person of <u>some interest</u>, one comes to you	
	And takes strange gain away:	
Pledges	<u>Trophies</u> fished up; some curious suggestion;	
	Fact that leads nowhere; and a tale <u>for two,</u>	Why
Bosh	<u>Pregnant with mandrakes</u>, or with something else	
	That might prove useful and yet never proves,	
	That never fits a corner or <u>shows use</u>,	Idiom: wear
Nothing!	|Or finds its hour upon the loom of days:|	
	The tarnished, gaudy, wonderful old work;	
Work?	Idols and <u>ambergris</u> and rare inlays, [. . .] (ll. 14-23)	

Frost emends "pledges" for "trophies" and "wear" for "use" on account of diction, not meter. He does not offer alternatives, however, for the overwrought phrase "Pregnant with mandrakes" or the infelicitous word "ambergris" (it is a natural product, not a kind of "work"). Although Frost does not say so, the words seem chosen to satisfy the meter, rather than for sense or tone. As polysyllables, they rigidly lay down stresses in the expected positions (including a regular trochaic inversion) in a way that Frost would have found suspicious not least because Pound had hunted for such infelicities in *A Boy's Will*.

That Frost is interested in how Pound derives his rhythm is best indicated by the jarring comment "Nothing!" This is not a complaint about diction subordinated to meter; rather, Frost seems to be noting that one cannot string together the words "its hour upon" without recalling Macbeth's famous soliloquy on his wife's suicide, in which life is personified as a "poor player/That struts and frets his hour upon the stage." Frost's judgment echoes Macbeth's final judgment of life as a "tale/Told by an idiot, full of sound and fury,/Signifying nothing." Frost locates more bad borrowings in the line "and the slow float of differing light and deep," which he calls "Miltonic." The hendiadys (here "adjective noun and adjective") is a dominant stylistic marker in Milton, there tied to a certain faith in flexible Latin syntax. The hendiadys obeys meter rather than rhetoric or other stylistic demands. Ironically, "Miltonic" was one of Pound's own "derogatory epithets," applied in 1913 to Yeats's rhetorical style, including "straddled adjectives" like "differing light and deep."[37] Many of Frost's annotations emphasize the promiscuity in Pound's returns to iambic rhythm; his edits have no compunction about "spoiling" Pound's meter, for instance, in "Your mind ~~and you are~~ is our Sargasso Sea" (1); "And bright ships left you this or that ~~in fee~~" (3). Frost no doubt believed the poem's meter to be evidence of Pound's hypocrisy. He apparently missed Pound's generic use of meter as riposte, as means and object of satire.

Of the poem's thirty lines, just over half place stresses only in even positions (or at the beginning of the line as part of a standard trochaic inversion). Some of these lines have weakened stresses, as in the first line: "Your mínd and yóu are our Sargásso Séa." But the main flexibility comes in lines where the alternating stress pattern tilts toward an ionic pattern (sometimes called a double iamb)—x x / / or / / x x—as in the end of "London has swept about you this score years." Although this movement of stresses constitutes a more fluid form of pentameter, Pound is fairly consistent in assigning the rigid lines to descriptions of the women and flexible lines to descriptions of men and London. The "flexible" lines are not necessarily rhythmically attractive, even if not "metronomic." Lines 14-15 defiantly but also spuriously warp the meter: "one comes to you" would satisfy the meter easily if printed at the beginning of the following line. The lineation for rhyme (you/two) signals an arbitrary marriage of sounds, all the stranger given that the poem has only three other rhyme pairs (1/3, 13/15, 21/23). Pound also plays up a rhythmic monotone, as in the description of monogamy (which the woman eschews) as "One dull man, dulling and uxorious,/One average mind—with one thought less, each year." The passage from lines 16-21 describes the woman in unflattering terms with a regularity of rhythm that even in its irregularity—missing stress midline—remains repetitive. The finale of this passage at line 21 ("Or finds its hour upon the loom of days"), before the speaker relents and tries to find value in the woman, is at once metronomic and derivative.

The poem's eclectic rhetorical mix of Milton, Shakespeare, and Browning indicates less ownership of style and more susceptibility to meter's vestigiality than earlier works like *Hilda's Book* and adjacent pieces in *Ripostes*. The style and meter are instead a symptom of modern poetry's adjacency to its antitheses. The proximity of poet-poem and feminized object can be adduced in the imagery of jetsam and floating waste, seemingly aligned with the lady but that is itself derivative of Tristan Corbière's "Épitaphe" (1873). Corbière describes a similar prodigal, a "Flâneur au large,—à la dérive,/Épave qui jamais n'arrive . . ." (A lounger at large,—drifting,/Jetsam never arriving . . .).[38] As in the metrical allusions to Laforgue or Gautier in Eliot, allusion or echo demand a well-constructed coterie. Frost's annotations show no interest in this club and provocatively claim Pound's deafness to his borrowings— and to general matters of diction and syntax. But given Pound's thorough attention to the pentameter and the dramatic monologue after Browning, it strikes me as more appropriate to read the poem as a meditation on the authority and autonomy of modern prosody. In its own words, the poem wonders what sort of "strange gain" one now takes away from metrical vestiges. If the lady is a denigrated target, she is also an embodiment of Pound's constrained poetics, moving between rigid and slightly modulated iambics, and between blatant echo and sudden changes of lineation.

Both the figure of the lady and the metrical form, even in their moments of brightness, perform only the un-muse-like function of aiding circulation: a usurious process of "gain" undertaken by a person of "some interest." Yet however shallow the woman and versification are separately, their connection runs surprisingly deep. The poem's derivative, if vaguely flexible, verse form may be read additionally as a satirical embodiment of the "One dull man, dulling and uxorious" that culture tries to foist on the lady. Frost thought Pound to be describing the woman's "polyandry," which makes her an intriguing figure for Pound's own multiple marriages to forms and figures throughout *Ripostes* (Sapphics in "Apparuit," the sonnet in "A Virginal," ballad stanzas in "Pan Is Dead"). In these other poems the gendering of verse form authorizes the poem's anachronism precisely by denying authorship and poesis to women. "Portrait" reconnects its lady's protean affinities to Pound's own.

Eliot's judgment of *Ripostes* implies the centrality of "Portrait d'une Femme" to Pound's maturing diagnosis of modernity's inability to hear:

> By romantic readers the book would be considered less "passionate." But there is a much more solid substratum to this book; there is more thought; greater depth, if less agitation on the surface. The effect of London is apparent; the author has become a critic of men, surveying them from a consistent and developed point of view; he is more formidable and disconcerting; in short, much more mature.[39]

The poem's Sargasso-like rhythmical inertia is the "mature" form of Pound's accentual-syllabic meter. The poem if not volume reaches an important conclusion in its final line, when the speaker pauses to reflect that the lady has "Nothing that's quite your own./Yet this is you." This is also the poem's beginning: the realization that the poem has nothing that is its own yet comes into being by virtue of this nothingness. The woman is a muse for a surprisingly mechanical, inorganic poetics. Pound wrote in *The New Age* (1915), "The difference between man and a machine is that man can in some degree 'start his machinery going.' [. . . H]e can produce 'order-giving vibrations.'"[40] Perhaps all the poet could or should do is start up the iambic machine and its ordered vibrations. If so, the lady becomes more than the portrait's object. She is a guide in the effort to inhabit and feel its vestigial life rather than own, master, modulate, critique, or otherwise stand outside of modernity's mechanized rhythmic order.

The final lines recognize this debt both in tone and by abandoning the controlled prosodic masquerade:

> No! there is nothing! In the whole and all,
> Nothing that's quite your own.
>   Yet this is you.

Set off typographically as the quasi-completion of a shared line, "Yet this is you" insinuates the poem's move toward acceptance of the lady as a subtle mental shift, a lyrical gesture. Its pivotal "yet" is one of dramatic lyric's oldest tricks for signaling what Wordsworth called the "fluxes and refluxes of the mind when agitated by the great and simple affections of our nature."[41] The line break contributes ambiguously to its lyrical turn, evoking either the Pindaric ode's free catalexis or merely the second half of a pentameter line.[42] It might seem a cheap effect, compared to Wordsworth's desire to achieve the feeling of a mind at liberty through logical transitions and "the impassioned music of versification"[43]—that, is, a vibrant blank verse. It could also signal an incipient dialogism. The partial indentation, compared with complete ones in the split lines of Frost's dialogue poems or Elizabethan drama, preserves the ambiguity between random typographic break and metrical precision. That it is hard to choose between these competing prosodic gestures—between Romantic lyricism, a return to techniques found in Renaissance drama, or simply the sort of slapdash typographic efforts for which Pound and Eliot later critiqued free verse—suits not only the poem's theme but its tonal ambiguity as well. If a clunky blank verse safely marks stagnation for Pound, the riot of trying to move past it is anything but secure. "Portrait d'une Femme" remains a prosodic masquerade into a gendered form, but it also reveals how that very satire could only be produced by the "dull" and ironically "uxorious" man who presumes, like the Duke in Browning's "My Last Duchess" (1842), to possess the woman through his act of portraiture. Rather than judging the gendered sin of having "nothing that's quite your own," the final lines appreciate the lady's middle voice—her half-active, half-stagnant amplification of the poet's metrical "riposte" to the world around him.

Pan, Syrinx, and Sappho: Pound's Editorial Control and H.D.'s *HERmione*

What is missing from "Portrait d'une Femme," as from the anima poems, is a direct encounter with women's literary production. The nearest Pound comes in *Ripostes* is "Pan Is Dead," which begins with an address to "maidens":

> "Pan is dead. Great Pan is dead.
> Ah! bow your heads, ye maidens all,
> And weave ye him his coronal." (*PTEP*, 243)

Pan's death symbolizes the dissipation of Bacchic, masculine energies in modern poetry; it also hints at the limits of myth and metamorphosis, specifically the transformation of Syrinx into a reed and then pan pipe, an instrument of male performance. Pound is aligning himself with Pan, or wishing to do so, with the apostrophe to the maidens as his main device. But the masculine self-crowning depends on Pound's unacknowledged displacement of two poems about Pan by Elizabeth Barrett Browning. "The Dead Pan" (1844) has a primary refrain of "Pan, Pan is dead" which it modulates (echoing Plutarch) to "Great Pan is dead." Browning's "A Musical Instrument" (1862) begins almost every stanza with a question about "the great god Pan." Pound echoes these poems, yet it is hard to imagine a poem less sensitive to Browning's Hellenism and her subtle interrogation, in the later poem, of Ovidian sexual violence and its reproduction in the gendering of poetic authority.[44] "Pan is Dead" follows its opening echo with a hint toward Keats's "Belle Dame sans Merci," "withered are the sedges" (Keats: "the sedge is withered"). Another poem of uncanny sexual union, Keats's poem leads Pound from merciless Pan and his helpless consorts to a merciless faery and enervated knight. The latter echo aligns his worry over Pan's death with his worry over cultural effeminacy.

The authority over self and form that Pound laments in "Pan Is Dead" is maintained instead through the displacement of Browning herself (Robert at least gets referenced in *The Cantos*). Where Pound does elevate women poets, he first asserts the intervention of his critical and poetic intelligence. For example, Pound celebrates Mina Loy's "arid clarity" and goes so far as to invent a poetic mode, "logopoeia," or the "dance of the intelligence among words and ideas and modifications of ideas and characters," to characterize Loy as well as Marianne Moore's early work. Pound's review of these two "girls" and "americaines" (Loy was not American) highlights their succession, "possibly in unconsciousness," of the ironic spirit of Laforgue already channeled by Eliot, Pound himself, and others.[45] This subtle bit of historiography preserves the male subject position of satire even as criticism becomes the more pressing genre in which to assert control.

There is no need to enumerate Pound's (or Eliot's) efforts to control the literary capital often held by women in the 1910s (Amy Lowell, Harriet Monroe, Margaret Anderson, Harriet Shaw Weaver, Dora Marsden).[46] Most relevant here is how aggravation by poetry's female critics and gatekeepers leads Pound to repeated efforts at control of women poets' prosody (both theory and practice). For example, "Amy-just-selling-the-goods" Lowell's poetry is completely absorbed by commodification and repetition: she produces "amygism" and "Amy[s] it out by the barrel" in a "gush" of "fluid diarhoea [sic]." John Gould Fletcher at least produces "diarhoea of bent nails and carpet tacks." Pound's obsessive references to Lowell's weight ("300 pounds and a charmer") and physical-literary bowel movements intentionally or unintentionally defines women's experimental poetries as an undifferentiated fluid mass requiring hard boundaries. In his letters to Alice Corbin Henderson, the coeditor of *Poetry*, Pound cordons off the malign influences of another, sentimental gush: the endless profusion of iambs in "Sara Teasdale or any other one of the 9000 illustrious American imbeciles."[47] In its place he tries to instill a more careful stylistic and metrical repertoire. A year before he praises Loy's Laforgian style, he tells Henderson "we should take a course in laforgue, those of us who have not done so, BUT ONLY the very elect. I do not think we should mention him to anyone but ourselves. Publicity is too dam'd democratic."[48] His comments on her manuscript poetry extend the influence tracing to Eliot (by "shall I go on" he notes "I think Eliot in Blast did almost the same thing as part of this with more grip + tenseness") and phrasing "derivative" of Yeats. Similar comments emphasize meter directly. Pound's lesson in Yeatsian "rhythm" contrasts poignantly with those of Florence Farr, who defended the "monotone" and chanted performance.

> I should say RHYTHM, watch the rhythm. Dissect good lyrics. Cut out Yeats' limited vocabulary. "'And an old man appeared in the dusk' etc. Dissect Yeats. 'The Danan [sic] children laugh.'" Note how rarely he is uniform. In the feet. Iambs. Anapests, quantitative feet alternating with stressed. I think its probably nothing but his wonderful ear for really long syllables that does much of the trick for him. You must make your own studies and dissections.[49]

The hasty description of Yeats's "feet" depends not on faith in Yeats but on his apostle Pound, whose "dissections"—here of Henderson's verse—reproduce an ear training ostentatiously aware of "more about poetry of every time and place. Than any man living. [. . .] nine months on Arnaut for polyphonic rime. [. . .] 6 months on Sapphics. 400 sonnets destroyed." He aims this critical "artillery" at all comers, though his control is most frequently leveled at women poets, and one of its central gestures is management of Sappho as one of Imagism's "parents." When he clarifies that Imagism "owe[s] more to the *metres* of the melic poets than to France," he pulls away from the recent past and toward a linguistic realm with deeper divisions of access. He observes Henderson's linguistic limitations: although he

"No Feet to Walk On"

knows she has "read as much french as I have," he asks, "what classics are you to read, without greek or latin?"—or Anglo-Saxon, which is "harder." Lacking these other languages, and stuck with Yeats, she hasn't "a language of [her] own."⁵⁰ Similar comments about bad-because-accidental "Sapphics" and a lacking "sense of quantity" pervade Pound's letters to Mary Barnard, though they seem to share disdain toward academic study of classical prosody (Pound offers a mock Guggenheim application "for the investigation of Greek metres and music. Research [. . .] for prehistoric indications of the 1/8 tone scale by the minotaur, Daedalus' invention of the pre-jazz saw").⁵¹

In isolation such scattered comments on classical languages and meter might be little more than Pound's admitted "braggadocio." But there is reason to see it as a continuation of a much older feeling that foreign, non-iambic, non-metronomic meter was, like access to Laforgian irony, a masculine province. In 1908 Pound observed to William Carlos Williams how Anglo-Saxon and "Greek metric" stand apart from "the English of Milton or Miss Austin's [sic] day."⁵² These visions of metrical Hellenism deliberately avoid Elizabeth Barrett Browning and the modernized Greek identity she designed in *Aurora Leigh* (1856). Pound, with his "classicizing ear," insinuates himself into the position of Leigh, who Yopie Prins describes as a "self-classicizing figure."⁵³ Leigh's suitor and cousin, Romney, reads her poetry ("poems, by the form," he unwittingly sneers) and fixates on some Greek marginalia: "Lady's Greek, without the accents." Pound's letters to Henderson reenact this scene. In accidentally playing Romney, Pound continues the male delimiting of formal lineages available to Victorian and modern women poets alike. Prins notes how the prior generation of fin-de-siècle women writers found an "exemplary claim to female authorship" in Browning. For Browning, Leigh's "Lady's Greek" makes translation of Greek into an expressive force—into the translation of "letters imprinted [. . .] in the heart, mind, and soul of woman."⁵⁴ There is no evidence that Henderson sensed any immediate foreclosure of Sapphic or other Greek lineages. For one thing, she was far more interested in southwest Native American materials, over which Pound also played expert. H.D., by contrast, was at once more deeply Hellenistic and more directly objectified as Pound's "Sapphic fragment" and "Galatea-like figure."⁵⁵ She articulates and responds to Pound's gendered determination of modern prosody, specifically his control over Greek meters and their Victorian afterlife.

As Cassandra Laity has shown, H.D.'s retort against masculine modernism includes her reclamation of fin-de-siècle figures like the decadent femme fatale and male androgyne found in Swinburne's poetry. In her roman à clef, *HERmione*, the recovery and redevelopment of Swinburne's poetics is a way to negotiate a relationship to classical prosody unmediated by Pound. *HERmione* burlesques Pound as Hermione's (usually called Her or Her Gart) wildly coifed fiancé, George Lowndes. Her escape from George into a lesbian relationship with Fayne Rabb (Frances Gregg) relies upon a steady stream of echoes and quotations of Swinburne's poetry. Other engagements with the Victorian fin de siècle as a feminist origin include a defense of her mother, Eugenia's, amateur painting as a legitimate affective object: "Think of the fun she had putting that pine tree by that pine tree until way up at the top of the mountain the last pine tree is just one speck of colour"; "you must see how she loved it." "Love doesn't make good art" replies George/Pound, rejecting the recent past as sentimental atavism.[56]

However, Eugenia's painted pines are not about romantic love but about the love of the final brushstroke, "one speck of colour" that becomes a tree by pigment and relation. Though still "Victorian" and rooted in mimetic art, Eugenia's painting sets the stage for modernist abstraction and medium specificity. To George, however, Hermione seems too proximate to the Victorian (m)other. When Eugenia tells her, "George has a new vocabulary, Rossetti, Burne-Jones-odd distorted creatures" (referring either to the artists or to their painted subjects), Her immediately internalizes the comment as a judgment from George upon her person: "Odd distorted Hermione descended the hall steps. She moved odd, distorted like a mermaid with no feet to walk on" (113). The male gaze as literary-historical vision makes her sea change into a wrong-footed stumble.

Eugenia's painting represents Her's maternal as well as Victorian lineage. George makes this connection and reacts violently—"Painted? You call that painted?"—then refuses to help with "her bally writing." He polices genre and meter when he discovers Her's poetry: "It's like—like—Theocritus. [. . .] It's like an epilogue"; when Her suggests, "Bucolic?" he responds, "No. The other thing. *Not* Tityrus tu titulae. [. . . I]t's like the choriambics of a forgotten melic." H.D. has George misquote Virgil (his first eclogue begins "Tityre, tu patulae"), which may be a canny satire of how Pound's investment in classical genre and meter exceed his linguistic grasp (148–49). In this sequence George mentally wanders from Her's actual writing—which we do not see—to imagine his recovery of lost song (*melos*) through choriambic nuclei: these, highlighted in Sapphic stanzas, became critical to Pound's poetics in the years following his relationship with H.D.

The scene reads as a satirical revisiting of the early moment in *Aurora Leigh* when Romney discovers Aurora's poems. There is no direct evidence that H.D. had read *Aurora Leigh* or had Browning in mind (Robert Browning's *The Ring and the Book* gets a mention). But I cannot otherwise explain the remarkable proximity between her famous poem "Oread" (1914) and Romney's description of the streamside hollow where he finds Leigh's book of poems: "That beach leans down into [the hollow]—of which you said, / The Oread in it has a Naiad's heart / And pines for waters."[57] Susan Stanford Friedman notes the parallel and, although she too cannot confirm the homage, argues that Browning could have been the sort of "literary 'grandmother'" Browning herself knew to be absent.[58] *HERmione* suggests that this particular grandmother's value would be to model an incisive rejection of patriarchal prosody even as Browning's metrical poetics would appear not to have interested H.D. Neither did Sappho's quantitative patterns. Far more important was the capacity to thematize and translate prosodic ideals—a capacity that, as Prins has shown, was already richly developed through Browning in fin-de-siècle women's poetry.

Her's response to George is not to vet her lines or claim their prosodic lineage. Within a short span of time she will realize that George's comment is flattery, a way of saying that women and women's verse is merely "decorative" rather than "something of somewhat-painful angles that he would not recognize": "George saying 'Choriambics of a forgotten Melic' was flattering her, tribute such as some courtier might pay to a queen who played at classicism" (172). The remark unites Pound's treatment of H.D. as an anima figure with his treatment of female meter as separate from his own rigorous classicism. "To George, Her was Dian or Diana, never Artemis," a distinction between Greek and Latin that Pound aims to transcend in *The Cantos* when he admits to using Andreas Divus's Latin translation of the *Odyssey* and in doing so bolsters his claim to critically mediating literary history. Late in the novel George's comments echo in Her's fever state, losing whatever coherence they might have had as prosodic judgment: "George called them forgotten lyrics of a lost Melic or iambics of a forgotten Melic. I have forgotten. I am the lost iambics of a forgotten Melic" (205). Her's fever state symbolizes women poets' heavily mediated encounter with modernism's lingering "melic" ideals. Not coincidentally the feverish confusion of metrical terms reverts to "lyrics" and "iambics." If she is "lost iambics," then the male poet can too easily find her: Pound's *Hilda's Book* is the obvious model, a playful encounter with a woman's versified, diminutive body. No surprise that George's remark finally makes Her feel "doomed [. . .] for the message you carry is in forgotten meters" (220). Pound too had to make peace with and overcome this feeling of vestigiality, but H.D. has to do so against Pound and his judgment that women poets can produce only half-conscious, atavistic encounters with the same tradition.

We do not see the "white pages" written by Her, so we cannot scan their "forgotten" meters. Following George's flattery, Her refuses to play the game of who can produce the right choriamb; she turns away from the Poundian poetics of "6 months on Sapphics" and toward a chiastic syntax that mimics the shape but not quantities of choriambic feet. At first, following his metrical judgment, she obsessively repeats his words and even rhythm:

> Choriambics of a forgotten Melic. Choriambics of a forgotten Melic beat rhythm and rhythm through the alert avid out-watching mind of Her Gart. "Choriambics," she repeated valiantly swaying with the jerk and sway of the trolley. "Choriambics," she said to herself, sustained against the bulk of a huge negress. [. . .] "Choriambics of a forgotten Melic" sustained Hermione against a broad-shouldered sort of butcher. [. . .] "Choriambics," she said, "Choriambics, this part of town is dreadful" and sustained and pushed and pushed and sustained and pushed finally into a corner. (149-50)

The actual utterance of "Choriambics, this part of town is dreadful" may echo George's accidental hendecasyllabic line as his phrase "beats" at her. But this episode is more important for its thematic discovery of the choriamb as a structure of mirrored unity: "sustained and pushed and pushed and sustained." The choriamb, transformed into chiastic figures, channels Swinburne's poetry, especially "Itylus" (1866) a poem that modulates in each stanza the chiastic, enveloping refrain of "Swallow, my sister, O sister swallow." More than any thematic echo of Greek myth or Swinburne's dramatic monologue, it is this syntactic rhythm that allows Her to negotiate her relationship with Fayne, who she renames Itylus:

> "I only said *O sister, my sister, O singing Swallow, the heart's division divideth us*. And then that afternoon I was sure that your name was Itylus." Her Gart spoke and read, read and spoke, her words made rhythm to the poem, the poem made rhythm suitable to her swift words. Words came from nowhere, tumbled headlong somewhere. (179)

Hermione takes the rhyme of "us" and "Itylus" from Swinburne's poem and uses it to stitch together identity through sound. The rhythmic language of

Victorian poetry catalyzes an affective bond, freeing Her from the strife of having to create new language or meters. The chiasma proliferate from the Swinburnian origin:

Spoke / read / read / spoke
Words / rhythm / poem / poem / rhythm / words
Nowhere / tumble / headlong / somewhere

Rhythm in such passages is not a "lost melic" fragment to be recovered or repeated; neither H.D. nor her verse is, in her own quotation of her critics, "chiseled as to seem lapidary."[59] With the syntactic choriamb Her recovers from her earlier stumbles. As she fixates on Fayne's sleeping heartbeat, Her finds that even this autonomous rhythm relies upon her own generative power: "Her seemed to be dragging beat on beat out of that heart by her very static willpower. I will not have her hurt. I will not have Her hurt. She is Her. I am Her. Her is Fayne. Fayne is Her. I will not let them hurt Her" (181). The chiasma transform syntax into a singular, paragrammatical, choreographed declaration of love.

The chiasmus helps Her prepare the final salvo against George, "accusation making fire and spark to wither George and defiance making George quiver beneath spark and fire of accusation" (186). We never see this moment of accusation within the novel's dramatic action. But H.D. has already resisted Pound's precise quantities, as well as previous decades' accentual analogues for Greek meter. Her lost Melic poet is Swinburne, not Sappho, nor Sappho as a Victorian or modern construction (including Swinburne's and Pound's).[60] Whereas Pound, Eliot, and Frost saw Swinburne's "musical" verse as a dead end, H.D. reclaims Swinburne's melopoesis by transforming its technical virtues into a symbolic mode.[61] Swinburne's real value is as a vestige to be remediated in a new genre, a melodic, rhythmic, and thematic base from which to escape gendered ideas of historical form and literary history.

Hidden in the title of H.D.'s "Oread," Carrie Preston discerns, is the command "O read."[62] *HERmione* exposes modernism's web of male editorial, personal, and prosodic overreading. It marks the un-reading of Elizabeth Barrett Browning and of the prosodic history she once grounded through works like *Aurora Leigh*. That said, H.D.'s personal investment "in forgotten meters" does not pull her toward writing in them, most likely because she was listening for Greek patterns but not reproducing them in ways we can scan. As I show in my next chapter, however, many other women poets did write in "lost iambics," despite the regime implied by Pound's metrical historiography. They share Pound's ambivalence toward the metrical vestige but with the added burden of his and others' presumptions about the conservatism and automatism of women's metrical traditions.

4 Metristes

Formal Feeling in Sara Teasdale, Georgia Douglas Johnson, and Louise Bogan

> Look what Eliot does to everyone from the Elizabethans down. [. . .] Anything that is conscious and acknowledged is all right. It's the horrible unconscious lifting [. . .] that is truly reprehensible.
>
> —Louise Bogan to Theodore Roethke, November 6, 1935

> And as for this line I stole it from T. S. Eliot
> And Ezra Pound and A. C. Swinburne. All very good
> Poets to steal from since they are all dead.
>
> —Veronica Forrest-Thomson, "Cordelia; or, 'A Poem Should Not Mean, but Be'"

The previous two chapters traced how T. S. Eliot and Ezra Pound developed literary authority through satires in and of meter that treated it as a feminized form. These masquerades in meter finally provide neither an ordering subject position for the satirist nor an ordering object in their metrically framed women. As my closing study of H.D.'s *HERmione* suggests, Pound's and Eliot's self-destructing metrical games circumscribed meter's conceptual and affective possibilities for women poets invested in and avidly experimenting with traditional prosody. Complicating twentieth-century divisions of form and sentiment, Tasha Eccles has shown that the desire for "sentimental sociability" and "sensibility lie at the very center of the formalist project."[1] This is readily apparent in Pound's and Eliot's early poetry and in Eliot's criticism. For modern women poets, the converse was as essential: the desire for genre and prosodic form lies at the center of their effort to persevere in and transform the sentimental and poetess traditions. The goal of this chapter is to understand how women poets' practice of meter reconfigures traditions of women's writing, including sentimental tropes, against prosody's gendered codes.

H.D. largely skirts the metrical arena by pursuing her own Hellenistic vision and free verse prosody. Her Greek translations, as Yopie Prins describes them, develop a spare "alternative to translations by 'clumsy metrists.'"[2] Mina Loy similarly developed her own non-accentual syllabic feminist prosody, in her case satirical neo-Skeltonic rhyme leashes. Although Loy and other non-iambic poets are not my primary subject, it matters how H.D., Loy, and others were initially read as an exception to the rule that women poets defaulted to meter. An appearance in a West Village theater production led to Loy's discovery by the New York press and her prompt naming as an icon of the "modern woman." Her first achievement: "She can and does write free verse and hold the intuitional pause exactly the right length of time."[3] According to Loy's editor Roger Conover, Harriet Monroe contrasted Loy with a more suspiciously modern West Village figure: "She immediately sensed that Mina Loy bore no resemblance to the lady love poets of the Edna St. Vincent Millay school."[4]

Despite her social and political radicalness, Millay was censored under the mark of the "sentimental." The sonnet I. A. Richards selected from *The Harp Weaver* (1923) for *Practical Criticism* was, he found, not only "demonstrably bad" but "a trap for the naïve, the unpractised, the unsophisticated reader." One of Richards's experimental readers ("protocolists"), most likely F. R. Leavis, is singled out for correctly identifying Millay's poem as a "play for easily touched off and full-volumed responses," leaving readers "in danger of sentimentality and kindred vices." Much of what drives this sentimental response is meter: Millay's poem cannot be saved by "giv[ing] decent prominence to the natural speech rhythm." Her "superficial rhythm" invites only superficial comments on rhythm.[5] Richards contrasts D. H. Lawrence's "The Piano" (1913) as a subtle meditation on sentimentality and memory; his meter, moreover, is apt to be "victimized by [readers'] imparted rhythm"— a bad music they supply and then, it seems, align with bad sentiment.

Mina Loy, though never included in the bad canons of metrical poetess verse, consistently aims her satire at the modern gendering of form. Emerging from the misogyny of Futurism, Loy's erratic rhymes and variable catalexis constitute a verse body that mocks modernist satire's failed transcendence and patriarchal tendencies. In her characteristically sharp "Apology for Genius" (1922), she figures the male reader as a kind of ornithologist, so fixated on female ornament that women artists' genius becomes "lacy bustles" and "tassels of the soul."⁶ The poet may create the "imperious jewelry of the Universe/ —The Beautiful"—but that is not what the male reader sees:

> While to your eyes
> > A delicate crop
> of criminal mystic immortelles
> stands to the censor's scythe⁷

The female poet or "immortelle" becomes a "crop," provoking Loy to make her own "crop" of the verse line in vertiginous, slant-rhymed, enjambed verse columns:

> Onyx-eyed Odalisques
> and ornithologists
> observe
> the flight
> of Eros obsolete⁸

This morphological rhyme (-isques, -ists, -ight, -ete) invents something like slant rhyme riche (now audible in hip-hop, including the feminist rhyme leashes of Missy Elliot or Lauryn Hill). Mirroring this descent from semantic to unmusical rhyme, all of Loy's subjects are built around the mouth-shaped absence of the "O" (as in her long roman à clef *Anglo-Mongrels and the Rose* (written 1923-1925 but not published until 1982), where she names herself O̱va and her mother Ro̱se). Loy captures both men and women in this cage of distorted and unsynthesized sound.

Meter's cage presents a more difficult medium for resisting modernism's gendered prosodic field. Bogan's worry about "lifting" and Forrest-Thomson's cagey theft suggest both the value and strain of self-consciously entering Eliot and Pound's privatized tradition of metrical borrowing. Forrest-Thomson's poem hints through anagram that T. S. "Stole it" Eliot should be more honest about his derivativeness. Her poem, lapsing repeatedly into the vestigial form of iambic heptameter and mocking its own "very satisfactory refrain," sounds most like Pound's earliest and most ambivalent metrical vestiges. It points to what has been lost: a tradition of metrical writing more honest about its uneasy debt to prosodic history (especially Victorian prosody) and the artifice of their meters. Her subtitle, "or, 'A Poem Should Not Mean but Be,'" alludes to Archibald MacLeish's dogmatic "Ars Poetica" (1926) to convey how her poems cannot "be" until they have understood the gendered constraints and processes of their production.

Modernism's early configuration of meter as a mass-cultural object made it "somehow associated with woman while real, authentic culture remains the prerogative of men."[9] Sandra Gilbert marks the stereotyping of "'bad' verse" as "'feminine (i.e., formally conservative)" and "'good' poetry" as "'masculine' (i.e., formally innovative)"—and the contrast between "verse" and "poetry" here is essential to the defensive rearticulation of genre.[10] As Rita Felski notes, the gendered logic of modernist formalism consistently "polarizes 'feminine' repetition and 'masculine' rupture and revolt."[11] As a result, women poets like Millay were "exiled so sternly from tradition that [they were] not privileged to charge the prosodic nuances of a traditional lyric genre with the force of male literary history."[12] That same sense of exile led Pound and Eliot to rearticulate "male literary history" with the support of an antithetical and further exiled female tradition now associated with meter. Put another way, we might read the early twentieth century as the moment when women poets began, finally, to build confidently on the heritage of Elizabeth Barrett Browning's iambic pentameter (blank verse and sonnets) and to thus escape the nineteenth-century association of iambic pentameter with a "patriarchal poetic tradition";[13] the reconception of meter as a "metronome" destroys the ground of that literary-historical renaissance.

Our inheritance of modernism's narrative about meter means even feminist reevaluations have had difficulty asking the "right questions about how traditional poetic forms such as the sonnet may serve the needs of women poets."[14] How can we read traditional form in poets like Millay as something other than pleasant restraint or the mark of gentility and instead as a negotiation of sentimentalism, the genre of poetess verse, and what Elissa Zellinger calls the modern "problem that faced the woman poet: the impossible and self-diminishing practice of professing privacy"?[15] In this chapter I ask how meter served three poets from different literary spheres and with different investments in private sentiment: Sara Teasdale, Georgia Douglas Johnson, and Louise Bogan. Each transforms meter into a formal response to a gendered literary history in which women poets remained, in Edna St. Vincent Millay's cutting words, "distressed / by all the needs and notions of [their] kind."[16] Through the "stolen" and "obsolete" metrical vestige, they explore and redeem the inauthenticity, artifice, and sentimentality with which they have been charged.

It bears adding that a full study of the historical prosody of modern women poets writing in traditional meters—sometimes labeled "formalists"—would itself be a book-length undertaking. I choose Teasdale, Douglas Johnson, and Bogan because their metrical practices converge despite writing for three very different audiences and thus under distinct but parallel pressures. Sara Teasdale was a Pulitzer Prize-winning poet, one of the most popular poets of the 1910s, and so unsurprisingly she is a consistent target of formal and generic distrust. Georgia Douglas Johnson experienced the unique strain of managing her "genteel" identity within the New Negro Renaissance and its swiftly changing dynamics of formal innovation and vernacularity. Bogan's highbrow distaste, as a prominent literary critic, for the genteel tradition would seem to make her a poor comparator. But her quarrel with the idea of defining or anthologizing "women poets" belies a sustained quest to understand, through her own meter, the feeling of alienation and psychic disturbance that comes from writing in the anti-sentimental, anti-Victorian, and often anti-metrical poetry culture I have detailed thus far.

Sara Teasdale and the Labor of the Line

In a 1920 editorial Harriet Monroe contrasts Teasdale and Millay with underappreciated new work by two male Imagists: "If Edna Millay sings to the lyre, and Sara Teasdale to the lute, must we be deaf to the delicately emotional lyric solos played on a reed by such younglings as Mark Turbyfill or A. Y[vor]. Winters—tunes of thistle-down texture?"[17] Within this odd comparison of lyricists is an important contrast between women poets who merely accompany music and men who, like Pan, play their own wind instrument. What value Monroe finds in Teasdale requires an ideal of a "real lyric cry" with the "grace and fragrance of flowers."[18] In 1933, following Teasdale's death, Monroe describes

> poems of a finished and delicate, if narrow technique. [. . . I]n all these five books she uses the simplest lyric forms. Two or three quatrains of three- or four-footed iambic lines, each quatrain emphasized by a single rhyme, form usually the metrical structure of her songs. Her instrument is not rich and powerful, capable of chords; it has the aching quality of a violin played with soft tenseness by feminine hands at twilight.[19]

For a canonically "lyric" woman poet like Sara Teasdale with prizes and a popular following, there might have been no cause to care about elite dismissal of her poetic form. Yet her poetry bears traces of the limits on what poetic capital she could claim. Like H.D. and Aurora Leigh, Teasdale invests in "melic" origins. Her journals hold a range of poems written about Sappho, including the poem titled after and spoken by Sappho that concludes *Rivers to the Sea* (1915). The poem's speaker reflects meta-poetically upon the demands placed on poetesses by imagining herself as Syrinx: "I will not be a reed to hold the sound / Of whatsoever breath the gods may blow, / Turning my torment into music for them."[20] In the poem's final section, the speaker tells Aphrodite that she has overcome, through maternal love for her daughter, the fiery and nonreciprocal loves "that made my life a lyric cry" and "turned my lips to lyres of thine." The speaker escapes lyric reading only through motherhood, a mercurial embrace of an alternate mode of reproduction that conforms to other gendered expectations about the themes and priorities of women poets.

Teasdale's drafts show how prosody takes part in her uneasy negotiations of the poetic and prosodic tradition. She excises the subtitle "Sapphics" from "September Midnight" (1913), a poem written in that meter and investing in permutations of choriambic stress patterns. It carefully detaches the speaker from the "lady nightingale" poetess tradition by aligning "lyric summer" not with birdsong ("never a bird") but with the "passionless chant of insects / ceaseless, insistent."[21] Reinforcing the turn to motherhood in "Sappho," Teasdale's decision to excise "Sapphics" avoids authoritative claims to both technical sophistication and a Hellenistic vision of the poetess. Her early notebooks repeatedly erase genealogies of poetic form. The "Ballad of the Carpenter's Son" becomes "The Carpenter's Son" (1915). She replaces a stanza in the early poem "Union Square" (1911) because it clearly alludes to Housman's "Loveliest of trees, the cherry now"—indeed, she had penciled "Housman" above the stanza. "A Provençal Song" seems to have been accepted by *Poetry* but was returned and not published until 1915 as "A Castillian Song," though whether that has anything to do with Pound's own claim to medieval French is pure speculation. The unpublished poem "Darkness at Noon" clearly fuses Hardy's "Darkling Thrush" (1900) with both the theme and stanza forms of Keats's "Belle Dame sans Merci." The decision not to publish was not due to the stanza form, which also occurs in the opening poem of *Rivers to the Sea* but more likely because of the very recent example of Hardy's well-known turn-of-the-century elegy.[22] Although there might be many reasons not to publish such poems or to exclude subtitles or specific stanzas, the pattern of erasure reinforces Monroe's and others' sense of a poet who avoids polymetricality in favor of lyrical quatrains. Teasdale's verse of the 1910s is written in many forms, including free verse, a range of sonnet structures, various ballad stanzas or quatrain, and blank verse. Yet her turn toward greater formal variety around 1911 was no more recognized or valued than Millay's metrical experimentation. Monroe's review of *Rivers to the Sea*, for instance, appreciates (ironically, given "Sappho") the "real lyric cry" of the quatrain poems, "the simplest tune in the language" sung with "girlish delicacy" (by a woman in her thirties). "It is a pity" she tries free verse, and in fact it would be a pity to analyze the poems at all: "It would be like analyzing the flowers of June."[23]

Such impressions reinforce a core irony of Teasdale's reception: she was imagined as a lyric poet even as the mass and commercial appeal of that role sparked ambivalence. Her changed titles suggest the strain of addressing herself to a different media environment as an American ballad poet, a path charted, Meredith McGill notes, by previous generations of American poets seeking in the ballad "a canon of popular works that they could claim as their own, a prehistory of British letters."[24] Teasdale's revisions and reception reveal the difficulty of escaping from lineages of the Syrinx-like "melic" woman poet for an alternate mode of circulation. She imagines that mobility in an unpublished elegy entitled "Mary Trevor's Sampler."[25] The first two stanzas evoke simple sentimental regret at the death of a young, pretty, and frail woman. There is no sense that Mary's death had any impact on the world or on the poet. The third stanza changes tack:

> Yet on the sampler that she made
> Red roses round her name are set
>   Square roses made of silken thread
>   A hundred years since she is dead
> Still keep the name that men forget

Mary died and left no trace other than what the poet might choose to sentimentally recover. "Yet" she made an embroidery sampler, a minimal bit of craft that sets her name moving across the hundred years since her death and that necessitates Teasdale's attention. Why this unheralded "yet"? There is no tension or contradiction between her young death and the fact that she stitched her name into a sampler surrounded by silken square roses. By the stanza's end we find the rhyme and reason for "yet": the sampler and its material details "still keep the name that men forget." The conflict is between sampler and history, between the merest trace of the proper name and a male history that forgets such names and the forms they take.

In the last stanza, the subtle "yet" grows into a meditation on literary genre, on the fraught relation between sentimental poetry and an inhospitable literary history:

> She died before her day of days
> And she was frailer than the snow
> > But since her fingers labored thus
> > She is not wholly dead to us
> Who read her name and dream and know.

The stanza makes a discovery about sentimental objects: they do not need to be repudiated so long as they mediate their own memory. Here that mediation occurs through the female labor of needlework, a labor that stands against other kinds of historical mediation. The "us" is a collective and clearly female position characterized both by an understanding of needlework and a feeling for sentimental verse. The final line stitches together two acts of reading and two signatures in a foursquare metrical figure: read, name, dream, know. We read a "Mary" and a Teasdale of both ink and thread. The poem is their needlework, its four stanzas the four roses of the sampler, and the fate it imagines transcending is not only Mary's but also Teasdale's restricted path in literary history.

The poem's search for a new concept of line-work reflects the absent solution that Pound developed in his time with Yeats and that Eliot concocted by letting Pound be his "Sage Homme" or male midwife.[26] Those same men actively "forgot" a sentimental tradition and left few avenues for its recovery. In Suzanne Clark's summary, "The revolt against the sentimental buried that tradition [of the novel or poem of social issues]. Women writers found themselves gradually cut off from the very past that might nurture them."[27] "Mary Trevor" cannot redeem sentimentality or its poetic form. It tells us why sentimentality cannot be redeemed. The figure of the sampler could only be an improbable and vestigial model of female metrical poetics. Teasdale's unpublished poem articulates an erasure of residual literary and social history. It marks the limit of meter's power to compel attention to alternate literary lineages.

Georgia Douglas Johnson's Metrical Bars

Georgia Douglas Johnson, one of the best established of the women poets now associated with the New Negro Renaissance, was often compared to Teasdale and understood in similar terms. Her explicit, thematic embrace of prosodic innovation connects her to both the poetess tradition and to the broad use of traditional Anglo-American prosody in modern black poetics. Douglas Johnson's engagement with discourses of gender and sentimentality serves as her entry point to the more explicit discussions of race as her career progressed. This makes her a critical counterpoint to a black poetics that, reproducing a gendered modern poetics, effaces the sentimental or poetess tradition and in doing so loses a means for understanding double consciousness.

To some extent we must find Douglas Johnson where early anthologists like Elizabeth Lay Green and recent critics like Michael Nowlin place her, in what Houston Baker calls a black cultural world "bent on recognizable (rhyme, meter, form, etc.) artistic 'contributions' where familiar structures such as ballads and sonnets presented the greatest 'use.'"[28] Yet recognizable forms signal a mode of self-recognition that anticipates how better-known works like Sterling Brown's *Southern Road* "point to artistry itself as a means of self-realization. Not simply as the articulation of myths and idioms but as prosody and craft."[29] Douglas Johnson ran her "S Street Salon" or "Saturday Nighters" in Washington, DC, for decades, with nearly every major figure in the Harlem Renaissance attending (Jean Toomer, Langston Hughes, Anne Spencer, Alain Locke), thus both encountering and facilitating the Renaissance's full range of styles and forms. In individual poems and in developments after her first book, Johnson's heightened consciousness of prosody transforms her lyricism and participation in a sentimental tradition. Her "subversively 'minor' forms" anticipate the "synthetic vernaculars" that Matthew Hart finds so central to black modernists like Melvin Tolson and that drive the critique of racialized form in Jean Toomer, James Weldon Johnson, and Sterling Brown.[30]

Sentimental verses on the sympathy of a mother and her child, written in traditional meters, now appear an odd place to look for the characteristic prosody of the New Negro Renaissance. Douglas Johnson's first volume, *Heart of a Woman* (1918), is full of such verse, which as William Stanley Braithwaite notes in his introduction the volume, remains closely linked with the fin-de-siècle poetess verse of Amy Levy. Braithwaite presses the allusion beyond Levy to Elizabeth Barrett Browning, Sappho, and even Ruth gleaning in the fields of Moab—Johnson, we learn, makes of "sadness a kind of felicity" as only a poetess can.[31] That Langston Hughes, in a headnote to *Fine Clothes to the Jew* ("A Note on the Blues"), defines the mood of the blues as "almost despondency, but when they are sung people laugh," and that the blues singer Ma Rainey, in the hands of Sterling Brown, will be said to accomplish much the same transformation of sighs into laughs, should, however, begin to suggest a commonality behind otherwise divergent poetics. Johnson, moreover, would have been keenly aware that she was eschewing explicitly racial concerns; in her best-known poem, "Heart of a Woman" (in *Heart of a Woman*, 1918) she adopts the same figure of the caged bird that Paul Lawrence Dunbar develops in "Sympathy" (1899), a poem that concerns the barrier of race rather than gender.[32]

In *Heart of a Woman*, literary tradition enters above all through Tennyson and his meters. The collection is braced by two poems—the first and the penultimate—that unmistakably allude to Tennyson. Few ears would have missed the allusion in the final line of the opening, titular poem, "Heart of a Woman":

> The heart of a woman goes forth with the dawn,
> As a lone bird, soft winging, so restlessly on,
> Afar o'er life's turrets and vales does it roam
> In the wake of those echoes the heart calls home.
>
> The heart of a woman falls back with the night,
> And enters some alien cage in its plight,
> And tries to forget it has dreamed of the stars
> While it breaks, breaks, breaks on the sheltering bars.[33]

The classical lilt and regularity of the triple meter serve both to elevate the subject matter and to prepare the turn of the final line. The final line quotes Tennyson's "Break, Break, Break" (1842) a poem famous precisely as a metrical experiment and even as an "exercise in metrical blockage" of voice and voicing.[34] The line may seem strange because it is both entirely sincere and a blatant echo. The lack of any concealment is evident in Sterling Brown's study questions for the poem: "a. Notice the verse form. [. . .] c. What poem is suggested by the last line?"[35] Yet the line is interesting precisely because of the obviousness and belatedness of the echo: poetess poetry as early as the 1880s played with meters that Tennyson had conspicuously adapted from classical sources.[36]

The echo of Tennyson reframes Braithwaite's introduction to the volume. Braithwaite identifies Douglas Johnson with Ruth ("amid the alien corn," as Keats had it, and Braithwaite may have been led to this association by Johnson's own use of the word "alien") rather than identifying her as the poet responsible for depicting the woman's "alien cage." Johnson's allusion to "Break, Break, Break" affirms, against Braithwaite's lyricized twentieth-century version of the poetess, the difference between poem and poet, between sentimental subject and the writer, not just in but above the sentimental tradition—between the rhythmic subject or body that "breaks" and the creator and breaker of rhythms.

This difference expands when the precise prosody of the Tennysonian line is considered. In Tennyson, "Break, break, break" forms an entire four-beat line (three feet, each containing a pause and a final rest). Johnson's line converts Tennyson's accentual meter into a triple meter and sets the three "breaks" into the more confined space of two anapestic feet. The pauses between "breaks" are therefore shorter than in Tennyson, and the effect is one of halting a line in progress through the substitution of heavy stress (the second "break") for two short and unstressed syllables (as in "of the" in the previous line). I give Derek Attridge's scansion of Tennyson, with B marking beats and O marking the implied offbeat:

```
Break,  break,   break,
  B   O   B   O   B      [B]³⁷
```

The final [B]eat is silent. Attridge points out that the poem as a whole can be "read either as duple or triple," an ambiguity making possible substantially different performances. That is, the offbeats could hold the place of either one or two syllables: roughly, "they break and break" or "and they break and they break." Douglas Johnson picks up on this ambiguity in the final line of each stanza, perturbing the otherwise triple rhythm:

```
In the wake of those echoes the heart calls home
   2      B    2     B      2    B    1    B

While it breaks, breaks, breaks on the sheltering bars
   2     B     1      B      2    B    2    B
```

Johnson's rhythmic shifts, akin to spondaic substitutions, syncopate Tennyson's already innovative prosody, marking her own position outside of or crossing the metrical "bars" (probably another Tennysonian word-echo from "Crossing the bar") of the woman's heart. It is not hard to imagine that position expanded to the circuit of elocutionary performance in which Tennyson's poetry participated. That context would afford (younger) readers both the energetic and pleasantly repetitive dactyls and the opportunity to make an unavoidable, emphatic break. Although there is no evidence that Johnson's soundscape includes the musical strategies of the "break" as self-reconstituting rhythmic rupture, the celebratory revisioning of Tennyson aligns with that strategy for alternate community and historical understanding.

The penultimate poem of *Heart of a Woman*, "Love's Tendril," again tropes on Tennyson to separate the poetess-as-object from the poetess-as-prosodist. Speaking of her infant, Johnson's speaker finds that "Deeper than the ocean's roll / Sounds her heart-beat in my soul" (ll. 7-8). The collocation "ocean roll" applied to rhythmic sound echoes Tennyson's "To Virgil" (1882), where he marks the contrast between the end of Rome and the immortality of verse: "thine ocean-roll of rhythm sound forever of Imperial Rome." Through the allusion Johnson reframes the sentimental moment, placing it at the end of a chain of immortality from Rome to Virgil to Tennyson. The moment is almost bathetic, as Rome and epic measure cede ground to an unknown infant and simple rhyming tetrameter, and yet the sheer audacity of the gesture itself measures the scope of the poet's imagination. Johnson cannily links the poet's far-reaching imagination to the figure of the child by adapting the natural and even exclusive link readers would have granted between maternal feeling and poetic power. This is borne out in both Braithwaite's introduction, which asserts that Johnson's work is "deeply human" because "intensely feminine" (vii), and in Du Bois's introduction to *Bronze*, which sees "a revelation of the soul struggle of woman of the race" issuing not "in fact" but "in feeling" that captures "the history of a generation."[38] If then the rhythm of the infant's "heart-beat" is "deeper" than the Virgilian ocean-roll that Tennyson binds to narratives of nation building, it is because readers were ready to hear in that heartbeat and perhaps only in that heartbeat Johnson's imaginative portrait of a time and people. Johnson's innovation here depends upon both the metrical execution and the thematic elevation of rhythm; she intertwines widely disparate rhythms (the infant's heartbeat, epic rhythm) and in so doing reinvents the scope of her own verse, written in knowingly homely tetrameter. Though the tetrameter of "Love's Tendril" and many other works is not as aesthetically adventurous as the syncopated triple measure of "Heart of a Woman," the poem nonetheless shows itself highly conscious of the symbolic and cultural value of meter. It is this awareness that transforms the conventional meter and conventional theme of motherly love into an unconventional relation to literary tradition. The incongruous comparison of baby and Virgil at once indexes and traverses the distance between the woman poet and the poetic tradition.

Douglas Johnson's prosody reflects the exigencies of the tight literary marketplace for African American authors and women. Her best avenue to wider reception would have been the clear middle-class posture of the "lady poet" that precluded avant-garde forms that would mark her work as definitively black.[39] Yet as my readings of "Heart of a Woman" and "Love's Tendril" suggest, her forms and posture need not be ironic to be knowing vestiges. Circumscribed by restrictions, Johnson folds them into the subject matter of her poetry. Tennyson's prosody becomes the "bars" at once sheltering and alien to "women"; for the poet, however, metrical bars stand for a patterning that the poet manipulates, tropes upon, breaks against but never breaks. Meter is not, as Braithwaite hears it, the form of woman's "saddest songs" but a figure for the power to transcend that association of poet, song, and suffering.

In her second volume, *Bronze* (1922), Johnson's mastery of sentimental tropes and meters opens a window onto the triple consciousness she experienced as an African American woman. As Claudia Tate has suggested, approximately a third of this second volume is composed of traditional lyrics that do not directly treat race; then, in those poems that do discuss race, Johnson repeats the themes from these lyrics and "marks them slightly with racial signifiers like 'veil,' 'sable strain,' and 'dusky child.'"[40] An uncharitable reading might understand these "raced" poems as afterthoughts guilty of borrowing their form from a nonblack tradition. Yet this misses the point of the performance, of an act of appropriation that reinterprets the present's racial issues through a sentimental poetess mode. Her third consciousness as a black woman becomes a purchase on double consciousness and racism. That perspective can be blunt, as when she renamed her poem "Motherhood," published in the *Crisis* (1922), as "Black Woman" when published in *Bronze*. But the changed title manifests how Johnson's engagement with race grew from a "critique of the naturalness of gender" more common to New Negro Renaissance women writers than racial themes.[41]

As she expands a sentimental framework of intersubjective feeling to encompass the pain of America's racial history, Douglas Johnson turns increasingly to figures of meter and rhythm. *Bronze* has near-constant references to feet, gait, step, and more than a half-dozen invocations of "rhythm" specifically. From slavery's victims we hear "the rhythmic chaunting of their pain" (35), and from freed slaves "the rhythmic chanson of their eager feet" (15). We are called to repeat, in our "throbbing heart," "a chanson for the feet/ That stumble" in the present (17), while the speaker promises to "stride" personally against that which "impede[s] my feet" (23). Her "credo" is faith in the "rhythmical conscience of men" (53), but she also appeals to the unwilled "rhythm of ages," the "cycle of seasons, the tidals of man," to bring African Americans into the light of both modernity and salvation (56). Douglas Johnson intensifies the New Negro Renaissance and spiritual tradition's language of fetters, stumbling, weary feet, and strident longing, affirming a faith in and need for metrical repetition even as she begins experimenting with free verse. The unmetrical or variable-length poems of *Bronze* are complemented and sustained by metered poems without any sense that metrical poems signify entrapment or that free verse means freedom. Both her cosmology and prosody entail training in meter and recurrence. A sonnet she dedicated "To William Stanley Braithwaite" makes explicit this sense of meter as the ground for both poetic and historical transcendence:

> When time has rocked the present age to sleep,
> And lighter hearts are lilting to the sway
> Of rhythmic poesy's enhanced lay,
> Recurring sequences shall fitly keep
> Your fame eternal [. . .] (*Bronze*, 91)

These "recurring sequences" point to both Braithwaite and Johnson's verse. Their strangeness—who wants to be eternally "recurring"?—is redeemed as part of a rhythmical trajectory of "enhanced" if somnolent "sway." That trajectory now feels anathema: as I have been arguing, the space between the valued "recurring sequences" of meter and a mechanical rocking or lilt was already collapsing at the dawn of Douglas Johnson's and Braithwaite's careers. In defining Braithwaite's poetics through this oddly technical phrase, Johnson projects a future readership with a very different prosodic competence than our own. Having preserved Tennyson's fame in her own meter and diction, she imagines here a future soundscape that resonates with, rather than overrides, an "enhanced" version of her own iambic, triple, and variable-length lines.

To "sway" its racist present, however, *Bronze* returns to the metrical vestige and its limits. Simple iambic couplets like "My heart is pregnant with a great despair/With much beholding of my people's care" warp the sentimental note by corrupting previous associations of care with childbirth and childrearing ("Moods," 32). The pregnancy is in the wrong place, and "beholding" of care prevents holding an infant. Broken metaphor similarly estranges lines about a motherless child "seeking the breast of an unknown face" ("To Samuel Coleridge Taylor," 95) and a command to a child to "sing your song, my bonny lark,/Before it melts in tears" ("My Boy," 46).

"Black Woman" is the volume's most direct abrogation of the responsibilities of sympathetic motherhood and its most strident critique of triple consciousness. In it the poet addresses her unborn or unconceived child: "Don't knock at my door, little child,/I cannot let you in." To the degree that the child can be addressed, it must exist, but if it exists it would need to be let out, not in. If unconceived and thus not yet "in," some hidden conception cruelly lurks in the poem, animating the child that must be "stilled." The poem obsesses over the ambiguous word "still" too much to preserve the child in an unconceived "still eternity"; the second stanza is a horrific revelation that the child must, after all, be gestating:

> Don't knock at my heart, little one,
> I cannot bear the pain [. . .] (ll. 9-10)

> Be still, be still, my precious child,
> I must not give you birth" (ll. 15-16).

Again the pregnancy is in the wrong place, to the point where it both exists and does not exist. The racism of "monster men/Inhabiting the world" (ll. 13-14) destroys both the mother's hope and the poem's figures.

In her reading of Gwendolyn Brooks's "The Mother" (1945) Barbara Johnson observes how abortions become a "lost, anthropomorphized other" that "eternally addresses" and possesses the self. Brooks's poem "attempts the impossible task of humanizing both the mother and the aborted children while presenting the inadequacy of language to resolve the dilemma without violence."[42] In her apostrophe to her child, Douglas Johnson animates her unborn listener with the threat of abortion or near-stillbirth into a monstrous world. To speak to the child is at once merely a generic convention and a revelation of the violence of genre as it compels her to speak to and therefore animate a child. As evident in the title change to "Black Woman," to be animated in this context is to be interpellated into a racist world by the mother's call. The result is poetic stillbirth, a speaker who, like Brooks, has "written herself into a poem that she cannot get out of without violence. The violence she commits in the end is to her own language."[43] The confluence of Brooks and Douglas Johnson depends not only on their gender but on their shared interest in formal vestiges: it is this commonality that makes Brooks's poem at once an admission of lyric failure and a rewriting of a male tradition of lyric address, and Douglas Johnson's poem an overwrought reinvention of the sentimental tradition through which Braithwaite and Du Bois framed her subjectivity and racial consciousness. In other words, Johnson does not renew the sentimental mode she celebrated metrically in *Heart of a Woman* but rather shows how sentiment withers and takes with it any lingering expectations for a feminine respite from modern racism.

Metrically, "Black Woman" alternates between iambic tetrameter and trimeter lines, organized into two octaves. The effect is predictably "lilting," except for the opening lines of each octave, "Don't knock at the door, little child" and "Don't knock at my heart, little one." Each line has a strategic mismatch of stress and unusual caesura:

```
                 x    /
Don't knock at the door, little child
  W      S    W   S    W    S  W   S
```

The line fits better into a triple meter, but this pattern doesn't hold for the rest of the poem:

```
Don't knock at the door, little child
  W      S    W  W   S    W  W   S
```

The triple meter that, in "Heart of a Woman," transcends the sentimental subject position, fails to take hold. The roughest line is, appropriately, "The world is cruel, cruel, child" (l. 7), which must be performed with a slowed disyllabic "cruel" to avoid both hypometricality and the conclusion that the second "cruel" is a prenominal adjective for "child" rather than a predicate of "world." In this line, metrical expectation slows reading to a "cruel" sway before the trimeter drives us speedily on: "I cannot let you in!" Iambics here dominate over triple meter, once celebrated in "Heart of a Woman," over articulation and over the ultimate desire of the speaker to be "still" and to make still. Dactyls and creative "breaks" infuse the metrical vestige of "Heart of a Woman" with hope; in "Black Woman" the vestige of meter shows its distress, performing an enthrallment that cannot be distinguished from the work of "monster men."

An escape from meter, and sentiment, toward modernist ideals of free verse rhythm proved a challenge because Douglas Johnson cannot know whether her own rhythmically grounded poetess tradition will ever "count." She desperately invokes rhythm in "The Ordeal" (1925) as a counterpoint and backstop to the masculinist negotiation of race. After urging her "brothers" to "pass me not by so scornfully/I'm doing this living of being black," she becomes militantly focused on her own gendered fate:

> [. . .] The planets wear
> The maker's imprint, and with mine
> I swing into their rhythmic line;
> I ask—only for destiny,
> Mine, not thine.[44]

These lines are split between a regularly ordered "rhythmic line" composed, like the heartbeat of her infants, in iambic tetrameter, and a movement into the private form and destiny hinted at by the rough cadence of the penultimate line and the bare-bones final line. It is not then entirely accurate to see in Johnson a Victorian "refusal to abandon poetic convention," as Tate writes,[45] even if Johnson certainly did resist the movement from traditional forms to the modernist forms that contemporaries like Hughes and Toomer were exploring in the 1920s. We can read this resistance as critical to the other resistance Tate notes: a "modernist impulse" to see the "sublime not [as] a state realized but one sustained by desire."[46] If the sublimity found in Johnson's "rhythmic line" and her soul's "heart-beat" is "modernist," it is because she transforms meter into a constant reminder of her endurance in a world far from the Utopian vision of "enhanced sway." In the two chapters that follow, I study how meter exposes the complications that occur when racial becoming gets grounded through modernist ideas of black rhythm; in "The Ordeal" Johnson reminds us that a patriarchal poetics of rhythm runs parallel to racialized concepts of rhythm. Her resistance to post-metrical prosody is resistance to a concept of lyricized black rhythm that can work only by effacing the poetess tradition. Her poetry expresses that effacement by composing the metrical vestige while constantly troping on and disfiguring the poetess's available mode of expressivity. "The Ordeal" recalls "bearing" a brother's load, uniting stress and pregnancy. Rhythm, in Douglas Johnson, is meter: not the living or transcendent force that modernism insists upon but a vestige of poetess verse that must be strenuously recollected to feel out the limits of gender and racial consciousness.

Louise Bogan's Precise Pentagon

In his retrospective on Louise Bogan's poetry, Theodore Roethke begins with a long list of the generally agreed-upon flaws of women poets: the "spinning-out; embroidering of trivial themes; a concern with the mere surfaces of life," and so on. "Louise Bogan is something else," but this throat- and ground-clearing operation indicates the bias faced by modern women poets, not least those who invite formal anxiety by affiliating themselves with that "great tradition" of English metrical poetry and who must therefore prove themselves "true inheritors."[47] Bogan herself refused "to edit an anthology of female verse" for the unpleasant "thought of corresponding with a lot of female songbirds. [. . . I]t is hard enough to bear with my own lyric side."[48] Where Teasdale wrote but did not publish her handiwork poem, Bogan mocked any of her own strident or sentimental verse as "Ella Wheeler Wilcoxism."[49] Yet despite her Pound-like formal sense that "once rigidity or efflorescence has set in [. . . t]he whole encumbered ground must be cleared,"[50] Bogan knew that repudiating a "songbird" past and its prosodic forms could not possibly revitalize modern poetry as a genre for individual voice. Instead, as Cheryl Walker observes, she builds a "stoic persona" in response to the "nightingale tradition" of women poets, which she at once valued for its emotional richness and disdained because it might license a lack of intellectual rigor.[51]

Meter, I argue here, is the medium and icon of that stoical response. Like Thomas Hardy, Bogan wrote in many idiosyncratic stanza forms (as well as free verse), and like Hardy she perceived how the metrical vestige denied the possibility of an expressive and shared prosodic ground. Her metrical form defers the combative wit and prosodic play of Millay, Elinor Wylie, or Dorothy Parker ("Never shall I give the feminine sonneteers any competition")[52] for an ideal of precision and statuary that inclines to rigor mortis. In this section, I consider how this metrical practice follows from and expresses her awareness of how the woman poet, sharing Millay's fate, tended to be assigned as "a poet for young girls, and poetry societies of married ladies" while male poets like Sandburg, Pound, and Frost were easily "cited as American's great poets."[53] Her careful and often ambivalent concern for traditions of women's poetry is most evident in her imagery, which emphasizes how a Romantic tradition of male authorship forecloses the possibility of female lyric voice. This imagery requires a soundscape in which the freedom of Romantic versification (blank verse, odes) is conspicuously undone.

Bogan wrote relatively little free verse; her first published poem, "Betrothed," is one of just three free verse poems in her first book (*Body of This Death*, 1923). Among the book's metrical and mostly stanzaic majority there is only one moment where stanzas change form. This stanza of "Medusa," one of Bogan's most-studied poems, conspicuously adds one line to its second quatrain (xAxA rhyming becomes xAxxA, with a hint of rhyme between the third and fourth lines):

> When the bare eyes were before me
> And the hissing hair,
> Held up at the window, seen through a door.
> The stiff bald eyes, the serpents on the forehead
> Formed in the air.[54]

The encounter with Medusa forecloses the lyrical quest narrative, transforming the poem into a loco-descriptive series of quatrains doomed to describe "a dead scene forever now." The process of transformation begins in this deformed stanza: in the hendiadys that delays and isolates "the hissing hair"; in the absence of a main clause in that sentence; in the metonymic return of bare eyes as bald eyes and hair as serpents that "formed" where they already were. This stanza's formal eccentricity, including the half rhyme of "door" and "forehead," comes from the mythic female figure inhabiting it. Like Eliot's broken quatrains in *The Waste Land*, this excessive and unrepeatable stanza is beyond the power of the poet or speaker.

The last stanza, beginning "And I shall stand here like a shadow," frames the speaker in its echo of "La Belle Dame sans Merci" ("And that is why I linger here"). Like Teasdale, Bogan creates stanzas that approximate Keats's famous 4-4-4-2, xAxA pattern, yet these never quite settle into place. Whereas Keats plays interlocutor in his poem, enjoying his elfin plot and eerie music, Bogan refuses to mark herself or her form outside the crisis of experience. Suzanne Clark characterizes Bogan's struggle as that between "the text itself [. . .] feminine, hysterical, a rhetoric of embodiment" and the male modernist's "symbolic mastery."[55] As the previous chapters showed, the dominant mode of that symbolic mastery was not just control of myth but control of mythic female figures and their degraded modern counterparts. Bogan rejects the disingenuous disavowal and aestheticization of the feminine but manages no reclamation of the sentimental. Instead, through metrical vestiges and correlate figures of aridness, rigidity, and infertility, she reinvents the woman poet as simultaneously Medusa and her victim.

Bogan's encounter with the Medusa follows from the intended entry point into her work, "A Tale," which opens her first book of poems (*Body of This Death*) as well as *Collected Poems 1923-1953* and *Blue Estuaries: Poems 1923-1958*. "A Tale" is a meditation on genre, engaging with Robert Frost's canny gesture of beginning his first volume, *A Boy's Will*, with the poignantly archaic sonnet "Into My Own." In that poem the middle-aged poet wears the mask of the boy who will successfully achieve his planned voyage into poetry. Bogan would have recognized the salesmanship of the poem, its ease in tricking the reader into believing what the final heroic couplet says in polished verse: "They would not find me changed from him they knew—/ Only more sure of all I thought was true." This voyage from and back into restraint lacks the salt of Bogan's not-quite sonnet:

> This youth too long has heard the break
> Of waters in a land of change.
> He goes to see what suns can make
> From soil more indurate and strange.
>
> He cuts what holds his days together
> And shuts him in, as lock on lock:
> The arrowed vane announcing weather,
> The tripping racket of a clock;
>
> Seeking, I think, a light that waits
> Still as a lamp upon a shelf,—
> A land with hills like rocky gates
> Where no sea leaps upon itself.
>
> But he will find that nothing dares
> To be enduring, save where, south
> Of hidden deserts, torn fire glares
> On beauty with a rusted mouth,—
>
> Where something dreadful and another
> Look quietly upon each other. (*CPLB*, 9)

Like Yeats's "The Second Coming" (1920) from which the fourth stanza draws its imagery, the poem reads as an allegory of poesis faced by catastrophe. The "still lamp" represents the spirit of the mature Romantic poet, but the man's fear of water, change, and the violence of the ocean also evokes a wasteland without experiences of the sublime.

Bogan does not adopt the absolute separation of H.D.'s "sea garden" from the formal enclosure celebrated in the male poetic tradition.[56] Nor does she merely ironize the (already arch) Romanticism of Frost's "Into My Own" but rather asks why she cannot inhabit that position. Frost's poem was sentimental about youth, following Longfellow's sentimental recovery in "My Lost Youth" (1855). The problem is that such sentimentality in a twenty-six-year-old woman poet writing in 1923 would have read not as prefiguration of a mature career but as natural to the poetess. No surprise that "Betrothed," published when Bogan was twenty, takes the perspective of a more mature, critical present—"What have I thought of love?/I have said, 'It is beauty and sorrow'"—and that it dismisses such thoughts in favor of a refined sound-image: "the sound of willows/Now and again dipping their long oval leaves in the water" (*CPLB*, 13).

In "A Tale" the sentimental quest belongs to a man, while reflection belongs to the poem's genderless and distant speaker. The interjection "I think" comes bluntly from nowhere, as does "this youth." This is a half-blind oracle, like Tiresias in *The Waste Land* but lacking his mythic role. The meter is the real agent of control. The youth wishes to escape "breaks," seeking the "indurate"; the poem responds with a hyper-enjambed finale. The male Romantic seeker is ill prepared to meet rough beasts like the Medusa or Sphinx. His soundscape clicks with the noise of "lock on lock" and the "tripping racket of a clock." These metronomic sequences echo in the rigid meter and grammatical rhyme of the final couplet. Brought together in the disjointed syntax of hendiadys, "something dreadful and another" silently look at each other the way the lines and rhymes do. This "quiet" looking displaces the sonic encounter of poet and himself in poems like Yeats's "Lake Isle of Innisfree" (1890) or poetic imagination and apocalyptic beast in "The Second Coming," leaving only the uncanny soundscape.[57]

In Clark's reading, the poem tells a story about "alienation from the male heroic quest."[58] It is one of several "nightmare" tales of "melancholy hysteria" that become doubly nightmarish in finding no potential narrative voice for the experience of gendered modernity that would not fall into the easily "dismissed" and "recognizable [. . .] seductive madness of woman."[59] Clark finds some "compensation" in "the body of song," but the straitened quatrains and silenced rhymes constitute a body controlled by inhuman powers. By contrast, Bogan's pentameter sonnets, somewhat like Millay's, strain against bonds by marking the mastery of form. For instance, "Fifteenth Farewell," a double sonnet whose title hints at a persistence beyond the closure of the fourteenth line, begins by alerting us to its own power over breath and thus reading: "You may have all things from me, save my breath,/The slight life in my throat will not give pause/For your love" (*CPLB*, 30). The actual refusal to pause at the "pause" prepares the reader of each of the final three sonnets in *Body of This Death* to read enjambment as a form of self-presence freed from romance. Yet as in "A Tale," such freedom is fleeting and isolated to these few lines in these few sonnets. Bogan's later meta-sonnet "Single Sonnet" prefers to celebrate its "staunch meter," not the abstract mastery of form.

A less triumphant development of traditional form as gendered space emerges in the three quatrains of "The Romantic":

> Admit the ruse to fix and name her chaste
> With those who sleep the spring through, one on one,
> cool nights, when laurel builds up, without haste
> Its precise flower, like a pentagon. (*CPLB*, 18)

The laurel is mountain or sheep laurel, whose small five-lobed white flowers bud out in fall and winter. A deciduous evergreen, the mountain laurel presents unusual greenery at the top of its range in southern Maine. The "Romantic" addressee is not intimate with this New England native and its life cycle; he dreams of more poetic laurels. The laurel briefly figures both woman and form, yet this precise formal life dissipates amid real-world formations of gender. In a later poem Bogan fumes, "Get the hell out of the way of the laurel. It is deathless / And it isn't for you." ("Several Voices out of a Cloud," *CPLB*, 99). But neither does this specialized laurel quite belong to the woman poet. As Bogan's poem continues, it encounters instead Medusan readers, with their sense of women's form, and thus new metaphors of enclosure for the woman:

> In her obedient breast, all that ran free
> You thought to bind, like echoes in a shell.
> At the year's end, you promised, it would be
> The unstrung leaves, and not her heart, that fell.

The obedience is a male projection. Bogan might have said, in some fashion, that this "you" sought to make the breast obedient, but instead she absorbs that projection into her own description. In the final quatrain, the projections of male Romantic fantasy become explicit:

> So the year broke and vanished on the screen
> You cast about her; summer went to haws.
> This, by your leave, is what she should have been—
> Another man will tell you what she was.

We do not know what "this" is, exactly, but presumably it is the bound and chaste "screen" woman of the first two stanzas. The idiomatic distance between the colloquial "went to haws" (the apple-like fruit of the hawthorn, or perhaps the laurel's seedpod) and "by your leave" divides the Romantic addressee from the natural order of time and season. The woman "went to haws" in a double sense: she has gotten older as a result of fertility and she has left the Romantic realm of poetic diction. The same image in "The Changed Woman," "the light flower leaves its little core," represents a transient state that will not lead to a restored "dream, ever denied and driven" (*CPLB*, 28). The inevitable, seasonal end of chastity and natural beauty condemns as "ruses" all Romantic efforts to preserve them. In "Ad Castitatem" (To chastity) the speaker celebrates infertility: "Hear me, infertile, / Beautiful futility" (14). The syntax makes infertility belong to both the addressee, "Beautiful futility," and to the speaker herself. In "The Romantic," however, the female subject does not determine herself through apostrophe. She is the object of the speaker, addressee, and "another man's" discussion.

The only escape from neo-Romantic ideology is to become reified on one's own terms, in kinship with meter. In "Fifteenth Farewell," when the speaker refuses to surrender breath's "slight life in my throat," she reimagines herself as rigid statuary: "Better, from time's claws, / The hardened face under the subtle wreath" (*CPLB*, 30). In "A Letter" Bogan celebrates the "dried beauty of women," "body as arid, as safe as a twig / Broken away from whatever growth could snare it."[60] This dark but triumphant version of the Syrinx myth courses through the book; in "The Crows" Syrinx becomes "a stem long hardened, / A weed that no scythe mows" (23). This protection is as unhappy and ineffective as it is necessary. The painful metamorphosis never ends for female statuary, which remains exposed to observation. The "marble girl" of "Statue and Birds" has hands "flung out in alarm / or remonstrances"; the speaker hopes that "what is forsaken will rest. / But her heel is lifted,—she would flee—" (20). *Body of This Death* ends with a final metapoetic "Sonnet" about "reedy traps" from which the "desperate mind" must escape to be "thrown"

```
Straight  to   its  freedom  in  the  thunderous cloud.
   W      S  W    S    W   S   W      S    W     S
                                        (CPLB, 32)
```

With this line the poem and book end in an exceedingly rare metrical flourish, a glimpse of freedom nevertheless contingent on a half-willed "thrown"-

ness. The absolute control Bogan seeks for herself and for women is elsewhere secured only in death, in the form of the epitaph where a "romantic woman" can "attain[] the permanence/she dreamed of."[61]

The "bitter spell" cast over voice in Bogan's mythic telling of gender has a constant analogue in her meter. In "The Romantic" the sequence of pentameter quatrains lacks the couplet or volta that makes the sonnet a space of combative cohabitation with the male literary tradition. Bogan thematizes this prosodic quietude in "My Voice Not Being Proud," whose speaker lacks the "strong woman's" voice that "cries/Imperiously aloud/That death disarm her" (*CPLB*, 19), and in "Men Loved Wholly beyond Wisdom," which finds wisdom in being "quiet in the fern/Like a thing gone dead and still." The true form of song in this poem is the cricket's "terrible, dissembling/Music in the granite hill." These lines, with what Roethke called "an intolerable tension, a crescendo in rhythm," silence voice in enjambment and erratically spaced stress.[62] "The Romantic" produces a different inhuman sound in the chiseled, metrical "pentagon" of pentameter. Where Mina Loy's overwrought rhyme sequences satirized the desire to control delicate female "crops," Bogan tightens and hardens her verse to the point where no blade finds entry. Her Medusan stare suspends the flow of rhythm into statuary or relief. With rhythm no longer experienced as a temporal art, the phenomenology of poetic breath comes undone. In "The Romantic" we encounter not breath but anagram or visual game (the slant rhyme of "haws" and "was"); in "A Tale," the entropy of morphological rhyme (another/other); in "Medusa," the deformity of the single extra line and half rhyme.[63] There is a poem called "Song" composed of two rhyming yet rhythmically asymmetrical stanzas, which ends by fleeing as far as it can toward prose: "Love Me,—I tell you that it [my heart] is a ravaged/terrible place."[64] Another poem, about mythic women who have forgotten their divinity, is willfully under-described by the title "Stanza." The isolated or distended stanzas, prosaic songs, bluntly shortened lines, and forceful enjambments signify at once the powers and limits of formal design as a means of poetic authority.

Clark notes that Bogan's later position as a prominent poetry critic for the *New Yorker* (1931–1970) provided a different because differently gendered source of authority:

> She acquir[ed] at a stroke the patriarchal maturity that might shelter her. But her poetry constantly works to rupture the ideology that lends her judgments credibility. The lack which threatens her psyche with psychosis is the lack of a public

position for the poet that is neither patriarchal nor sentimental—a position that could limit the processes of abjection and provide a remedy for strangeness.[65]

As this book has been arguing, the metrical vestige always points to the mercurial necessity of criticism in a culture of audile technique. In Pound and Eliot, the critical faculty, with its masculine authority, is brought as close as possible to their poetics. Bogan leaves the chasm in place. In each of the poets discussed in this chapter, meter's estrangement repeats rather than restores "the processes of abjection." Teasdale figures meter as a kind of unpublishable handiwork rather than a claim to patrimony, as reflected by the unstable claims to prosodic capital in her archive. In Douglas Johnson, meter begins as a proving ground for maternal and sentimental authority but comes to express the alienation of voice and selfhood in a racist and sexist world. For Bogan, meter is at best a means of more successful repression, of paradoxical mastery through "beautiful futility."

The necessary inadequacy of mastered but limiting form is most poignant in Bogan's poem "Women." Leslie Wheeler reads the "deformation" of the poem's "little rooms or cells"—a clear and traditional metaphor for stanzas—as the product of gendered frustration.[66] The poem concludes:

Their love is an eager meaninglessness
Too tense, or too lax.

They hear in every whisper that speaks to them
A shout and a cry.
As like as not, when they take life over their door-sills
They should let it go by. (*CPLB*, 25)

As in "The Romantic," the tone catches between ironic riposte and internalized self-identification with the male perspective. The same ambiguity suffuses Bogan's criticism, caught between disinterest in traditions of women's writing and keen "awareness of the male literary world's attitudes toward women's art as being a limitation imposed from without, not from within."[67] The only given is constraint itself. In "Women" the problem of mismeasure—the lines "too tense" and "too lax," the volume wrong, the borders mismanaged—inflects performance at a visceral level. The stanzas distend and interrupt common meter like an extreme version of Emily Dickinson's hymnal stanzas. In a 1939 interview, Bogan lists Dickinson as an early influence, a rare American and woman among Greek and Latin poets, Arthur

Symons, Yeats, and the newly in-vogue metaphysicals. She also observes that the liturgy of her Roman Catholic upbringing saved her from Protestantism's "dreadful hymnody."⁶⁸ Bogan's version of hymnody in "Women" reclaims that feeling of dreadful and alien prosody with its constant imbalance between shorter even lines ranging from four to seven syllables and longer odd lines ranging from nine to thirteen syllables. One barely catches the beat before willful disruption, as in the third and most regular stanza:

> They wait, when they should turn to journeys,
> They stiffen, when they should bend.
> They use against themselves that benevolence
> To which no man is friend. (ll. 9-12)

The choice of "benevolence" instead of "kindness" precludes stable rhythm with its mass of unstressed syllables that cannot be easily promoted by meter:

```
x  /     x  \       x   x / x x    x    x    x    /
        against themselves that benevolence to which no man
```

The absence of metronomic stiffness does not make the lines flexible. To be a master of form, for Bogan, is not to undo but to master the "stiffness" she sees in women. Elizabeth Frank suggests that the poem is envious of men, who are "capable of broad, unfettered, unselfconscious action," and is anxious that women are "given to formlessness, ineffectuality, and, therefore, immobility." Formlessness is bad, but immobility proves necessary. Literalized rigor defines the ideal of impersonality she adapts from Eliot. She imagines the ideal poet "claimed" and "identified rigidly" by a "stern countryside."⁶⁹

In her review of Allen Tate's early poems, Bogan discerns a late Romantic too indebted to Eliot and lacking "pure form or formal feeling."⁷⁰ The judgment echoes Dickinson's famous poem, "After great pain, a formal feeling comes." Bogan identifies her desired "formal feeling" with that poem's paradoxical embrace of "mechanical" movement and "freezing" as forms of feeling:

> This is the Hour of Lead -
> Remembered, if outlived,
> As Freezing persons, recollect the Snow -
> First - Chill - then Stupor - then the letting go -⁷¹

It is hard to identify a "letting go" in Bogan other than her acceptance of leaden meter. Tate, in Bogan's critique, is stuck by the fire in the sort of pre-formalized, overwrought feeling that modernism read as effeminate Victorian sentiment. "Not only can the feeling be in excess to the matter," she writes Tate with a critique of his work, "but devices, crotchets, and all skilled traps for the unwary, can exceed [. . .] these poems struck me as elaborate ruses."[72] In this judgment and elsewhere, Bogan provides an implicitly feminist perspective on Eliot's canonical decree that "poetry is not a turning loose of emotion, but an escape from emotion; it is not the expression of personality, but an escape from personality. But, of course, only those who have personality and emotions know what it means to want to escape from these things."[73] Bogan's version turns simple escape into an active process of repression:

> The poet represses the outright narrative of his life. He absorbs it, along with life itself. The repressed becomes the poem. Actually, I have written down my experience in the closest detail. But the rough and vulgar facts are not there.[74]

Eliot's dictum assumes that the poetic shape of personality will be Romantic or sentimental gush. Bogan agrees but also absorbs Eliot's implicitly gendered literary-historical judgment of sentimentality, the "eager meaninglessness" she indicts in "Women." She writes, in an early 1923 essay, of actively pursuing emotional "reticence" so that "passion is made to achieve its own form."[75] Behind this ideal lies a subtle response to the dogma of impersonality. To take seriously the passive voice in her formulation, we have to stop asking recurrent questions about how poets and especially women poets give form to their feelings and to think instead about their feeling for form. This is a challenge to formalism's desire, stemming from ideologies of rhythm, to find an expressive relationship between poets, their passions, and their forms.[76] "Formal feeling" is not a feeling expressed in suitable form but a feeling or passion felt in the process of formalization (for Bogan, always "stiffening") that has little to do with mimetic effects and more to do with the resonance of a given form or deformation within literary history.

There can be no Poundian "absolute rhythm" for women poets when its expressive ideology depends on the negation of feminine expressivity. H.D. enters Hugh Kenner's account of American modernism when her "cadences" are "perceived" by Pound; Kenner then ventriloquizes Amy Lowell: "Why, I too am an *Imagiste*"; for "unreadable" Millay there is only disdain: "what's her name, the candle woman, Miss Millay, Edna St. Vincent" (referring to her excellent epigram "First Fig" [1920]).[77] John Crowe Ransom mutilates another of Millay's epigrams to eliminate the word "compromise" because it seemed compromised by sentimental discourse, proving Cheryl Walker's observation that "patriarchal criticism disparages the personal when that personal is gendered female."[78] Before Adrienne Rich and other feminist poets imagined taking a knife to such patriarchal poetics, other marginal late modernists like Lorine Niedecker "absorbed an imperative not to be sentimental, not to let the 'I' dominate the poem."[79] As in the case of Pound's editorial midwifery, it is likely that this imperative derives from Niedecker's abandoned relationship (and pregnancy) with Louis Zukofsky and his critique of her poetry's "personal" nature. The haunting final lines of her stoical "[Keen and lovely man moved as in a dance]" evoke the gendered constraints Bogan transformed into a poetics. The poem is about a woman, probably the poet, applying for a secretarial job:

> And the neighbors said "She's taking lessons
> on the dictaphone" as tho it were a saxophone.
>
> He gave the job to somebody else.[80]

The female stenographic or gramophonic voice persists here, mastered only in the utter dryness that refuses any alternate lyric genealogy of voice. A. E. Stallings describes the poem's "chariness with syllables, a sly sense of humor, the 'I' condensed out of existence, an awareness of gender and social injustice, and a refusal to sentimentalize"[81]—all, save the explicit interest in class, features of Bogan's writing. Bogan defines her anti-lyricism as the practice of writing "in the closest detail" and "behind clenched teeth, subsidiz[ing] emotion by every trick and pretense."[82] This is different from the masculine authority of "impersonality": Bogan turns from Eliot's abstract talk of the poet's mind "expressing a medium"[83] to the most local stutters of meter and stanza. This is the unconventional basis of Bogan's ideal of "pure form": she develops meter's stiffened vestiges to expose poetry and poets in a state of distress and alienation. In this regard, she shares her "formal feeling" with Teasdale or Douglas Johnson even though she avoids the affective relationship to prosody seen in their work. Each poet writes and scans "the closest details" to reveal how the modern woman poet lacks a way of circulating in or out of modernism's anti-sentimental but still expressivist ideal of rhythm.

5 The Prosody of Passing

Jean Toomer and

James Weldon Johnson

> what is inward
> wanting to get out
> prey to the lard
> trying to pass for butter
>
> cakewalk matrix
> tapping the frets
> dubbed and mastered
> tucked into folds
>
> —Harryette Mullen, from *Muse & Drudge*

In the previous chapter I showed how Georgia Douglas Johnson's identification as a prosodist superseded determinations of identity along lines of gender and race. Her own nods to the rhetoric of passing confirm the importance of poetics and prosody in negotiating and defining the terms of racial discourse. In "The Passing of the Ex-Slave" (1922), for example, "lighter hearts" forget slavery's "mounded bodies," yet there remains kinship between the last ex-slaves, "Gnarled sentinels of time and tide," and the poet-sentinel who might echo their "rhythmic chaunting."[1] My final chapters focus on the poetics and prosody of the New Negro Renaissance, specifically the role of traditional Anglo-American prosody in a black poetics critical of the a priori and externally determined racing of forms. I articulate a practice of the metrical vestige that refutes modernist rhythm's racial essentialism and specifically its frequent recourse to imagined non-Western, African, or black rhythms. In this chapter, I show how Jean Toomer and James Weldon Johnson interrogate the latent minstrelsy of these formal conditions, but with divergent methods and results. Each powerfully deconstructs what

Harryette Mullen brilliantly condenses as the "cakewalk matrix": the malformed conception of Anglo-American metrics as a white form in which black poets sought a prosodic passing, rather than (as with the cakewalk) a simultaneous parody and enjoyment of only nominally white forms.

I begin with Toomer because of *Cane*'s particularly prominent role in modern literary history. Compiled in 1923, it earned Toomer consideration as a "harbinger" of a distinctly modernist black art.[2] This predication of race was for Toomer a deeply personal constraint on his own development of a black genealogy, and it clarifies his repeated resistance to the idea of a "black" rhythmic tradition. I contrast Toomer's quest for generic innovation, tormented by the racialized logic of lyric, with James Weldon Johnson's work anthologizing, critically framing, and teaching African American poetry—and with the poetry and prose he wrote out of that critical consciousness. Toomer and Johnson reveal in different ways the danger of and early responses to what Anthony Reed calls "racialized reading": "a selective account of the project of black aesthetics" that produces "reductive, commodity versions of black 'folk.'"[3] They respond to a field of raced forms by marshalling the logic of passing to complicate implicitly and explicitly raced prosodic traditions.

Both writers reconceive black rhythm and musicality in light of what Johnson called the "problem of the double audience": "It is a divided audience, an audience made up of two elements with differing and antagonistic points of view. The audience of a Negro writer is always both white America and black America. The moment he takes up his pen or sits down to his typewriter he is immediately called upon to solve, consciously or unconsciously, this problem of the double audience."[4] In the *Autobiography of an Ex-Colored Man* (1912), the double audience generates the narrator's double consciousness, expressed through his anxiety about the raced reception of both his music and his person. The *Autobiography* famously begins and ends with the narrator's choice to pass, and one of the foremost markers of passing is not only his marriage to a white woman but their Chopin duet, followed by his failure to participate in a community centered on spirituals. He becomes an entrenched observer, as Noelle Morrissette notes, rather than participant;[5] even the duet, which the narrator embraces as music but scorns as passing's "mess of pottage,"[6] reveals how the pain of the veil is enhanced, not overcome, by performances of musical passing. The *Autobiography* is a long meditation on the heavily mediated sociality of rhythm as a raced concept. Johnson's critical work, poetry, and fiction place him at the center of efforts to articulate black poetics in that deeply raced field of formal discourse. This effort requires another revelation about white poetics—namely, that white forms are racialized in their non-markedness. To mark out the contingency of modern sound, as Johnson and Brown do through their metrical satires, is to denature white canons of form.

Where Johnson intervenes in the racing of literature by drawing constant attention to the framework of production, reception, and analysis, Toomer's literary effort in *Cane* immerses itself in raced forms and arrives on the page scarred by the resulting encounter with self-difference. Put another way, *Cane*'s poetic speakers and characters seem to come from inside Johnson's *Autobiography*, repeating in diverse ways his narrator's struggle for racial identity. This is also true to some extent of Toomer's biographical materials, especially his letters to Waldo Frank. Toomer shares Johnson's narrator's desire for musical and rhythmic modes of identification, and he is equally aware of his failure to fulfill that desire, ultimately seeking to define his poetic modernity through that very alienation. The metrical vestige is a key means of that self-definition, marking out a space where no one belongs and where all poets in some sense "pass." *Cane*'s prosody, in both prose and verse, metrical and not, defines the work's modernity not as an abstract formal achievement but as an intense revelation of double consciousness in the scarred foreclosure of aestheticized sound. *Cane* has been considered modern in part because it mixes prose and poetry, and because its poetry diverges, like *The Waste Land*, into a multiplicity of prosodic and poetic styles. But *Cane*'s effort to synthesize a range of genres and prosodies is best considered modern in its failure of synthesis. It shares this with *The Waste Land* but even more so with *The Cantos* (Canto 116, "I cannot make it cohere," 1962), a project whose impossible task is also to "contain history," albeit on a different scale. The reason for Toomer's negative synthesis is that he exposes but never makes peace with the lack of homology between literary form and racial genealogy.

I go against chronological order in order to read Johnson's *Autobiography of an Ex-Colored Man* as a reading of Toomer's search for identity through musical collectivity. Johnson's maneuvers in the field of the "double audience," his reading and displacement not only of cultural nationalism (as in his willingness to see the white appropriation of ragtime as a positive hybridity) but also of racialized reading itself, refute a racialized hermeneutics of which Toomer seems less conscious, and certainly less inclined to treat sociologically. As Paul Gilroy notes, hermeneutics extends the reach of cultural nationalism: ideas of white or English cultural life "typically construct the nation as an ethnically homogeneous object and invoke ethnicity a second time in the hermeneutic procedures deployed to make sense of its distinctive cultural content."[7] Johnson, I suggest, opens up moments of nonwhite reading by doubling back to the non-givenness of Anglo-American prosody. Johnson's pedagogy and satirical metrics create the possibility of reconstructing Anglo-American traditional prosody as something alien to white audiences: as their mode of passing. This potent irony is already visible in the *Autobiography*'s presentation to white audiences not of the advertised and expected "inner life of the Negro in America" but, as Aldon Nielsen wryly notes, of "an ordinarily successful white man who has made a little money" and by extension "a world in which 'white' does not 'know' the truth of its own blackness."[8] The *Autobiography* as well as the satire "Saint Peter Relates an Incident of the Resurrection Day" (1930)[9] remap the white world by emphasizing the non-immediacy, rather than given otherness, of blackness. They reveal the alienness of a priori racings of black music and prosody and then resituate readings of race as shifting genealogical and intertextual efforts amid a sea of disentitled and vestigial forms.

Spirituals after the Victrola

Cane indirectly comprehends the crisis of usable aesthetic history for the individual poet burdened by double consciousness. Sterling Brown, even with his skepticism and irony, imagines a broad field of forms and prosody available for poaching and versioning. *Cane* gives us unprocessed generic indeterminacy that should not be mistaken for willful bricolage. This indeterminacy is not a function of the overall text's mix of verse and prose, of its assembly from already published work, or even the multiple prosodic styles of its poems. None of this would necessarily have seemed in need of special reconciliation (Williams's *Spring and All*, a notable prosimetrum, was published the same year). Rather, I focus on two flawed valedictions to black folk life: "Song of the Son," a poem in traditional stanzas that attempts to constitute an African American history and literary genealogy by singing a swan song, and "Kabnis," a short story that narrates and denatures the same attempt. These sections of *Cane* point to a modernism best understood, as in previous chapters, for its tenuous affinity with forms now seen as vestigial. They center on deafness to or alienation from the metrical forms that might record and generate racial affiliation. Consistent with his personal resistance to presumptive race, Toomer's adoption of traditional stanzas and devices in "Song" makes all formal belonging seem a matter of passing: he insists that as slave traditions "pass" out of history, they "pass" into him so that he can pass in and out of them without biologically joining them. Vestigial prosody is a space where everyone passes, awkwardly but productively. *Cane* then becomes an act of self-preservation in the form of the vestige: nostalgic but incomplete, legible but often mute. With "Kabnis" he shows what happens when the vestige fails to achieve a prosodic and generic form. Kabnis experiences the pain of having to inhabit more-concrete categories of identity and form caused by modernity's insistence on racial and class boundaries.

The reception of Toomer's work has always been framed by the question of how race—including that of the author—should or must figure into (Afro) modernist poetry. Despite his own ambivalence toward the way influential peers like Waldo Frank, Sherwood Anderson, and the publisher Horace Liveright cast his work as that of a "Negro," he criticized Georgia Douglas Johnson as one unlikely to uniquely express or reconsider race (he had in mind her first volume, *Heart of a Woman*, and likely not the poems published in *Bronze* in 1922). She labored, he wrote to editor John McClure in 1922, under "inhibitions and taboos and life-limitations [. . . that] make even her modest achievement remarkable."[10] Toomer is referring, ironically, to the same genteel position that enabled Douglas Johnson to host "Saturday Nighters" for artists, including Toomer, in her Washington, DC, "Halfway House." Toomer's chauvinism is not atypical for a male writer of the Harlem Renaissance or, as Pound and Eliot's satires suggest, modernism more broadly. But Toomer's shoehorning of Douglas Johnson betrays anxiety about his own ambivalent racing and about the fetishistic emphasis on race within an American literary culture he fervently hoped to enter.

Toomer's ambivalence extends to representations of African Americans by contemporary white authors he respected. In adjacent sentences of a letter to Sherwood Anderson, Toomer praises Anderson for "evok[ing] an emotion, a sense of beauty that is easily more Negro than almost anything I have seen" and then critiques Anderson's claim that "[the Negro] by educating himself [has] cut himself off from his own people" (160). From these comments it would seem that Toomer sees broad continuity and an essential racial aesthetic within African American culture. Yet while he critiques Anderson for viewing these qualities as the property of the uneducated or rustic, he himself espouses a similar view. Toomer's views of African American heritage stem in large part from his experience of folk songs and spirituals during a two-month stint as a school principal in Sparta, Georgia. In a letter to Waldo Frank, Toomer writes:

> There for the first time I really saw the Negro, not as a pseudo-urbanized and vulgarized, a semi-Americanized product, but the Negro peasant, strong with the tang of fields and soil. It was there that I first heard the folk-songs rolling up the valley at twilight, heard them as spontaneous and native utterances.[11]

A second letter describes Negro church music as pure "feeling [. . .] sincerely, powerfully, deeply. And when they overflow in song, there is no singing that has so touched me."[12] Yet the idealized immediacy of folk song provokes for Toomer a sharp sense of its practical distance and mediation. His ideal of folk authenticity comes less from personal experience than from nineteenth-century ballad theory and twentieth-century practices of ethnographic collection. His own process of collection and recollection via writing are what might preserve folk authenticity, but like Hart Crane's similar (auto-)ethnographic participant observation, the result is strained.[13] We can already sense what Anthony Reed identifies in his reading of the contemporary poet Douglas Kearney: the critical reframing of "black genius as the unfolding of a unitary folk spirit" whose expression is no longer consummated in a "unitary moment of lyric understanding."[14] In Kearney's work this follows from his acute sense of how media history, especially radio and recording, refracts black voices even as it collects and codifies them. Where Kearney remediates those voices via typography, lexical play, and the polyvocality of his performance technique, Toomer tries to embody them himself. Yet his inspiration for *Cane* depends from the beginning on a sense of the loss that comes with lyricizing the folk—with accommodating cultural practices to more legible and tractable poetic genres such as what we now think of as first-person lyric. Six months later Toomer writes to Frank:

> Don't let us fool ourselves, brother: the Negro of the folk-song has all but passed away: the Negro of the emotional church is fading. A hundred years from now these Negroes, if they exist at all will live in art. And I believe that a vague sense of this fact is the driving force behind the arts movements directed towards them today.[15]

Toomer largely dismisses these "art movements" for their "vague sense" of sociocultural change, but his own work remains intensely anxious as to whether he himself has found a "usable past" (in Van Wyck Brooks's 1918 phrase) or whether he is separated from the "folk" by history, social status, and perhaps most importantly, by a sense of his own racial difference. What Toomer describes first as a historical change ("passing away") and then as a failure of historical understanding (the "vague sense") is a cypher for his own sense of personal alienation. Every positive association with a "Negro" past developed in *Cane* gets countered by consciousness of the disruption of vernacular continuity.

The editors of the second Norton Critical Edition of *Cane* have shown Toomer's complicated relationship with race; their contention that Toomer "was a Negro who decided to pass for white" puts the matter in terms much starker than Toomer would have accepted or admitted.[16] How might *Cane*, plainly the work of a poet who circa 1923 "did not wish to 'rise above'/or 'move beyond' [his] race,"[17] thematically and formally reflect Toomer's unstable racial identity? The speakers and characters do not attempt to pass as white but rather fail to begin and end in blackness; my argument is that that the cause of this is the specialized mode of double consciousness in which embracing black forms aligned Toomer with a largely white, nineteenth-century tradition of constructing and collecting black folk authenticity and its aesthetic characteristics. At once dependent upon this tradition and discontented with its hardening of race and racial forms, Toomer tries to imagine passing as a normative condition for poetry and poetic form—if not yet personal identity. Below I show how *Cane*'s approach to the vernacular forms Toomer heard while in the South leads to an experience of constitutive, deracinating and de-racing distance.

While emphatic about Toomer's biographical ambivalences, the Norton editors conceive the South as a usable, organic past for Toomer. They take him at his word when he writes of his sojourn and the songs he heard as his and *Cane*'s "seed." This image of a seed, the editors note, reappears "as one of the unifying, fecund conceits in his poem 'Song of the Son,' in which he celebrates the ancestral past and cultural landscape of Sparta [Georgia]."[18] For Vera Kutzinski it guides *Cane*'s "pastoral journey back to the source," though she notes the complication of this recovery after part 1.[19] Such views echo an early review by Montgomery Gregory as well as Sterling Brown's later opinion that the poem "expresses the return of the younger Negro to a consciousness of identity with his own, a return to folk sources."[20] "Song" does emphatically profess the notion that black art stems or should stem from a racial heritage, even as Toomer expresses ambivalence at being considered a "Negro author." On the one hand, he emphatically refuses to be advertised as black, hoping he might be thought of as racially "American."

The diverse colors, classes, locales, and literary forms of *Cane* are an expression of this hope. On the other hand, nearly every male character in the work is described as having been uprooted from soil and tradition. What diasporic promise there is seems mainly located in the figure of the Jew and Jewish cantor. *Cane*'s women are either sexual objects identified with the earth (in the case of southern women) or hysterically disassociated from that sexuality (northern women). The former read easily within the project of black re-rooting emphasized by early critics. The portrait of Fern, for instance, presents both the speaker and reader with images of a woman's eyes into which "the whole countryside seemed to flow. [. . .] Flowed into them with the soft listless cadence of Georgia's south."[21] Fern's eyes are replaced by a cadence or rhythm, a substitution that repeats in another portrait, "Carma," which presents women as passive catalysts for converting the land into an ancient, African place. The narrator's mind provides the imagistic energy for the reaction: "Pungent and composite, the smell of farmyards is the fragrance of the woman. *She does not sing; her body is a song.* She is in the forest, dancing. Torches flare [. . .] juju men, greegree, witch doctors [. . .] torches go out. [. . .] The dixie pike has grown from a goat path in Africa."[22] The protagonist of "Box Seat," an alienated DC man, must "place his palms on the earth to cool them" after recoiling in a mix of desire and terror at the touch of a "portly Negress." He smells her "soil soaked fragrance" and watches with paranoia as "through the cement floor her strong roots sink down," "spread under the asphalt streets," and "sink down and spread under the river and disappear in blood-lines that waver south."[23]

These are the moments that made critics think that not just *Cane* but Toomer himself were "sprung from the tangy soil of the south."[24] Yet *Cane* is too busy constructing metonymies of the South for his own voice, person, or literature to then be its organic outgrowth. Toomer strains as much as *Cane*'s critics to imagine folk song transposed into modernity without a loss of authenticity. Just as songlike women catalyze sudden spatiotemporal linkages of an African past with a southern present, so did the experience of hearing folk songs catalyze for Toomer the pastoral linkage of the South and its history with his urban and urbane perspective. Describing his two-month stint as a schoolteacher in rural Georgia, Toomer reads history in terms of a transformation of genre:

> A family of back-country negroes had only recently moved into a shack not too far away. They sang. And this was the first time I'd ever heard the folk-songs and

spirituals. They were very rich and sad and joyous and beautiful. But I learned that the negroes of the town objected to them. They called them "shouting." They had victrolas and player-pianos. So, I realized with deep regret, that the spirituals, meeting ridicule, would be certain to die out. With negroes also the trend was towards the small town and then towards the city—and industry and commerce and machines. The folk-spirit was walking in to die on the modern desert. That spirit was just so beautiful. Its death was so tragic [. . .] and this was the feeling I put into *Cane*. *Cane* was a swan-song.[25]

The beginning of this passage is predicated on Toomer's difference from rural African Americans, a difference that produces sublime regret and lyrical nostalgia. But the end of the passage erases this difference as Toomer takes upon himself the task of singing a distinct culture's "swan-song." Critics repeatedly embrace this idea of *Cane* as swan song: his ethnographic mission of memorialization becomes both actual preservation and individual expression. Yet the lyrical pseudo-genre of the swan song obscures the underlying politics of the practice of collection and of folk song as, in Ana María Ochoa Gautier's terms, a "racialized category of being."[26] In the Victrola's displacement of African American song, Toomer marks not only the limits of modern aurality but also his sense of cultural displacement by modern aurality's racialized aesthetics. Friedrich Kittler observes that the earliest commercial cylinders prominently advertised "negro songs and dances," recorded as if in situ; this displaces song from being a function of subjective memory and performance to being "part of their acoustic environment."[27] That is significant to Toomer and his avatar Kabnis because the "acoustic environment" is never neutral: it encodes one commodified version of black sound and repeats it as the real. The contrast with Weldon Johnson, Sterling Brown, or later Kamau Brathwaite's sense of media is stark: the player piano and gramophone for Toomer mark the passing and reification of culture rather than the transatlantic, "stereophonic" recirculation of LPs and other material transcriptions.[28] Toomer avoids dialect spelling in his poems and songs for a similar reason: he adopts an abstract sense of orality rather than exploring the productive "tension" between orality and literacy that Nadia Nurhussein locates in late nineteenth- and early twentieth-century dialect verse.[29] In the section that follows, I suggest that Toomer's media-effacing attraction to folk song, coupled with his self-conception as the singer of a "swan-song" for a vanishing race, brings him uncomfortably close to the racially overdetermined tradition of ballad collection.

Cane as Collection

Attempting a lyrical rather than material preservation of oral folk culture, *Cane* mourns its way into modernity with a beautiful, nostalgic marking of a tradition's complex death. Rather than think of Toomer's work as reproducing or reinventing folk song, as reviewers, critics, and Toomer himself have, we can see how it reproduces the history of collecting and interpreting folk song. The transformation from passing culture to present expression that Toomer narrates in his letters and autobiography traces a path from folk form to personal lyric that characterizes ballad theory from Wordsworth and Hegel through Francis Barton Gummere and modern anthologists. Building on Susan Stewart's diagnosis of the ballad as a "distressed genre" constituted by its invention of orality and the folk, Michael Cohen has shown how the collection of supposed oral cultures forms a "history of the present." We can see in Toomer exactly the "fantasy of plenitude through the pathos of loss" that drives ballad theory's "paradoxical process of restoring fragmentation." And we can hear in Toomer the exact worry of collectors and ballad theorists like Francis Child that "genuine ballads of the people" would cease to circulate, necessitating acts of critical preservation that had to appear transparent.[30] In Toomer's southern turn we find what Meredith Martin calls the "ballad-theory of civilization":

> Ballads were at once imagined to be the authentic record of a nation's earliest poets as well as evidence of early songs that appeared at the beginning of every culture. Now collections of fragments, authentic ballads had to be in some way corrupted or faded so that their re-creation could accommodate the nostalgic projection onto the past of a purer form of connected society, via poetry.[31]

The African American South was to Toomer what Scotland and India were to British collectors like Thomas Macaulay: a periphery, Martin observes, "elevated as the primitive and brought into the whole fabric of the nation as an imagined common past." That Toomer is not explicit about nationalism is a quintessentially American nationalism; what matters is his ability to imagine, along pathways laid out by the ballad, the South as other and therefore material for poetic remediation.

In the nineteenth century the idea of the "folk" comes through investments in Herder's *Volksgeist* theory and practical efforts of collection like Child's ballads or Thomas Wentworth Higginson's memoir *Army Life in a*

Black Regiment (1869). Higginson assigns himself the task of recording the spirituals he heard while commanding the first black regiment in the Union army. His explicit model is Walter Scott's eighteenth-century collection of Scottish ballads. Higginson refers to the songs as "specimens" and describes how "it was a strange enjoyment to be suddenly brought into the midst of a kindred world of unwritten songs, as simple and indigenous as the Border Minstrelsy, more uniformly plaintive, almost always more quaint, and often as essentially poetic."[32] Higginson adopts the eighteenth- and nineteenth-century practice of ballad collecting in service of what he took to be America's native history and culture. In the midst of a challenge to America's national unity, driven by disputes over the rights of African Americans, Higginson looked for "indigenous" culture in African American song. In the mid- to late nineteenth century the collection of folk songs held significance not only for national identity but for defining the "essence" of modern poetry and of lyric, modernity's essential genre. Recent work by Erin Kappeler and Virginia Jackson shows how ballad theorist and Anglo-Saxonist Frances Gummere in particular had an outsized influence on American academic and popular thinking about poetry and its social origins. Kappeler observes that Gummere's ideal primitive "throng," synchronized through "rhythm," is entirely Anglo-Saxon, and that even the apparent cosmopolitanism or diversity of theories of poetry influenced by Gummere may "champion racialist logics" in their treatments of modern, "individual" poetry.[33] Jackson, building on this point, observes the persistence of Gummere's fetishization of premodernity in more palatable critical celebrations of "rhythm" as lyric's communal force. The growing body of scholarship on the ballad reveals in particular how twentieth- (and now twenty-first-) century theories of poetry remain rooted in idealized primitive, rhythmic kinship. It is this racialized genre logic that determined Toomer's participation in a seemingly "multicultural" poetic modernity.

Gummere's *Handbook of Poetics*, published in 1885 and reprinted numerous times, clarifies the terms of that participation—terms Toomer adopts and adapts in his own poetics. The *Handbook* places considerable value on authentic, non-"imitative" ballads as the lost wellspring that modern lyric yearns for but cannot return to. Folk forms, particularly ballads, are the dragon's teeth of the epic tradition. The epic is determined by its impersonality, lack of authorial presence, lack of reflection, and its mirroring of nature. Gummere looked to folk song as a mediating term or genre in the "development" toward lyric and away from epic elements missing from *Paradise Lost* or Keats's *Hyperion*:

> The old wheat field of epic poetry, long after it was ploughed under, kept sending up scattered blades, which we call ballads or folk-songs. [. . . F]olk song is something made by the whole people, not by individual poets.[34]

As the epic genre and spirit become vestigial and modern lyric necessary, folk song and the lyrical ballad hold out some hope for a vestige of cultural and racial unity. Gummere thinks of lyric in terms he derives from the genre definitions Hegel develops in the *Aesthetics* (1835): it is "essentially *individual*. We cannot claim, even for the so-called folk-lyric, or ballad, that spontaneous growth in the popular heart that we claimed for the epic folk-song."[35] He gives central place to the hybrid genre of the lyrical ballad. Robert Burns earns special note for his evocation of place and culture through his mastery of Scots dialect. Lyric, for Gummere, succeeds when it sings in a popular tone, sincerely and with simplicity but without conspicuously imitating ballads.

Gummere's critical inheritors embraced his stadial theories of genre. After the stage of communal expression, write the authors of the 1913 handbook *The Art of Versification*, "came the development of the individual poet with his increasingly personal expression, culminating in the lyrical form."[36] Early anthologists of African American poetry like R. T. Kerlin also follow his genre logic. Kerlin praises orality but relegates it to what Gummere called the primitive "throng"; that good but now impossible rhythmic collectivity was to be transcended, albeit with ample nostalgia, through the new, more conscious and individuated literature emblematic of America's national formation. Kerlin argues for a greater proximity of the "Negro" to that rhythmic throng and thus to the capacity to bind together collective and lyrical rhythm: "The Negro nature is endowed above most others, if not all others, in fervor of feeling, in the completeness of self-surrender to emotion. Hence we see the marvelous display of rhythm in the individual and in the group."[37]

This racialized logic of rhythm overdetermines whatever potential there may have been in the model of Burns, the Scots dialect, and the lyrical ballad. The Burns-like or vernacular African American poem will still signify the throng, given its presence in Kerlin's anthology. Stephen Henderson observes how such modern anthologists "thought of refining the folk materials, in the manner of the *Lyrical Ballads*, or of absorbing them into forms deriving from European music."[38] Numerous African American poets, and James Weldon Johnson in particular, anticipate this critique and recognize that given America's racial conflicts, Burns or the lyrical ballad could not provide an unambiguous generic model. Where Gummere's conception of lyric depends on the prop of racial unity, Toomer must seek that unity through the unsteady ideal of the lyrical "swan-song." This must be both a valediction to orality and a concession to literate modern individualism. Even as "Song of the Son" translates Gummere's "scattered blades" as "ripe plums," imagining the epic past of a "song-lit race," Toomer cannot make his own lyric practice contiguous with (much less an inheritance of) that tradition. Like Whitman, Toomer collects the nation's blades of grass, or ripe plums, into his own lyrical song. But his representation of folk song is also a form of specimen collecting, a mowing or picking in which black folk and black folk song become aesthetic capital.

The importance and success of literary collections like Du Bois's *Souls of Black Folk* (1903), Anderson's *Winesburg, Ohio* (1919), and possibly Masters's *Spoon River Anthology* (1915) all suggest reasons why Toomer would invest in collection and depend on folk forms as a measure of authenticity. Doing so allows him to hold close the powerful idea of an epic and objective representation of a racial and even national spirit. It allows Toomer to reimagine his own lyric poetry outside the lyricism he criticized in Douglas Johnson. Yet the idealized modern lyric poem was, as we see in Gummere, conceptually vague. Unlike the epic, it cannot be spontaneous or originate in a communal heart, must never try to imitate genuine folk song, and yet must be sincere and common in tone and is most ideally developed in the lyrical ballad. This definition of lyric is not a positive articulation but the defensive gesture of generic collapse that Jackson calls "lyricization"; unable to articulate or defend a logic of expressive genre, the "awkward, transitional form" of the lyrical ballad polices an improvised border between authentic balladry and modernity's genres.[39] Toomer cannot cross this border, because he agrees that folk song is being annihilated by the nascent culture industry symbolized by Victrolas and player pianos. But this leaves him without an operative genre: he cannot create or imitate folk songs, but neither can he write expressive lyric "swan-songs" without becoming either an imitator or another collector of (black) folk tradition.

Contrary to its insistence on continuity between oral culture and lyrical preservation, *Cane* questions the authenticity or presence of a "folk" and folk song in modern genres. It is as much a story about the unavailability of folk sources as it is a valedictory re-rooting; or rather, it obeys the paradoxical logic of the valedictory, as articulated by Justin Sider, in which poetry strives for its greatest connection to an audience at the moment of leave-taking. The pseudo-genre of the swan song papers over that difference, over an impossible occasion of performance.[40] The characters in *Cane*, as well as its narrators and poetic speakers, yearn for but fail to access the music that we discover throughout the text hovering in dusks, trees, and women.

"Fern," for example, tells the story of a black woman idolized by and sexually available to men but who remains strangely alien to the community and ultimately marries a Jewish man. The narrator depicts Fern as an extension of her geography but not without a strange, dislocated impression of her as song:

> At first sight of her I felt as if I heard a Jewish cantor sing. As if his singing rose above the unheard chorus of a folk-song. And I felt bound to her. I too had my dreams: something I would do for her. I have knocked about from town to town too much not to know the futility of mere change of place. Besides, picture if you can, this cream-colored solitary girl sitting at a tenement window looking down on the indifferent throngs of Harlem. Better that she listen to folk-songs at dusk in Georgia, you would say, and so would I.[41]

The passage attempts to overcome the speaker's itinerancy through the complex treatment of Fern as a static, female subject. The male gaze becomes an organic experience echoing that of its object: the sight of Fern creates imagined sound; that sound calls forth "unheard" folk song; the narrator's fantasy is briefly undercut by the image of Fern re-"framed" by his life; to overcome this dissonant image the narrator imagines Fern as not only song but its listener. The narrator's dream for Fern is exactly what he wishes her to provide for him: a pathway from the imaginings of vision to the immediacy of listening in a group. He forgets that the songs are imagined and "unheard," and he fails to realize that they are "unheard" precisely because of the cultural itinerancy Toomer describes in his letters and autobiography. In the absence of real song, the narrator dreams up a phantasmal combination of individuality (represented by the cantor) and rootedness (represented by the folk song at dusk). Fern's figuration of hybrid song is unfulfilling, however, and her final rechristening as "Fernie May Rosen" signifies a too-literal form of hybridity. While Fern has the temporary ability to catalyze the divinity of place for the narrator, her identity and voice nonetheless remain "tortured" and "broken," her throat "spatter[ing] inarticulately in plaintive,

The Prosody of Passing

convulsive sounds."[42] Her strangled rooting in place recalls how, in Johnson's *Autobiography*, it is a southern lynching that "roots [the narrator] to the spot in horror" and propels him to pass and occupy a role of pained "observer, not composer."[43] In "Fern" that veiled threat is present for each character and effects the stark distance between the narrator's observation and Fern as object. Indeed, a very different reading of "Fern" would be that the narrator simply projects his own failures while Fernie May Rosen manages a cosmopolitan escape. In either reading, the narrator is too naively romantic about folk authenticity to capture his southern objects. This is how *Cane* figures the conditions for a native swan song; why should Toomer's poems be more stable valedictions?

"Song of the Son," a valedictory poem that renders leave-taking as "lyrical" recovery, complicates that recovery in its strange figuration of the history of slavery as organic fruition:

> Pour O pour that parting soul in song,
> O pour it in the sawdust glow of night,
> Into the velvet pine-smoke air to-night,
> And let the valley carry it along.
> And let the valley carry it along.
>
> O land and soil, red soil and sweet-gum tree,
> So scant of grass, so profligate of pines,
> Now just before an epoch's sun declines
> Thy son, in time, I have returned to thee,
> Thy son, I have in time returned to thee.
>
> In time, for though the sun is setting on
> A song-lit race of slaves, it has not set;
> Though late, O soil, it is not too late yet
> To catch thy plaintive soul, leaving, soon gone,
> Leaving, to catch thy plaintive soul soon gone.
>
> O Negro slaves, dark purple ripened plums,
> Squeezed, and bursting in the pine-wood air,
> Passing, before they stripped the old tree bare
> One plum was saved for me, one seed becomes
>
> An everlasting song, a singing tree,
> Caroling softly souls of slavery,

> What they were, and what they are to me,
> Caroling softly souls of slavery.[44]

This poem of self-expansion and self-discovery is not a swan song in the sense of an organic formal embodiment of the tradition of the spirituals. Most obviously, the heavily alliterative pentameter lines do not reflect the "caroling" described in them. The poem fails to aesthetically resemble the spirituals or folk songs that slaves sang before they became plum seeds—pits—for Toomer to replant. This is not to say, of course, that Toomer *should* mimic the form of the spirituals. Yet the poem repeatedly frames itself as a genetic continuation of "song" and thus invites the comparison.

The folk orientation is most emphatic in the final refrain stanza, which looks like a ballad stanza stretched out into pentameter. Whereas spirituals most commonly follow a four-beat, four-line prosodic form with xAxA rhyme scheme,[45] Toomer's "Song" is defined by its apostrophes, parallelisms, meter, and ABBAA/ABBA rhyme scheme (excepting the final stanza): all of which sound like vestiges of English traditions. The poem's prosody is a paradox at the level of stanza. It seems finally to achieve ballad rhyme in the final stanza, but such stanzaic development is itself alien to folk song or ballad. Even the repetition of the fourth line in the first three stanzas diverges from the musical tradition it approximates. In the first stanza the repetition is exact, in the second the change is slight, but the third alters both the iambic rhythm and the syntax. In this stanza the "leaving" soul-soil becomes the speaker's leave-taking: "To catch thy plaintive soul, leaving, soon gone, / Leaving, to catch thy plaintive soul soon gone." For the speaker to simultaneously embody the soul-soil and progress to lyrical reflection, the poem must distort the musical repetition. This persists to the poem's final syllable, as the final quadruple rhyme invites strain between sound and pronunciation by forcing stress on the final *y* in "slavery."[46]

Cane contains other poems whose prosodic forms pay closer homage to spirituals, as in the extradiegetic quatrains framing "Karintha" and "Carma" and the poem "Cotton Song." The book also has free or Imagist verse that bears no immediate resemblance to folk forms ("Face," "Nullo," "Portrait in Georgia") and traditional forms in "Georgia Dusk" (ABBA, pentameter), "Reapers" (pentameter couplets), and "November Cotton Flower" (sonnet in pentameter couplets). This diversity suggests that "Song of the Son" as a single poem may uneasily strive for a lyric syncretism that *Cane* prefers to pursue through collection and juxtaposition. Yet its effort to join traditional

English form with the speaker's reflection on lost slave culture is not itself counterintuitive. That it parallels, with only slight shifts of register and tone, Georgia Douglas Johnson's "The Passing of the Ex-Slave" (1922) confirms Toomer's participation in the New Negro Renaissance's diverse investment in poetic forms rather than his prescription of a priori raced folk forms. The difference is that Toomer so potently apostrophizes the raced origins of his own voice and song that it seems impossible not to register the fissures of the composite form. Those fissures return us to "Song of the Son" as an act of collecting, rather than lyricizing, the tradition it evokes. As a narrative of folk collecting, it symptomatically fails to absorb, reconcile, or signify on its own almost fetishistic pursuit of a usable past. Whereas poems like Countee Cullen's "Heritage" (1925), Claude McKay's "Harlem Dancer" (1922), or Sterling Brown's later "Cabaret" (1932) signify on spectatorship, Toomer remains in the awkward position of trying to turn a recognizably foreign past into his own lyrical becoming. More importantly, however, the poem places the reader in that same awkward position, waving something like folk song in front of us like ripe fruit we cannot eat: a song whose "everlasting" nature is undermined by the poet's failure or refusal to reproduce it formally.

The fourth stanza extends this anti-mimetic process, dropping the formal echo with a surprising stanzaic enjambment ("one seed becomes // An everlasting song"). The stanza invites us to think of the folk-lyric relationship as a botanical metamorphosis. The "song-lit race of slaves" is a plum tree from which the speaker plants a new "singing tree" that must be both him and something singing to him of its own accord. The metonymic chain recalls "Fern," now compressed into syntactic gymnastics and sudden changes in stanza form. The slaves seem to transform into their apposition ("dark purple ripened plums") even as a mysterious "they" that we presume to be the slaves "strip the old tree bare" of all but a single plum. Toomer models his own human and poetic being on the inhuman image of slaves plucking themselves for posterity. "They" need not refer to the slaves, yet no other subject presents itself. Nor is it said who "squeezed" the plums or "saved" one for the speaker. The answer from Toomer's memoir, and from the prose portions of *Cane*, would be the genius of the place, the Georgia air and hillsides. Not so here, though Toomer does apostrophize "O soil." The poem wants us to translate the enjambed "one seed becomes / An everlasting song" as "I plant this everlasting song in myself, through my poetry." The enjambment adds a sense of the seed as entelechy and isolates the "everlasting song" as if it were another self-sustaining subject. The author-collector's literate function of recovering, translating, and transcribing hides in the stanza break. The syntax muddles agency more directly; the speaker is presumably the poem's titular "son," yet it is the tree, not the speaker, that carols "souls of slavery / what they were, and what they are to me." Nowhere in the poem does the son/speaker himself collect, plant, or carol, and yet everywhere we know him to be doing so. Only through the occlusions and disruptions of formal mimesis can the poem's lyrical subject remain a member of an oral and collective tradition.

The poem begins in a confusion of agents, addressing something only later identified as "land and soil," "plaintive soul," and finally "Negro slaves." The alliterative opening address, "Pour O pour that parting soul in song," rhetorically attaches song to organic soil but performatively appropriates it to its own voice. The rest of the poem as I have been reading it works to resolve this paradox of the swan song, of modern lyric as native to but also alienated from tradition. The poem's overwhelming confusion of agency, address, syntax, and prosody suggests, however, that there is no simple conduit from spiritual or folk song to a modern lyrical subject tasked with embodying and representing that tradition. This mediation and withholding of folk song is for *Cane* part of a larger problem: Toomer's work cannot seem to decide whether folk song is a living part of black aesthetics or a figure for an absent past. However much *Cane* may seem to offer or try to offer us folk song via swan song, at the critical moment represented in "Song of the Son," *Cane*'s folk song—and its claim to being a "swan-song"—arrives only as figure.

This reading captures the appeal, for both Toomer and subsequent criticism, of conceiving *Cane* as modernist epic escaping the limits of subjective lyric. It also tries to capture the strain of that escape as evidenced in the poetics and prosody of "Song of the Son." *Cane* has the "elusive poetics" C. D. Blanton observes in the modernist "negated epic," "devised under the force of the injunction to include history, but caught simultaneously in a history too complex and often too menacing to include straightforwardly."[47] "Song of the Son" captures such paradoxical demands of genre formally, through the potent but never-quite-legible vestigiality of its meter, stanzaic development, syntax, and structures of address.

Kabnis's Unheard Blues

The narrative of "Kabnis" turns on the strain of hearing and parsing such prosodic vestiges. *Cane*'s characters are alienated from a specifically audile heritage; folk forms in *Cane*'s short stories act as distorted, painfully silent ghosts lurking within their psyches. Toomer diagnoses, through Ralph Kabnis, the destabilization of lyric experienced in "Song of the Son" as the product of the historical impermanence of folk song itself. Kabnis strives to silence and distance the past he encounters during a stint as a rural schoolteacher in Georgia. Although Kabnis's speech becomes inflected by local dialect over the course of the narrative, there is no real suggestion that Kabnis is becoming rooted in the south. At the end of the story he is training to become a carriage repairman: not a great job in 1923, nor is Kabnis any good at it. He is described as a failing "promise of a soil-soaked beauty; uprooted, thinning out. Suspended a few feet above the soil whose touch would resurrect him."[48] His antagonistic relation to song emphasizes this uprootedness. He prays to Jesus, "Do not chain me to myself and set these hills and valleys, heaving with folk-songs, so close to me that I cannot reach them."[49] Song confronts Kabnis not only in its presence but in its absence; at his nadir Kabnis fails to recognize a folk song—and very nearly a blues form—sung right at him and for him.

In the final scene of the narrative, Kabnis joins several men and women for a night of drinking in the basement of a repair shop. With them is a largely mute, sibylline figure named Father John who keeps muttering the word "sin." Another character, Lewis, reads Father John as the "symbol, flesh, and spirit of the past." But Kabnis can see him only as a "done up preacher," a sort of wind-up toy who "aint my past."[50] These different attitudes toward John reflect divergent ways of understanding folk song; in terms of poetic genre, they reflect divergent visions of lyric as founded in collective song: Lewis, like Gummere, sees it as the living heir to an epic universalism; Kabnis, against Gummere, sees it as an imitation of a nonuniversal, falsely constructed history with no culminating moment in Kabnis's (or anyone else's) individuality.

John's last words confirm his status as a symbol of folk song's tense historicity. He speaks three times, interrupted first by a virginal figure named Carrie and then by the more cynical Kabnis. Put back together, his dialogue reveals its crypto-form:

> Th sin whats fixed upon the white folks
> —f tellin Jesus—lies
> O th sin th white folks 'mitted
> When they made the Bible lie (114)

If we look just at John's prose message, as Kabnis does, we too might question the importance of such an old truth. It is a commonplace that proponents of slavery manipulated religion in defense of their cause. Kabnis's jeering response is therefore not unreasonable. But had he heard in Father John's mumbling the rhymes and rhythms of a spiritual or the blues, his response would then seem to be a dismissal not of a truism but of a historical response to slavery. John's song is formally alien to "Song of the Son." It scans as a rhyming ballad stanza with a 4-3-4-3 stress pattern, rather than pentameter. Compared to the fourth and fifth lines of "Song's" stanzas, Father John's stanza develops a natural parallelism between two pairs of lines (or one pair of heptameter lines). The lines recall the repeated "A" lines of the three-line AAB blues stanza. The final, culminating line that would provide a twist or interpretation is silenced by Kabnis. Perhaps most important is the shift in the "O," not artificially apostrophic as in "Song" but simply a lament. These formal markers frame Father John's message as part of a deeper history unavailable to Kabnis. He is an uprooted subject, outside of the shared history implied by the folk song. As in Toomer's autobiographical writings, that uprootedness is caused by the lack of a coherent literary history or genre through which to ground identity. If this makes Kabnis a paradigm of the modern lyric, defined by its distance from notional epic, it also prevents him from expressing any sentiment other than disdain and anger.

The figure of Kabnis as a reader forces a further reconsideration of *Cane*'s genre, which is neither a lyrical, modernist swan song nor an epic collection of fragments such as Father John's refrain stanza. Kabnis is a powerful model of the modern lyric reader precisely because his inability to hear the past's song becomes the reader's deafness, enforced through Toomer's physical setting of the song on the page. It would be one thing if modernity were decisively driven to the new by a willful repudiation of historical forms, as in Toomer's own rejection of Douglas Johnson or the broad rejection of meter as metronome and atavism. But the truth of Kabnis's disconnection, like the reality of meter as vestige, lies not in a substantial rejection of historical form but in his deafness to its existence. He reads his proximity to folk song as being "chained to myself," but he cannot really hear those songs because of his preexisting sense of race and class. Kabnis's failure is one of embodiment, a failure to be entrained in rhythm. As with the formal intention of "Song of the Son" not to be a recognizable kind of prosodic object, Toomer's character stands outside the Gummere-influenced modern demand to build lyric consciousness out of the aesthetics of vernacular song forms. Kabnis reveals, in his non-hearing, how the internal divisiveness of race (rather than some general modern malaise) makes lyric (or its modern renaming as "poetry") an impossible target. Kabnis does not merely reject the south as a locus of racial continuity but outright rejects the hybrid and paradoxical literary genre—modern lyric—that offers to underwrite this continuity. Toomer rhetorically invests in the lyrical "swan-song" even as he formally undermines its universality. While Kabnis may seem pathetic or regrettable in his disdain compared to Lewis (Toomer's more benign representative in the text), he is hardly wrong to distinguish himself from Father John's past. Kabnis simply doesn't recognize the song: he is defined by his inability to hear the traditional genre or accept it as anything other than a distressed one. Father John's song may evoke the seemingly universal truths of slavery, but it lacks symbolic force for him because it has not received the editorial and anthology treatment that could bring it to audition. The only figure who might remediate John's utterance with its mystical force intact is Carrie, but she cannot make Kabnis listen.

Figures like Kabnis and poems like "Song of the Son" reinforce Jeremy Braddock's argument that one of the foremost aesthetic practices in the New Negro Renaissance (and modernism more broadly) is the collection and institutionalization of art and literature.[51] *Cane* registers the troubled dependence of prosody and prosodic genre on aggressive forms of collection and abstraction. It does this by generally obscuring the music in its stories. In "Esther," a story in which an itinerant preacher's song floats within prose narration, Toomer interweaves spirituals without any commentary from the narrator or characters. Splitting apart and de-lineating the song again threatens the reader with Kabnis's failure of audition, suggesting that even if *Cane* were a fitting "swan-song," we might not recognize it. *Cane*, as a collection of disparate forms and styles, challenges the reader's relation to tradition by insinuating that the reader is like another collector searching out the blades of grass and plums and specimens of folk song. To my knowledge the only critic to concatenate Father John's stanza is Paul Anderson, who hears a "halting and cryptic manner" transcended by both Kabnis and Toomer.[52] The necessary prose scansion never feels quite authorized but is not therefore dispensable. Whatever kind of prosodic reading *Cane* desires, Kabnis doesn't perform it. As Anderson notes, the story parallels Du Bois's "Of the Coming of John," in which the "frustrated hero die[s] prematurely" having been unaffected by the spiritual "Go Down, Moses" and preferring instead Wagner's *Lohengrin*.[53] Kabnis's transcription of the spiritual "My Lord, what a mourning" (91) denies even the ambiguity and poignant choice that comes with the homophone "morning" (as the spiritual is often titled, though not in Toomer's most proximate source, *The Souls of Black Folk*).[54] Even in such minimal and inevitable failures of transcription, *Cane* works neither as a defiant break with the past and its prosodic and musical forms nor as the lyrical "swan-song" Gummere and Toomer's peers anticipated. Rather, it manifests the necessity and impossibility of defining a relation (whether continuum or break) with the vernacular past without radically rebuilding the relations between prosodic form, genre, and race.

James Weldon Johnson: Re-scanning the Anglo-American Tradition

In a recent article, Michael Nowlin argues that James Weldon Johnson's critical and editorial efforts attempt to lay a "groundwork" for more experimental or "modern" African American poetry.[55] Nowlin is undoubtedly right in seeing Johnson, Alain Locke, and others trying to increase the literary circulation and value of black writing; at some level it is also true that Johnson sought to prove that black poets were capable of writing in "conventional" forms. A more thorough study of Johnson's professional activities suggests, however, anything but a simplified notion of conventional form as "groundwork" to be supplied, then transcended. He recognizes what Kamau Brathwaite, writing about Claude McKay and the acceptance that comes with traditional metrics, calls the "terrible terms meted out for 'universality.'"[56] That recognition does not, however, require that African American writing see itself recapitulating, in an accelerated development, the still "terrible terms" that would mandate movement away from historical and conventional forms. *Cane*'s generic self-conception as a swan song—rather than the modernist "break" it would become—bears this out. Where we do see Nowlin's schematic, it comes largely from white critics and anthologists like R. T. Kerlin who, whatever their motives, remained indebted to nineteenth-century ballad scholarship and its racial ideology. Weldon Johnson, Nowlin notes, contrasts Georgia Douglas Johnson's "conventional lyric forms" to Joseph Cotter's "free and bold" move beyond them;[57] but the increased valuation of the modern here comes from Nowlin more than Johnson and is belied by Weldon Johnson's pedagogy, criticism, and poetics, by kindred poet-critics like Countee Cullen and Sterling Brown and, crucially, Douglas Johnson's own poetics. On the one hand, Nowlin is right that Johnson and others faced the "fundamental aesthetic problem [of] how to transfer African American cultural power" from the achievements in music and oral forms to "a racially 'original' literature."[58] But Johnson saw the shape of the solution not in being "modern" but in reconceiving the relation of black poets and modern audiences. Toward that end he enforced a broad formal tradition whose racing depended on careful reading, not presumptive identity. Johnson's modernism breaks not with form but with racialized models of reading and listening for it.

In the courses Johnson taught at Fisk in 1932-1933, one discovers an analytic of form and prosody independent of historical narratives of progress. In both subtle and explicit ways Johnson invites students to read their own raced identity in traditional forms, rather than taking them as markers of politics or containers for racial content. For Johnson, even a poet as (seemingly) hermetic as Gerard Manley Hopkins could be radically separated from putatively white literary history. The James Weldon Johnson Collection at the Beinecke Library contains lecture notes, assignments, and other course materials from two courses: a 1932 course in creative literature and a 1933 course in contemporary American literature.[59] Johnson's literary history in his courses clearly diverges from our inherited narratives. For example, he begins his lectures on American literature by noting William Vaughn Moody's 1910 death, then turning to important divergences of literary opinion between E. A. Robinson and Robert Frost. When he does speak of Imagism, he anticipates recent critical focus on manifestos in arguing that the aesthetic conflict had less to do with the poetry than with claims made about it. He is less familiar to us in finding that "the principles set down in [Imagist manifestos] are not incompatible with the principles of traditional poetry." These include "the exact word, economy of expression, avoidance of monotony of rhythm. To produce poetry not blurred." But it is his non-chronological sense of literary history that is most striking. Good Imagist poems, he writes, "may be found in the works of the traditional poets."

Here, as in the speculation that Poe might have developed his "rhythmic patter from the Negroes in Virginia," we see a repeated invitation to do a revisionary reading of the history of prosody. Johnson chooses his words carefully in critiquing the seemingly easy road of "free" verse that "abolished" tradition, hinting that the "droves" of young Imagists may have been following an ideological drive to leave behind the past and the not-yet-complete abolitionist struggles manifest in Jim Crow. Johnson had spent several years in the 1920s fighting for the ultimately unsuccessful Dyer anti-lynching bill, and the more contemplative opportunities afforded by his position at Fisk could not have dulled his acerbic sense of American history as it related to African American strivings. His verb "abolish" emphasizes the very real danger of a formal amnesia embodying a historical failure to grapple with the outcome of abolition and reconstruction.

The most immediate concern of the courses was to reevaluate and reconceive literary history, more specifically, the history of prosody. Early in his 1932 course on creative literature, Johnson jabs at historical practices of scansion: he asks, "How many of you have studied English prosody? Then you know all about iambic, trochaic, anapestic, dactylic feet. Well, for the purposes of this course, forget them! NO practicing poet knows much about them." He proceeds with this mocking definition of scansion: "Drumming the meter out with your fingers to see if all the feet are of the proper size and length is not practiced by real poets." Such comments look like a typically modernist rejection of meter as something metronomic and pedantic. While Johnson explicitly prefers the term "rhythm" to "meter," his definition of rhythm as "the combination of accent groups into artistic and effective sequence" is designed to let him scan not only metrical verse, including Edna St. Vincent Millay's "varied rhythm" in her sonnets, but also Hopkins's sprung rhythm and even prose. His approach to prosody was certainly influenced by I. A. Richards's *Practical Criticism* (1929), the source of several poetic examples used in class. Richards wryly observes his students' "desperate efforts to apply the fruits of the traditional classical training" and, more severely, critiques the overall bias of students toward the regularity Johnson calls "drumming."[60]

While Johnson shares Richards's modernist belief that meter can and must be saved from pedantry, his version of practical criticism differs crucially in its orientation away from speech and oral performance and toward practices of scansion. Johnson describes the work of versification in terms that by no means exclude metrical experimentation and would even seem to encourage it: rhythm occurs "much like a musician establishes a theme and then varies it—but the theme must be established and in the variations never lost." His ranking of poets in terms of their skill in metrical variation subtly resists Richards, who encourages his readers to recognize sophisticated rhythmic patterning yet persistently decries prosody as superficial description removed from the "mind of the reader." No less important is Johnson's resistance to Richards's canon through his own exercise in practical criticism: three poems, A, B, and C, handed out without author's names. Perhaps in recognition of Cullen's kinship with Millay, he lauds the "power"

```
Margaret, are you grieving
Over Goldengrove unleafing?
        - - -
Ah! as the heart grows older
It will come to such sights colder
By and by, nor spare a sigh
Tho' world of wanwood leafmeal lie;
Yet you will weep and know why.
Now no matter, child, the name.
Sorrow's springs are the same.
Nor mouth had, no, nor mind express'd
What heart heard of, ghost guess'd:
It is the blight man was born for,
It is Margaret you mourn for.
```

James Weldon Johnson's transcription of Gerard Manley Hopkins's "Spring and Fall." Courtesy of the Beinecke Rare Book and Manuscript Library, Yale University.

of her "varied rhythm," retaining her as a metrically gifted model for innovative writing rather than Richards's "demonstrably bad" and sentimental writer.[61] Johnson's revised canon of taste, ordered along prosodic criteria, demotes instead the prolific newspaper poet Edgar Guest.

Johnson reserves highest praise for Hopkins's sprung rhythm poem "Spring and Fall: To a Young Child." Special attention to his transcription and printing of the poem is merited given the poem's central and sustained role in the course. The handout Johnson gave his students is missing lines 3-4 of the poem, almost certainly because those lines were excluded in *Practical Criticism* (without ellipses) and in Bridges's 1916 *Spirit of Man* (with two ellipses after line 2). Johnson was aware of the omission, given his inclusion of the ellipsis in at least one typescript copy. If he had at hand one of Bridges's 1918 or 1930 editions of Hopkins, he would also have seen the famous stress markings to which Richards briefly alludes, though it seems most likely that he noticed the ellipses in *Spirit of Man* and knew of the marks

Jan 21-1932. A   Lecture 5

    You will probably not be surprised to see us going back occasionally throughout the course to Spring and Fall to a Young Child. That will be because I feel that we have found in that poem a key to the understanding and appreciation of poetry — If we have, we cannot use the key too often.

    I gathered that most of you had found some trouble in marking the metrical scheme of the poem. More trouble, at least than you had with poems A & B. Will someone volunteer to put the scheme on the blackboard.

1. — ∪∪ — ∪ — ∪
2. — ∪ — ∪ — ∪ —
3. — ∪∪ — ∪ — ∪
4. ∪∪ — — ∪ — ∪
5. — ∪ — ∪ — ∪
6. ∪ — — ∪ — ∪ —
7. { ∪ — ∪ — — — — = You persist in weeping & knowing why
   { ∪ — ∪∪ — ∪ — = Some day you will weep & know why
8. — ∪ — ∪ — ∪
9. — ∪ — ∪∪ — ∪
10. ∪ — — ∪ — ∪ —
11. ∪ — — ∪ —
12. ∪ — ∪ — ∪ — ∪ — = { The things you mourn for are:
13. ∪∪ — ∪ — ∪ — ∪   { The blight man was born for & Margaret

    Note the two possible readings of line 7 — according to the accent given to the word "will"

    1st "will" is not a future, but a present use of the verb "to will." = You persist in, you continue to want to. — examples — You simply <u>will</u> do it, so there is nothing more I can say.

    2nd = When you are older you will weep and know why. Two totally different meanings — Which one do you think correct? prefer?

James Weldon Johnson's scansion of "Spring and Fall." Courtesy of the Beinecke.

from Richards. Perhaps an awareness of the poem's odd editorial trajectory of erasure and reprinting made Johnson even more inclined to attend to its metrical difficulty, though I believe he places more emphasis on the materiality of scansion and accentuation than Richards does because the ultimate aim of his teaching—as of his criticism—was to apprise his students of the many forms of inscription, mediation, and reproduction involved in the reception of poetry. The importance of the rhythmic pattern to Johnson emerges both from this scansion and from an initial transcription of line 2 as "Over the Goldengrove unleafing," an error that gives the line the choriambic (/ x x /) pattern available in lines 1 and 3 as well. Johnson's own scansion in lines 1 and 3 shows that he heard this pattern, even as he scans the second instance of "Margaret" in line 13 with a second stress (Margarét). His overall focus on sound can be seen in his attention to consonance. In his notes, and perhaps for the class, Johnson isolates each consonant in the first lines with periods between them. While Johnson theorizes this pattern as an unconscious presence for the "sensitive" poet, he clearly values the critic's role in physically schematizing and revealing such patterns.

This pattern of consonance, together with Johnson's editing and scansion, suggests a focus on rhythmic variations even though no obvious metrical norm is available. Johnson reconstructs the poem's meter and prosody as he hears it, half-finding and half-inventing the quality he attributes to Hopkins's rhythm: "ever changing modulations. [. . .] No monotony. Hardly any two consecutive lines in the same rhythms, and yet what perfect music." This "music" becomes visible as Johnson uses Hopkins's poem to expose the inadequacies of traditional scansion. Johnson's scansion dynamically reconstructs Hopkins's sprung rhythm as a riff on iambic verse, visibly marking a distance from accentual-syllabic meter. There is no obvious precedent for hearing sprung rhythm as a technical pivot against iambic meter—but it makes sense for Johnson to have heard it that way and to have invited his class to think of the poem as beginning with a modulation of traditional meter. The first six lines of his scansion, all embodying rhythmic variations found in the iambic tradition, show something more visibly iambic than Hopkins's original, with its added accent marks, and overall provide a metrical framework in which the very regular sixth line of the (emended) poem works as a pivot for the complexity of line 7 and the much wilder rhythms of the poem's second half (i.e., lines 9, 11, and 12). He may have detected a large-scale modulation from regular counterpoint to dissonance that roughly

1st line of Collins's <u>Ode</u> <u>to</u> <u>Evening</u>:

    If aught of oaten stop, or pastoral song.

Recurring consonants:

    f . t. f. t (n) st. p. r. p. st. r. (l. ng.)

Vowel sounds played on consonants:

    aw - oh - ŏ - ŏ - ŏng -

If aught of oat — stop — stor

2nd line: 1st version:

    May hope, O pensive Eve, to soothe thine ear.
        (hope - ope) (ive - Eve)

2d version:

    May hope, chaste Eve, to soothe thy modest ear.

\#

    Margaret —

1. m - r - g - r - t - r - y - g - r - r - ng -
2. r - r - g - l - d - n - g - r - r - l - f- ng.

\#

To the poet with a sensitive ear, the making of such music is not though a <u>conscious effort</u>.

James Weldon Johnson's consonant diagram of lines 1–2 of "Spring and Fall." Courtesy of the Beinecke.

maps to the poem's shift in focus from Margaret's naive sorrow at falling leaves to her future reckoning with man's internal blight.

The double scansion of line 7 deserves special emphasis both for the reading it enables and for the way it reevaluates Richards's pedagogy of misreading. The more common performance and interpretation of the line, especially without Hopkins's accent mark on "will," stresses "weep" and "why": "And yet you will *weep* and know *why*." In this hearing, as Richards puts it, "'will' may be read as giving future tense. [. . . T]he sense being that in the future she will know the reason for a sorrow that is now only a blind grief."[62] Things get messier—literally messy in Johnson's scansion—when we follow the "hint" of Hopkins's accent mark on "will": "When 'will' is accentuated it ceases to be an auxiliary verb and becomes the present tense of the verb 'to will.' She persists in weeping and in demanding the reason for the falling of the leaves." Richards gives no further help in determining what the effect of this strange conjugation would be or how to best balance the competing imperatives, leaving readers like Johnson with the assertion that what is paramount is not scansion or print convention but the subordination of rhythm to sense: "The rhythmical difference made by the change of sense is immense."[63] Richards does not indicate what "sense" is best or how performance might enable it: only that "will" must have some stress.

Rather than guess at Richards's interpretation, we can note that his driving interest is the reorientation of prosody around the new law of "sense" and what Richards calls "speech situations." As Meredith Martin has noted of Hopkins's appearance in *Practical Criticism*, and of critical approaches to meter more generally, the effect of this reorientation is that "poetic meter becomes merely voice's vehicle without an expressive capacity of its own."[64] Nowhere is this so glaring as in the "erasure" of Hopkins's material markers, which Richards plainly takes as disposable cues to be internalized (ideally without even seeing them) by performance. Anxious about modern audile technique, Richards wished to cultivate close attention to "sense" in order to avoid the mechanistic scansions and performances proliferating in his students' responses. Scansion and prosodic training are important to him because they perpetuate an outdated, Victorian response to the crisis of poetic sensibility, attention, listening, and literacy caused by modernity's dispersal of communities of shared language.

Although Johnson, as noted above, can be almost as critical as Richards of atavistic prosodic understanding, he does not view metrical schemas as anathema to the aesthetic appreciation or interpretation of Hopkins's poem. His practice in teaching is shot through with exercises in scanning both poetry and prose less for precision than to "stimulate [students'] powers" through attention to prosodic features of language. Unlike Richards he is not interested in proving his students' failings as prosodists. The chronology of his lectures and assignments suggests that he showed the students his scansion of Hopkins before asking them to submit their "metrical schemes" for a second series of poems. He does not wait to see whether his students will catch the "hint" of the accent on "will." What he does instead is to deliberately frame the challenge of interpretation as one of scansion. His scansion, written on the board, is the basis for the lesson, with the bracketed double scansion showing an ambiguity that need not be resolved into a unitary voicing.

Johnson tries to reckon with the oddity of Hopkins's stress mark on "will," knowing that college students encountering these words without typographic assistance would certainly not have stressed the auxiliary verb. The more obvious reading that Richards thought wrong is given in Johnson's second scansion ("and *yet* you will *weep* and know *why*"). This reading avoids consecutive stresses and thus comes off as a minor loosening of iambics or an anapestic rhythm. Johnson is more interested in the almost impossibly dense five-stress rhythm of the first scansion: "And *yet* you *will weep* and *know why*." We can see that the scansion challenged him. It may be that he is testing out the decision by one of Richards's students to make the "accent fall on 'will weep' and 'know why.'" Accents cannot "fall" on adjacent monosyllabic words: they may both receive stress, perhaps even equal or "hovering" stress, but this hardly amounts to a final parsing of rhythm through careful attention to sense-based accentuation. Johnson gives Richards's reading ("Will is not a future [. . .] but a present use of the verb 'to will'") but finesses Richards's incomplete explanation: "You persist in. You continue to want to. You simply <u>will</u> do it." Johnson's recourse to idiomatic expression does not actually give us a "present use of the verb 'to will,'" which, as Empson notes in his reading of the line, does not work grammatically.[65] But Johnson does tidily foreground a pun on "will" that obsessed not only Shakespeare but many Victorians.[66] He retains the auxiliary for the sake of grammar but adds, through the force of idiom, the insistence on the limits of the human "will"—"you simply will." He suggests that Margaret's weeping not only foreshadows adult cares but also embodies, in its jejune willfulness, a measure of fallenness. This latter meaning may feel distant from the line's intention, yet it resonates with the end of the poem. There we find that Margaret, with neither knowledge nor words, "guessed" and even performed the imminence of blight in her present. Johnson reveals the essence of Hopkins's ambiguously stressed "will": the gap between one's "will" and what "will" be. That too-human gap is embodied in the word, in a pun even, and in the monosyllables' absence of definite stressing. The limit of will emerges in the space between two scansions.

In contrast to Richards, what Johnson shows his students is that no performance reveals the "meaning" of "will" because the "two totally different meanings" offered by the scansions do not resolve in a single voicing. Rather, they produce the complexity of an interpretive engagement (mirroring Margaret's natural theology) rooted in the multiplicity and inconclusiveness of scansion. Thus, although Johnson does help us toward a reading of the line, its particular meaning seems less important to him than exposing the interconnected rhythmic and interpretive challenges it poses to the modern reader. "I gather," Johnson writes, "that most of you had trouble in making out the metrical scheme of the poem." Johnson provides both scansions because he wants his students to feel positive, provocative uncertainty at the level of rhythm—and to suggest that local uncertainty about rhythm augers deeper uncertainty about issues of literary sound such as dialect writing that were pressing to his and his students creative and analytical practices.

It becomes clear, moving forward in the course, that a heightened but also skeptical hearing of literary sound is Johnson's preferred way to start his students thinking about how they might consider race in their own creative compositions. His assignment of a chapter from *Brown America*, a 1931 work of sociology by Edwin Embree, turns out to be an exercise in scanning for prose rhythm. Also assigned are the first three verses of Genesis. In marking the success of Robert Burns in avoiding overwrought diction and rhyme—a repeated concern in the class—he contrasts Burns's ability to write in "Scottish dialect" (thus avoiding English artifices) with the more ominous case of black dialect: "the problem," as he jots in notes adjacent to the discussion of Hopkins. When critiquing his students' limited facility with rhyme, their error of "mistaking assonance for rhyme," he notes this fault is "extremely common in Negro folk poetry—so common, in fact, that it can hardly be called a fault. The Negro folk poets appear to prefer assonance to rhyme—and so assonance instead of rhyme becomes their scheme for lines endings." This remark reflects the complexity of the "problem." It suggests that both the "folk" and a sufficiently aware poet could develop such a new "scheme" but that when done unconsciously it becomes either "fault" or atavism. The "problem" then is not in the form but in students' understanding of form's history. In contrast to theorists of the folk like Gummere and Kerlin, Johnson prioritizes conscious over spontaneous soundings. Johnson's comment on assonance-rhyme frames all rhyme, potentially, as an engagement, desired or not, with "Negro folk poetry." He wants students to make clear-eyed decisions about how they choose to embody prosodic heritage, just as they must decide how and whether to write in dialect. Johnson does not insist that students write in dialect or not, or that they rhyme a certain way, but forces them to frame their formal choices in light of racial history. If they develop assonance or even slant rhyme, they will for better or worse be read in connection with "Negro folk poetry" (and not, say, with Dickinson).

This attention to the history of literary form is made explicit in two of the options given for students' final "practical work": either an essay discussing "what limits, if any, should the Negro novelist impose upon himself in choosing and making use of material from Negro life?" or a short story with a predetermined theme:

> Mozart Brown a little colored boy, so named by his mother because of her ambitions he become a great musician. Mozart is shortened into Moze by his playmates and friends. A. Moze has real talent and does through a series of experiences develop into something beyond his proud mother's expectation, perhaps even her comprehension. B. Moze has no exceptional talent and fails in spite of the hopes and efforts of his fond mother.

The detail of the name seems more important than the plot. "Moze" suggests either a literal foreshortening of musical possibility by circumstance or the promise of a Mosaic exodus into (as well as out of) vernacular music. This is again the "problem" of dialect and of the "double audience" whose classical standards of taste denigrate the vernacular or, equally bad, fetishize it. The double naming in "Moze" figures the tight and overdetermined space of black poetics and musicality that the students are to explore narratively. I imagine Johnson hoped this detail would become a focal point, pressing students to engage music's racial logic in every paragraph. Both this creative assignment and the analytic assignment elaborate the imperative behind the double scansion of Hopkins: they each reframe musical and prosodic tradition as a space of personal, political, and now explicitly racial intervention.

In the next section, I argue that the rhythmic and exegetical uncertainty visible in the scansion of Hopkins and in the plural signification of "Moze" registers Johnson's own poetic divergence from both the conventional and modern conceptualizations of black form. Disruption here occurs not only in the past, in an already constituted literary history to be claimed or disavowed, but in precisely calibrated moments of present reading that test out how Mozart becomes Moze, how language and folk expression become dialect, and how certain rhythms become "black." What enables Johnson's own work to serve as a "solution" to the problem of that present is what I call his rhythmic exegesis, in the double sense of a critical interpretation of rhythm and an interpretation that, like the sermon poems of *God's Trombones* (1927), works by creating new rhythms out of old structures. Such rhythms dissolve the binary of conventional and modern in favor of that attention to the practice of poetry reading that Richards desired but also, in his modernist antipathy toward prosody as a study and discourse, disabled.

Rhythmic Exegesis

Johnson's *Autobiography* constitutes an ars poetica for his poetry, offering both negative and positive scenes of musico-rhythmic training.[67] The young narrator can neither embrace his (absent, white) father because he imagines the gesture to be "melodramatic"—an atavistic sort of musical emotion—nor play piano for him without anticipating the reception of every note. That tense encounter, defined by the breakdown of musical sympathy, contrasts sharply with the narrator's later visit to a congregation being addressed by a rhythmically gifted orator named John Brown:

> He seized the Bible and began to pace up and down the pulpit platform. The congregation immediately began with their feet a tramp, tramp, tramp in time with the preacher's march in the pulpit, all the while singing in an undertone a hymn about marching to Zion. Suddenly he cried, "Halt!" Every foot stopped with the precision of a company of well drilled soldiers, and the singing ceased. The morning star had been reached. Here the preacher described the beauties of that celestial body. Then the march, the tramp, tramp, tramp, and the singing was again taken up. Another "Halt!" They had reached the evening star. And so on. [. . .] He took his hearers through the pearly gates, along the golden streets, pointing out the glories of the City, pausing occasionally to greet some patriarchal members of the church, well known to most of his listeners in life, who had had "tears wiped from their eyes, were clad in robes of spotless white, with crowns

of gold upon their heads and harps within their hands," and ended his march before the great white throne. [...] I was a more or less sophisticated and non-religious man of the world, but the torrent of the preacher's words, moving with the rhythms and glowing with the eloquence of primitive poetry swept me along. (92)

These feet may be well drilled, but they are not overdetermined or disciplined in their rhythm like the World War I footslog (we're hére becáuse we're hére becáuse we're hére) which Meredith Martin scans for its "footbeat rhythm becoming almost maddingly repetitive"[68]; or Gerard Manley Hopkins' generations who "have trod, have trod, have trod"; or the work rhythms of a chain gang. As in Hopkins, Johnson's re-scansion of Hopkins, or Sterling Brown's wry version of chain-gang song in "Southern Road" (1932), John Brown's sermon develops a mode of counterpoint that intentionalizes the otherwise rote repetition. For instance, the rhetorical journey taken by the parishioners looks strange given that the morning star and evening star are both Venus. This journey is circular or static, however, only from the perspective of location, not time. By "tramping" from the morning star to evening star, the preacher renders place dynamic by injecting return with difference: the journey is metaphysically charged by the symbolism of westward movement from morning to evening to a new morning in Zion and the "New Jerusalem."

The heightened rhythm of the prose parallels this rhythmic vision of space as iterable. The preacher's own words form a well-regulated but fluid iambic hymnal stanza that can be lineated through stress count as either 3-4-4-3 or 7-7 ("fourteeners"):

[had] *tears wiped* from their *eyes*,
were *clad* in *robes* of *spot*less *white*,
with *crowns* of *gold* upon their *heads*
and *harps* with*in* their *hands*

Though lacking full rhyme, the substantial assonance and consonance further structures these "lines": wiped/eyes/white; heads/harps/hands; clad/crowns. These sound repetitions help create what the narrator calls "tone pictures." The sermon is certainly not recognized as having prosodic structure, and yet I believe Johnson, in contrast to Toomer, desired his own evocation of the ballad stanza to be as rhythmically effective to the reader as it is for the narrator. The drama of deliberate and effectual rhythm anticipates

Johnson's effort to train readers in the drama of scansion, in its hunt for a different kind of "figure of vocalization."

Whereas the narrator of the *Autobiography* tends, like Toomer, to alternately dissociate from or overinvest in his experiences of black sound, Johnson's poetic oeuvre neither eliminates nor fully invests in the possibility of a meaningfully (rather than peremptorily) raced rhythm. Brent Hayes Edwards characterizes Johnson's poetics as "discarding the mediating figure of music" and "transferring the swing from the vernacular, performing black body or bodies into the very formal body of the poem; in the manipulations of line, measure, and punctuation, the poem itself begins to be sketched out as a 'breathing,' 'syncopating' body."[69] In keeping with this transfer from musical figure to poetics, Johnson's anthologies of spirituals and sermon poems remain profoundly different from other "folk" collections because of his skepticism about the translation back from text to sound: "I doubt that it is possible with our present system of notation to make a fixed transcription of these peculiarities that would be absolutely true; for in their very nature they are not susceptible to fixation."[70] In the drafts to *God's Trombones*, he is similarly skeptical about cueing stress contours for the reader: "I would be tempted to indicate by italicizing the words [where] the voice stresses fall except for the fear that it would [be] a clumsy if not confusing chore."[71] The drafts are more explicit on the matter of scansion than is the final preface: "The number of syllables makes no difference—Just as in music—any number of syllables may be syncopated into the rhythm." In its final form the preface tells us only that there is "a decided syncopation of speech—the crowding in of many syllables or the lengthening out of which must be left to the reader's ear."[72] That so much must be left to the ear and not typography is worrisome when readers like Harriet Monroe heard Johnson's "Creation" as an "ironed out [. . .] version of the folk-lore subject" she had heard orally from an unnamed "lady."[73] But it should also complicate acceptance of the very different audition of Leopold Senghor, who understood *God's Trombones* in terms of the jazz "pocket"; certainly intriguing from a prosodic perspective, this idea shouldn't overwhelm New Negro Renaissance poets' as well as Senghor's own insistence on the figurality and instrumentality of rhythm and music.[74] The inadequacy of sound as it reverberates for the double audience is also, paradoxically, a moment of great possibility akin to (or simply participating in) the modernist breakdown of genres. Because, as Morrissette concisely puts it, "Sterling Brown, Johnson, and others were wary of the reception of their poetry as pure performance, the response to their use of vernacular as mere vaudeville, mere source, mere transcription, not poetry,"[75] Johnson celebrates productive interruptions such as his creative writing students' "trouble in making the metrical scheme" of Hopkins's sprung rhythm.[76] If confusions of sound are disabling but necessary for the variegated audience of the spirituals, they also held the potential to initiate new modes of collective hearing.

The question then is what the "formal body of the poem" can look like when it has "discarded" pure music in favor of new rhythmic and rhetorical design. In this final section I study how Johnson's satirical mock exegesis "Saint Peter Relates an Incident of the Resurrection Day" creates a medium as "sharp," "surprising," and "electric" as that of Jasper Jones, the singer-preacher who originally framed the poems of *God's Trombones*. Jones embodies the duo of John Brown and "Singing Johnson," an "indispensable" aid who pulls together diverse congregations by knowing all the hymns (not just the refrains) and when to sing them. Yet because Johnson's poetic performance occurs without antiphony or a musical analogue, he turns sharply to the mercurial prop of poetic prosody. As "Saint Peter" reinterprets the white myth of the Unknown Soldier, he modulates and mutilates an equally legible white myth: the English metrical tradition. The poem builds its trenchant critique of America's historical self-understanding in its powerful revocation of the formal and generic contracts it seems to set up.

"Saint Peter" is written largely in quatrains of heroic couplets that make no effort to mimic any particular dramatic performance or occasion. Like *God's Trombones*, "Saint Peter" both builds and interrogates its own prosodic performance. The priority of the latter is evident in Sterling Brown's response to the poem's "notes of irony":

> I think the ironic approach is excellent. It isn't at all one of those "damn you, take that" sort of things. [. . .] There is quite a swing to the lines; they catch you up before you know it. [. . .] The whole poem keeps to its tone of high wit, and tempered irony. And it's not "wise-cracking"—it's the spirit best seen in Dryden and Pope, at their best. I think the use of the couplet form was well chosen; they are fluid, and pointed—and to me at times "drawling"—which accents the wit—and the other stanzaic variations lend variety—and each form suits the function it performs in the narrative—the raillery may be gentle—but it is trenchant:—there's so much real social criticism compassed in such a small space—
>
> [. . .] The note of irony which is so frequently struck by our people is missing in our poetry.[77]

Brown's genealogy of satire focuses on English origins because these are the high-water mark for the couplet, the crucial medium for the Augustan wit of Pope, Dryden, and Swift. Eliot and Pound recognized the couplet's high entry cost, as Eliot removed his Pope- and Swift-inspired "Fresca" couplets because, as Pound noted, he lacked Pope's skill in the form. The "drawling" here is not some native syncopation belonging to Johnson's voice, or Brown's ears, but the same fluid relation to the couplet tradition for which Brown would later praise Cullen.[78] Johnson's "drawl" nonetheless suggests that his lines might become a literary embodiment of the (shockingly black) Unknown Soldier's "loose, long stride." The goal then might seem to be a positive form of rhythmic racing that does not depend on presumed folk source or nativeness. These were already co-opted in the blunt cadences of Vachel Lindsay, the popularized form of the cakewalk, or the "chaotic parades of arpeggios" in "pseudo-rag."[79] Like the cakewalk's mockery of white pretensions, Johnson's drawl and stride are raced only at a second order, a figurative syncopation of America's military-poetic footsteps that Brown identifies as his "note of irony." This version of rhythmic, racial becoming proceeds through the double irony of adopting a mode of satire marked as white to mock white nationalism and its racial spectatorship.

The process of drafting the poem shows how Johnson builds on and modulates the Anglophone metrical tradition. As with Hopkins there is variation but not of the sort he celebrated as akin to when a musician "varies a theme." With the exception of a few shortened lines, the first four sections and thirty quatrains are written in heroic couplets. The drafts suggest that although the poem was written quickly, Johnson did take the time to return almost obsessively to certain lines to manipulate their rhythm, usually within the constraints of meter. The drafts are littered with synonym lists meant for putting together metrical lines. Yet the metrical revisions are idiosyncratic. The draft moves from anger to wit not by smoothing out irregular lines or even by introducing the conventional variations Brown likely has in mind when he calls the couplets "fluid" (caesurae, limited inversions or counterpoints, enjambments, shifts of stress) but by making lines jagged and acoustically confrontational. These revisions do not follow Johnson's own ideal of "establishing a theme" without losing it in necessary variation; rather, they parody meter's illusion of order, despairing that its harmonic resolution of dissonance aestheticizes a broken world. Johnson does so to detach meter from its tradition and audience, equated here with the KKK and nationalist groups, to parody their use of meter and scansion. Outside the rhetorical realm of the half-sung and antiphonal sermon, Johnson's black meter brings irony into its very core, a disfiguring presence that figures meter as a symbol if not engine of a racist order.

Several of the revisions suggest that Johnson was trying to make his poem a bouquet of blunt, arch-Augustan metrical and rhetorical effects. Before settling on the heavily alliterative and bouncily metrical second line "Hung heavy on the hands of all in heaven" Johnson tried out five different ornate, bad, less metrically regular lines, including "Hung like a heavy opiate in heaven" (requiring a three-syllable "opiate"—and are there light opiates?) alongside a list of metrically distinct adjectives—"tedious, soporific, monotonous, somnolent"—so monotonously florid that Johnson could not have missed the irony of using them to help render his line metrically tedious. One quatrain, concerned with the gathering of peoples for revelation day, stands out for its prosodic, rhetorical, and descriptive hyperbole:

> Swift-winged heralds of heaven flew back and forth
> Out of the east, to the south, the west, the north,
> Giving out quick commands, and yet benign,
> Marshaling the swarming milliards into line.

Johnson heavily worked and reworked these lines. The first line came about in part after Johnson played with several patterns of scansion, indicated through the same classical symbols he forbade in his teaching. The mock-epic collocation "swift-winged heralds" was for Johnson a choriambic (— ˘ ˘ —) or dactylic (— ˘ ˘) opening leading into a triple rhythm. Here — = long and ˘ = short, though Johnson converts this pattern into stress and unstress: / x x /, with "wingèd" made disyllabic. The second line had several incarnations, each with different ordering of the directions, suggesting that the final form exists largely for its rhythmic contour. This, like the previous line, begins in triple feet before shifting back to iambs. The third line is more metrically regular but was heavily modified to contain the flourish of a syntactically ornate hendiadys. Drafted as some variant of "directing and guiding every tongue and nation," the final form chooses the syntactic transformation that pushes the adjective "benign" to the end of the line and in so doing regularizes the meter. The fourth line brings these lines "into line" with the more regular rhythm that guides most of the quatrains. It is as if he invites us to scan so that we can assure ourselves that the meter is there (which it is).

The Prosody of Passing

James Weldon Johnson's draft of a quatrain in "Saint Peter Relates an Incident of the Resurrection Day." Courtesy of the Beinecke.

    Why, if Johnson excluded traditional scansion from the poet's toolbox, preferring (in typically modernist fashion) a more "musical" ideal, do his "modulations" here seem so canned and vestigial? He is in part parodying metrical culture—the angels "chanting the selfsame choral aeon after aeon"—and yet Johnson knows how poets like McKay, Cullen, and he himself in poems like "O Black and Unknown Bards" (written 1908, published 1917) carefully modulate meter to great effect and not as an escape from questions of race. How then does Johnson's parody become a parody of whiteness and racism, rather than the typical modernist rejection of older forms? The answer comes at the end of the poem in the new black rhythm figured by the soldier's "loose, long stride." At that moment we see the full fruits of Johnson's rhythmic interpretation, the way he lends his feet (no longer classical, but almost literal) to the Unknown Soldier's embodiment. This sets in relief Johnson's willful failure to "modulate" the white meters that frame the angels, the KKK, and other nationalist groups. He parodies meter's reception and production by the double audience, which hears black meter as a mode of passing and anything with swing as authentic.

The drafts show that Johnson also edited lines to disfigure metrical regularity. These are not "variations" that enhance the sense of musicality but rather marked refusals to secure the couplet form. As such they bear the trace of their former homogeneity, and they do so both in sonic raggedness and in content that itself concerns rhythmic movement or linear organization. In each case I have underlined the irregular moments—namely, additional syllables between stresses or stresses in normally unstressed positions. Supplementary accents show the underlying pentameter:

"their voices show the strain" → "their tone revealed voice strain."

"and then the line was thrown into the flurry" → "Then, through the long line ran a sudden flurry

"Gave rise to another puzzling question" → "Gaveríse to a ráther mètaphýsical quéstion" → "Gave ríse to a ráther níce metaphýsical quéstion" ("nice" forces the first syllable of "meta" out of its previously stressed position)

"directing, guiding [every tongue and nation]" → "guiding and shepherding [every tongue and nation]" → "directing and guiding every tongue and nation" → "Giving out quick commands, and yet benign" (see above)

Beneath these lines Johnson writes out a distinctly non-iambic five stress pattern: ᵕ ᵕ — ᵕ — ᵕ ᵕ — ᵕ — ᵕ ᵕ — . This pattern of inserted double offstresses nearly matches the alternative that begins "directing and guiding." The scansion reflects how these examples all overload, counterpoint, or stretch the iambic line found in their first iterations (the fourth eventually resolves into regular meter but ornate syntax). Pairing anti-metrical distortion with the overdose of vestigial rhetoric and pseudo-classical inventions, Johnson creates a deliberately frayed poetics that sets in relief the false relation elsewhere between metrical and social order. Angels "chanting the selfsame choral, aeon after aeon" and "The G.A.R., the D.A.R., the legion" line up "compliantly" in plot and form: these were lines that Sterling Brown and his wife recited and laughed over again and again. Thinking back to Johnson's lectures on meter, one sees a poignant contrast between free "modulation" that allows meter to refresh itself and a composition that willfully disturbs the ground so the weeds of the "great white" tradition can grow. This occurs repeatedly in the poem, with alternate lines diverging from the base pattern before snapping back to attention with brutal consequences. For instance, after the Unknown Soldier is revealed to be black:

Bedlam: They clam<u>ored, they</u> railed, some roared, some bleated:	[extra syllables]
All of them felt that somehow they'd been cheated.	[strict]
The question rose: <u>What</u> to <u>do</u> with him, then?	[mismatches of stress]
The Klan was all for burying him again.	[strict]

Johnsons is cakewalking here, parodying the Klan's movements through the same mechanicity against which he cautioned his students. Going a step beyond the self-mocking rigidity of George Reginald Margetson, whose satire I discuss in the next chapter, Johnson plays with modulation itself, with the core historical defense of meter as capable of conveying musicality and natural speech. Through its vestigial obsolescence he mocks a nationalist racism (as embodied in the treatment of the Negro Gold Star mothers) that even when it plays at syncopation never truly skips a beat.

It is against this critique that the poem's other modulation takes form. The syncopation of section 5 is not merely "black" but a variant on variation. It is a modulation that goes to the heart of measure and wrenches the decasyllabic line into a heterogeneous form that is, like the sermons of *God's Trombones*, no longer trackable or scannable by ears trained for the syllable play of Dryden and Pope. As the poem shifts into antiphony, with the italicized text of "Deep River" printed as a quasi-antiphony for "singing" Saint Peter, the quatrains in regular typeface begin to "drawl" in a new formal sense: shifting from variation at the level of the line toward a large-scale stanzaic disturbance.

> I rushed to the gate and flung it wide
> Singing, he entered <u>with</u> a loose, long stride;
> Singing and swinging <u>up</u> the golden street,
> The music married <u>to</u> the tramping of his feet (ll. 146-49)

These lines are still near enough to heroic couplets that syncopation can be perceived in the missed beats on the underlined syllables "with," "up," and "to." The second and third lines still scan as iambic pentameter (mismatches of stress in bold):

```
Singing, he entered with a loose, long stride;
  W S     W S W    S  W  S    W   S
```

The following stanza, however, shifts to a completely different "singing" analogue:

> Tall, black, soldier-angel marching alone,
> Swinging up the golden street, saluting at the great white throne.
> Singing, singing, singing, singing clear and strong.
> Singing, singing, singing, till heaven took up the song:
> > *Deep river, my home is over Jordan,*
> > *Deep river, I want to cross over into camp-ground.* (ll. 150-55)

Returning to Johnson's drafts, we can see in process a striking transformation. In the first line he added and then removed the word "all" from "marching all alone," thereby avoiding more regular alteration of stress at the line end (a position where metrical regularity usually asserts itself). Into the second line he inserted the words "great white"—a massive addition of phonological material and weight, rendering the line completely excessive to the iambic pentameter base still present in the preceding stanza. The third line was initially "singing, singing, singing, so sweet and strong," which could still count as a highly counterpointed iambic line. The fourth "singing" makes that impossible and brings the line into parallelism with the fourth line, a full six-beat alexandrine that splits into two measures (three beats and an implied rest each). The fourth line was initially "The angels listened and heaven took up his song," an even more regular line. In other words, the entire stanza began like the rest of the "angry" poem as bluntly modulated heroic couplets. Scansion needs to be flexible to find iambics in the drafts—it might better scan as trochaic, though the rest of the poem is iambic—but they are certainly more present than in the final version:

```
    Tall, black soldier-angel marching all alone
(W) S      W   S W    S W   S   W    S W S
[hexameter, headless]

    Swinging up the golden street, saluting the throne
(W) S  W   S  W   S W    S       W S W  x    S
[hexameter, headless, one unfooted/syncopated
syllable]

    Singing, singing, singing, so sweet and strong
    W S      W S      W S   |  W  S    W   S
```

```
[iambic with three inversions, or trochaic with a
syncopation of "so"]

The angels listened and heaven took up his song
 W   S W      S     x    W    S      W  S  W   S
[one unfooted syllable/syncopation]
```

The scansion clearly fails to show rigid iambics, but it does show the pull of isometric (equal length) accentual-syllabic verse (here, alternating stress). Like Hopkins—but not Millay—the final "Saint Peter" version overthrows iambic scansion. The first line is closer to pentameter but farther from the following lines and thus from isometricality):

```
Tall, black, soldier-angel marching alone,
 S     W       S   W      S   W     S   x  S
[unfooted syllable]
Swinging up the golden street, saluting at the great
 S   W   S   W    S     W        W S W    S   W    S
white throne.       [heptameter]
  W     S
Singing, singing, singing, singing clear and strong.
 S   W    S   W    S   W    S   W    S    W    S
     [hexameter]
Singing, singing, singing, till heaven took up the
 S   W    S   W    S   W    x    S     W   S  W
song:
 S
[hexameter with syncopation or heptameter with a
silent beat before "till"]
```

The drafts suggest a manic desire to have the word "singing" override whatever hint there was of an alternative, iambic meter. Like the word "whispering" in Frost's "Mowing," "singing" is at once a narrative figure that displaces an alien, formal sound and the material means for that disruption at the level of scansion. The long, looping cursive *g*s even serve to cross out the abandoned, iambic fourth line: there is no other mark to erase it. Like the crush of long syllables (and cross-outs) needed to scan Hopkins, anti-metrical "singing" visibly as much as acoustically repudiates the metrical line.

These couplets no longer permit iambic scansion. Though lacking the

⑨

Peter — I ran down to the gate and flung it wide,
Singing, he entered with a loose, long stride,
Singing, and swung up the golden street.
The music beat out a rhythm — to his feet
Tall, black soldier-angel march — alone
Swung up the golden street, saluting at the throne
Singing, singing, singing so sweet and strong
till heaven took up his song

   Deep River — My home is over Jordan
   Deep River — I want to cross over into campground.

The tale was done,
The angelic hosts dispersed,
But till after
There ran through heaven
Something that day
Twixt tears and laughter.

James Weldon Johnson's draft of the end of section 5 of "Saint Peter." Courtesy of the Beinecke.

direct allusion to musical support in the italicized refrain from "Deep River," Johnson's transformation into longer, two-measure lines brings us toward a quasi-musical measure of the sort seen in John Brown's hidden hymnal fourteeners. The drafts show a transformation within the final quatrain, which mirrors the poem's hoped-for "crossing over" into a post-Revelation, post-diasporic prosody. Indeed, the singular variation we see in the transcribed spiritual is the insertion of "Lord" and an accompanying relineation similar to Johnson's stretched final quatrain:

> *Deep river, my home is over Jordan,*
> *Deep river,*
> *Lord,*
> *I want to cross over into camp-ground.* (ll. 142-45)

The rhythmic convergence of Saint Peter's sermon and the spiritual in the form of the poem is more asymptotic than suggested by the line "heaven took up the song." Johnson's horizon of circulation, both the two hundred people to whom he sent the original printing and the wider audience of the 1935 edition, is hardly equivalent to the "angelic hosts" who take up the spiritual. Babylon is still hovering over prosody, as it does in "Lift Every Voice and Sing," also reprinted by Johnson in 1935: "lest our feet stray from the places [. . .] where we met Thee." All of the anxieties Johnson expresses through his career about audition (the "long convention" that dictates the hearing of dialect, the continued dependence on the reader's uncertain "ear," the figurality of "black music") persist in the formal fissure between Saint Peter's speech and the italicized song of the unknown soldier. We cannot see his "loose, long stride" and we cannot hear him "singing clear and strong," and so the new "marriage" of "singing and swinging" is at once spectacular and phenomenologically obscure. The final emotion of the poem is appropriately "something that quivered/'twixt tears and laughter":

> The tale was done,
> The angelic hosts dispersed,
> But not till after
> There ran through heaven
> Something that quivered
> 'twixt tears and laughter. (ll. 156-61)

What Johnson accomplishes, both personally in the revisions and formally in the poem, is a new trajectory for a black poetics of the metrical vestige, which hovers 'twixt the piercing prosodic satire with which the poem begins and the spiritual with which its penultimate stanza closes. The final stanza, an isolated sestet, leaves heaven resounding with a rhythm that has no obvious prosodic form at all: an embodiment of a "something that quivered/ 'twixt tears and laughter." Johnson's poem is a sustained rhythmic interpretation of this amorphous laughter-suffering: a prosodic analysis of how black forms and subjects (including the Negro Gold Star mothers) circulate in contemporary America. Like Toomer's "Song of the Son," and working in full awareness of the problem of the double audience and Kabnis's crisis of audition, "Saint Peter" ultimately knows what Frost, Douglas Johnson, and other poets of the metrical vestige recognize: that it has departed from given rhythmic and performative traditions before an alternate phenomenology is in place. Resetting the conditions for audition and performance against modernity's racialized genealogies of form was central to Johnson's career as teacher, scholar, and poet; as the next chapter shows, this radically heterogeneous conception of the prosodic tradition defines Sterling Brown's critical and poetic response to the African American poetic tradition.

6 Folk Iambics

Sterling Brown's *Outline for the Study of the Poetry of American Negroes*

> Why should the world be over-wise,
> In counting all our tears and sighs?
>
> —Paul Laurence Dunbar, "We Wear the Mask"

In the previous chapter, I studied how Jean Toomer and James Weldon Johnson mark the inadequacy and dangers of rhythmic conceptions of black subjectivity and collectivity. They prove how, from its earliest and most recognizable moments, the poetics and prosody of the New Negro Renaissance emerges from a tense interchange with then-prevailing cultural ideals of black embodiment, musicality, and rhythm. The vestigial presence of traditional versification in each writer's oeuvre undermines the modernist turn to racialized rhythms of presumed organicism and authenticity. This is an ironic fulfillment of Kofi Agawu's speculation that "a determined researcher" could "quite easily invent 'European rhythm'" just as easily as they invented "African" rhythm.[1] Working in vestigial form shows all rhythm to be invention, usually from an Anglo-European position.

In this chapter I bring that argument forward into the 1930s and beyond through attention to the poetry and critical writings of Sterling Brown, whose sophisticated adoption of traditional Anglo-American prosody registers an integral part of African American heritage. Not only Brown but the diverse set of poets he studies counter the identification of racialized, vernacular rhythm as the necessary medium of black expressivity. Like the "elastic" concept of rhythm Jaji observes in the case of Léopold Senghor, modernist definitions of rhythm—and certainly black rhythm—proved too expansive and programmatic for Brown.[2] Elasticity permitted the primitivism of Pound or Vachel Lindsay and the general conflation of form with musical style that critics like Brent Hayes Edwards have been at such pains to disentangle and reread. Once blackness and rhythm are intertwined, other historical prosodies face withering accusations of mere gentility or passing. Brown's poetry, essays, letters, and editorial work perform a prosodic balancing act between such overdetermined pasts. He sensed from the beginning of his career the potential collapse of black poetics under the weight of racialized ideologies and responded by actively constructing his own metrical vestiges rather than letting others discover their own projected roots.

Following Edwards, who assigned James Weldon Johnson's *Book of American Negro Poetry* a "central role" in the New Negro movement,[3] I argue that Brown's study companion to the second (1931) edition of Johnson's anthology (*Outline for the Study of the Poetry of American Negroes*) demands a reevaluation of Anglo-American prosodic form as a productive force within the New Negro Renaissance. This chapter reveals not only the *Outline*'s formalism but its effort to reveal nuanced relations between traditional form and race as the latter is framed within American society. In the spirit of Brown's guide, I revisit some of the anthology's poetry in terms of its (frequently explicit) formal investments. I have already explored, in chapter 4, how Georgia Douglas Johnson's poetry manages the overdetermination of prosody by both gender and racial discourses. Brown's *Outline* points to the engagement with prosodic traditions—especially Victorian prosody—that let poets like Douglas Johnson situate themselves in and against expectations for raced and gendered form. In the second half of this chapter, I emphasize how Brown's own poetry builds upon this genealogy of an African American metrical vestige. His heterogeneous prosody responds, like the tradition detailed in the *Outline*, to the homogenizing demand for a native, vernacular poetics rooted in ideas of black rhythm.

"Black" Rhythm's Double Audience

The reception of African American poets in the 1910s and 1920s was conditioned by works like Vachel Lindsay's 1914 *The Congo*, a poem Brown later parodied as "The New Congo" ("with no apologies to Vachel Lindsay").[4] Lindsay strove to produce black- or African-sounding rhythms with sequences of trochees, meant to imitate tom-toms, like "Boomlay, boomlay, boomlay, boom." The poem instructs us to chant in a "deep rolling bass" as natives, now in double-timed trochees, "béat an èmpty bárrel wìth the hándle òf a bróom." As Lorenzo Thomas has shown, Lindsay and others hoped modernity might be "revitalized by an infusion of energy from more instinctual peoples"; this hope, however, "comes uncomfortably close to replicating the exploitation of the same people by modern capitalism"[5] even among "negrotarians" like Waldo Frank, who were "well-meaning but compromised by voyeuristic primitivism."[6] It is no small testament to the lasting impact of such rhythmic exploitation that Melvin Tolson, decades later in "Dark Symphony" (1941, included in Brown's coedited anthology *The Negro Caravan*, 399), disdainfully marks it as a crux for black poetics:

> The centuries-old pathos in our voices
> Saddens the great white world,
> And the wizardry of our dusky rhythms
> Conjures up shadow-shapes of the ante-bellum years. (ll. 19-23)

The crux is that African American poetry's drive toward vernacular form is framed by the demands of an alien audience for black poets and bodies to perform a rhythmic, musical, and linguistic vernacular. Tolson, like the earlier poets of the New Negro Renaissance, experienced the restrictions of reception primarily in the difficulty both black and white audiences had with a poetics that wasn't markedly raced; Michael Bérubé notes how his style was viewed as an "appropriation rather than an inheritance."[7] Rhythm, I would argue, is at the core of what could count as an "inheritance" but was for this reason far from being an open form for African American poets. What Michael North has shown with regard to dialect—that its adoption by white modernists ironically restricted its availability to modern black writers—was partly the case with regard to rhythm.[8] It is less that white modernists coopted "black" rhythms, though that was certainly the case, than that white audiences had ideologically constructed expectations for "black" rhythm.[9]

Where one understanding of African American poetics sees a crucial movement from the mastery of traditional forms to mastery of the vernacular (largely blues and jazz), the poetry discussed below anticipates Tolson's modernist flattening-out of time and tradition, his folding of traditional metrics and "dusky rhythm" into each other. The lesson of Brown's study guide and Johnson's anthology as a whole is that rhythm, despite its "dusky" appearances, is not raced until its audience marks it so.[10]

The notion of rhythm and song as an organic ground for racial community has been viewed positively (and even as a necessity) from Du Bois's *The Souls of Black Folk* to critical writings of the 1920s (Hurston and Hughes, especially), the Negritude and Black Arts movements, vernacular criticism of the 1980s, and contemporary critical work on poetry and hip-hop.[11] As Meredith Martin has shown, questions of meter and rhythm have been imbricated with English national identity, imperialism, and race since at least the mid-eighteenth century,[12] and so it should not be surprising that African American poets faced by a culture of ballad collecting and prosodic prescription inherited from England and invested in the "native" would need to strain against existing prosodic ideologies.[13] For this reason it is crucial to listen to how New Negro Renaissance poets destabilized the prosodic vernacular and its relation to Anglo-American traditions. Michael Manson has argued, modifying Henry Louis Gates Jr.'s formulation, that poets do not "'mediate' or 'resolve' the black vernacular and standard English literary tradition. [. . . I]nstead they worry the line between those traditions and hence worry the line between black and white, country and city, folk and modern, oral and written."[14] The central worry I attend to here is that of an alien audience's demand for and consumption of lines in a putatively black vernacular. An explicit portrayal of this demand and its destructive effect on song emerges in the character of Eustace from Wallace Thurman's 1932 roman à clef *Infants of the Spring*. Eustace would prefer to sing a classical repertoire, refusing spirituals even "as a sop": "These darky folk songs had become his *bête noir*."[15] Eustace's abortive career represents a failure to sidestep (much less transcend) race in the search for an alternate, in this case classical and lyrical, tradition.

The painful limitations of Eustace and fellow residents of "Niggerati Manor" would seem to legitimate the recent critical shift away from the 1920s and the New Negro Renaissance as a seminal site of cultural or political development.[16] If this chapter runs retrograde, it is because Sterling Brown figures pivotally between the two decades and is thus the best place to look for patterns and trajectories (outside of Hughes's towering influence) that might have emerged from earlier twentieth-century poetry and poetics. There is no question that Brown has been central to black poetry and scholarship: as "poet, critic, scholar, activist, and head of Negro Affairs for the WPA Federal Writer's Project," he was "*the* most important black literary figure in the United States" through the early 1940s.[17] And yet it is too easy to read Brown's influence as primarily folkloric, as Hurstonian native ethnography. He certainly had access outside of middle-class and northern culture, and his diverse after-hours gatherings at Howard University had a tremendous and well-acknowledged influence. But it is easy to overplay Brown's broad interests as "a program of racially subjective folk-oriented literature" or as a lyrical apotheosis of formerly unconscious, collective poetry.[18] Brown anticipates, rather, recent critics like David Nicholls who consider the "folk" an overused "organizing trope" in African American criticism when it is in fact a "contested vision of collectivity."[19] Far from seeing pre-1930s writing as coherent because of its relative folk grounding, Brown describes early twentieth-century African American authors as "closer to O. Henry, Carl Sandburg, Edgar Lee Masters, Edna St. Vincent Millay [. . .] than to each other. The bonds of literary tradition seem to be stronger than race."[20] In a similar gesture of inclusion and heterodoxy, Brown's introduction to *Negro Poetry and Drama* (1937) is critical not so much of Victorian or Pre-Raphaelite poetry than of the uncritical adoption of past styles. Brown writes of 1930s poets, "They confine their models to the masters they learned about in school, to the Victorians, and the pre-Raphaelites. Almost as frequently they have been unaware of the finer uses of tradition."[21] This criticism parallels the multitude of nineteenth- and early twentieth-century works worried about poetasters' errant prosody. Brown eschews bad iambics or hexameters, not absent folkways, reflecting a broader cultural desire for prosodic mastery that Brown did not want equated with the presumption that nonwhites were naturally rhythmic and capable of guiding civilization away from canned meters. The instances of canonical metrics discussed here are less about proving oneself in white techniques than about avoiding equally canned "native" rhythmics that did not reflect African American poets' heritage.

Too easily fetishized and stereotyped "folk" rhythm leads Brown again and again—and leads him to show us other poets turning again and again—to the Anglo-American prosodic tradition. Brown was not alone in the 1920s and 1930s in worrying about the idea of the "folk" and its music. A number of poets, including Brown, register anxiety about the fetishistic reception of folk song and folk rhythm through allusions to Psalm 137 and its lament, "How shall we sing the Lord's song in a strange land?" As David Stowe has shown, the psalm has long represented "cultural dispossession and exile" but has had special significance for African Americans and colonial subjects in the Caribbean attempting to "challenge traditional European binaries."[22] To challenge these binaries is, this chapter argues, to challenge (rather than depend on) the racing of rhythm: however compelling the tradition of vernacular rhythm may be to poets and critics, rhythm is antedated and threatened by Babylonian demands for it. Tolson writes, just after describing the "wizardry of our dusky rhythm," "They who have shackled us / Require of us a song" (ll. 38-39). In "Lift Every Voice and Sing" (1900) James Weldon Johnson invokes rhythm and meter in the psalm's mnemonic effort: "Keep us forever in the path, we pray. / Lest our feet stray."[23] The experience of diaspora is here metrical—"weary feet" to be combatted with a "steady beat."

The challenge for Sterling Brown was to locate a "steady beat" stemming from yet altering Anglo-American traditions. His response to Johnson's "Saint Peter Relates an Incident," discussed in the previous chapter, is characteristic. When a simultaneously traditional and syncopated beat, incarnated in the "loose, long" stride of a black Unknown Soldier, becomes a source of racial identification and pride in Johnson's poem, Brown explicitly notes an ironic "wit" generated through the "fluid, and pointed, and to me at times 'drawling'" flow of the "couplet form."[24] Brown recognizes that Johnson stretches the couplet form in precisely the way the soldier surprises surrounding Klansmen—through his gait, his rhythmic pace—and hopes that Johnson and others would look for such prosodic cues in his and other poets' work.

In his first published essay, on the African American tenor Roland Hayes (1925), Brown sees in Psalm 137 and Hayes's performance a strident critique of how the black or folk vernacular was thoroughly conditioned by the demands of an audience alien both in class and race. He anticipates Johnson's definition of the black and white "double audience" in "The Dilemma of the Negro Author" (1928): the black writer's rhetorical dilemma of whom to address given an audience with "opposite and often antagonistic points of view."[25] Focusing on Hayes's rendition of Psalm 137, Brown reveals the stress fractures caused by the double audience but then finds in Hayes's repertoire a cleverly veiled assault on the appropriation of black music:

> The whites start at the wild summoning of beautiful distress. Why is there arranging of them in a cantor's song—sung by a Negro? What histrionic ability in this man to so feign passionate despair! [. . .]
>
> The Negroes brood; are stirred by something deep within, something as far away as all antiquity, as old as human wrong, as tragical as loss of worlds. What does he mean—and why are we so stirred—
>
> [. . .] required of us a song
> And they that wasted us
> Required of us mirth
>
> And a thousand of our girls prostitute their voices singing jazz for a decadent white and black craving.[26]

For Brown this scene reveals not only an obvious commodification of the black voice but a deeper irony involving the white audience's own heritage. The white audience recognizes the psalm as its own, and so Hayes's subjective expression must then be inauthentic, "feigned"; yet Brown finds it ironic that this logic is applied to a song about diaspora's threat to cultural heritage. The white audience clearly does not see this irony or the connected irony of becoming the present's Babylonians. Where they view the present as a continuation of the past, the African American audience members—in Brown's eyes—view this song of the past through the lens of the present. In Hayes's concert Brown discovers what Kimberly Benston has called the "radical historicity" of his poetry: an alternate relation of past and present that "make[s] the past available as a *hypothetical* (hence *prophetic*) version of the present."[27] Not continuity but repetition with a difference.

Hayes's complex setting of the psalm suggested to Brown a strategy for disrupting and re-encoding notions of heritage in order to defy restrictive notions of racially marked music and rhythm. The performance preempts the demands of the white audience by ironizing their efforts to set limits on the genealogy of song; at the same time, it sets in place a new form of heritage at odds with white expectations. The performance scene suggests how carefully African American poetry would need to navigate its notional vernacular tradition, a tradition offering both empowerment and danger. Whatever pride might be taken in the "spontaneity and ease" of black musicians and dancers, the visions of an unstudied, "primitive form of self-expression" noted by Thurman are a short hop from one critic's judgment of Hughes's verse as "notably self-conscious."[28] Thurman's response was characteristically blunt—"now what the hell does that mean"—but Brown engages in the subtler irony found in Hayes and, like Hayes, does so by appropriating white traditions.

Brown's letters to Weldon Johnson concerning the *Outline* couple substantial discussion of poetics, including Johnson's "polyrhythmic cadences," with heavily ironic descriptions of a literary scene defined by expectations for racially marked style. Brown's playful send-up of society hostesses who "poodlize" him and "craves to hyeah me recite my worses" lead him to a more heavily satirical version of Roland Hayes's concert:

> If I were to pull out a dialect piece on some of these Bahstonians or the word Nigger they'd swoon.—so I read them with great feeling all I can find of Watts' hymns, and Felicia Hemans: Oh Mr. Brown, we have heard of slim greer. Do let us have his exploits." So I go on dolefully—
>
> > It was in the gloaming
> > > When the moonlight it did creep

> Across the misty moorland
> Where Slim's inamorata
> Lay asleep
> Asleep
> Asleep
> In the deep.
> Peep, peep.[29]

As in Hayes's psalm performance, Brown is giving his audience the past as version and vision of the present. Slim Greer embodies (for the Bahstonians) the stereotype of the "naturally musical black"[30] but here wears Victorian drag to signify his audience's vestigial tropes (just as elsewhere he parodies fourteeners, the metrical form of balladry, "a'pattin' the time/ with No. Fourteen shoes"[31]). Brown's nonce poem is a parody of a "Bahstonian" parlor scene still reading Hemans in spirit though clamoring for new "worses" and also a pastiche of his own refusal to reject supposedly vestigial Victorianisms.

Brown's wrangling with expectation is not limited to his white or bourgeois audience. He is equally cautious with Johnson's efforts to define his poetics. In his counter-definitions he anticipates the fine-tuning that would go into the questions of the *Outline*; above all Brown is concerned that he not be taken as a bardic continuation of the "so called folk epics." He repeatedly refers to his own formal efforts as "congruous" to rather than imitations of folk form. His lexical and rhythmic vernacular—what Michael Harper calls his "poet's vernacular"—is a "variation" on folk elements, a search for "fitting structures [. . .] such as the clipped line, the blues form, the refrain poem, etc—all with my own variations."[32] He takes folk ballads as "indices to folk life, never [. . .] ultimate sources."[33] Brown's vocabulary of congruity, variation, and index all recall the mediatedness of the past. In terms of Brown's poetics, this means that contemporary forms and meters can generate "congruity" though lacking explicit "folk" heritage. Congruity contrasts with presumptive vernacular lineage, and in Brown's *Outline* we see a crucial effort to systematically explore its diverse instantiations across New Negro Renaissance poetry.[34]

Brown's *Outline* and Johnson's *Book of American Negro Poetry*

Johnson suggested the *Outline* to Brown in the fall of 1930, thinking it might be modeled after Elizabeth Lay Green's *The Negro in Contemporary American Literature* (1928). Green's guide gives brief descriptions of poets, separating "rather conventional" poets like Georgia Douglas Johnson ("Note the absence of racial self-consciousness") from "modernists" and "black renaissance" poets who either experiment "as does the white modernist" (Fenton Johnson's free verse) or, in the case of Cullen, can be compared to Millay owing to his "effective handling of metre and rhythm." The categories of "conventional" and "modernist" are predictable, though Cullen's and Millay's inclusion in the latter camp is intriguing. The guide says nothing about how to scan or, more importantly, interpret prosodic choices, though Langston Hughes does receive mention for his "use of jazz rhythms and colloquial phrasing."[35] The prosodic acumen so important to poets like Douglas Johnson becomes here an opaque signifier for grouping.

By contrast, the *Outline* avoids grouping by redefining heritage as a heterogeneous prosodic field charged, as a whole, with responding to the corruptive expectation for raced rhythms. Brown's *Outline* begins by asking students to reflect on Weldon Johnson's two prefaces (1922 and 1931). Four of Brown's first six questions concern Johnson's attitude toward black music, in particular ragtime and spirituals. Ragtime matters to Johnson and Brown because its racial origins could be obscured by subsequent appropriation;[36] spirituals were appropriated, by contrast, as positive evidence of a native American folk form:[37] "In the 'spirituals,' or slave songs, the Negro has given America not only its only folksongs, but a mass of noble music."[38] In the case of spirituals, Johnson, unlike Eustace or Roland Hayes, is happy to grant this appropriation.

Brown is far more ambivalent about associations with earlier folk forms. His comments suggest that the category of the "folk" problematically circumscribes aesthetic practices that are not defined by race. Through a set of fairly open-ended questions posed in connection with Weldon Johnson's second preface, Brown invites readers to challenge or at least complicate the preference for "genuine folk stuff":

> 4. Explain (p. 6): "Several of the group have dug down into the genuine folk stuff—I mention genuine folk stuff in contradistinction to the artificial folk stuff of the dialect school."
> 5. Discuss (p. 7): "An artist accomplishes his best when working at his best with material he knows best."[39]

The questions mark the imprecision of "genuine folk stuff": Is it the underlying "racial conflict and contact" out of which "the best poems rise," or is it "folk sources [like] the blues and work songs"?[40] Johnson likely means both, identifying the best work—including his poems modeled on spirituals and sermons—as driven by racial conflict to embrace raced, vernacular forms.

Though Brown's poetry and much of what is now associated with the New Negro Renaissance may seem to follow this formula, many of the poets in Johnson's anthology assert themselves in relation to other literary "material" without by that act separating themselves from the complexities and conflicts of race. Like the epigraphs in *The Souls of Black Folk*, which bring Byron and Arthur Symons to bear on civil rights, Brown's *Outline* as well as his poetry work toward a broader recognition of the New Negro Renaissance's intertextual underpinnings. The primary means by which both the *Outline* and his poetry do this work is by attending to and practicing prosodic diversity.

Brown's approach to prosody is not intrinsically raced. He derives his definition of "accent" from R. F. Brewer's popular textbook *Orthometry*; to explain "feet" he scans lines from both Fenton Johnson and Longfellow. For most of the anthology's sonnets, Brown asks some variation of "Notice the form and tell the type." R. Nathaniel Dett's idiosyncratic "The Rubenstein Staccato Étude" is described as "a metrical *tour de force* or experiment";[41] Brown asks, "How does the rhythm suggest the subject matter?"[42] and then evokes a longer history of experimental prosody by inviting students to consider debts to Poe and Sidney Lanier, nineteenth-century prosodists interested in musical scansions. Though Dett's poem is not about race, the question of how prosodic form intersects with "subject matter" prepares the reader to ask how diverse prosodic forms might intersect with race in the anthology's racially themed works.

Where Green's guide limits appreciation of verse form in poets like Georgia Douglas Johnson or William Stanley Braithwaite to vague lyricism, Brown heightens the student's sense of formal intertextuality. George Reginald Margetson's "Fledgling Bard and the Poetry Society" (1916) satirically employs traditional forms in an ironic quest to "find the new, the modern school/Where science trains the fledgling bard to fly."[43] Brown asks the reader to "Notice the verse forms" and points toward Margetson's frequent use of Wordsworth's stanza from "Resolution and Independence."[44] The poem then turns to its own verse form, mocking its author as "A rustic ranting rhymer like by chance/Who thinks that he can make the muses dance/By beating on some poet's borrowed lyre."[45] Margetson's use of a Wordsworthian stanza shows a preference for borrowed and markedly inadequate forms, yet the decision to dwell in historical meters turns out to be caused by the incongruity of race and form in America:

> The Scotchman tunes his pipe and drum,
> Old Ireland's Harp is never dumb,
> We make our rag-time banjo hum
> To Uncle Sam's swift pace.[46]

Where Weldon Johnson admires Synge's Irish literary nationalism,[47] Margetson exposes the rift between racial vernacular and national form in America. The gap between the "rag-time banjo" and "Uncle Sam's swift pace" pushes Margetson toward traditional iambic forms: a conscious, satirical investment in prosodic vestiges similar to Brown's Victorian Slim Greer poem.

Brown's *Outline* leverages traditional form and prosody against presumed racial lineage most directly when it arrives at Countee Cullen. Though Weldon Johnson's headnote calls Cullen's race "pure irrelevance," Brown persists in asking students, "Is Countee Cullen a 'Negro' poet?" That Brown poses the question despite Johnson's and Cullen's own reticence forces a reconsideration of what the question entails. In his comments on "Yet Do I Marvel," Brown asks his reader to reconsider the question of Cullen's race not from the poet's perspective but in terms of reception: in terms of the de facto racing that must occur in the context of an anthology of "Negro" poetry.

In response to the poem's epigrammatic finale—"Yet do I marvel at this curious thing:/To make a poet black, and bid him sing!"—Brown asks, "Why would the irony of 'this curious thing' be especially striking to a poet of the Keatsian type?"[48] The question is a difficult one because it is not immediately clear what the relation is between a poet of the "Keatsian type" and a poet who is black. The answer to Brown's question is that to be Keatsian is to be made for song, but that to be black is to be barred from an affiliation with Keats (and thus with song). Cullen's poem counters this logic by suggesting that before God made the poet black, the poet made himself Keatsian. Previously, the poem had found divine logic behind a range of seemingly painful facts (why "the little buried mole continues blind"). In the last couplet, however, God's plan seems truly at cross-purposes with itself, and only the poet's self-legislative prowess can overcome the dissonance. Yet Brown's question, focusing on an English poet synonymous with innate and melodious lyricism, suggests that the divine plan is less at stake than are the contingencies and expectations of contemporary reception. The poem reflects the perspective of a broader reading public that saw no "curious thing" at all in bidding a black poet sing—but that held a highly specialized notion of black song. In asking his readers to note the "especially striking" irony, Brown suggests that prevailing notions about the role of the Anglo-American tradition in African American poetry are what generate Cullen's irony. The "curious thing" is not song but expectations for specific kinds of song and a resistance to African American ownership of other cultural capital. Throughout his *Outline* Brown pushes readers to find nothing curious in the agency of traditional Anglo-American forms.

Cullen is well known for refusing, as he puts it in his introduction to *Caroling Dusk* (1927), "nebulous atavistic yearnings toward an African inheritance" in favor of the "rich background of English and American poetry."[49] Brown would also seem reject "atavistic yearnings," yet when he introduces himself in *Caroling Dusk* he also parodies his yearnings for traditional metrics: "From early years I have lisped in numbers but the numbers seem improper fractions."[50] The allusion to Pope's "Epistle to Dr. Arbuthnot" ("I lisped in numbers") hints at Brown's own "rich background" but then allows the archaism for verse—"numbers"—to disintegrate into "improper fractions." The joke implies that what makes his poetic "background" "rich" is a degree of impropriety and syncopation, but whether that is Popean or derived from a black tradition is a toss-up. Although Brown shares Cullen's desire to counter simplified notions of vernacular tradition and although he, like Cullen, sees traditional prosody as a means to this end, his verse and criticism seek to balance and play vernacular and traditional form against each other. The result is a poetics that renews the vernacular by inviting traditional forms to operate playfully (as in the mock Slim poem) in and against a context overdetermined by an expectation for vernacular forms.

"When de Saints Go Ma'ching Home"

Michael Manson has elegantly shown the extent to which Brown's oeuvre traverses the "hard line" drawn by much criticism between his vernacular practices, commonly associated with musical black collectivity, and the "flexible rhythmic line" of traditional meter that historically supported a "lyrical" or "individuated subjectivity."[51] Both past and contemporary critics have rejected absolute divisions between folk culture and poetic "subjectivity." But the most common critical effort to cancel this divide has been to suggest, as did the reviewer of Langston Hughes mocked by Wallace Thurman, that some black poets somehow transcended the collectivity insinuated by their rhythms and became "notably self-conscious." R. T. Kerlin's 1923 anthology *Negro Poets and Their Poems*, for instance, raises the model provided by Wordsworth in the *Lyrical Ballads*: black poets might continue to recover and render lyric—against an "artificial age"—the "simplicity, sincerity, veracity" of America's native folk form.[52] The idea that Brown and other New Negro Renaissance figures rendered folk tradition as lyric is, in Virginia Jackson's formulation, a critical "lyricization" of historical poetics; as discussed in chapter 5, lyricization and especially modern ballad theory overdetermine Jean Toomer's poetics; but in Brown's case, the notion of becoming "lyric" crucially fails to account for the irony with which he treats both ostensible "folk sources" and, as the following readings show, supposed lyrical apotheoses. To conceive of modern black poetry along the generic lines of the "lyrical ballad" is to overlook English literary history's vesting of "explanatory power" in that otherwise "awkward, transitional form" and to miss the formative potency of awkwardly hybrid modes in Brown.[53] More accurate is John S. Wright's point that "Brown treated the products of folk imagination as [already] *self-conscious* wisdom,"[54] and yet this formulation may still sideline the intertextuality of Brown's poetics and prosody. David Anderson, attempting to redefine Brown's view of folk culture as non-static, continues to read the traditional prosody of "Vestiges" (the final section of *Southern Road* [1932]) as an "aesthetic dead end" that can only mark the "gulf separating poetic creation from community interest."[55] If Brown saw such a gulf, he certainly refused to restrict it to "vestigial" poetic creation; his "improper fractions" rupture the continuity of genre, tradition, and voice latent in both Anglo-American "lyric" and communal "folk sources."

Brown's first published poem, "When de Saints Go Ma'ching Home,"[56] represents a trenchant effort to discompose the generic and prosodic options being pressed upon African American poetry. It exemplifies what Michael Harper calls the "both/and" choice of tradition and vernacular in Brown's work but adds the critical "neither" that Manson has traced across a broader range of poems. This "neither" is not, of course, a refusal of either tradition; as Kimberly Benston has argued, Brown gives us a "modernization" and "reconstruction" of the past that refuses lyric's notional immediacy and continuity. In place of an abstract lyric voice emerging naturally from folk tradition, Brown's "quest is for a performative and declamatory moment that supersedes immediate experience and invites exploration of *selfhood as possibility*."[57] Benston also notes the pressures that forged this poetics; Brown's problem with dialect, for example, lies less in its debased portrayal of black subjects (James Weldon Johnson's position) than in its "covertly totalizing" force for "the reading public." The hybrid prosody of "Saints" rejects that totalizing force within contemporary reception.

Brown wrote a number of poems that seem to treat folk singers as authentic, individualized, lyric performers of folk collectivity. Yet although Brown undoubtedly gives special place to singers like Ma Rainey, who "sings our song" and "jes' gits hold of us dataway," Brown take pains to differentiate his poetry and person from authenticity grounded in a racial collectivity. The poem's subject is the power of the blues, sung here by Big Boy Davis, to express both individual and collective yearning. This might augur an archetypal instance of modern black poetics transforming a vernacular tradition into written lyric. Yet the transformation, though desired, obscures rather than reinforces a narrative of synthesis. Robert Stepto has elegantly described how the poem arcs from its dedication to Davis, "Chased Out of Town for Vagrancy," to the possibility of new forms of community birthed by Brown's own written echo of Davis. In the first section of the poem Davis's "singing re-creates the conditions in which shared performative events may fittingly close"; in the fifth section "Big Boy sings himself into the chant" and "a certain exhilarating vision of community in both this and another world is complete"; in the final section, when Davis leaves his audience and the narrator alone with their thoughts, "the primacy of the total group performance over and above an individual's singing of a song is once more underscored."[58] Stephen Henderson finds, in Davis's concert, "a microcosm of the musical tradition [of the blues]" and in the "series of portraits evoked by the music [. . .] an emblem of folk society framed by the consciousness and craft of the poet."[59] This reading suggests not only the unity of a musical tradition and its folk, but an equally unified presence of folk and tradition within the mediating poetic "consciousness" and "craft" that give the reader access to Davis's song. Yet although Davis's performance does create a vivid collective portrait that the audience hopes to echo, there remains the fact of Davis's final removal from the narrator. And how precisely does Brown's "craft" transform the blues tradition that the narrator encounters (and that we encounter through the narrator)? How might the poem's prosody, echoing the narrative distance between Davis, narrator, and audience, negotiate the poem's own performance: not the song Davis sings but our collective performance as historically situated readers?

Although Brown uses accentual verse to represent Davis's song for the reader, he consistently frames both Davis and narrator in iambic pentameter. This metrical mediation questions the poem's vision of collectivity, as does Brown's active reframing of Davis's words and song through the narrator. The refusal to unambiguously represent the blues man in a moment of lyrical self-transformation leads, at the end of the poem, to a conspicuous separation of Davis from the narrator, audience, and reader. If Brown can be said to create the improvisational written form Stepto finds, it is not through shared blues prosody but through the heterogeneous poetics at work in Johnson's anthology and Brown's *Outline*—a poetics that needed to be taught, practiced, and actively recognized.

In the poem's first section the narrator sets the stage for Davis's concert. The second section directly transcribes Davis's song. Though this division of folk song and interpreter is blurred in later sections, what blending there is initially tends to transplant Davis's voice into iambics. The thirty-seven lines of the first section are written largely in strict or loose iambic pentameter, as when the speaker describes Big Boy's preparations: "He'd tune up specially for this. There'd be / No chatter now, no patting of the feet. / After a few slow chords, knelling and sweet—" (ll. 12-14). The enjambment of "There'd be" is one of several that help fill out the traditional line by breaking apart syntax, indicating that prosody is following neither song nor the rhythm of speech but rather breaking speech into preformed metrical units. The mild metrical inversions ("After," "knelling") recall traditional manipulations of iambic verse. Brown further differentiates metrical speech from what could be called "vernacular" by framing both Davis's speech and song within the fixed verse form: "He'd say, / 'My mother's favorite.' And we knew / That what was coming was his chant of saints" (ll. 5-7). Davis does not sing a "chant of saints": this is a rephrasing oriented toward meter. Even Davis's lyrics seem to fit into an iambic cadence, sometimes more regularly than the speaker's words:

```
For he would see
A gorgeous procession to "de Beulah Land,"—
Of saints—his friends—"a-climbin' fo' deir wings."
   W   S    W      S       W   S  W   S    W    S
```

The division between Davis's song and its poetic emergence is reinforced by the initial description of Davis's voice, which comes not in pentameter but in an extremely stiff pair of fourteeners: "Deep the bass would rumble while the treble scattered high, / For all the world like heavy feet a-trompin' toward the sky" (ll. 25-26). Oddly enough, Brown's use of a metrical form associated with the Plantation school[60] aligns him with Davis's own participation in stereotypes (a saint's pomade of "hoggrease," for instance). Stepto notes how Brown "willingly runs the risk of creating 'plantation' stereotypes" in such moments to affirm the everyday nature of his saints,[61] but it is not clear what sort of "everyday" element the fourteeners, not to mention the pentameter, admit into the poem. The "heavy feet" of the fourteeners may gesture to poetic song, but if so, they suggest a written form struggling toward a musical form free from either outright mimicry or off-putting historical echoes.

The poem's second section is composed entirely of Big Boy's verses, which vary widely in syllable count and stress location:

Ole Deacon Zachary
With de asthmy in his chest,
A puffin' an' a-wheezin'
Up de golden stair; (ll. 39-43)

The challenge of forming these rhythms is the challenge of knowing Big Boy's style, and the accentual-syllabic verse of the first section cannot prepare the reader for this task. The poem asks, with its sharp prosodic shifts, What reader could scan the subtleties of the blank verse, sense the historical resonances of fourteeners, and perform the text-setting operation necessary to hear Davis's song? What reader has the critical distance of Slim Greer, gleefully "a'pattin' the time / with No. Fourteen shoes," not shackled in tradition but "pattin" on it—unlike Vachel Lindsay's "Barrel-house kings, with feet unstable"?

Sections 3 and 4, as if aware that transcribed music is unstable on the page, reverse the movement toward musical prosody and folk form; they transform the song first into an iambic pentameter dialogue (Davis responding to unvoiced questions about whites who might deserve to march alongside black saints) and then into a variably rhyming, loose iambic free indirect discourse (Davis speculating about folks who will not make it into heaven):

"Whuffolks," he dreams, *"will have to stay outside*
Being so onery." But what is he to do
With that red brakeman who once let him ride
An empty, going home? Or with that kind-faced man
Who paid his songs with board and drink and bed?   (sec. 3, ll. 92-96)

> Sportin' Legs would not be there—nor lucky Sam,
> Nor Smitty, nor Hambone, nor Hardrock Gene
> An' not too many guzzlin', cuttin' shines,
> Nor bootleggers to keep his pockets clean. (sec. 4, ll. 106-9)

Although the narrative form of these sections suggest different strategies for creating a more dialogic consciousness that might include Davis, they also push him away from accentual song meter into an alien prosodic tradition.

The fifth section seems to recognize this internally divergent prosody and to attempt some synthesis between the shifting narrative perspectives of sections 3 and 4 and Davis's song, marked by shortened lines, accentual meter, and italics:

> *Ise got a dear ole mudder,*
> *She is in hebben I know—*
> He sees:
>> Mammy,
>> Li'l mammy—wrinkled face,
>> Her brown eyes, quick to tears—to joy—
>> With such happy pride in her
>> Guitar-plunkin' boy.
>> *Oh kain't I be one in nummer?*
>
> Mammy
> With deep religion defeating the grief
> Life piled so closely about her,
> *Ise so glad trouble doan last alway,*
> And her dogged belief
> That some fine day
> She'd go a ma'chin'
> *When de saints go ma'chin' home.* (ll. 118-34)

The section contains both generic and prosodic hybridity without synthesis. In terms of genre, there is Davis's lyric recollection of his mother but also the narrator's intervention in framing a previously self-sufficient song. Davis's song becomes what "he sees" rather than what he sings. If the metaphor of perception marks Davis's subjective moment, the visionary ideal of subjective lyric must also mark a shift away from folk music. The chimerical result blends italicized reproductions of song with narrative masquerading as Davis's vision. What if Davis's lyric turn is in fact the narrator's intrusion, and what if Davis's "seeing" is less his emergence as lyric subject than the narrator's effort to move deeper into the singer's mind than his song, of itself, permits? This is the dilemma of lyricization: the reframing of Davis by the narrative consciousness is not a passive moment in the generation of folk collectivity or the emergence of a lyric mode but an active, even violent mediation. Between the ideal generic concepts (folk and lyric) and Davis stands the intervening figure of a narrator whose receptivity is at once a model for our own and a limit placed on our access to the original performance.

The disjunction between the narrator's reframing and Davis's "lyric" song is borne out prosodically, as the non-italicized lines, composed in irregular length and rhythm, fail to be metrical in either a traditional or a blues sense. There is only the roughest echo of Davis's three-beat lines and dialect, as in the "Guitar-plunkin' boy," but it would be very demanding of the reader to hear blues cadences across the multiple dashes and enjambments. The difficulty is exacerbated by the rhymes' refusal to enforce rhythmic parallels and by a general abandonment of the double quatrains previously structuring Davis's transcribed song. The lines "With deep religion defeating the grief" (128) and *"Ise so glad trouble doan last always"* (130) are rhythmically parallel, but "grief" rhymes instead with "belief" a line too late and thus disrupts the emergent ballad stanza that could have united Davis's italicized song and the narrator's language. Similarly, the rhyme between "always" and "day" is massively slanted in its typography, lexical stress ("way" lacks full stress), the enjambment of "day," and in the metrical difference between each line. Where rhyme does hint at greater order ("joy"/"boy" in the first stanza), the lines have no metrical or rhythmic parallelism.

Thus, if this fifth section elevates Davis's folk song to lyric expression, the speaker's desire to close the gap with Davis spawns polyvocal, polyrhythmic confusion. Although Davis may remain a model for becoming-lyric, he cannot be Brown's model of the paradigmatic modern black poet. The sudden confusion of genre and prosody when Davis sings does not transform the narrator or Brown; the poem instead, in Benston's terms, "explicates and stages the model of authentic expression which constitutes the touchstone of Brown's subtle poetics."[62] This might suggest a mimetic aim, but for Benston the poem avoids mimesis in favor of "an unending enactment of an unending drama."[63] "Staging" and "explicating" are anti-mimetic processes; Brown is not entering an "authentic" expressive tradition and

Folk Iambics

then, as James Weldon Johnson saw it, "taking the raw stuff and turn[ing] it into conscious art."[64] As I have argued, Brown's prosody works anti-mimetically, making Davis's song a model not for imitation but rather for the ongoing revision of folk and other poetic material: "a text/voice calling for its own revised performance."[65]

But what constitutes this "revised performance" in "Saints"? If the poem is not merely a descent into confusion, a polyvocal tale of fragmentation, what lesson does it provide about modern African American prosody and its relation to vernacular form? The poem's final section, when Davis takes his leave, provides one possible answer: Brown, counterintuitively, treats iambic pentameter as a vernacular African American form. Section 6, which follows the polymetrical pseudo-synthesis of Davis and narrator, proceeds in irregularly rhyming loose iambic verse:

> He'd shuffle off from us, always, at that,—
> His face a brown study beneath his torn brimmed hat,
> His broad shoulders slouching, his old box strung
> Around his neck;—he'd go where we
> Never could follow him—to Sophie probably,
> Or to his dances in old Tinbridge flat. (ll. 142-47)

It might be possible, even preferable, to scan many of these lines as simply sharing Davis's four-beat musical measure. Adopting a simplified Attridgean beat scansion, for example:

```
His broad shoulders slouching, his old box strung
 1   B       2        B        2    B  1   B
```

But every line save the fourth could also scan as complex iambic pentameter. Bold indicates mismatches of stress and position, and underline indicates elision or resolution:

```
He'd shuffle off from us, always, at that,—
 W    S W    S    W  S   W  S    W   S
His face a brown study beneath his torn brimmed hat,
 W   S    W    S   W S    W    S   W      S
His broad shoulders slouching, his old box strung
 W   S      W S     W    S     W   S   W    S
Around his neck;—he'd go where we
 W S    W   S    W   S   W   S    [tetrameter]
```

```
Never could follow him—to Sophie probably,
W S     W     S W     S W     S W     S W     S  [hexameter]
Or to his dances in old Tinbridge flat.
W     S     W     S W     S     W     S     W          S
```

Given the complexity of this scansion, it is fair to ask why the four-beat scansion is not to be preferred. The answer, much as in the case of Toomer's "Song of the Son" in chapter 5, is that too many prosodic aspects signal distance from that musical analogue: the interposition of "always" that makes the first line distinctly pentametric, the sheer length of the second, the enjambment of the third and fourth lines, and the irregular rhyme scheme (AABCCA). The scansion as iambic pentameter points not to a performance but to a loosened but still-present metrical substrate carried over from the poems' earlier sections but now inflected by Davis's song.

Yet Brown revises Big Boy's performance not through mimicry or further prosodic and generic intermixing but through a new sort of "brown study." The pun here is telling: whatever else Davis represents, he is also a "brown study" like the poets in Brown's *Outline*. As the "brown study" leaves the stage, turning away from his audience, Brown's study turns away from Davis's music; and just as Davis returns to "*his* dances" after his concert for a middle-class audience, Brown turns from imitations of musical performance to poetry's broader historical performances of sound. Davis's separate "dances" reveal the telescoping inauthenticity of "folk" art, as Brown freely admits that his narrator (and to some extent proxy) "never could follow him," yet Brown reveals that neither these "dances" nor Davis's "chant of saints" were ever the ground of the poem's authenticity. We recall at this moment that Davis was "chased out of town for vagrancy" and could no more follow Brown into print publication than chain gangs could tour like the Fisk Jubilee Singers.

Brown's world has its own dance, however, in the movement of stress and syllable in the final section. Rhythmical effects abound: the "slouching shoulders" framed by falling feet, the lines that wrap the "old box strung/ Around his neck," and the sharp, mimetic enjambment in "we/ Never could follow him." The section's rhythms are as diverse as its clever effects, yet they are anything but the blues forms for which Pound praised Langston Hughes's early work: "The strength of folk song gets into it because everything unnecessary is forgotten in the oral transmission, and simply drops out. I think you were dead right in starting with the 'blues' as model."[66] In

Pound's view, to start with the "blues" is to be automatically inducted into the realm of "oral transmission" and to thereby avoid the pitfalls of written verse, including rigid meter. For Brown, however, the foremost "written" form of poetic sound—its meter—remains as central to his representation of the vernacular as it was to his pedagogical efforts to introduce African American poetry to broader audiences.

The poem's final line is the most significant in establishing the role of meter in Brown's poetic song, paralleling many of the *Outline*'s prosodic emphases. The line permits several performances, with the most likely being "Ór to his dánces in óld Tìnbridge flát." The line's nascent triple rhythm, laid over a perfectly scannable iambic pentameter, is crucial. Its mild swing and drift toward four stresses, emerging from the relatively iambic cadence of the previous lines, fittingly suggest dance and music. Yet the pattern belongs as much to Keats ("Síngest of súmmer in fúll-thròated éase") as it does to Hughes's bluesman playing his "sád ràggy túne like a músical fool." This rhythmic effect is not innately "blues" or black but a long-standing strategy for varying the rhythms of metrical verse. This rhythm could be taken to mark race, yet in Brown's final line this rhythm does not mark race or folk authenticity but rather the constructedness of this authenticity. By concluding with the traditional artifice of meter, half swung and half Keats, rhyme colliding with rather than completing rhythm, Brown refuses a demand for definitively raced folk form; he suggests not only the heterogeneity of early twentieth-century prosody but a heterogeneous participation in that prosody.

The length and polymetrical surface of "Saints" renders it an outlier in Brown's oeuvre and yet central in its emphasis on rhythmic shifts, generic indeterminacy, and the need for the reader to listen for the African American metrical vestige. Brown's poetry insists that we be aware of meter and rhythm as technical performances rather than intrinsic, racial properties of the poet; prosody both forms and deforms racial identity. Nowhere is this more evident than in "Southern Road," a poem widely read as an adept mimesis of chain-gang song synthesized with a speaker's lyrical reflections.

> White man tells me—hunh—
> Damn yo' soul;
> White man tells me—hunh—
> Damn yo' soul;
> Got no need, bebby,
> To be tole. (*Collected Poems*, 52)

Brown notes that bitter chain-gang songs, unlike "slave seculars," could not be easily overheard: "Only to collectors who have won their trust [. . .] and only when the white captain is far enough away, do the prisoners confide these songs."[67] Brown's literary audience has not earned such trust, so a true mimesis of the genre would revoke the right of a broad readership to "overhear" (or oversee) either the chain gang or the speaker's lyrical musings. As Margaret Ronda observes of Paul Lawrence Dunbar's Georgics, the specter of forced labor "strains" poetic genre and rhythmic fluency.[68] Nadia Nurhussein locates a similar challenge to lyricism and presumptive orality in the "constructedness" of Dunbar's dialect work, which "requires work from both the reader and the writer."[69] In the *Outline* Brown suggests the hard limit to that dialect work posed by lynching. He notes that Dunbar's poem about lynching, "The Haunted Oak" (1903), is not written in dialect and despite metrical appearances is not even a ballad but a "literary ballad." Anticipating Virginia Jackson's argument that the stanza form "would (and did) prompt turn-of-the-century readers to think of 'The Haunted Oak' as an Anglo-American border ballad," Brown disquiets our sense of genre by sending us to his appendix, where the poem is resituated in a post-Romantic genre alongside Longfellow's "Wreck of the Hesperus" and Brown's own darkly ironic "Slim Greer" poems. In Jackson's reading, Dunbar's feint is to wrap the ballad's historically fungible "communal folk story" around lynching's "contemporary violence"—a violence too easily recognized despite the complete silencing of human voices or details about the victim's "old, old crime." This makes the illusion of the border ballad so much more effective and that effectiveness all the more haunting as we discover ourselves complicit in the second-order violence of spectatorship and ignorance of history. To Brown's question, "Have you any theory to explain [the lack of dialect]?" Jackson answers, "It would be taken to represent the indigenous 'Negro' perspective." Whatever voice we do create for the ballad's tree-speaker reveals our "guilty pleasure" in designing voices of witness and pathos abstracted from history.[70]

Brown's chain-gang poem is not a ballad but shares that genre's strong temptation to simplistic recognition. By 1930 we are well into the era of race records and the corresponding illusion that one can access the "real" black voice or body remediated by mass production. As Friedrich Kittler notes, an 1898 recording of "Down on the Swanee River" was advertised not only for "Negro songs and dances" but also for the action of "pulling in the gangplank" and the sound of "a steamboat bell." For Kittler this is a "hallucinatory wish fulfillment" that poetry as a symbolic, verbal medium could only promise. But lyricization, by 1930 if not earlier, performed the same extrication from format, medium, and genre. The practical challenge of prosody, however, offered Brown and the poets he studied a way to deepen and complicate the reader's encounter with spectral and racialized voices. What we find inside the stamping rhythm of "Southern Road" is skepticism about *our* transformation of a musical or "folk" tradition into lyric performance and lyric reading. The medium of this skepticism is prosodic: whereas the first four lines cited above encourage a call-and-response performance through heavy beats and typographic indications of pause, the final "to be tole" is phonologically lighter than any other line in the poem. To give it two or three beats is to ride roughshod over the dark humor of the speaker's final, individuated turn. We cannot synthesize the rhythmic prerogatives of work song and vernacular speech, and there is no triumphant return to artsong via iambic technique.

Brown's brilliance was to reject the discourses of folk collection and lyric oversight in favor of the discourse of prosody, where his manipulations of song illuminated fetishistic, racist spectatorship while exploring new forms of poetic and prosodic community. The vision of community in Brown is always marked by exile, whether of Big Boy Davis or the speaker of Brown's closing poem, "Mill Mountain," who worries about search parties while camping outside town with his child. That speaker reflects, in his extended blank verse soliloquy, about his own "strange pastoral for poor city dwellers." Although this would-be pastoral swain is a victim of modern enclosure and exclusion, the poem's prosody reaches across time, space, and genre through a delicately cultivated iambic pentameter drawn from the English techniques Brown had praised. Fully 20 percent of the lines follow a pattern known as the "Italian" line, split in half with two stresses on each side, creating the illusion of a simpler dipodic form. The joy and fluidity of this verse form resonate with the apostrophe to the child, calling out for some unknown new pastoral at complete odds with the socioeconomic and racial history in which the speaker is situated.

Brown's oeuvre prepared the way for works like Gwendolyn Brooks's "The Anniad" (1949) with its range of allusions, prosodic forms, and oxymoronic final "sonnet-ballad," and the polyvocality and prosodic heterogeneity of Robert Hayden's "Middle Passage" (1945) The critique of race by way of the metrical vestige has a broader hemispheric (and perhaps broadly postcolonial) context, which I can only hint at through John Figueroa's scathing poem "Problems of a Writer who does not quite . . . ", which contextualizes itself as written "after reading Helen Vendler's Review of Walcott":

> Bwoy, you no hear wa de lady say?
> Watch di pentameter ting, man.
> Dat is white people play!
> [. . .]
> Yu arse goin swing
>
> Like metronome, yu'd say,
> But a black bwoy should play
> Widout dem mechanical aids
> Full of rydhm like all true spades (ll. 2-4; 12-16)[71]

Figueroa, a Jamaican poet who makes complex investments in classical and traditional forms and who writes only infrequently in dialect, identifies the whiteness of the proscription of regular meter or prescription for "patois" and for the rhythm to "break loose." Walcott would certainly disapprove of "mechanical aids" for the composition of those pentameters that Vendler finds too "harmonious" and "derivative" for such an "explosive subject" as colonial history.[72] But Figueroa's poem suggests that even a relatively benign lesson in form polices prosody and genre along unacknowledged racial lines. Thus, even as Figueroa pretends to agree with Vendler's sense of an early poem as less a poem than "an essay in pentameters," he turns against the non-Vendlerian meter "breakers" (W. C. Williams, Ezra Pound, perhaps Kamau Brathwaite) who prescribed more "explosive" measures: "See what dat pentameter an ESSAY do/ Yu bwoy! Long time I school yu/ To break/ up yu/ Lines."

Figueroa's poem exposes the still-unresolved relationship between meter, innovation, and race. He counters, in a sense, Kamau Brathwaite's now-canonical sense that iambic pentameter "carried with it a certain kind of experience, which is not the experience of a hurricane. The hurricane does not roar in pentameters." But at a deeper level neither Figueroa nor Brathwaite follows the modernist narrative that could equate the antimetrical work, the *avant-garde*, and anti-colonial struggle. Brathwaite's manner of listening to T.S . Eliot (or the Middle English *Piers Plowman* for that matter) is certainly more important than his participation in modernist ideas of rhythm; recalling the radio transmission of Eliot's "riddims of St. Louis," Brathwaite decides that "what T. S. Eliot did for Caribbean poetry and Caribbean literature was to introduce the notion of the speaking voice, the conversational tone." He continues by emphasizing the sound of "Eliot's actual voice," recorded and broadcast, as opposed to its textual instance.[73]

With this attention to local timbre and medium, Brathwaite destabilizes, in the service of what he calls Caribbean "nation language," what we might call the canonical reading or transmission of Eliot's verse as a written artifact. There is a willfully anti-historical element in Brathwaite's midwesternizing of the late Anglican poet-critic. It is a deracinating sample of modernism far more provocative than his conventional narrative of the rise of free verse. Investing in a regionalism Eliot had no truck with further exposes modernism's racial fantasy of orality, so distant from the postliterate orality mediated by LPs and radio—that is, actual fragments, loops, and samples of sound newly heard across distance.[74]

Brathwaite's version of Eliot and Figueroa's mock-up of late twentieth-century formalist criticism mark an ongoing struggle to navigate twentieth-century poetics and its prosodic narratives. For Brown and his inheritors, the question of how black voices fit into world-historical narratives is again and again a question of the caesuras and silences imposed by the history of prosody. Brown helps us read poems like Elizabeth Alexander's "The Venus Hottentot" (1990), in which Georges Cuvier's scientific racism issues in feverish trochees: "Science, science, science!/Everything is beautiful! (ll. 1-2)."[75] He reports, in 1825, that her genitalia will rest above "Broca's brain" (l. 23). Broca, who discovered which area of the brain controlled language, died in 1880. Cuvier, detached from history, thus ironically guides us to the Hottentot's transcendence of physically and historically fixed language. Her voice, so alive in Alexander's rendering, proclaims, however, that in its historical moment it could only speak as silence:

> In my silence I possess
> mouth, larynx, brain, in a single
> gesture. (ll. 102-4)

If Cuvier's voice exists transhistorically yet speaks its own undoing, the Hottentot's voice exists in no time, in the space of paradox and enjambment. Recovery comes through the sonic battle between "Science" and silence, between Cuvier's manic feet and the poise of the Hottentot's written but prosodically rich presence:

```
\   x   / x    \   x   /
In my silence I possess
S  W    S W    S   W   S
```

As in Brown's "to be tole," the downbeats of this line mute the forced beats of "Science" and "Everything." Brown lays out a poetics and a course of reading that redirects us to the "Xhosa/clicks" of African American poetry's "flexible tongue" (ll. 110-11). Alexander is one of many poets in whom we can find this legacy of vestiges that speak from seeming silence, from prosody's range of now-hidden, intralineated content, and against rhythmic givens whose seeming virtues conceal their fetishism.

Conclusion
Prosody after Form

> Nor would I be a Poet -
> It's finer - own the Ear -
>
> —Emily Dickinson, *Poems*

This book has shown how modern poetry and poetics were decisively influenced by debates over meter and the work of genre it at once still performed and could no longer perform. Meter's vestigiality reveals the instability of modern ideas and fantasies about poetic form. Perhaps the most important conclusion to be drawn from meter's aftermath concerns the Anglo-American formalist methods and theories of genre that emerge after modernism. In this conclusion, I suggest that the study of prosody is itself a vestige, a discourse haunting New Criticism and subsequent formalisms' key concepts of form, structure, and the tense unity of the poem as aesthetic object. The process by which formalism is abstracted from prosodic discourse accelerates with modern poetry, but the limits of our formal and hermeneutic attention to metrical practice can only be explained by midcentury conceptions of meter and rhythm as kinds of form, with rhythm the more ineffable and thus valuable, and of poetry as a genre defined by formal or rhythmic unity rather than metrical practice.

The advent of rhythm as form and form as the ground of lyric required a double move, the first being the rejection of meter and its technical apparatuses, which I have detailed throughout the book. This runs in parallel to the widely acknowledged distancing of twentieth-century criticism from scholarly work in philology and textual criticism.[1] The second is the invocation through rhythm of an ideal of expressivity and embodiment. As scholars of historical prosody have observed, this begins at least with Romanticism, especially in Coleridge's conspicuous and often-cited preface to *Christabel*

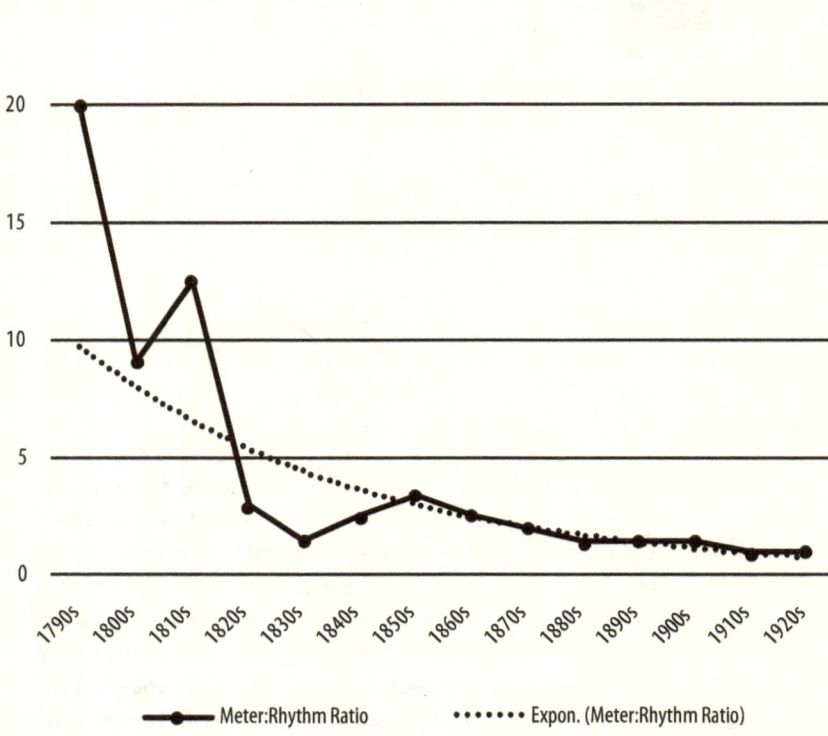

Meter to rhythm ratio in the Princeton Prosody Archive, between 1790 and 1923.

(1816), building across the nineteenth century from Hegel's ideas about prosody in his *Aesthetics* (1835) to Coventry Patmore's influential affective metrics and Whitman's drive toward "line length [. . .] determined by the thought," culminating in Pound's prescription of "absolute rhythm" in which "every emotion and every phase of emotion has some toneless phrase, some rhythmphrase to express it."[2] Amy Lowell describes rhythm as a matter of "curves" and even more abstractly as a "quality of *return* [. . .] produc[ing] the effect of music on the ear"; she also argues that the "new rhythms" of free verse "express new moods" and constitute a "principle of liberty" and "individualism."[3] Her proof lay in scientific recordings of her own performances. This study confirmed for Harriet Monroe not only the scientific basis of free verse, but rhythm's existence as "an element of unalterable law:

Conclusion

from the electron to the most enormous sun in space, every object moves rhythmically."[4] A blunt measure of rising investment in rhythm can be seen in the falling ratio of appearances of "meter" (and "metre" and "metrical") with "rhythm" (and "rhythmical") across the Princeton Prosody Archive.[5] Such prominence masks rhythm's odd value to literary criticism, especially in its post-metrical formation. As Hans Gumbrecht observed several decades ago, "The association of 'rhythm' both with literature *and* with the body has never been seen as a problem by literary scholarship." He points to rhythm as a means of bypassing the phenomenological uncertainties that accompany the study of temporal forms ("time objects," in Husserlian terms). Rhythm lets criticism transcend already represented forms like metrical feet, "minimal units of form [. . .] experienced even by inexperienced listeners as form."[6] This prospect of phenomenal but also numinous unity protects and sustains New Criticism's treatment of prosody as supplying some of the interlocking poetic and linguistic features making up the poem as an aesthetic object. Rhythm allows the critic to be, like Donne in Eliot's "Whispers of Immortality," "expert beyond experience."[7]

As a puzzle piece of rhythmic sensibility: this is how meter gets heard and analyzed within the institutions of lyric reading. Poetry criticism in the twentieth century idealizes formalist (or formalizing) listening yet at the same time distrusts the pedantic drift of technical treatments of prosody. Northrop Frye, in a moment highlighted by Jonathan Culler in his recent *Theory of the Lyric*, discovers the "rhythm of lyric" not in the brilliance of Elizabethan metrics but in his own relineation of Shakespeare's blank verse. This suggests that the idea of lyric involves not only, as Culler puts it, a mode of "hearing differently, attending to sorts of patterning that might not compel attention in narrative poetry," but also the poet or critic's subjective reconstruction of historical prosody. Frye must "arrange the fragments as a kind of free verse" to "create lyric rhythm."[8] Lyric theory has observed how Frye's idea of lyric's "concealment of its audience" is a critical backformation; no less important, however, is his critical construction of "emancipated lyrical rhythm" that "associates" and unifies sound and sense in the age of prose.[9]

The ideal of unity, especially organic unity, has been extensively studied in histories of the discipline and most recently in lyric theory. Mary Poovey has traced the dependence of formalist reading on organicist tropes surrounding the Romantic lyric. Lyric remains such an amenable critical genre because the ideals of "textual autonomy and critical expertise [are] the cornerstones of modern formalism."[10] The mutual incompatibility of these cornerstones is mitigated, as John Guillory has argued, by the New Critical reconception of literary criticism as a sacred space figured and allegorized in turn by the texts it reads. The poem's obligatory "retreat before the act of interpretation"[11]—its critically endowed defense against paraphrase and the acquisitive scientific or philological mind—demands a critical retreat from preceding generations' pragmatic, local, and heterodox discourses of versification. By flattening historical poetics and prosody into a range of coexisting and static forms or structures, New Critical formalism retains the ideals of difficulty without the errant challenges presented by elocution, scansion, and notation; this assures that complexities such as paradox or irony will occur at the level of interpretation rather than linguistic performance, even as that interpretation privileges material and linguistic "forms."

Guillory observes that the real shape of "form" tends to be "the form of paradox"—a genitive formulation that echoes twentieth-century criticism's many "rhythm of" formulations. Just as actual historical concepts of poetry as para-doxical (in the sense of remaining outside given beliefs) winnow, in formalism, to mere "reconciliation of any apparent antitheses,"[12] so does the heterodoxy of historical prosody winnow to the generalized sense of a schism between metrical and prose language or between lyrical rhythm and the mixed prose-doggerel of mass culture. The discourse of form and paradox-as-form elides practices of generic and prosodic recognition which, as the editors of the *Lyric Theory Reader* recall, demand historical knowledge: "'poetry as a thing in itself' requires no special knowledge of the reader."[13]

Debates over prosody were the primary medium for debates over poetry as a genre, and so the New Criticism's repeated attacks against what it took to be an irredeemably decentralized and conflicted theorization and pedagogy of prosody should read as a tactic by which to retain short lyric poems as prized hermeneutic objects despite the modernist annoyance with all things "lyrical." Although nominally oriented toward technical expertise, the abstraction of meter partakes in a general resistance to a perceived "narrowing of sensibility in philological and historical specialists."[14] Few scholars today would wish to revive the 1922 MLA Committee on Metrical Notation, which determined, unsuccessfully, that a system of common notation would reconcile embattled musical and syllabic scanners.[15] But we should nonetheless worry that when New Criticism "erases doubts about the progress of [prosodic] scholarship," as Donald Wesling finds, it does so by limiting the role of meter in criticism: "Metrics indeed achieves a twentieth century form of authority, based on scaling down its assumptions and purifying its methods." The modernist cordoning-off of meter and metrical culture lets New Criticism "separate[] off and reif[y] meter."[16] This is manifest institutionally when Rene Wellek distinguishes his history of criticism and George Saintsbury's by the latter's "professed lack of interest in questions of theory and aesthetics," leaving aside his prominent histories of prosody as presumably not "aesthetics."[17] The subordination of meter is epitomized pedagogically in Brooks and Warren's *Understanding Poetry* (1938), which while disdaining prior efforts to "isolate certain aspects of poetry for special investigation," presents meter as "one factor" contributing to "effects" through relations with other factors.[18] The difference is in how "organically" ("like a plant") and not "mechanically" ("as bricks are put together to build a wall") the pieces get put back together.[19] Organic or mechanical, the poem is in pieces, but the critic has an easier job of bringing the poem back to life without mechanical iambs serving as its pulse. *Understanding Poetry* is typical in refusing generic distinctions or definitions based on prosody. Rhythm is in all language; poetry has a "tendency [like a plant] toward a high degree of organization"; therefore, rhythm must be organized, and the result tends to be metrical verse. Poetry and prose are now species of "unregularized" and "regularized" rhythm.[20] Just as modern poets adopted rhythmic conceptions of poetic genre to defend against audile technique and meter specifically, critics adopted a post-metrical "sensibility" to secure a sense of disciplinary authority. Rhythm-as-sensibility becomes both the telos of poetic form and excessive to formalist analysis. Harvey Gross writes, for example, "We cannot subject rhythm and rhythmic values to the kind of precise analysis that scansion accomplishes for meter. The notation of scansion defines with comfortable accuracy metrical structure; the rhythms of even the simplest poem are too complex to be ever completely analyzed."[21] Meter is preserved only because "every element in poetic structure contributes to rhythmic feeling," but metrical scansion is no more than a propaedeutic to surrounding claims about rhythm or structure.

The reification and then isolation of meter away from the definition of poetry entails abstraction less from history—the common complaint against New Critical and formalist criticism—than from historical reading. Despite John Crowe Ransom's emphasis on the particularity and even "insubordinate character" of meter and other poetic detail, his conception of writing and reading subsume prosodic parts into a generalized "medium" and medium into the greater goal of defying paraphrase and developing emotional purposes.[22] In Doug Mao's account of Ransom:

> Poems become the distinctive things they are thanks to a certain resistance of the medium: the poet sets out with some point to make, but as writing proceeds, formal constraints (stanza, meter, rhyme) turn the poem into something other than a simple statement of the intended argument. Interwoven with the structure of argument in the finished poem, in other words, is always a texture of irrelevancies, of "incessant particularity" in which "each fresh particular is capable of enlisting emotions and attitudes."[23]

Meter's value here comes from its ability to complicate paraphrase, and that complication involves "emotions" that cannot and need not be specified. This account of poesis and reading is not antagonistic to meter but is hard to square with its historical articulations. It is hard to adapt this account to poetry that has an overriding intention to be metrical or which makes its "intended argument" about prosody itself. Prosody gains the power to save the poem from paraphrase only *after* it has been reconceived as ancillary to argument. Ironically, the resistance to paraphrase depends utterly on paraphrase for its definition of poetry's "distinctiveness," while also depending on meter's inaugural separation from both linguistic medium and genre.

Through its abstract logic of formal particularity, the New Criticism displaces still-resonating questions about audience, performance, and elaborate notation. It institutionalizes, as a method of reading, precarious modernist ideals such as Clive Bell's "significant form," whose coherence devolves upon "a spiritual experience for the initiated."[24] The initiation into poetic form and away from prosodic recognition characterizes New Critical outliers as well, in particular I. A. Richards. Concerned in *Practical Criticism* with the psychosomatics of meter and the inadequacies of its performance, he had nevertheless resolved in the subsequent *Principles of Literary Criticism* (1924) that the "adequate reader" will be able to grasp both stress and pitch contours. This leads him to a prescription against italics and other notation in poetry: "What can be done with sound should not be done otherwise or in violation of the natural effects of sound."[25] The prescription extends to Richards's criticism, despite its pragmatism, in that no scansions support his claims about rhythm or mimetic form. In this regard, Richards's concept and practice of post-metrical reading achieves what meter is said to achieve—namely, "isolating the poetic experience from the accidents and irrelevancies of everyday existence."[26] This is what rhythm, with meter as its foil, does for modern poetry as a genre, suggesting again that New Criticism's reconception of poetry as a formal object took modern poetry's cue in leveraging a repeated break with the particularities and heterodoxies of the previous decades' and century's prosodic discourse.

W. K. Wimsatt and Monroe Beardsley's "The Concept of Meter: An Exercise in Abstraction" (1959) is explicit about meter's separation from mere acoustical fact and the contingencies of individual performance. Although the essay has a productive schema of meter as an abstract mental pattern, it works hard to turn from historical practices of reading and scansion and establish a universal reader (or practitioner) of meter. The same difficult encounter with historical reading emerges when they define diction in "The Affective Fallacy" (1949) or when Cleanth Brooks treats allusion in *The Well Wrought Urn* (1947). In reference to a line from Frost's "Mowing," "The Concept of Meter" argues that critics who record poetry in search of timing or intonational patterns or who use elaborate indications of intonational stress (i.e., the four-level stress system developed by George Trager and Henry Smith) perform a circular rediscovery of what "another person might know through boyhood experience on a farm, or through a footnote."[27] Yet these are very different readers and very differently mediated pathways to phonological fact—pragmatic differences that Frost himself explores throughout his poetry, as does Eliot in his notorious footnotes to *The Waste Land*.

Even when critics do attend to the social dimension of form, they isolated their own formalist practice from historical prosody. R. P. Blackmur's 1952 essay "Lord Tennyson's Scissors," for instance, provocatively conceives of poetry's "social" history as the effort of "readers catching on to new rhythms or new relations between rhythm and metre." Blackmur participates nonetheless in the modernist abstraction of prosody into rhythm and form, defining meter as the "foot and hand holds" for rhythm, which is poetry's means of "moving meaning into words." This pivot to a Coleridgean sense of meter as an adjunct or prop to a specialized mode of language prevents worry that meter's laws are only "partly knowable" and that prosody is of "first but not necessarily conscious importance."[28] More important than his theory of meter is Blackmur's situating of Yeats, Pound, and Eliot as ideal readers with a thoroughgoing grasp of the metrical tradition. They are the readers that matter, the ones who might still understand Tennyson's once-profound claim that "scissors" was the only word for which he did not know the correct quantity. The actual question of syllabic quantity is irrelevant to Blackmur's discussion, which is odd given his concern that most of

Eliot's, Pound's, and Yeats's successors "do not understand what Tennyson meant and many would repudiate the statement [. . .] for its irrelevant nonsense." Yet like those modernists, Blackmur continued to worry about the limits of technique in post-metrical prosodic culture. Pound was to blame for "the general prosody of the teens and twenties [. . .] perhaps the weakest and least-conscious in English since the dead poetry of the mid-sixteenth century."[29] Pound might have agreed. What we do get of prosody in Eliot, Pound and Yeats is, for Blackmur, still "just enough metre to make a patter, just enough rhyme to make a noise"; even as Pound's "Medallion" (from *Hugh Selwyn Mauberly*) sings a "song of syllables," he is mute outside his rhythmic coterie: Pound "got to play a very complicated stylistic game by ear."[30] Blackmur can only overcome his realizations about the troubled prosodic horizon of the 1910s and 1920s the way Pound and others did: by critiquing the metronome in favor of the musical phrase. Despite the brilliance of its typologies of modern poetry, including an intriguing discussion of syllabics, Blackmur's essay forecloses further navigation of meter in favor of a fixed modernist canon and ideal of poetic form. What we take away is the idea that the modernist trio "made form and substance possible" for late modernist and midcentury poetry.[31]

Michael Wood observes that Blackmur "cherished" the word "form" but "cannot plausibly be called a formalist" in part because of his emphasis on technique and recognition of its "disorder."[32] In his early 1930s assessment of Marianne Moore, he is more skeptical and pragmatic about the need for "special terms" for "form." After an approving citation of T. S. Eliot's description—"the poems are in exact [. . .] complicated formal patterns, and move with the elegance of a minuet"—Blackmur backpedals: "As [the pattern] enlivens it becomes inextricably a part of the material [. . .] the only difficulty in apprehending this lies in our habit of naming only the conventional or abstract aspects of the elements of the pattern, naming never their enactment."[33] A footnote here invites I. A. Richards to weigh in on the precise linguistic, cognitive, or social reason for such failings. But the footnote is a dead end, and Blackmur must accept his critical expediencies. The poem being studied, "The Past Is the Present" (1915), ends with the lines "Ecstasy / affords / the occasion and expediency determines the form." Blackmur reads this as an allegory of the ecstasies and expediencies of formalist criticism: "We perceive the occasion and seize the nearest peg to hang the form on, which happen[s] to be the very slight peg of inverted commas." He wants to believe, in sympathy with Eliot, that the poem has found a more elegant form, and yet he grasps for handholds in Moore's iconic use of quotation marks. It doesn't help that the poem's most prominent rhyme—a more recognizably prosodic "peg"—pairs "rhyme is outmoded" with "goaded." Moore's enticements to recognizable form at once goad and embarrass the questing reader. Poet and critic alike are confronted by the "methodically oblique" form she praises in Elizabeth Bishop's early work.[34] As Robert Beloof observed in 1958, Moore's syllabics induce an unusual systematic attention to prosody in an otherwise apathetic criticism: "Critics are likely to speak of the tautness of her form, the precision of her sensibility."[35] His primary observations about that form involve rhyme and Moore's disruption of the "usual rhythmic possibilities for syllabic structure," by which he means the iambic tendencies of English.

Moore's evident rigor presents a special challenge to criticism that aims for technical virtuosity with vestigial organs of prosodic expertise. Recent critics have more cautiously observed Moore's "inaudible syllabic measure" and penchant for "mechanical pattern."[36] As discussed in chapter 1, poets like Frost and more recent critics have observed that free verse, despite its rhythmic self-conception, expresses the same feelings of rhetoricity and disembodiment that critics like Blackmur admit.[37] Free verse's feeling of mediation, and recourse to metadiscourse and efforts to train readers, brings it much closer to metrical practices than has been recognized. Blackmur's early understanding reveals how Moore's syllabics, and non-iambic verse in general, is not a prod back to rhythmic or speech-based understanding of poetry as a genre or tradition but a reminder of the arbitrariness of both poetic and critical pattern. William Empson, in his earliest assessments of the modern conditions of literary form, also points in this productive direction. He finds, for instance, that the "dogma of Pure Sound often acts as a recipe for aesthetic receptiveness, and may be necessary."[38] The intuitionism present in early Eliot and many of his contemporaries strikes Empson as "surreal." His historicized view of literary criticism sees only gradations of dogma's necessity. Thus, Pope must have had "critical dogmas" but "could afford to forget [them], so deeply had they become part of his sensibility." What Empson then says of faith in "sensibility" applies not only to Eliot but to the entire field of modern prosody and poetics: "To say that the dogma does not influence the sensibility is absurd. People only say it when they are trying to put the sensibility in a peculiar state of control over the dogma."[39]

I hope to have shown, however briefly, that New Critical formalism radically revises and compromises early twentieth-century prosodic discourse.

More recent efforts toward a "new" formalism might take note of this specific disciplinary history and pick up on Blackmur's and Empson's early wariness, or Yvor Winters's kindred critique of both Brooks's view of "poetry purely as structure" and of R. S. Crane's belief that poetry's only goal was "the perfection of its own form—whatever that may mean."[40] We have yet to satisfy Donald Wesling's 1996 call for formalist and historicist criticism to work against the New Criticism by "raising the issue of the relation of exegesis to formalization" and subjecting those formalizations to "historical critique."[41] Awareness of formalization and its impact on concepts of genre could advance Jonathan Culler's and Richard Cureton's disciplinary critique of how, in the latter's terms, "not understanding linguistic form critics of poetry have just avoided the issue entirely by treating poems as stories, plays, or some other sort of language primarily concerned with meaning rather than linguistic form."[42] As Herbert Tucker notes in his response to Caroline Levine's concept of "strategic formalism," even useful correctives to a generation's "antiformalist crouch" can overlook the "generative conflicts" of versification.[43] What matters, per Tucker, is not merely to be formalist, or to look for new kinds of "form" or new relations between them (i.e., between social and literary forms), but to ask what sort of concept of form one's critical practice depends upon or enables and what that concept's disciplinary history reveals. This entails the recognition that form is a deliberate and necessary abstraction from, for example, phonemic facts or subjective experience, but also an "abstract, aloof" concept within our discipline.[44] Recent essays by Rob Lehman and Nicholas Gaskill show the value that comes with more pragmatic understandings of form and its contingent determinations by aesthetic judgment and the history of aesthetics.[45] My point here is that the need for such reevaluations, especially when it comes to modernism and poetry, follows from modernism's displacement of meter by rhythm and form. As I have been arguing, it is specifically modernism and then New Criticism that abstracted form and the poem as formal object from prosody; this disciplinary trajectory necessitates historical prosody as a methodological means of navigating genre, circulation, and reading practices across periods.

Modernism spurred on the idea that the creative destruction of prosody occurs within and even proves the perseverance of a unitary genre of poetry. This is the outcome, for example, of Eliot's reevaluation of Milton as a model of formal idiosyncrasy. Recent criticism too often treats modernism's uneasy concepts of form as if they were final proof of its aspirations rather than a result of the twentieth century's disavowal of prosody as a discipline. For instance, Ben Lerner has embraced the disjunction between the "virtual" poem's "song of the infinite" and the actual poem that suffers its pedestrian formal means.[46] There is certainly a kind of torment in being exiled from a history of coherent and internal prosodic development, but it belongs to modernism's specific aesthetic formation and not to poetry as such. Oren Izenberg similarly derives a canon of poetry "in the general sense" from such conflicts as that in Yeats between meter as limiting material and rhythm as liberatory concept. He argues that Yeats's "To Some I Have Talked with by the Fire" (1893) desires a "rapturous music" that "cannot be identified with its own 'fitful' rhymes; it beats out a loud and regular rhythm that cannot be heard in the strangely patterned pentameter of the lines that house it."[47] Perhaps this conflict is a real one, although I think Yeats was more capable than most of hearing, performing, and writing "rapturous" meter—or at least of not finding meter to be the problem. But more at issue is the tacit acceptance of an idea that modernism did not yet take for granted: that meter is a limited mode of rhythm and that (musical) rhythm ultimately forms the ideal generic baseline for poetry.

Both Lerner and Izenberg develop Allen Grossman's idea of "the bitter logic of the poetic principle," a concept Grossman evidences in Hart Crane's sense of formal inadequacy. If Crane's metrical and other vestiges mark desire in excess of structure, it is not because he has exceeded given "forms" like meter in Izenberg's sense, but because Crane is alienated from the logic of rhythm, structure, and form that took root by the 1920s. Crane, like all poets working with the metrical vestige, writes fragments of what C. D. Blanton has described as the "late modernist or negated epic": "a poem that cannot remain a mere poem, one that has already begun to participate dialectically in the critical labor of historical reading."[48] In this formulation, as in Grossman's, modern poetry survives its poems, and form survives its limited manifestations. But the modern metrical vestige questions this logic of genre thriving in the dissolution of readers' formal contracts. When the vestige conceives its reader's labor, it is with small certainty that poetry could "participate" in its increasingly post-metrical conception.

Modern metrical poets wrote in response to changing terminologies and practices of reading—in response, effectively, to the absence of a functional formalism. Literary criticism eagerly stepped in to provide one, mining modernist poetics to do so, but has consequently been deaf to the endemic uncertainties and ambivalences provoked by the very need for such reinventions of poetry and poetics. My hope is that this book's renewed attention not only to the meanings and tactics of meter in the early twentieth century but to a field of poetics at odds with critical formalism will allow further study of the dialectic between historical practices of reading what we now call poetic "form" and the poems that address their listeners with such loving unease.

Appendix
Scansion and Metrical Notation

It is helpful, especially in teaching, to define meter in terms of a binary approach in which *rhythm* constitutes the flexible performance of an abstract *metrical* pattern. This understanding of meter is good at describing the stylistics of the accentual-syllabic tradition, and represents a reasonably well-established understanding in prosodic treatises from at least Edwin Guest's *History of English Rhythm* (1832) through to contemporary linguistic approaches.[1] The binary scheme has limits, however, both practically and conceptually. It offers little help and potential harm when one looks at something like the long medieval alliterative tradition. It does little service to free verse, more or less by definition.[2] Sixteenth-century accentual-syllabic verse had not necessarily regularized itself to the point of having a clear abstract pattern. Sorting out what counts as a flexible incarnation of such a pattern, a truly new pattern (as I find in the case of Frost), or an unmetrical line is not likely to be resolved even with greater collaboration between linguistic and literary approaches.[3]

However, for much modern metrical poetry—largely iambics—a straightforward notation drawn from Morris Halle and Samuel J. Keyser's seminal *English Stress: Its Form, Its Growth, and Its Role in Verse* (1971) proves useful. I give an abbreviated primer here to facilitate understanding of scansions throughout the book. Where scansions use a different system, such as Derek Attridge's beat metrics, I explain them in context. I am grateful to Robin Sowards for his inspiring short guide to scansion and generative metrics.

Iambic meter (and the English language) prefers to alternate unstressed and stressed syllables. The resulting pattern looks like this for pentameter:

```
W   S   W   S   W   S   W   S   W   S        (W for Weak position,
                                               S for Strong)
```

One can scan most accentual-syllabic meter by comparing possible performances of the line (which differ, of course) to this pattern. This pattern is not "correct" or better or even normative: just nominally *regular*. Indeed, as I suggest in my introduction, one of the main flaws in modernist retheorization and sometimes practice of meter is to understand the "W S" template as a mechanical prescription. Scansion using this template is a heuristic, a way to conceive the actions of verse.

Once the line's syllables are aligned above the template (sometimes a challenge because of resolution and elision), the *rhythm* can be indicated using accent symbols. Here is a famously metrical line beginning Thomas Gray's "Elegy Written in a Country Churchyard," with abstract template beneath and actual stress above:

```
x   /   x   /   x   /   x   /   x   /
The curfew tolls the knell of parting day
W   S   W   S   W   S   W   S   W   S
```

It should be clear that there is an exact correspondence between strong positions and stress. The two stresses in polysyllabic words are "lexical" stresses and obey the primary rule of this meter as articulated in Paul Kiparsky's foundational 1977 article, "The Rhythmic Structure of English Verse": "Polysyllabic words must have their strongest stress in S position."[4] Kiparsky elaborates several other important points, including the availability of monosyllables and compounds in any position, and the nonrequirement that S positions have any particular stress. Of course, there are many exceptions, particularly at the beginnings of phrase boundaries (and thus most lines), which explains the common "trochaic inversion" at the beginning of iambic lines and after caesurae. Then there is the crucial question of relative stress. Whether one should use only *x* and / or add secondary stress is a matter of debate and ultimately preference. All stress in English is relative, though the number of levels of stress probably does not exceed four. I find it useful to employ \ for a syllable that has *relatively* less stress because it is adjacent to a stronger stress, as well as for secondary stress in polysyllabic words. This can clarify the metricality of unusual lines and suits Halle and Keyser's important concept of the "stress maximum." Scanning with

Scansion and Metrical Notation

stress maxima justifies lines like the following from Donne, in which "God" has more stress than "behóld":

```
  x     x \   /    x   / x   /     \      /
Shall behold God, and never tast Deaths woe
  W    S  W   S    W   S W   S     W      S
```

The line's metricality is less important than its unusual qualities—indeed Donne was famous for his metrical difficulties. Kiparsky's rule, and its amendment in such instances, generates a sensitive scansion that can recognize difficulty, especially when joined to statistical, cognitive, or reception study. Reuven Tsur argues that our "rhythmical performance" must navigate and create a "perceptual solution" to such complex lines through a "knowledge of phonologic and versification features"; I agree, and I believe that the tool of binary scansion is part of that performance and solution.[5] For a concise overview of the how meter gets generated by "specific regularity in the rhythm of language," how readers make intuitive judgments about metricality using their linguistic competence, and how we might better speak across disciplinary lines about judgments of complexity and style, see Kristin Hanson, "Generative Metrics: The State of the Art."

I conclude with a particularly germane example: Pound's infamous claim, in *The Cantos*, that "To break the pentameter, that was the first heave." Scansion, if hazarded, suggests it is well outside iambic norms (clear mismatches in bold; elisions and resolutions underlined):

```
 x     /    x     / x     /   x   x   /     /
to break the pentameter, that was the first heave
 W     S    W     S W     S   W   S   W     S
```

Requiring two unusual compressions, two mismatches of stress, and a caesura breaking the line in half, this is a violent breaking indeed. Or it is simply another meter. Or it is such a heave that it muddies the line between meters, hinting at Pound's skill in transforming one more recent part of English tradition into an older tradition, either Anglo-Saxon verse or Greek Adonics, which are certainly part of *The Cantos*' development. Meredith Martin argues that Pound's line can be read, "of course, in pentameter, or can be read as pentameter without much wrenching, rising from an iamb to three anapests to a final, emphatic, stressed syllable." One could cavil here about the propriety or historicity of foot substitution, but Martin's argument is that what matters in such cases is not whether the line is "in pentameter" but how it might come to appear so.⁶

Indeed, the line has "come to appear" metrical through one of scansion's embarrassing cousins: misremembering and mishearing. I hope I will be forgiven for pointing out the telling version by Michael Golston and Susan Stewart: "To break the heave of the pentameter." Seamus Heaney also refers to the pentameter's "heave" when assessing Pound's influences on modernist poetry. Antony Easthope celebrates Pound's free verse for "breaking with pentameter." A recent review of Langdon Hammer's biography of James Merrill argues that Merrill simply bypassed modernism and the "'heave' that broke the back of the pentameter."⁷ Though to be fair, Merrill also recalls the line incorrectly. Like this reconstruction, Stewart and Golston's version of the line ironically pulls Pound's remark back toward metronomic pentameter:

```
 x   /   x    /   x   x   x  / x  \
To break the heave of the pentameter
 W   S   W    S   W   S   W  S W S
```

Christine Brooke-Rose finds it ironic that both this and the line "And as for those who deform thought with iambics" (Canto 98) are "good iambic pentameters."⁸ But scansion struggles here too:

```
 x   /   x    /    x   x  \    /      x    x / x
And as for those who deform thought with iambics
 W  S   W    S    W   S W    S      W    S x
```

Even if we let the "rhythm rule" stress "déform," the line is far rougher than this counterfactual:

```
 x   /   x    /   x   / x    /     x   / x
and as for those who deform thought with iambs
 W  S   W    S   W   S W    S     W   S ...
```

As I argue in chapter 3, by the late cantos Pound is no longer interested in satirizing meter in meter as he does in the Ur-Cantos (1917) and *Ripostes* (1912). While Pound still disdained meter's deformations, his post-metrical versification no longer sought to spur and challenge the English ear's metrical fervor. Pound's early anti-metrical Imagist dogma did, however, as I observe in my introduction: "As regarding rhythm,"

Scansion and Metrical Notation

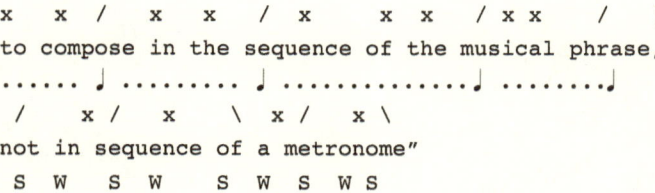

Such musical notation belongs to a different tradition of temporal and musical scansion. The first half of the dictum sounds more musical because of its almost triple rhythm. The second half is iambic, especially if we promote "of" and "ome" to some stress, which tends to happen in both metrical and natural language contexts.

There are many, many guides to versification, both its description through scansion and its production in writing and performance. I offer this basic practice of binary scansion as historically justified (it is how Frost scanned, as I show in chapter 1) and, most importantly, as a good balance of complexity and accessibility.

Notes

Introduction

1. Pound, "A Retrospect," 84. Published in *Pavannes and Digressions* (1918).
2. Williams, *Marxism and Literature*, 123.
3. Levenson, *A Genealogy of Modernism*, 76. Critics including Oren Izenberg, C. D. Blanton, Andrew Goldstone, and Ben Lerner have recently theorized late or alienated style that limits poetry's sense of its own formal autonomy. See Goldstone, *Fictions of Autonomy*.
4. Epstein, *Sublime Noise*, xx, xvii.
5. Already in the eighteenth century, Paul de Man notes, one finds "'music' substituting for 'poetry.'" "Lyric and Modernity," 168.
6. Peter Howarth argues that Hardy, Robinson, and several other poets permitted blatant instances of "rhetoric" in their poetry because they wished to mark the "disparity" between poetic selves and language. *British Poetry in the Age of Modernism*, 10. John Timberman Newcomb returns to the lost decades of 1890-1910 in *Would Poetry Disappear?*, pushing against the logic of a great formal divide circa 1912 and arguing for the modernity of poets like E. A. Robinson who "exploit disparities between traditional styles and modern subjects [to] offer new ways for artistic 'form' to embody social 'content'" (xxvii). In his sequel, *How Did Poetry Survive?*, Newcomb suggests that meter might work within a "strategy of subversion and critique," though the mechanism is unclear (3).
7. For a concise critique of the bad historiography behind the formal divide narrative as well as a critique of Newcomb's and other revisionist efforts to overcome it, see Kappeler, "Editing America." Joseph Harrington is blunt in his attack both on New Critical ideas of poetry that codify evaluative criteria alien to historical circumstances and on criticism that can read "non-modernists" only by considering them modernist. His method of "social formalism" seeks to historicize poetry as a genre (or range of generic practices), though he is inattentive to the discourses of form that in my view of the period take priority over questions of the "meaning of 'poetry'" (often still

called verse). *Poetry and the Public*, 2–5. More recent is Sarah Ehlers's skepticism about efforts to recover the Victorian (its authors, forms, sentimentality, and so on) as the modern. "Making It Old." As Herbert Tucker notes, familiar modernists let in the Victorian only under "heavy ironic guard"; he notes moreover the ironic "reverse sentimentality" of this anti-Victorian, anti-sentimental stock response. "Doughty's *The Dawn in Britain* and the Modernist Eclipse of the Victorian," 2. Tucker pushes scholars of modernism to see through irony and anti-sentimentalism to deeper formal lineages such as those between Imagism and the Edwardian Charles Doughty's "purged language" and "radical prosody" (25, 9).

8. Nelson, *Repression and Recovery*, 4. Nelson emphasizes the almost total loss of the leftist and communist poetry tradition—poetry frequently written in traditional meters.

9. Cavitch, "Slavery and Its Metrics," 110.

10. Cavitch, "Stephen Crane's Refrain," 33, 38.

11. For a thorough overview of the "modern consolidation of lyric as a genre of critical reading," see the general introduction to Jackson and Prins, *The Lyric Theory Reader*.

12. The *Edinburgh Dictionary of Modernism* has an entry for free verse and, happily, "syllabic verse" but not for meter. Rebecca Beasley's 2007 *Theorists of Modernist Poetry* never uses the word, contrasting free verse with "regular patterns of rhythm" (26). Michael Whitworth observes that poets can "engage with modernity" in "traditional poetic techniques" and helpfully notes metrical echoes but accepts that "predetermined metres [iambics or classical experiment] suggested a kind of rigidity which precluded really open-ended experimentation." *Reading Modernist Poetry*, 2, 73–74. The 2015 *Cambridge History of Modernist Poetry* has essays by Fiona Green and Helen Carr that push back against, respectively, the legibility of "absolute rhythm" and the idea that Imagism inaugurated "poetic transformation," but meter is nowhere foregrounded, and modernist prosody remains a practice of rhythm. Davis and Jenkins, *A History of Modernist Poetry*.

13. Finch, *The Ghost of Meter*.

14. Holder, *Rethinking Meter: A New Approach to the Verse Line*, 14.

15. Gross, *Sound and Form in Modern Poetry*, 49.

16. Gross, *The Structure of Verse*, 77.

17. Gross, *Sound and Form in Modern Poetry*, 5.

18. Meredith, *Earth Walk*, 68.

19. Beyers, *A History of Free Verse*, 9.

20. Fussell, *Lucifer in Harness*, 12. Fussell uses this claim to argue for Frost's overall insignificance to the American revolt against English poetics (led by Whitman, succeeded by William Carlos Williams). Fussell's discontent focuses on figures like William Cullen Bryant, which makes some sense given Bryant's Anglocentric concep-

tion of literary history; Bryant, however, also had an acute understanding of the internal diversity of English accentual-syllabic prosody.

21. The precise link between "extreme metrical conservatism" and Keatsian lyric "discursiveness" is never given. Davie says the two are "part and parcel," and Perloff that they go "hand in hand." Nor do Davie's claims that Stevens "never made [Pound's] break" and that his meter is "quite regular" bear out—even if we are skeptical of J. V. Cunningham's claim, contemporary with Davie's, that Stevens attains "the stability of a new metrical form [. . .] out of the inveterate violation of the old." Davie, "Essential Gaudiness," 14. Perloff, "Pound/Stevens," 137. Cunningham, "The Poetry of Wallace Stevens," 164.

22. Gross, *Sound and Form in Modern Poetry*, 243.

23. Duffell, *A New History of English Metre*, 237.

24. Duffell, *A New History of English Metre*, 213. In *The Life of Metrical and Free Verse in Twentieth-Century Poetry*, British poet Jon Silkin tries to "heal" the rift between meter and free verse by helping poets regain an "active choice" (2) between "interrelated modes" (6), which share "imaginative capacity" and "rhythmic impulse" (19, 272).

25. Adams, "Pound's Quantities and 'Absolute Rhythm,'" 105. Perloff, "English as a 'Second' Language."

26. Blount, "Caged Birds," 227.

27. Barkas, *A Critique of Modern English Prosody (1880-1930)*, 3.

28. Lewis, *Selected Literary Essays*, 114.

29. Chasar, *Everyday Reading*, 6.

30. Martin, *The Rise and Fall of Meter*, 183, 107. Martin reveals in particular George Saintsbury's massive influence on early twentieth-century English prosody. His metrics constitute an "attempt at stabilization for the healthy, collective, patriotic view of English meter and, by extension, English poetry's role as a stabilizing, patriotic force in national culture" (103).

31. One critic determined that "all prolonged experiments in [hexameter] break down" and adds that we lose the "measure" of blank verse to enjambment; another thought that experiments in unrhymed meters "will not bear repeating" (i.e., Longfellow's *Hiawatha*, "McPherson's *Ossian* and the labored efforts of Tennyson to imitate Greek modes"). Qtd. in Gillis, "American Prosody in the Eighteen Nineties," 134. Rhyme was hardly a safe alternative, however, as one article on "Browning's form" regrets how prosodists "insist upon lugging in considerations of quantity, alliteration, and assonance, and devices from classical tongues. [. . .] [T]hey are led astray by tricks of rhyme and fail to mark the distinction between rhythm and meters." Francis Howard Williams, "Browning's Form," 300.

32. Longenbach, *Modernist Poetics of History*, 7.

33. R. John Williams, *The Buddha in the Machine*, 100. Williams details modernism's complex investments in a concept of Asian "techne" that might cut the "apron

strings of the mechanical" (as phrased by an editorial in *New Age*). Relevant here is his study of Ernest Fenollosa's theory of Asian art, which sought an escape for "debilitating minds" that "crave a perfected machinery for learning art" (91).

34. Monroe, Introduction to *The New Poetry*, vi. On the strategic reimaginings of Whitman as a ground for free verse and, by extension, a unified and transracial American poetics, see Erin Kappeler, "Constructing Walt Whitman."

35. Pound, "A Few Don'ts by an Imagiste," 204. As late as Canto 98 he threatens, "and as for those who deform thought with iambics." *Cantos*, 687.

36. Harriet Monroe to T. S. Eliot, April 2, 1934, Poetry: A Magazine of Verse, Records, Box 33, Folder 11, Special Collections Research Center, University of Chicago Library.

37. Parody "keeps cultural stereotypes in circulation even while holding them up for critique" (xiv). Williams's book very usefully develops a formalism rooted in genre theory. She attends to processes of formalization, especially how parody raises social forms into recognition precisely as "forms": "The operas treat social formations as a variety of 'preformed material,' available to parody insofar as they may be seen as forms already mediated by representation." *Gilbert and Sullivan*, 15. Meter in modernism works as such a "preformed" literary material.

38. The initial attribution is to Flint, in his essay "Imagisme" published in *Poetry*, March 1913, followed by Pound's "A Few Don'ts by an Imagiste." Monroe's editorial note links the two, and given Pound's absorption of Flint's rules into his 1914 essay "Vorticism" and his 1918 *A Retrospect*, I would not be surprised if they were written by Pound originally or in committee. All three versions end "not in sequence of a/the metronome" ("the" in 1914); only Pound's 1918 version begins "to compose in the sequence" rather than "to compose in sequence." This adds to the small but palpable rhythmic contrast I describe. Pound, "Vorticism"; "A Retrospect."

39. Qtd. in Leighton, *On Form*, 153. Of particular interest are Florence Farr's tonal performances of Yeats and critical defenses circa 1910 of those performances and of Yeats as the "master of subtly modulated monotone." *The Music of Speech*, 5.

40. Ford, *Critical Writings*, 157.

41. Prins, "Victorian Meters," 98.

42. Woolf, "Aurora Leigh," 228.

43. Lowell, "Some Musical Analogies in Modern Poetry," 141.

44. William Carlos Williams, introduction to *Illustrated Leaves of Grass*, 12.

45. Monroe, "What Next," 37.

46. Kenner, *The Poetry of Ezra Pound*, 114.

47. Donoghue's mention of counting is not intended as a judgment about meter as beautiful form, but it does come just after a challenge to the authenticity of "common form": "Hardy, Graves, Frost, A. E. Housman, Edward Thomas, and—for the most part—Yeats and Stevens thought the common forms were adequate," but "the most exacting poets, notably Eliot, Pound, and Crane," did not. This "formal" divide

is a metrical one. Donoghue, *Speaking of Beauty*, 121, 118. Angela Leighton cites Donoghue's discussion as an example of how definitions of form "steer the argument away from questions of verse-form or metre. Form is not a matter of correct technique; it is a force of creativity generally." Leighton, *On Form*, 23.

48. The challenge of simply counting syllables recurs across the history of English prosody from at least sixteenth-century debates over Chaucer's meter through Robert Bridges (see below) to Kenneth Goldsmith's *111*, a syllabic poem that he tried to write with a computer-based dictionary but ultimately had to work out by hand as "the rules determining syllable counts are extremely idiosyncratic." Perloff, "A Conversation with Kenneth Goldsmith." In his survey of English prosodic theory from 1880-1930, Pallister Barkas hints at the chicken and egg problem of philologists and literary historians looking to each other to determine what counts as a syllable, an elision or resolution, or correct historical pronunciation. He was overly optimistic, it seems, in finding that "the one proposition on which most authorities would agree is that we cannot determine *a priori* how many syllables a heroic line must contain." *A Critique of Modern English Prosody (1880-1930)*, 3-4.

49. Martin, "Picturing Rhythm."

50. Newcomb, *Would Poetry Disappear?*, xv.

51. Ziff singles out Trumbull Stickney for his "almost automatic dependence upon the traditional arsenal." *The American 1890s*, 317.

52. Even in the Renaissance, Omond finds, "critics were preaching an 'arithmetic' view of blank verse," and "rhythmus became merely the alteration of stronger and weaker accents. This mechanical view of meter, founded on no sufficient induction of instances, spread and flourished without challenge." *English Metrists*, 29. Edward Bysshe's 1702 *Art of English Poetry* later formalized this "mechanical" and "arithmetic" approach to blank verse; similar attitudes can be found in Samuel Johnson or even Thomas Jefferson, "Thoughts on English Prosody." Bysshe's work was reprinted eight times by 1762. Jefferson's short treatise dates to roughly 1789.

53. Omond, *English Metrists*, 48.

54. Mayor, *Chapters on English Metre*, 7.

55. Brewer, *Orthometry*, 9.

56. Sarah Ehlers argues for a late 1800s dating of this manuscript essay, originally titled "Modern Tendencies in Poetry." Monroe amended the title on the carbon copy to "Victorian Poets." In her discussion of how seemingly "modern" critics "idealize, preserve, and recirculate" Victorian poetry, Ehlers suggests that Monroe's patronage, nationalism, and canon align better with Victorian than (proto)-modernist priorities. "Making It Old," 39. I would call her "modernist" in the restricted sense that she adopts an anti-technical theory of rhythm as the basis of poetry.

57. Monroe, "Editorial Comment: Rhythms of English Verse," 61. Esenwein and Roberts, *The Art of Versification*, 39.

58. Lanier's musical notation marks different quantities, or lengths of syllables as

well as rests, in contrast to scansion focused on the placement of stressed and unstressed syllables. Citations to him appear in Esenwein and Roberts, *The Art of Versification*, x, 83, 215, 291. Monroe and the manual share an investment, ultimately, in metaphysical concepts of rhythm found in nineteenth century treatises such as Thaddeus Bolton's long 1894 essay "Rhythm," which according to Michael Golston "marks the beginning of Anglo-American investigations of rhythm." Bolton links literary and "cosmic rhythms" amid more compelling discussions of how meter helps long poems resolve the Kantian question of "how the mind made a unity out of a manifold." "Rhythm," 156. As I discuss in chapter 5, following the work of Virginia Jackson and Erin Kappeler, Francis Barton Gummere's *Handbook of Poetics* (1885) is the more immediate source for ideologies of rhythm and lyric. Especially influential in early twentieth-century ideas of rhythm and lyric, Gummere describes how "rhythm is found everywhere in nature: the beat of the heart, the ebb and flow of the sea, the alteration of day and night. [. . .] It lies at the heart of things." *Handbook*, 134-35. After quoting this passage, Esenwein and Roberts's otherwise very technical manual contends, "We are all more or less affected by the rhythm of recurrent sounds and movements in nature: by the surge and withdrawal of the waves on the beach, or by the moan of the wind in the trees" (61).

59. Bridges, *Milton's Prosody*, 113.
60. Eliot, *Selected Prose*, 271.
61. Pound, "A Retrospect," 84.
62. Robinson, *Poems*, 15.
63. Cornford, *Spring Morning*, 17.
64. Masters, *Spoon River Anthology*, 93.
65. Qtd. in Rogers, *Georgian Poetry, 1911-1922*, 35.
66. Martin, "Rupert Brooke's Ambivalent Mourning, Ezra Pound's Anticipatory Nostalgia," 186.
67. Brooke, *The Collected Poems*, 260-63. Pope explicitly mocks the rhyme of breeze/trees in his *Essay on Criticism*. Given the presence of "Grantchester" in a 2004 audio collection *England's Favourite Poems* without any tone of sarcasm, such ironic and conscious effects of prosody are lost to many present readers.
68. Eliot, *The Waste Land*. Henceforth cited parenthetically as *TWL*.
69. Tiffany, *My Silver Planet*, 11, 17.
70. Cavitch, "Stephen Crane's Refrain," 48.
71. Halliday, *Sonic Modernity*, 27. Frattarola, *Modernist Soundscapes*, 13.
72. Mao, *Solid Objects*, 4.
73. Murphet, Groth, and Hone, *Sounding Modernism*, 14, 4.
74. Prins, "Victorian Meters," 91-92.
75. Rudy, *Electric Meters*.
76. Hall, *Nineteenth-Century Verse and Technology*, 240.
77. Gitelman, *Scripts, Grooves, and Writing Machines*, 52.

78. Qtd. in Ellmann, *James Joyce*, 476.

79. Joyce, *Ulysses*, 7:369. Henceforth cited parenthetically by chapter and line.

80. MacHugh's scansion is sparked by Myles Crawford's outburst of "Ohio, My Ohio," a variant of the ballad "My Maryland," a song that had been parodically adapted as "My Ohio" and performed in Dublin by a blackface Irish group. Simpson, "Ohio." "Ohio" is not really a cretic (perhaps a molossus or bacchius). This may reflect MacHugh's limited understanding, or Joyce's, but my sense is that linguistic accuracy is subordinated to musical hearing and that this is Joyce's point. To be very precise—more precise than MacHugh or any Anglophone reader—the phonology of the Iroquoian language family may not even treat the phonological word as the appropriate prosodic domain for determining stress. It is impossible to say exactly how, out of context, "Ohio" would scan in Seneca. See Dyck, "Defining the Word in Cayuga (Iroquoian)."

81. Vincent Cheng notes that the beginning of "Proteus" represents for Stephen a moment of trauma and alienation, and that Stephen frequently in such moments turns to metrical poetry. "Twining Stresses," 392.

82. Sterne, *The Audible Past*, 155.

83. Sterne, *The Audible Past*, 167.

84. Kittler, *Gramophone, Film, Typewriter*, 22–23, 33.

85. Murphet, Groth, and Hone, *Sounding Modernism*, 8.

86. Longenbach, *Stone Cottage*, 12. Pound, *Poems and Translations*, 194.

87. Eliot, *Ezra Pound*, 11, 9.

88. Winters, *In Defense of Reason*, 146.

89. Hammer, *Janus-Faced Modernism*, 43–44.

90. Winters, *In Defense of Reason*, 104.

91. Hall, *Nineteenth-Century Verse and Technology*. Golston, *Rhythm and Race*, 4.

92. Hartman observes, "The invention of free verse required, and implies, a new awareness of prosody as part of the communication a poem offers to its readers. Besides allowing poets to use new techniques prosodically, this awareness has also encouraged directly rhetorical uses of form to establish a special community between the maker of the poem and the reader who 'uses' it." *Free Verse*, 81. Each "new awareness" must be deeply precarious if it demands an operating "rhetoric" of form within the poem. Cushman diagnoses the non-coherence and absent "inherent auditory dimension" of W. C. Williams's prosodic theory, especially the "variable foot." *William Carlos Williams and the Meanings of Measure*, 48. Chris Beyers argues that free verse had to grow out of initial anxiety about absent metrical contracts: "By the thirties [. . .] poets in general became less intent on announcing their rhythms. This suggests that something changed in the general approach to poetry. [. . .] Historically, what happened was that free-verse poetry started evincing less concern about guiding the reader because new contracts between free-verse poets and readers familiar with Modern poetry began to emerge." *A History of Free Verse*, 37.

93. Brinkman, *Poetic Modernism in the Culture of Mass Print*, 36.
94. Sider, *Parting Words*, 195. Prins, "Metrical Translation," 230, 252.
95. Du Bois, *The Souls of Black Folk*, 264.
96. Farr, *The Music of Speech*, 21.
97. Richards, *Practical Criticism*, 326, 229, 224.
98. Buckley, "Talking Machines," 24.
99. Kane, *Sound Unseen*. Josh Epstein, reflecting on Schaeffer as well as George Antheil's belief in the pure formalism of the *Ballet mécanique*, observes that only the "purveyors of doctrine actually experienced" this form. *Sublime Noise*, xxiii.
100. Napolin, "The Fact of Resonance," 177, 183.
101. Skinner, *The Shaping of a Behaviorist*, 175. Skinner published his research as "The Verbal Summator and a Method for the Study of Latent Speech." I am grateful to Mara Mills for bringing Skinner's phonographic device and auditory testing protocols to my attention. On the auditory projective test in the context of media history, disability studies, and the history of medicine, see Mills, "Evocative Object."
102. Bromwich, *Skeptical Music*, 7–8.
103. See Jarvis, *Wordsworth's Philosophic Song*, 4. For Jarvis's most programmatic statement on the importance of verse "repertoire" to historical poetics, formalism, and criticism more generally, see "For a Poetics of Verse."
104. Hardy, *Jude the Obscure*, 21.
105. Hardy, *Complete Poems*, 430.
106. Taylor, *Hardy's Metres and Victorian Prosody*, 200.
107. Hanson, "Generative Metrics," 59. As Natalie Gerber has argued, Wallace Stevens similarly tests and provokes our ears through word-level phonological experiment; he "winkingly refuses our desire to impose certain *iambs*" with a flexible blank verse that can feel "both obvious and nearly irrelevant." "Stevens' Prosody."
108. Winslow, *Trial Balances*, 76. The same dialectical reversal grounds Tate's own poetry. Langdon Hammer finds that Tate's "determination that Milton could not write epic were he to stand in Tate's place points to the presence of the complementary fantasy that Tate, because *he* cannot write an epic, stands in Milton's [place]." *Janus-Faced Modernism*, 44–45.
109. Grossman, *The Long Schoolroom*, 87.
110. Grossman, *The Long Schoolroom*, 120, 101.
111. Ray, "Object of Destruction."
112. Agawu, *Representing African Music*, 56.
113. Jaji, *Africa in Stereo*, 69.

1. Modernist Scansion

1. Frost, *Collected Poems, Prose, and Plays*, 116. Henceforth cited parenthetically as *CPPP*.

2. For a rare study of modern investments in syllabics, which turns out to be another untold history of versification beyond lyric "rhythm," see Meredith Martin on Bridges, Crapsey, and William Carlos Williams in "Picturing Rhythm."

3. Walcott, "The Road Taken," 103.

4. Steele, *Missing Measures*, 61.

5. See Glaser, "Modernist Scansion." It was Frost who coined the term "loose iambic," arguing that "there are virtually but two [meters], strict iambic and loose iambic" but it is unclear whether he had in mind the later linguistic definition. "The Figure a Poem Makes," 776.

6. "Beyond Meaning," 227-28, 237.

7. Qtd. in Gould, *Amy*, 170.

8. Aldington, "Review of *North of Boston*," 248.

9. Ford, "Mr. Robert Frost and *North of Boston*."

10. Pound, "Review of *A Boy's Will*," 72.

11. See Wheeler, *Voicing American Poetry*, 4. Frost mentions the "hearing ear" in *Letters*, 140. "The Imagining Ear" is the title of a 1915 lecture.

12. Robert Frost to John T. Bartlett, July 4, 1913, *Selected Letters*, 79-81.

13. Frost, *Notebooks*, 99. An important contrast to analysis focused on Frost's dramatic representation of place and language can be seen in critics like Marie Borroff and John Lynen, as well as Richard Poirier (discussed below). Each suggests that Frost forces the historical reader into a series of uncomfortable determinations, including choices about sound. Lynen affirms the importance of the written medium to Frost, specifying that "rhythm" is no guarantee of audibility and mimetic accuracy: "Frost is working in the printed, not the spoken word. He cannot reproduce the intonation of Yankee speech but must imitate it, and no particular rhythm will accomplish this" *The Pastoral Art of Robert Frost*, 88. Borroff notes that Frost uses few regionalisms or colloquialisms, suggesting that he adopts instead a "common level of style" representing a "selection from the spoken language rather than a reproduction of it." *Language and the Poet*, 29.

14. Frost, *Notebooks*, 112.

15. Frost, "Letter to Sidney Cox," December 1914, in Evans, *Robert Frost and Sidney Cox*, 54-56.

16. Frost, "Letter to Sidney Cox," December 1914, in Evans, *Robert Frost and Sidney Cox*, 54-56.

17. Frost, "The Figure a Poem Makes," 776.

18. Robert Frost to John Cournos, July 8, 1914, *Selected Letters*, 128.

19. Frost, *Notebooks*, 95.

20. Robert Frost to John T. Bartlett, July 4, 1913, *Selected Letters*, 79-81.

21. Frost, *Notebooks*, 139.

22. Using alternating stress and unstress markers underneath the line to indicate the metrical template is not ideal because it conflates actual phonological stress with

an abstract grid that lacks a clear phenomenological presence. For further discussion see the appendix.

23. Frost, *Notebooks*, 132.
24. Frost, *Notebooks*, 120.
25. Frost, *Notebooks*, 110. Although many metrists indicate "secondary" stress—often marked by \—and a four-level approach is somewhat common, the eight or more implied by Frost's half step has no precedent. Jespersen's system, which Frost seems unlikely to have known, had four levels: weak, half-weak, half-strong, strong. Trager and Smith, *An Outline of English Structure* (1951), establishes four levels in the domain of syntax, and some linguists applied this schema to verse as well.
26. Although Chaucer is generally thought of as the forefather of accentual-syllabic (iambic) verse in English, he and poets of the following generation like Hoccleve and Lydgate are best treated as a separate case for both formal and literary-historical reasons. The appendix to this book takes a more deliberate approach. For an extended exploration of both (1) how these "rules" emerged in linguistic approaches to meter since the 1960s and (2) their sensitivity to vicissitudes of historical practice and taste, see Marina Tarlinskaja's recent "What Is 'Metricality'? English Iambic Pentameter." The essay is equally useful in providing an array of "meter-fixing" vs. "meter-fixed" rhythmic "figures" that to varying degrees recall or distract from our recognition of meter (62). She provides many examples from Frost's strict iambics showing how far he could "complicate recognition" (72). I diverge from Tarlinskaja primarily in my theory of how Frost's loose iambics perform this complication.
27. Pound, "Review of *A Boy's Will*," 72–73.
28. Brower, *Constellations*, 19.
29. Brower, *Fields of Light*, 71.
30. Pinsky, *Democracy, Culture and the Voice of Poetry*, 26.
31. Eliot, *Selected Prose*, 150.
32. Hopkins's "counterpointed" verse is best treated as an extreme case of metrical tension. Browning's prosody achieves what Simon Jarvis calls a "rich corrugation" unheralded in his other work or in Victorian poetics. His avoidance of fixed accent in key positions achieves an effect similar to that of Frost. Jarvis, "Sordello's Pristine Pulpiness," 60. In direct contrast with Frost, Stevens's metrical play occurs at the level of the word; he "harnesses the force of meter to focus our attention on the sounding and resounding of the sounds of words." Gerber, "Stevens' Prosody," 178.
33. Randall Jarrell finds the sequence of four "don'ts" "exactly accurate, perfectly effective," compared to three or five, though this "perfection," like the metrical exactness, is a register entirely alien to the woman. "Robert Frost's 'Home Burial,'" 49.
34. Kearns, *Robert Frost and a Poetics of Appetite*, 77. Kearns notes the line "She took a doubtful step and then undid it" as a fitting the meta- and extra-metrical example of "uncontrol" over language made ironic by the controlling presence of meter.

35. Krauss, *The Originality of the Avant-Garde and Other Modernist Myths*, 9.
36. Jarrell, "Robert Frost's 'Home Burial,'" 48.
37. Jarrell, "Robert Frost's 'Home Burial,'" 49.
38. In five YouTube dramatic stagings reviewed in 2017, no one read the line twice. Three of three women read the line with stress on "man," whereas both men did not. No claims are made for the training of these ears, only the possibility for variance and the possibility, born out by the poem itself, that the speaker's gender or consciousness thereof galvanizes performance. Whether the later "man" in "any man can" is stressed varied. Readers were pulled to the final "can" despite its relative non-prominence and hypermetrical position. It is an entirely unusual feminine ending for Frost, being the only stress-able syllable in the poem to come after a stressed tenth syllable, and thus uniquely destabilizes the all-but-universally fixed stress on the tenth syllable of every pentameter line in Frost. Jarrell observes the "triumphantly ugly dissonance" of this line ending (48).
39. Poirier, *Poetry and Pragmatism*, 176.
40. Markovits, *The Victorian Verse-Novel*, 105.
41. Cramer, *Robert Frost among His Poems*, 21-22.
42. Murphy, "'A Thing so Small.'"
43. Poirier argues that the famous question ("what to make of a diminished thing") cannot actually be answered by the bird but only by the poet, and specifically in his meter: "The steady iambic push against the trochaic falling" is a "metrical performance [that] shows what it is like to meet and answer the 'fall.'" *Performing Self*, 98.
44. Frost, *Selected Letters*, 248.
45. Tennyson saw the meter as primarily fitting for "sui-generis experiments which I wished to try with the public." *Letters*, 2:346. It was published in *Enoch Arden* (1864).
46. Martin Duffell argues that Tennyson "stumbled on this accentual metre by accident" and critiques the result for lacking the variable stress contours present in Catullus but effectively impossible in English. "Tennyson's 'Metre of Catullus,'" 28. Yet Tennyson is not just writing "in" the metre but performing a bathetic "metrification of Catullus." Duffell rightly notes how such accentual oddities must "remain a curiosity, unless some poet employs it in a major poem and transforms it into a canon" (28). Yopie Prins delightfully observes Tennyson's "performance of . . . mock-versification" in response to the Victorian "hexameter mania" and how he forced readers to sound like "barbarous hexamateurs." "Metrical Translation," 247.
47. This certainly did not prevent efforts to write quantitative hendecasylabics. Take, for example, Robinson Ellis's unfortunate 1871 effort to translate Catullus 5 ("Living, Lesbia, let us e'en be loving").
48. Catullus, *Poems*, 33, 27-28.
49. Ezra Pound, I note in chapter 3, uses double off-stresses modeled on the choriambic foot to good effect in "Apparuit" and possibly in some of the Cantos.

Hopkins's "counterpointed" verse, in which trochaic inversions are not limited to the beginning of the line or after caesuras, shows by convergent evolution why the SWSWWS opening of the hendecasyllabic line is so potent. Hopkins writes that the "reversal of feet" is "done freely at the beginning of a line and, in the course of a line, after a pause; only scarcely ever in the second foot or place and never in the last, unless when the poet designs some extraordinary effect; for these places are characteristic and sensitive and cannot well be touched." *Poems and Prose*, 8. Milton has similar lines, often with some mimesis of dissonance.

50. In Fabb and Halle's 2008 *Meter in Poetry*, this constitutes a "grid transformation" (28–32). Once a key syllable is discounted—the head of the line, in fact—iambic scansion can proceed. While their description helps show the contrast between hendecasyllabic and iambic verse, the discussion problematically naturalizes hendecasyllabic scansion, given the lack of any true corpus of these one-off experiments.

51. Tennyson, *Poems*, 2:652.

52. Frost's copy of *Catullus, Tibullus and Pervigilium Veneris* (Macmillan, 1912) is held at the Fales Library at New York University.

53. He has in mind Swinburne and Tennyson. His judgment is specifically trained on prosodic investment in "the music of words [as] a matter of harmonized vowels and consonants." This could entail both alliterative meter (potentially mock Anglo-Saxon) or quantitative meter. Frost, *Selected Letters*, 79–81.

54. Brower, *Constellations*, 138.

55. Talbot, "Robert Frost's Hendecasyllabics and Roman Rebuttals," 75, 82.

56. T. S. Eliot, a kindred spirit here, dismissed elaborate patterns (like Frost and Pound, he takes issue with Swinburne, who also wrote a poem in hendecasyllabics and several in Sapphics) because they do not permit the poet to "take liberties" with them. Eliot, "Reflections on *Vers Libre*," 33.

57. Dryden, *Poems*, 272. On Elizabethan prosody's awkward routing through classical scansion, see Attridge, *Well-Weighed Syllables*.

58. Poirier, *Poetry and Pragmatism*, 146.

59. Kearns, *Robert Frost and a Poetics of Appetite*, 43.

60. Poirier, *Poetry and Pragmatism*, 176.

61. Poirier, *Poetry and Pragmatism*, 146.

62. Mao, *Solid Objects*, 7.

63. Booth, *Trying to Say It*, 47.

64. The violence of the poem may reflect on the wounded deaths of Frost's wife and children in the previous decade: his son Carol, by suicide; Marjorie, from puerperal fever, a complication of childbirth; and his wife, Elinor, from surgery related to cancer.

65. Empson, *Seven Types of Ambiguity*, 30.

66. Forrest-Thomson, *Poetic Artifice*, 223.

2. Penty Ladies

1. Rob Lehman provides this characterization but argues that Eliot's poetry questioned the historical narratives that would make such recoveries and returns possible. Lehman, *Impossible Modernism*, 29.

2. Tucker, "Doughty's *The Dawn in Britain* and the Modernist Eclipse of the Victorian," 2.

3. Eliot, *Collected Poems*, 45. Henceforth cited parenthetically as *CPTSE*.

4. Schulze, *The Degenerate Muse*, 128.

5. In a kindred spirit, Aldous Huxley's *Brave New World* (1932) deploys "pneumatic" to describe particularly desirable women like Lenina Crowne, as well as a sofa, scent organ stalls, chairs, and shoes. *Brave New World*, 32.

6. North, *The Dialect of Modernism*, 10. I take the idea of metrical "masquerade" from both North and Rosemary Gates, "T. S. Eliot's Prosody and the Free Verse Tradition," 556.

7. Clark, "Arguments about Modernism," 103.

8. Gordon, *T. S. Eliot*, 37.

9. Larzer Ziff notes how Pound and Eliot, unlike the poets of the 1890s, return to the past to find leverage for "ironic comment on the present." *The American 1890s*, 311, 317.

10. Clark, *Sentimental Modernism*, 126.

11. Nicholls, *Modernisms*, 127.

12. McDonald, *Learning to Be Modern*, 83, 31.

13. McDonald, *Learning to Be Modern*, 64.

14. Holmes, "The Physiology of Versification," 319.

15. Untitled lecture from 1893 and December 1924 lecture on the "free-verse movement in America." Monroe, Harriet, Papers, Box 10, Folder 5, and Box 11, Folder 1, Special Collections Research Center, University of Chicago Library.

16. Nicholls, *Modernisms*, 184.

17. In her PhD dissertation, Amanda French observes how Saintsbury and others coded the form as effeminate. French, "Refrain Again."

18. Stephen and Orlando are prefigured by Emma Bovary, whose "career is the very embodiment of a second-hand desire derived from romantic fiction" against which "Flaubert's countervailing model of verbal precision—the novel itself—tacitly proposes a 'genuine' aesthetic as ground of critical distance." Nicholls, *Modernisms*, 20.

19. Mao, *Solid Objects*, 10.

20. McDonald, *Learning to Be Modern*, 83.

21. Nicholls, *Modernisms*, 4.

22. Bollobás, "(De-)Gendering and (De-)Sexualizing Female Subjectivities," 105-6.

23. Bogel, *The Difference Satire Makes*, 42.

24. Nicholls, *Modernisms*, 178.

25. Wilson's ear detects, for example, that "I grow old . . . I grow old . . ./I shall wear the bottom of my trousers rolled" is a metrical echo of Laforgue's "Légende": "Oh! L'automme, l'automme!/Les casinos/Qu'on abandone/Remisent leurs pianos." *Axel's Castle*, 97. Wilson and others would have been prepared for such linguistic crossings by F. S. Flint's encyclopedic essay, "Contemporary French Poetry," published in the August 1912 issue of the *Poetry Review*. In a 1914 letter to Harriet Monroe, Pound praised the essay as something "everybody had to get." *Selected Letters*, 74. Reinforcing the point is René Taupin's 1929 *L'influence du symbolisme français sur la poesie americaine*, which notes, with guidance from John Gould Fletcher, Richard Aldington, Ezra Pound, and others, how Eliot "imitated the rhythms of Gautier." *The Influence of French Symbolism on Modern American Poetry*, 189.

26. Eliot, *Facsimile*, 107.

27. Eliot, *The Use of Poetry*, 13.

28. Gordon notes Eliot's repeated "caricatures" of his friendship with this "emotional older woman [. . .] who used to serve tea to Harvard men in a home crowded with bric-à-brac." *T. S. Eliot*, 37.

29. Although this "Lady" is not Florence Farr, as in Pound's "Portrait d'une Femme," Farr and Yeats had in the previous decade elaborated a positive poetics of what one scholar called a "subtly modulated monotone." Yeats defends "a monotone in external things for the sake of internal variety [. . .] an asceticism of the imagination." Eliot's portrait inverts this complex monotone, giving us external cacophony and internal monotone. Farr, *The Music of Speech*, 5.

30. Powell, "The Two Paradigms for Iambic Pentameter and Twentieth-Century Metrical Experimentation," 567.

31. "Epistle to a Lady" (87).

32. *CPTSE*, 24.

33. Gordon, *T. S. Eliot*, 81. Eliot's recently released letters to Hale confirm the poem's extreme struggle toward impersonality.

34. Lehman, "Eliot's Last Laugh," 70. Lehman suggests that satire in *TWL* falls apart because it becomes a "satire of satire." The effect of this meta-satire is, he argues, an inescapable recognition of one's similarity to the object of satire. 75.

35. "Music is for dreaming, or for kissing, or for taking a shower, or for having your teeth drilled." "Music Discomposed," 202.

36. Bedient, *He Do the Police in Different Voices*, 55.

37. Bedient, *He Do the Police in Different Voices*, 54.

38. Eliot, *Facsimile*, 39. Swift rhymes "greasy stench" and "careless wench."

39. Gordon, *T. S. Eliot*, 173. Gordon makes this claim based on Anne Crisholm's biography of Cunard.

40. See Henri D. Davray's 1918 review of *Georgian Poetry, 1916–1917*, which Pound cites when rejecting some of Eliot's wordiness: "Cherchent-ils des sentiments

pour les accomoder à leur vocabulaire et non des mots pour exprimer leur passion et leur idées" (They sought out feelings to accommodate to their words rather than words to express their passion and ideas). *"Georgian Poetry, 1916-1917,"* 717, my translation. This was the cardinal sin of rhetoric against which modernism, like Romanticism, positioned itself. F. S. Flint, for example, praised the French symbolists for their attempt to "strip poetry of rhetoric." Qtd. in Naremore, "The Imagists and the French 'Generation of 1900,'" 358.

41. Eliot, *Facsimile*, 23.

42. Marvell's lines read "But at my back I always hear/Time's winged chariot hurrying near." Eliot drags out Marvell's swift tetrameter and even swifter extra syllables (chariot, hurrying) into the repetitive iambs of "from time to time."

43. Day's couplet ends with a line of only three stresses: "Actaeon to Diana in the spring"; Eliot loads up the trochaic names common to English—"Sweeney" and "Mrs. Porter"—to install a more palpable iambic rhythm. In the satires of 1920, Grishkin, Doris, Rachel, Bleistein, and Burbank serve the same roles, sometimes in particularly seamless falling verse ("Apeneck Sweeney spreads his knees," "Rachel *née* Rabinowitz").

44. Eliot, *Facsimile*, 11.

45. Sullivan, *The Work of Revision*, 138.

46. Koestenbaum, *"The Waste Land,"* 115.

47. Dante Gabriel Rossetti's paintings of golden-haired women like Elizabeth Siddal hover in the passage, especially given Eliot's contrast of Fresca with "The lazy laughing Jenny of the bard" and Eliot's allusion to Rossetti's description of Jenny's hair "all golden in the firelight's gleam." Other modern poets turned to such women and their hair to signal aesthetic escape. Loy found in Rossetti's poetry, with its "wide-eyed women stricken with fried hair," "so powerful an emetic of the spirit as to relieve a middle-class visionary [herself] of her adolescence." *The Last Lunar Baedeker*, 315. H.D. likewise imagined a composite identity of her and Siddal as a feminist reclamation of the queer energies of the Pre-Raphaelites from the Victorian-modern male collusions of Swinburne-Pound and Rossetti-Aldington. See Laity, *H.D. and the Victorian Fin de Siècle*, xvii. Laity notes Pound's starkly contrasting imagery, in *Mauberly*, of "a listless, barren, and ravaged Elizabeth Siddal, absorbed by 'sterile' language, with a 'half-ruin'd face' and wasted body, 'thin as brook water,' and with a 'vacant gaze'" (13).

48. Eliot, *Facsimile*, 27.

49. Eliot, *The Use of Poetry*, 31.

50. Eliot, *Facsimile*, 11.

51. Bedient, *He Do the Police in Different Voices*, 93.

52. Eliot records this entirely subjective perception of the clocktower at St. Mary Woolnoth. Note to l. 68, in *TWL*, 22.

53. Bedient, *He Do the Police in Different Voices*, 95.

54. Eliot, *Poems*, vol. 2. The letters are addressed to Conrad Aiken, Pound, Bonamy Dobreé, and others.

55. Eliot, *Facsimile*, 33.

56. Pound rallies Verlaine to his cause here, writing in the margin, "Qui dira les gaffers de la rime" (Verlaine: "O qui dira les torts de la Rime"). Eliot, *Facsimile*, 45.

57. Bedient reads Tiresias's Augustan quatrains and couplets as "not unlike the clerk's 'one bold stare,' just as histrionic and arrogant." Like the clerk, Tiresias must be "on his guard in the presence [. . .] of this slovenly female," and so Eliot "equips Tiresias with a style all aggression." Bedient, *He Do the Police in Different Voices*, 130, 138, 134-35.

58. Epstein, *Sublime Noise*, xxxv.

59. Sullivan, "T. S. Eliot—His Poetry."

60. Fabb and Halle, *Meter in Poetry*, 90. Duffell, *A New History of English Metre*, 199.

61. Eliot, *Ezra Pound*, 11.

62. Eliot, *Ezra Pound*, 21.

63. Eliot, *Ezra Pound*, 15.

64. Pound, *Ezra Pound and Music*, 47-48.

65. Pound, *Ezra Pound and Music*, 48, 37.

66. Eliot, "Isolated Superiority," 5.

67. Eliot, *The Use of Poetry*, 11.

68. Eliot, "Reflections on *Vers Libre*," 32.

69. Eliot, "Reflections on *Vers Libre*," 33.

70. Eliot, *Selected Prose*, 263.

71. Eliot, *Selected Essays*, 247.

72. Ramazani, *Poetry of Mourning*, 4.

73. Eliot, *Selected Prose*, 270.

74. Eliot, *Selected Prose*, 273-74.

75. Pound, *Ezra Pound and Music*, 288.

76. Eliot, *Selected Prose*, 271.

77. Eliot, *Selected Prose*, 273.

78. Guillory, *Cultural Capital*, 148.

79. Eliot, *The Use of Poetry*, 12-13.

80. Mill, "Thoughts on Poetry and Its Varieties," 83.

3. "No Feet to Walk On"

1. Martin, *The Rise and Fall of Meter*, 186.

2. Dennis, "Pound, Women and Gender," 266.

3. Pound, *Collected Early Poems*, 261. Austin Graham observes the oddness of "Pater's poor standing" as an "out of date embarrassment" given the importance of his aestheticism. Graham chalks this up to Pater's "overly abstract" conception of music,

"dead to the many actual possibilities of musical literature" in the twentieth century. I think it more likely that Pater fell victim to modernist antipathy toward Victorian "musical" poetics. Graham, *The Great American Songbooks*, 2.

4. Dubrow, *Genre*, 12.

5. Eliot, *Ezra Pound*, 170.

6. Pound, "Treatise on Metre," 200-203.

7. "One might call it a counterpoint, if one can conceive a counterpoint which plays not against a sound newly struck, but against the residuum and residua of sounds which hangs in the auditory memory." Pound, *Ezra Pound and Music*, 288-89.

8. Pound, *Selected Letters*, 322.

9. Pound, *Selected Letters*, 87.

10. R. John Williams traces Pound's development of Fenollosa's ideas in his own aesthetics; for example, how Pound's concept of the "vortex" translated Fenollosa's understanding of the ideograph's "abstract, dynamic energies" back to the mechanical (*The Buddha in the Machine*, 117). The abstract temporality of the ideograph's "rhythm" obviated further investment in the bad mechanicity of meter's linear parsing of poetic time.

11. Pound, "Vorticism," 463.

12. Albright, *Quantum Poetics*, 151, 148-49. For a diametrically opposed effort to trace a "developing theory" of absolute rhythm and the "great bass," see R. Murray Schafer's appendix to *Ezra Pound and Music*.

13. Poetry: A Magazine of Verse, Records, Box 39:31, Special Collections Research Center, University of Chicago Library.

14. Nicholls, *Modernisms*, 187.

15. McDonald, *Learning to Be Modern*, 82.

16. Pound, Ezra. "Three Cantos," 118.

17. Ezra Pound to Alice Corbin Henderson, May 1913, in *The Letters of Ezra Pound to Alice Corbin Henderson*, 44.

18. Latimer, Ronald Lane, Papers, Box 1 Folder 15, Special Collections Research Center.

19. Kenner, "Blood for the Ghosts," 345.

20. Pound, *Poems and Translations*, 173. Henceforth cited parenthetically as *PTEP*.

21. Pound, *Collected Early Poems*, 215.

22. Thomas H. Jackson, *The Early Poetry of Ezra Pound*, 146, 232, 236.

23. Clark, *Sentimental Modernism*, 41.

24. *PTEP*, 15.

25. Adams, "Poetics," 229.

26. In Greek or Latin these patterns would be quantitative. I indicate stress contours because that is how such patterns almost always occur in modern poetry. Scholars like Stephen J. Adams have skillfully parsed the "successive shifts of verse form," discerned the "characteristic lyric rhythms" of individual cantos, and found

the "whole explicable as combinations of Greek *metra*," but the logic of a "constantly evolving contract" appears either paradoxical or at the least an incredible challenge to the ear that simply "takes it all in" and "grasps it instinctively." "Metrical Contract," 67-68. The necessity of Adams's own extensive scansion and decades-long experience of *The Cantos* belies, in my view, the claim to phenomenological rhythm. In a separate article Adams agrees with D. S. Carne-Ross's 1967 judgment that the "rhythm" of *The Cantos* "is based on a number of well-defined rhythmic fragments [Carne-Ross: 'recurrent metrical cola'] which reappear freely." "Pound's Quantities and 'Absolute Rhythm,'" 105. Carne-Ross conceives Pound's Greek syllabic "phrases" as his "metrical signature." Kenner nominates the "terminal spondee" as this signature, in both 1909 and "five decades later." "Blood for the Ghosts," 336. Whichever pattern we choose, Pound's "formal homage" to Sappho requires that he extend such signatures in his "commendation [of the Sapphic stanza] to his disciples." Carne-Ross, "New Metres for Old: A Note on Pound's Metric," 221-22.

27. Rosenblitt, "Pretentious Scansion, Fascist Aesthetics, and a Father-Complex for Joyce," 181.

28. Adams, "Poetics," 229.

29. Burke, "The New Poetry and the New Woman," 46.

30. Thomas H. Jackson, *The Early Poetry of Ezra Pound*, 145.

31. Thomas H. Jackson, *The Early Poetry of Ezra Pound*, 234.

32. In 1909 Yeats wrote to Lady Gregory, "This queer creature Ezra Pound, who has become really a great authority on the troubadours, has I think got closer to the right sort of music for poetry than Mrs. Emery—it is more definitely music with strongly marked time and yet it is effective speech." *Letters*, 543.

33. DuPlessis, *Blue Studios*, 124.

34. The *North American Review* initially rejected "Portrait d'une Femme" in part because the first line is so awkward to pronounce. Pound's response, as conveyed by the editors of *Early Writings*, echoes "Phasellus Ille": "Pound understood this reasoning as proof of the compliance of American editors to fixed formulas of literary success" (351).

35. Sergeant, *Robert Frost*, 103.

36. Grieder, "Robert Frost on Ezra Pound, 1913," 302.

37. Ellmann, *Eminent Domain*, 66.

38. Corbière, *Selected Poems and Prose*, 7.

39. Eliot, *Ezra Pound*, 172-73.

40. Pound, *Selected Prose 1909-1965*, 376.

41. Wordsworth, *Major Works*, 598. Donald Wesling finds that in "Tintern Abbey" the mild turns of "And," "Therefore," and "Not only [. . .] but" help suggest a "mind almost entirely in possession of its experience." "The Inevitable Ear," 116.

42. Whereas Patmore theorizes catalexis as a natural "essence" of the "iambic ode" and not "irregular," in Pound and even more so in Eliot the irregularity of catalexis is blatant and precisely the point. *Essay on English Metrical Law*, 27-28. The exact inden-

tation of the last line varies somewhat by edition. In my reprinting I am following the 1917 Knopf edition *Lustra by Ezra Pound: With Earlier Poems*.

43. Wordsworth, Note to "Tintern Abbey" (1800), in *Major Works*, 692.

44. See Prins, "'What Is Historical Poetics?,'" 23-28. Browning looks to meter as her own musical instrument, but meter is something painfully "cut up" like the re-imagined reed (28).

45. Pound, "A List of Books," 57-58.

46. Pound plans, in a 1913 letter to Alice Corbin Henderson, to take poetry on "as our or at least my organ on this side the drink, and [I] shall control its literchure." *The Letters of Ezra Pound to Alice Corbin Henderson*, 52. According to Diana Collecott, it was H.D.'s promotion of women writers that led Pound to say she "is all right but shouldn't write criticism." *H.D. and Sapphic Modernism 1910-1950*, 166. In a 1917 letter to his father, Eliot writes "I struggle to keep the writing [of the *Egoist*] as much as possible in Male hands, as I distrust the Feminine in literature, and also, once a woman has had anything printed in your paper, it is very difficult to make her see why you should not print everything she sends in." Eliot, *Letters*, 1:228.

47. Pound, *The Letters of Ezra Pound to Alice Corbin Henderson*, 138-39, 198.

48. Pound, *The Letters of Ezra Pound to Alice Corbin Henderson*, 156.

49. Pound, *The Letters of Ezra Pound to Alice Corbin Henderson*, 21.

50. Pound, *The Letters of Ezra Pound to Alice Corbin Henderson*, 20, 4, 150, 29.

51. Pound, *Selected Letters*, 337, 345.

52. Pound, *Pound/Williams*, 8.

53. Rosenblitt, "Pretentious Scansion, Fascist Aesthetics, and a Father-Complex for Joyce," 181. Prins, "Lady's Greek," 594.

54. Prins, "Lady's Greek," 594-95.

55. Prins, *Victorian Sappho*, 5. Preston, *Modernism's Mythic Pose*, 192.

56. Doolittle, *HERmione*, 149. Henceforth cited parenthetically.

57. Browning, *Aurora Leigh*, 35.

58. Friedman, "Gender and Genre Anxiety," 212.

59. From *End of Torment*, qtd. in Preston, *Modernism's Mythic Pose*, 194.

60. See Prins, *Victorian Sappho*, especially chapter 3.

61. The symbolic chiasma of *HERmione* resonate as well in other echoes of Swinburne, such as Phaedra's speeches in *Hippolytus Temporizes*: "O swallow fair/oh fair sea-swallow." Qtd. in Laity, *H.D. and the Victorian Fin de Siècle*, 105.

62. Preston, *Modernism's Mythic Pose*, 197-98.

4. Metristes

1. Eccles, "Formalism and Sentimentalism," 13.

2. Richard Aldington, H.D.'s husband in the early 1910s, is responsible for the critique of other translators as "clumsy metrists." Prins, *Ladies' Greek*, 182-84.

3. Qtd. in Loy, *The Last Lunar Baedeker*, xliv.
4. Loy, *The Last Lunar Baedeker*, xxvi.
5. Richards, *Practical Criticism*, xx, 86, 117, 74.
6. Loy, *The Last Lunar Baedeker*, 316.
7. Loy, *The Last Lunar Baedeker*, 5.
8. "Loy, *The Last Lunar Baedeker*, 9.
9. Huyssen, *After the Great Divide*, 47.
10. Gilbert, "Female Female Impersonator," 299.
11. Felski, "Introduction," 613.
12. Fried, "Andromeda Unbound," 6.
13. Finch, "Dickinson and Patriarchal Meter," 166.
14. Fried, "Andromeda Unbound," 1. As recently as 2006 Rachel Blau DuPlessis continues the call for feminist criticism to study "gendered materials in the apparatus of *poesis*." DuPlessis's main examples of such material are "subject positions" such as (male) genius and (female) muse or poetess. *Blue Studios*, 122. Lesley Wheeler has also attended to the "modernity" of formalism in Millay and other women poets, including her "queering" and "bending" of the sonnet's "technical parameters." "Formalist Modernism," 633. Millay may be the exceptional example of a poet who can be safely said to have "used" metrical shifts to "dramatize" breaks with convention (632), though such a language of mimetic and political form requires, in my view, a sustained sense of form's historical valuations and of the author's participation in that discourse (here the gendered sonnet tradition).
15. Zellinger, "Edna St. Vincent Millay and the Poetess Tradition," 242.
16. Millay, "I, Being Born a Woman and Distressed," in *Collected Poems*, 601. Millay's poem focuses on sexual ideals but certainly does not preclude a reading of her sonnet as "distressed" by gendered notions.
17. Monroe, "What Next," 36. Turbyfill and Winters both published in *Poetry* in the 1910s.
18. From lecture notes on "The New Poetry," delivered July 1920. Monroe, Harriet. Papers, Box 12, Folder 9, Special Collections Research Center, University of Chicago Library.
19. Monroe, Harriet, Papers, Box 11, Folder 8, Special Collections Research Center.
20. Teasdale, *Collected Poems*, 103-9. I use the term "poetess" not in the derogatory sense it has in twentieth-century criticism (and for modernism) but to refer to the nineteenth-century tradition of women poets like Helen Hunt Jackson. Virginia Jackson has discussed both this tradition and the ways poetesses manipulated its generic elements. See "'The Story of Boon.'"
21. Teasdale, *Collected Poems*, 69. There is a possible echo or affinity with Emily Dickinson's displacement of birdsong by a "ceremonial mass" of insects. Louise Bogan also turns from birdsong to the sound of the "prisoned cricket." *Collected Poems 1923-1953*, 17. Henceforth cited parenthetically as *CPLB*.

Notes to Pages 112-124

22. Teasdale: "He seemed so brave, so blithely calm/Tho' nature cried aloud/That while I listened to his song/My heart was bowed"; Hardy: "That I could think there trembled through/His happy good-night air/Some blessed Hope, whereof he knew/And I was unaware." Teasdale liked her poem enough to include it in a 1912 letter to Orrick Johns, though she hedges that it is "worthless" and that she only includes it for its reference to a bird she had mentioned. Sara Teasdale Collection, Beinecke Library, YCAL MSS 746 Box 4.

23. Monroe, "Review of *Rivers to the Sea*, by Sara Teasdale," 148.
24. McGill, "What Is a Ballad?," 164.
25. Sara Teasdale Collection, Beinecke Library, YCAL MSS 746 Box 1.
26. Pound, *Selected Letters*, 180.
27. Clark, *Sentimental Modernism*, 33.
28. Baker, *Modernism and the Harlem Renaissance*, 87.
29. Sanders, *Afro-Modernist Aesthetics and the Poetry of Sterling A. Brown*, 39.
30. Hart, *Nations of Nothing but Poetry*, 18.
31. Braithwaite, introduction to *Heart of a Woman*, ix.
32. Margo Crawford notes that Dunbar's wife, Alice Dunbar-Nelson, writes a "sarcastic version" of "Sympathy," "I Sit and Sew," in which she too reconsiders the role of gender within poetic production. "'Perhaps Buddha Is a Woman,'" 130.
33. Georgia Douglas Johnson, *Heart of a Woman*, 1. Henceforth cited parenthetically.
34. See Jason David Hall's survey of critical responses to the poem, many of which emphasize its twin imperatives to "utter thoughts" and to parse and articulate the idiosyncratic flow of its rhythm. *Nineteenth-Century Verse and Technology*, 179. The poem continues to be used in many studies of English prosody as an example of line-internal pausing and the flexibility of accentual poetics. See Attridge, *Poetic Rhythm*, 35-36.
35. Brown, *Outline for the Study of the Poetry of American Negroes*, 23.
36. See Glaser, "Polymetrical Dissonance."
37. Attridge, "The Rhythms of the English Dolnik," 169.
38. Du Bois, forward to Johnson, *Bronze*, 7.
39. Tate, introduction to *Selected Works of Georgia Douglas Johnson*, xlvii.
40. Tate, introduction to *Selected Works of Georgia Douglas Johnson*, liii.
41. Crawford, "'Perhaps Buddha Is a Woman,'" 127.
42. Barbara Johnson, "Apostrophe, Animation, and Abortion," 32-33.
43. Barbara Johnson, "Apostrophe, Animation, and Abortion," 34.
44. The poem appears in Alain Locke's 1925 *New Negro* anthology. Georgia Douglas Johnson, "The Ordeal," 146.
45. Georgia Douglas Johnson, *Selected Works*, lvii.
46. Georgia Douglas Johnson, *Selected Works*, lvii.
47. Roethke, "The Poetry of Louise Bogan," 142, 150.

48. Bogan, *What the Woman Lived*, 86.
49. Bogan, *What the Woman Lived*, 86.
50. Bogan, *A Poet's Prose*, 227.
51. Walker, *Masks Outrageous and Austere*, 12, 185.
52. Bogan, *What the Woman Lived*, 86.
53. Bogan, *What the Woman Lived*, 15.
54. *CPLB*, 10.
55. Clark, *Sentimental Modernism*, 41.
56. In "The Gift," for example:

another life holds what this lacks,
a sea, unmoving, quiet—
not forcing our strength
to rise to it, beat on beat—
a stretch of sand,
no garden beyond, strangling
with its myrrh-lilies—

H.D., *Collected Poems*, 18.

57. In "Lake Isle" mimetic sound produces sympathetic magic: "I will arise and go now, for always night and day/I hear lake water lapping with low sounds by the shore [. . .] I hear it in the deep heart's core." This remembered sound evokes Yeats's belief in the symbol, and specifically a Celtic symbolism that appealed to Bogan.
58. Clark, *Sentimental Modernism*, 112.
59. Clark, *Sentimental Modernism*, 126.
60. Bogan, *Body of This Death*, 5. Bogan did not include the poem in later volumes.
61. Bogan, *Body of This Death*, 18.
62. Roethke, "The Poetry of Louise Bogan," 17.
63. Wheeler also sees this extra line as a deformation of the stanza, noting as well that in "Women" (*CPLB*, 25) "the little cells or rooms of this poem are deformed, as if by women's frustration, or Bogan's own." "Formalist Modernism," 642.
64. Bogan, *Body of This Death*, 25.
65. Clark, *Sentimental Modernism*, 106.
66. Wheeler, "Formalist Modernism," 642.
67. Dodd, *The Veiled Mirror and the Woman Poet*, 93. In response to a review request from Harriet Monroe, Bogan comes up with several excuses, including never having "tried to review a book of poetry by a woman contemporary." *What the Woman Lived*, 49.
68. Bogan and Limmer, *Journey around My Room*, 52.
69. Bogan, "The Springs of Poetry," 9.
70. Bogan, "Allen Tate's New Poems," 186.
71. Dickinson, *Poems*, 372.

72. Bogan, *What the Woman Lived*, 63.
73. Bogan, *Selected Prose*, 42.
74. Bogan and Limmer, *Journey around My Room*, 72.
75. Bogan, "The Springs of Poetry," 9.
76. Bogan would take issue, I think, even with the judgment that she "submits to the rigors (and pleasures) of poetic form." Frank, "The Pleasures of Formal Poetry."
77. Kenner, *Homemade World*, 14.
78. Walker, *Masks Outrageous and Austere*, 7.
79. O'Rourke and Stallings, "This Condensery," 224.
80. Niedecker, *Collected Works*, 169.
81. O'Rourke and Stallings, "This Condensery," 226.
82. Bogan, "The Springs of Poetry," 9.
83. Eliot, *Selected Prose*, 42.

5. The Prosody of Passing

1. Johnson, *Bronze*, 35. Jeremy Braddock suggested, in conversation, an allusion to passing in the lines "I want to die while you love me,/ While yet you hold me fair." "I Want to Die While You Love Me" in James Weldon Johnson, *The Book of American Negro Poetry*, 183.
2. The term "harbinger" belongs to Waldo Frank, but a range of more recent essays and retrospectives have echoed it. Michael North notes Gorham Munson's simultaneously "extravagant" and "condescending" praise of Toomer for, in North's arch paraphrase, "virtually solv[ing] the problem of modernity by pulling his own authentic speech from the 'folk ways' of his ancestors." *The Dialect of Modernism*, 149.
3. Reed, *Freedom Time*, 7-8.
4. James Weldon Johnson, *Writings*, 477.
5. Morrissette, *James Weldon Johnson's Modern Soundscapes*, 41.
6. James Weldon Johnson, *The Autobiography of an Ex-Colored Man*, 110.
7. Gilroy, *The Black Atlantic*, 3.
8. Nielsen, *Writing between the Lines*, 178.
9. James Weldon Johnson, *Writings*, 868-73.
10. Toomer, *Letters*, 46.
11. Toomer, *Cane*, 1987, 150.
12. Toomer, *Cane*, 1987, 152.
13. See Tapper, *The Machine That Sings*, chapter 3. Developments in the field of ethnography, especially those of Franz Boas, influenced Crane's effort to imagine himself as a "participant-observer" in common with "ethnographic fieldworkers" (115).
14. Reed, *Freedom Time*, 128.
15. Toomer, *Cane*, 1987, 166.
16. Toomer, *Cane*, 2011, lxx.

17. "Toomer," in Alexander, *Crave Radiance*, 237.

18. Toomer, *Cane*, 2011, li.

19. Kutzinski, "Unseasoned Flowers," 168. David Levering Lewis describes Toomer's experience of the south through *Cane*'s tropes of transformative soil and song: "In a cabin whose floorboards permitted the soil to come up between them Jean Toomer came down to earth, into the cotton and cane fields, for the first time in his life"; like Kutzinski he notes the brevity of the transformation, a mere "instant" of reconciled "racial duality." Qtd. in Paul Allen Anderson, *Deep River*, 70. Anderson describes the speaker as a "liberated racial amanuensis" (75).

20. Toomer, *Cane*, 1987, 193.

21. Toomer, *Cane*, 1987, 19 (my italics).

22. Toomer, *Cane*, 2011, 14.

23. Toomer, *Cane*, 2011, 65.

24. Toomer, *Cane*, 1987, 178.

25. Toomer, *Cane*, 1987, 130.

26. Ochoa Gautier's study of popular song in colonial Colombia shows how the concept of orality emerges from "the contradictory political obligations of the place assigned to tradition in the public sphere generated by modern colonial history"; this is to say that what is (mis)named traditional (i.e., folk song) becomes simultaneously a site of resistance and of the reification of racial difference. For instance, folklorists "trac[ed] popular song verses back to similar or equal samples to be found in the Spanish coplerío (collections of popular verse forms)." The ambivalent embrace of indigenous practices within an existing regime of value reinforces racial hierarchies in which "the failed phoné of blacks is a disglossia that acoustically delimits their linguistic competence while recognizing the musicality of the voice." Ochoa Gautier, *Aurality*, 90-97.

27. Kittler, *Gramophone, Film, Typewriter*, 37.

28. See Jaji, *Africa in Stereo*, 8. Toomer's logic of a vanishing musical tradition reproduces what Paul Gilroy calls "the dualistic structure which puts Africa, authenticity, purity, and origin in crude opposition to the Americas, hybridity, creolisation, and rootlessness"; Jaji's study of black sound from a "stereophonic" transatlantic perspective helps prove Gilroy's point that the dualistic structure is "explode[d]" by "the circulation and mutation of music across the black Atlantic." *The Black Atlantic*, 199.

29. Nurhussein finds that "the juxtaposition of elements that gesture toward orality alongside those exploiting literate forms [do] not necessarily impoverish the genre" (*Rhetorics of Literacy*, 8). This was of course hard to feel at the time, given the overdetermination of dialect by the minstrel tradition. Dialect spelling appears only twice in *Cane*'s poems. In "Cotton Song" it is contained in quotation marks with no speaker indicated, and in "Harvest Song" a parenthetical aside reads "(Eoho, my brothers!)."

30. Cohen, "Popular Ballads," 198-99, 205.

31. Martin, "'Imperfectly Civilized,'" 348.
32. Higginson, *Army Life in a Black Regiment (1870)*, 149.
33. Kappeler, "Editing America," 900.
34. Gummere, *Handbook*, 35.
35. Gummere, *Handbook*, 57. For Hegel's discussion of lyric as the essential genre of subjectivity, as well as modernity and western culture, see Hegel, *Aesthetics*, 1111-28.
36. Esenwein and Roberts, *The Art of Versification*, 16.
37. Kerlin, *Negro Poets and Their Poems*, 4.
38. Henderson, *Understanding the New Black Poetry*, 5-6.
39. Virginia Jackson, *Dickinson's Misery*, 7. Jackson defines lyric as the product of "reading practices in the nineteenth and twentieth century that become the practice of literary criticism" (8). The "expressive romantic lyric" dispatched not only a range of subgenres and historical practices, but modes of circulation (i.e., the prosodically focused readings of Brown's *Outline*) that "disappear behind an idealized scene of reading progressively identified with an idealized moment of expression" (7). The observation about the lyrical ballad comes in Virginia Jackson, "'The Story of Boon,'" 243.
40. There is a striking analogue to the Ghost Dance, which gets read as repeatable and essential Native American expression rather than a response to colonization and removal by the US government.
41. Toomer, *Cane*, 1987, 19.
42. Toomer, *Cane*, 1987, 21.
43. Morrissette, *James Weldon Johnson's Modern Soundscapes*, 41. In her reading of Johnson's autobiography *Along This Way*, Jacqueline Goldsby marks a parallel struggle to "find the language to partition off" his own near lynching "while preserving its transformative effect." *A Spectacular Secret*, 171.
44. The poem first appeared in the *Crisis* 23 (June 1922): 65. Here I follow the text of Toomer, *Cane*, 2011, 16.
45. A typical example is "Somebody's buried in the graveyard," from John Wesley Work's *Folk Song of the American Negro*, 34.

> Somebody's buried in the graveyard
> Somebody's buried in the sea
> Going to get up in the morning a shouting
> Going to join jubilee

A variable number of syllables are strung across four beats ("graveyard" gets a full two beats, "sea" gets two as well). The long third line works because "going to" is an extrametric pickup sung before the measure begins. The poem's syntax is repetitive and paratactic.

46. Cullen's "Heritage" provides an interesting contrast. He ends six lines with

"me," rhyming with "sea" "tree" "see" "tree" (enjambed), "tree," and lastly "humility." The entire poem plays with the question of whether to stress the "savage measures" of alternating trochaic rhythm, strongly hinting that the reader would err in thumping out "I belong to Jesus Christ, / Preacher of humility; / Heathen gods are naught to me." It is not nearly so obvious in Toomer whether one ought to foreground the rhyme of "me" and "slavery."

47. Blanton, *Epic Negation*, 4.
48. Toomer, *Cane*, 1987, 96.
49. Toomer, *Cane*, 1987, 83.
50. Toomer, *Cane*, 1987, 106.
51. See Braddock, *Collecting as Modernist Practice*.
52. Paul Allen Anderson, *Deep River*, 69.
53. Paul Allen Anderson, *Deep River*, 75.
54. See Sundquist, *To Wake the Nations*, 498.
55. Nowlin, "Race Literature, Modernism, and Normal Literature," 504.
56. Brathwaite, *History of the Voice*, 20.
57. Nowlin, "Race Literature, Modernism, and Normal Literature," 514.
58. Nowlin, "Race Literature, Modernism, and Normal Literature," 511.
59. Box 78: 573, James Weldon Johnson and Grace Nail Johnson Papers, Yale Collection of American Literature, Beinecke Rare Book and Manuscript Library. All further James Weldon Johnson citations are from this collection.
60. Richards, *Practical Criticism*, 224.
61. A comment not from *Practical Criticism* but from Richards's lecture series. See John Constable's introduction to the volume, xx.
62. Richards, *Practical Criticism*, 91.
63. Richards, *Practical Criticism*, 91.
64. Martin, *The Rise and Fall of Meter*, 49–52.
65. I am grateful to Meredith Martin for making this connection. In *Seven Types of Ambiguity*, Empson notes that the accent on will "intensifies" ambiguity. "Certainly, with the accent on *weep* and *and*, *will* can only be an auxiliary verb, and with the accent on *will* its main meaning is 'insist upon.' But the future meaning also can be imposed upon this latter way of reading the line if it is the tense which is being stressed, if it insists on the contrast between the two sorts of weeping." Empson, *Seven Types of Ambiguity*, 148.
66. See Campbell, *Rhythm and Will in Victorian Poetry*.
67. I make this argument at greater length in "Autobiography as Ars Poetica."
68. Martin, *The Rise and Fall of Meter*, 139.
69. Edwards, "The Seemingly Eclipsed Window of Form," 595.
70. Johnson, preface to *Book of American Negro Spirituals*, 30.
71. James Weldon Johnson and Grace Nail Johnson Papers, Box 59: 202.
72. James Weldon Johnson, *Writings*, 840.

73. Qtd. in Morrissette, *James Weldon Johnson's Modern Soundscapes*, 146.

74. Jaji, *Africa in Stereo*, 69. Sensitive to the multivalent circulation of sound in the black Atlantic, Jaji echoes Paul Gilroy's "lament over the instrumentalization of music as 'a cipher for racial authenticity.'"

75. Morrissette, *James Weldon Johnson's Modern Soundscapes*, 140.

76. James Weldon Johnson and Grace Nail Johnson Papers, Box 78: 753

77. James Weldon Johnson and Grace Nail Johnson Papers, Box 4: 66

78. See Brown, *Outline for the Study of the Poetry of American Negroes*, 32.

79. Qtd. in Baldwin, "The Cakewalk," 215.

6. Folk Iambics

1. Agawu, *Representing African Music*, 56.

2. This "elastic use of rhythm [. . .] render[s] the notion that 'le negre etait un etre rhythmique' so broad that it becomes virtually meaningless." Jaji, *Africa in Stereo*, 77.

3. Edwards, *The Practice of Diaspora*, 44.

4. Brown, *Collected Poems*, 175.

5. Thomas, *Extraordinary Measures*, 4.

6. Whalan, Review of *Brother Mine*, 661.

7. Bérubé, *Marginal Forces/Cultural Centers*, 109.

8. North, *The Dialect of Modernism*.

9. Pound, Yeats, and Eliot "criticized the poetry of their own time [. . .] for being fatally deficient in rhythmic technique, a situation they sought to remedy by listening closely to the body which was marked [. . .] by certain inalienable characteristics." Golston, *Rhythm and Race*, 10.

10. Similarly, Hughes's "Weary Blues" can largely be scanned as either four-beat accentual verse or loose iambic pentameter. While the first line ("Droning a drowsy syncopated tune") figures a "syncopated" rhythm, it could also be scanned as iambic. The point of both line and poem may be that rhythm, like the speaker's race and affinity for the blues, is not given in advance.

11. The cases of Hurston and Du Bois are more complex than can be treated here. Hurston's *Mules and Men* (1935) famously balances the objective methods of Boas-inspired anthropological observation with her embeddedness in the black culture of Eatonville, Florida. Du Bois moves in a single sentence from "the innate love of harmony and beauty" in the black artist to necessary doubt about how that beauty is deformed by the racism of that artist's "larger audience." *The Souls of Black Folk*, 5.

12. Martin, *The Rise and Fall of Meter*.

13. As North notes, white dialect writers like R. Emmet Kennedy found a source for "authentic national voice" in folk ballads belonging "only to the unlettered folk 'who have not lost the gracious charm of being natural.'" *The Dialect of Modernism*, 21.

14. Manson, "Worrying the Lines," 112.

15. Thurman, *Infants of the Spring*, 108, 110.

16. Smethurst, "Genesis and Crisis," 450.

17. Smethurst, "Genesis and Crisis," 451. Evan Kindley's recent *Poet-Critics and the Administration of Culture* suggests that Brown's sociological awareness of class and race, evident in his poetry's complex vernacular, influenced his later administrative projects.

18. Woodson, *Anthems, Sonnets, and Chants*, 6.

19. David Nicholls, *Conjuring the Folk*, 4.

20. Brown, Davis, and Lee, *The Negro Caravan*, 6-7.

21. Brown, *Negro Poetry and Drama*, 80.

22. Stowe, "Babylon Revisited," 96.

23. James Weldon Johnson, *Writings*, 874.

24. Sterling A. Brown to James Weldon Johnson, January 6, 1930. The poem was not published until 1935, but Brown read it in early 1930 while writing the study guide and working on *Southern Road*. In the previous chapter I discussed the poem at length in the context of Johnson's poetics.

25. James Weldon Johnson, *Writings*, 745.

26. Brown, "Roland Hayes."

27. Benston, "Sterling Brown's After-Song," 34.

28. Thurman, *Collected Writings*, 71, 104.

29. Sterling A. Brown to James Weldon Johnson, December 16, 1931, Box 4, Folder 66, James Weldon Johnson and Grace Nail Johnson Papers, Yale Collection of American Literature, Beinecke Rare Book and Manuscript Library. All further James Weldon Johnson citations are from this collection.

30. Sanders, *Afro-Modernist Aesthetics and the Poetry of Sterling A. Brown*, 73.

31. Brown, *Collected Poems*, 78.

32. Harper, "An Integer Is a Whole Number," 281.

33. Sterling A. Brown to James Weldon Johnson, February 17, 1932.

34. Several critics have registered alternate forms of literary heritage in Brown's work. See Gary Smith in "The Literary Ballads of Sterling A. Brown," Michael Manson on the idea of the "blues sonnet" amid the traditional poetry of "Vestiges" in "Sterling Brown and the 'Vestiges' of the Blues: The Role of Race in English Verse Structure," and J. Edgar Tidwell on the dialogue between Brown and regionalist "New American" poets like Robert Frost and Edgar Lee Masters in "Two Writers Sharing: Sterling A. Brown, Robert Frost, and 'In Divés' Dive.'"

35. Green, *The Negro in Contemporary American Literature*, 11, 19.

36. James Weldon Johnson, *Writings*, 690.

37. There was also interest in Native American folk songs, as evidenced by anthologies like George Cronyn's *The Path on the Rainbow* (1918). These songs are seen as at once vanishing and prefiguring modernist free verse: Mary Austin's introduction to Cronyn's anthology sees Native American song as having an "extraordinary like-

ness" to "the recent work of the Imagists" (Qtd. in Braddock, *Collecting as Modernist Practice*, 161.

38. James Weldon Johnson, *Writings*, 694.
39. Brown, *Outline for the Study of the Poetry of American Negroes*, 3.
40. Brown, *Outline for the Study of the Poetry of American Negroes*, 6.
41. Dett's poem is something of an experiment in quantitative meter. Most of its lines scan in triple meter.
42. Brown, *Outline for the Study of the Poetry of American Negroes*, 22.
43. *The Book of American Negro Poetry*, 108.
44. *Outline for the Study of the Poetry of American Negroes*, 17.
45. James Weldon Johnson, *The Book of American Negro Poetry*, 109.
46. James Weldon Johnson, *The Book of American Negro Poetry*, 110.
47. James Weldon Johnson, *Writings*, 713.
48. Brown, *Outline for the Study of the Poetry of American Negroes*, 47.
49. Cullen, *Caroling Dusk*, xi.
50. Cullen, *Caroling Dusk*, 130.
51. Manson, "Worrying the Lines," 120.
52. Kerlin, *Negro Poets and Their Poems*, 18.
53. Virginia Jackson, "'The Story of Boon,'" 243.
54. Wright, "The New Negro Poet and the Nachal Man," 103.
55. David Anderson, "Sterling Brown's Southern Strategy," 1024.
56. The poem first appeared in *Opportunity: Journal of Negro Life*, 5 (July 1927): 48.
57. Benston, "Sterling Brown's After-Song," 34.
58. Stepto, "'When de Saint Go Ma'chin' Home,'" 941, 944.
59. Henderson, "The Heavy Blues of Sterling Brown," 35.
60. As Jean Wagner has argued, the prosody of Plantation school poets like Irwin Russell had a paradoxical double purpose: first, along with dialect, to infantilize blacks and second, to "situate the work more convincingly within the Anglo-Saxon popular tradition." *Black Poets of the United States*, 59.
61. Stepto, "'When de Saint Go Ma'chin' Home,'" 942.
62. Benston, "Sterling Brown's After-Song," 35.
63. Benston, "Sterling Brown's After-Song," 39.
64. James Weldon Johnson to Sterling A. Brown, February 22, 1932.
65. Benston, "Sterling Brown's After-Song," 39.
66. Qtd. in Hughes, *Collected Poems*, 222.
67. Brown, "Negro Folk Expression," 57.
68. Ronda, "'Work and Wait Unwearying,'" 864.
69. Nurhussein, *Rhetorics of Literacy*, 11-12.
70. Virginia Jackson, "Specters of the Ballad," 180, 182, 187, 191.
71. Figueroa, "Problems of a Writer who does not quite . . .".
72. Vendler, "Poet of Two Worlds."

73. Brathwaite, *History of the Voice*, 30-31.

74. My thanks to Anthony Reed for reminding me of Brathwaite's unlikely pairing of Eliot with another global radio voice, that of cricket announcer John Arlott, whose regional "burr" also participated in a "riddmic" subversion of the BBC as colonial institution (Brathwaite, "History of the Voice," 31).

75. Alexander, *The Venus Hottentot*.

Conclusion

1. See, for example, Sullivan, *The Work of Revision*, 46, on the New Critical avoidance of genetic criticism, partly out of their objection to intentionalism.

2. Pound, "Vorticism," 463. Pound makes the same statement in his introduction to *Guido Cavalcanti*, *PTEP*, 193. Donald Wesling characterizes Coleridge's "idea of a prosody malleable to meaning [as] extremist, organicist, and avant-garde [. . .] such a prosody is incapable of being actualized in the strict sense, and though others later attempt to write in the beat-counting mode, Coleridge himself does not, despite the claims of his preface." *The Scissors of Meter*, 13. Steven Parrish contrasts Coleridge's sense of meter as "superficial form" with Wordsworth's poetics. See "Wordsworth and Coleridge on Meter." For an extended and excellent treatment of Coleridge's theories of poetic form, beyond the famous "Christabel" preface, see Jones, *Coleridge and the Philosophy of Poetic Form*. Hegel's prosody maps to modernist concepts of post-metrical rhythm: where the epic "rhapsode" can be "mechanical, rolling and flowing on in tranquil independence" such that there are no real choices made and the music is "remote from him as an individual" (1037), the lyric poet adopts the spirit of the "more varied" lyric or "Melic" meters to the extreme point in which "each poet makes his own syllabic measure to suit his own lyrical character" (1151). Coventry Patmore recognized that one meter can permit many "cadences" but also demands that the "remission, inversion, or omission" of the regular placement of accents follow "an emotional motive." *Essay on English Metrical Law*, 22. See Rudy, "Material Patmore." Lascelles Abercrombie follows Patmore in describing meter as "direct expression of the emotion which the words enclose. Not only does the underlying consistent beat keep our answering emotions in the necessary state of excitation, but the sudden varieties and modulations of metre, the momentary deviations from consistency, are most powerful suggesters of shifting changes." "The Function of Poetry in the Drama," 112. The comment on Whitman's prosody comes from Everett Gillis's dissertation on 1890s magazine verse prosody, which includes a study of Whitman's influence therein. "American Prosody in the Eighteen Nineties," 53. The most thorough study of how Whitman centers modern ideologies of free verse and rhythm is Erin Kappeler's "Shaping Free Verse."

3. Lowell, "Editorial Comment," 215-16; and preface to *Some Imagist Poets*, v-vi.

4. Monroe, "Dr. Patterson on Rhythm," 30.

5. The archive extends through 1923. Please visit https://prosody.princeton.edu/ for more information about the project. For extended studies of nineteenth- and twentieth-century investment in rhythm, I invite readers to explore *Critical Rhythm*, a collection of essays I coedited on the role of rhythm in post-Romantic poetic theory.

6. Gumbrecht, "Rhythm and Meaning," 170, 174.

7. Eliot, *Collected Poems*, 45.

8. Culler, *Theory of the Lyric*, 133.

9. Frye, *Anatomy of Criticism*, 272-73.

10. Poovey, "The Model System of Contemporary Literary Criticism," 428.

11. Guillory, *Cultural Capital*, 165.

12. Guillory, *Cultural Capital*, 160. In *Poetic Authority* Guillory notes how allegory's "great ambition, as its etymology indicates, is to bring sacred mysteries into the marketplace, to make the displacement of the sacred a triumph"; he warns, however, against the tendency of criticism to project that narrative onto itself, envisioning literary study (of any text) as a sacred space and triumphant resistance to modernity (44). *Cultural Capital* diagnoses precisely this error in Brooks and the New Criticism.

13. Jackson and Prins, *Lyric Theory Reader*, 160.

14. Mao, "Modern American Literary Criticism," 288.

15. See Morris Croll et al., "Report of the Committee on Metrical Notation Appointed at Philadelphia 1922."

16. Wesling, *The Scissors of Meter*, 16.

17. Qtd. in Menand and Rainey, introduction to *The Cambridge History of Literary Criticism*, 11.

18. Brooks and Warren, *Understanding Poetry*, xiii-xiv.

19. Brooks and Warren, *Understanding Poetry*, l, liv.

20. Brooks and Warren, *Understanding Poetry*, 105-6,108.

21. Gross, *Sound and Form in Modern Poetry*, 39.

22. Qtd. in Mao, "The New Critics and the Text-Object," 235.

23. Mao, "Modern American Literary Criticism," 299.

24. Jane Goldman, qtd. in Bromley, "Significant Form."

25. Richards, *Principles of Literary Criticism*, 142.

26. Richards, *Principles of Literary Criticism*, 145.

27. Wimsatt and Beardsley, "The Concept of Meter," 586.

28. Blackmur, "Lord Tennyson's Scissors," 6.

29. Blackmur, "Lord Tennyson's Scissors," 7.

30. Blackmur, "Lord Tennyson's Scissors," 4.

31. Blackmur, "Lord Tennyson's Scissors," 18.

32. Wood, "R. P. Blackmur," 235, 238.

33. Blackmur, *The Double Agent*, 144.

34. Winslow, *Trial Balances*, 83.

35. Beloof, "Prosody and Tone," 116.

36. Holley, "The Model Stanza," 186. Holley finds that certain stanzas derive their structure from syntax and theme but that Moore's practice of "duplicating" syllabic stanza structures "transforms a unique, relatively organic pattern into a replicated, relatively mechanical pattern, so that one and the same syllabic configuration appears natural to one syntax, and artificial to another." Martin Duffell notes the "peculiar mode of counting" entailed by Moore's syllabics—an "anti-rhythmic counting" that avoids the "intuitive composition" of Romance-language syllable-counted verse. What he calls the spirit of "modern English syllabics"—verse that "defeats the ear" and "a game played by the expert and missed by the general audience"—characterizes accentual-syllabic modernism as well. Duffell, *A New History of English Metre*, 208-10.

37. See introduction, note 92. Stephen Cushman's *Fictions of Form in American Poetry* ascends from his earlier critique of Williams's prosodic theory to modern fictions of "figurative significance" attempting to connect "forms" to worldly meaning (6). Donald Wesling locates the strain of claiming distinctive "form" much earlier, as the defining characteristic of Romantic poetry. Where the Augustans agreed that "literary innovation meant repetition and correction of existing forms and genres," in modernity it is the elimination of patterning that becomes "the true motor of stylistic dynamism and innovation." Wesling, *The Chances of Rhyme*, 48, 64. These critics share a sense of post-metrical poetic form (especially the rhythm of free verse) as rhetorical, fictional, or a matter of negation.

38. Empson, *Seven Types of Ambiguity*, 247.

39. Empson, *Seven Types of Ambiguity*, 254-55.

40. Winters, "Problems for the Modern Critic of Literature," 331, 333.

41. Wesling, *The Scissors of Meter*, 19.

42. Cureton, "Temporality and Poetic Form," 38. Culler critiques the narrativizing influence of the dramatic monologue in *Theory of the Lyric* and concisely in "Why Lyric."

43. Tucker, "Tactical Formalism," 85-87.

44. Leighton, *On Form*, 1.

45. Lehman, "Formalism, Mere Form, and Judgment"; Gaskill, "The Close and the Concrete."

46. Lerner, *The Hatred of Poetry*, 8. An interesting moment occurs when Lerner celebrates how Dickinson's fascicles and other hard-to-read material practices "throw a wrench in the bitter logic of the poetic principle by causing us to shift back and forth between modes of perception—we read one minute and look the next, the object refusing to become or to remain a typical poem" (34). This is less a "wrench" than an example of the recuperative energies of reading for "bitter logic." What could be more satisfying proof of the "powerful dissonance" of Dickinson's meter and rhyme than the fundamental impossibility of experiencing them as the properties of an "actual" material poem? The simpler explanation established by Virginia Jack-

son lies in a different dissonance: that between our practice of reading lyric and historical practices that include whatever games Dickinson is playing with how she and her readers listened for hymnal prosody. Lerner thus evidences the ultimately happy logic of lyric reading.

47. Izenberg, *Being Numerous*, 14-15.

48. Blanton, *Epic Negation*, 21.

Appendix

1. See Halle and Keyser, *English Stress: Its Form, Its Growth, and Its Role in Verse*; Kiparsky, "The Rhythmic Structure of English Verse." In "Modernist Scansion" I explore developments in generative metrics and apply them to Robert Frost's versification.

2. This is so despite the fact that, as Martin Duffell puts it, free verse "employed many of the same linguistic features as the traditional" (237). If a basis of comparison can be developed at the level of "the matching and the contrasting of linguistic units," scansion may again become a potent tool across traditions (210). That entails a separate question, not my concern here, of how far the tools of linguistic metrics (i.e., attention to higher levels of the phonological hierarchy) can extend. Duffell's own brief studies of Eliot and Moore perform scansions but also attend to our unusual protocols of reading and our limited perception of components like the syllable. My simple point here is that there were not even remotely adequate principles of scansion in play at the time, and that most poets saw nonmetrical verse as antagonistic toward scansion's largely pedagogical orientation.

3. The last substantial effort I know of to bring together scholars of linguistics and literary criticism was a conference on metrical theory organized by Paul Kiparsky at Stanford in 1984 and a resulting collection of essays published in 1989. In his preface, Gilbert Youmans observes the project to be a "rare collaboration" between "disciplines that tend too often to treat each other as adversaries." Kiparsky and Youmans, *Rhythm and Meter*, xi. One nice exception is the development of the program prosodic.py at Stanford by Arto Antilla, Josh Falk, and Ryan Heuser.

4. Kiparsky, "The Rhythmic Structure of English Verse," 191.

5. Tsur, "Metricalness and Rhythmicalness," 59.

6. Martin, "Rupert Brooke's Ambivalent Mourning, Ezra Pound's Anticipatory Nostalgia," 196.

7. Golston, *Rhythm and Race*, 9. Stewart, *Poetry and the Fate of the Senses*, 251. O'Driscoll, *Stepping Stones*, 127. Easthope, *Poetry as Discourse*, 60. Kleinzahler, "A Peacock Called Mirabell."

8. Brooke-Rose, "Gifts above Price," 11.

Works Cited

Abercrombie, Lascelles. "The Function of Poetry in the Drama." *Poetry Review* 1 (1912): 107-18.

Adams, Stephen J. "The Metrical Contract of *The Cantos*." *Journal of Modern Literature* 15, no. 1 (1988): 55-72.

———. "Poetics: Prosody." In *The Ezra Pound Encyclopedia*, edited by Demetres P. Tryphonopoulos. Westport, CT: Greenwood, 2005.

———. "Pound's Quantities and 'Absolute Rhythm.'" *Essays in Literature* 4, no. 1 (Spring 1977): 95-109.

Agawu, V. Kofi. *Representing African Music: Postcolonial Notes, Queries, Positions*. New York: Routledge, 2003.

Albright, Daniel. *Quantum Poetics: Yeats, Pound, Eliot, and the Science of Modernism*. Cambridge: Cambridge University Press, 1997.

Aldington, Richard. "Review of *North of Boston*." *Egoist*, July 1, 1914, 248.

Alexander, Elizabeth. *Crave Radiance: New and Selected Poems 1990-2010*. Minneapolis, MN: Graywolf Press, 2012.

———. *The Venus Hottentot*. Saint Paul, MN: Graywolf Press, 2004.

Anderson, David. "Sterling Brown's Southern Strategy: Poetry as Cultural Evolution in *Southern Road*." *Callaloo* 21, no. 4 (1998): 1023-37.

Anderson, Paul Allen. *Deep River: Music and Memory in Harlem Renaissance Thought*. New Americanists. Durham, NC: Duke University Press, 2001.

Attridge, Derek. *Poetic Rhythm: An Introduction*. Cambridge: Cambridge University Press, 1996.

———. "The Rhythms of the English Dolnik." In *Critical Rhythm: The Poetics of a Literary Life Form*, edited by Ben Glaser and Jonathan Culler, 153-73. New York: Fordham University Press, 2019.

———. *Well-Weighed Syllables: Elizabethan Verse in Classical Metres*. London: Cambridge University Press, 1974.

Baker, Houston A., Jr. *Modernism and the Harlem Renaissance*. Chicago: University of Chicago Press, 2013.

Baldwin, Brooke. "The Cakewalk: A Study in Stereotype and Reality." *Journal of Social History* 15, no. 2 (1981): 205-18.

Barkas, Pallister. *A Critique of Modern English Prosody (1880-1930)*. Studien Zur Englischen Philologie, Hft.82. Halle (Saale): M. Niemeyer, 1934.

Beasley, Rebecca. *Theorists of Modernist Poetry: T. S. Eliot, T. E. Hulme, Ezra Pound*. Routledge Critical Thinkers. London: Routledge, 2007.

Bedient, Calvin. *He Do the Police in Different Voices: The Waste Land and Its Protagonist*. Chicago: University of Chicago Press, 1986.

Beloof, Robert. "Prosody and Tone: The 'Mathematics' of Marianne Moore." *Kenyon Review* 20, no. 1 (Winter 1958): 116-23.

Benston, Kimberly W. "Sterling Brown's After-Song: 'When de Saints Go Ma'ching Home' and the Performances of Afro-American Voice." *Callaloo: A Journal of African American and African Arts and Letters* 5, nos. 1-2 (February 1982): 33-42.

Bérubé, Michael. *Marginal Forces/Cultural Centers: Tolson, Pynchon, and the Politics of the Canon*. Ithaca, NY: Cornell University Press, 1992.

Beyers, Chris. *A History of Free Verse*. Fayetteville: University of Arkansas Press, 2001.

Blackmur, R. P. *The Double Agent; Essays in Craft and Elucidation*. New York: Arrow Editions, 1935.

———. "Lord Tennyson's Scissors: 1912-1950." *Kenyon Review* 14, no. 1 (1952): 1-20.

Blanton, C. D. *Epic Negation: The Dialectical Poetics of Late Modernism*. Modernist Literature & Culture. New York: Oxford University Press, 2015.

Blount, Marcellus. "Caged Birds: Race and Gender in the Sonnet." In *Engendering Men: The Question of Male Feminist Criticism*, edited by Joseph A. Boone and Michael Cadden, 225-38. New York: Routledge, 1990.

Bogan, Louise. "Allen Tate's New Poems." *New Republic* 70, no. 904 (March 30, 1932): 186-87.

———. *Body of This Death*. New York: R. M. McBride, 1923.

———. *Collected Poems 1923-1953*. New York: Noonday Press, 1954.

———. *A Poet's Prose: Selected Writings of Louise Bogan*. Edited by Mary Kinzie. Athens, OH: Swallow Press, 2005.

———. "The Springs of Poetry." *New Republic*, December 5, 1923, 9.

———. *What the Woman Lived: Selected Letters of Louise Bogan, 1920-1970*. Edited by Ruth Limmer. New York: Harcourt Brace Jovanovich, 1973.

Bogan, Louise, and Ruth Limmer. *Journey around My Room: The Autobiography of Louise Bogan; A Mosaic*. New York: Viking Press, 1980.

Bogel, Fredric V. *The Difference Satire Makes: Rhetoric and Reading from Jonson to Byron*. Ithaca, NY: Cornell University Press, 2001.

Bollobás, Enikő. "(De-)Gendering and (De-)Sexualizing Female Subjectivities: Woman Hating and Its Revisions in Literature and Painting." *Eger Journal of American Studies* 8 (2002): 105-20.

Bolton, Thaddeus L. "Rhythm." *American Journal of Psychology* 6, no. 2 (1894): 145-238.
Booth, Philip. *Trying to Say It: Outlooks and Insights on How Poems Happen.* Ann Arbor: University of Michigan Press, 1996.
Borroff, Marie. *Language and the Poet: Verbal Artistry in Frost, Stevens, and Moore.* Chicago: University of Chicago Press, 1979.
Braddock, Jeremy. *Collecting as Modernist Practice.* Hopkins Studies in Modernism. Baltimore: Johns Hopkins University Press, 2012.
Braithwaite, William Stanley. Introduction to *Heart of a Woman*, by Georgia Douglas Johnson. New York: G. K. Hall, 1997.
Brathwaite, Kamau. *History of the Voice: The Development of Nation Language in Anglophone Caribbean Poetry.* London: New Beacon Books, 1984.
Brewer, Robert Frederick. *Orthometry: The Art of Versification and the Technicalities of Poetry, with a New and Complete Rhyming Dictionary.* Edinburgh: J. Grant, 1908.
Bridges, Robert. *Milton's Prosody.* Rev. final ed. Oxford: Oxford University Press, 1921.
Brinkman, Bartholomew. *Poetic Modernism in the Culture of Mass Print.* Hopkins Studies in Modernism. Baltimore: Johns Hopkins University Press, 2016.
Bromley, Amy. "Significant Form." In *The Edinburgh Dictionary of Modernism*, edited by Vassiliki Kolocotroni and Olga Taxidou. Edinburgh: Edinburgh University Press, 2018. https://search.credoreference.com/content/entry/edinburghnko/significant_form/.
Bromwich, David. *Skeptical Music: Essays on Modern Poetry.* Chicago: University of Chicago Press, 2001.
Brooke, Rupert. *The Collected Poems.* 4th ed., rev. London: Sidgwick & Jackson, 1987.
Brooke-Rose, Christine. "Gifts above Price: The Legacy of Ezra Pound." In *Make It New: The Rise of Modernism*, edited by Kurt Heinzelman and Thomas F. Staley, 11-13. Austin: Harry Ransom Center, University of Texas Press, 2003.
Brooks, Cleanth, and Robert Penn Warren. *Understanding Poetry: An Anthology for College Students.* Rev. ed. New York: H. Holt, 1939.
Brower, Reuben A. *The Fields of Light: An Experiment in Critical Reading.* New York: Oxford University Press, 1951.
———. *The Poetry of Robert Frost: Constellations of Intention.* New York: Oxford University Press, 1963.
Brown, Sterling A. *The Collected Poems of Sterling A. Brown.* Edited by Michael S. Harper. 2nd ed. Evanston, IL: Triquarterly, 1996.
———. "Negro Folk Expression: Spirituals, Seculars, Ballads, and Work Songs." *Phylon* 14 (1953): 45-61.
———. *Negro Poetry and Drama.* Washington, DC: Associates in Negro Folk Education, 1937.

———. *Outline for the Study of the Poetry of American Negroes*. New York: Harcourt, 1931.

———. "Roland Hayes." *Opportunity*, June 1925, 173-74.

Brown, Sterling A., Arthur Paul Davis, and Ulysses Grant Lee, eds. *The Negro Caravan*. New York: Arno Press, 1969.

Browning, Elizabeth Barrett. *Aurora Leigh and Other Poems*. Edited by John Robert Glorney Bolton and Julia Bolton Holloway. Penguin Classics edition. London: Penguin Classics, 1996.

Buckley, Jennifer. "Talking Machines: Shaw, Phonography, and Pygmalion." *Shaw: The Annual of Bernard Shaw Studies* 35, no. 1 (2015): 21-45.

Burke, Carolyn. "The New Poetry and the New Woman: Mina Loy." In *Coming to Light: American Women Poets in the Twentieth Century*, edited by Diane Wood Middlebrook and Marilyn Yalom, 37-57. Ann Arbor: University of Michigan Press, 1985.

Campbell, Matthew. *Rhythm and Will in Victorian Poetry*. Cambridge: Cambridge University Press, 1999.

Carne-Ross, D. S. "New Metres for Old: A Note on Pound's Metric." *Arion: A Journal of Humanities and Classics* 6, no. 2 (Summer 1967): 216-32.

Catullus, Gaius Valerius. *The Poems of Catullus: A Bilingual Edition*. Translated by Peter Green. Berkeley: University of California Press, 2007.

Cavell, Stanley. "Music Discomposed." In *Must We Mean What We Say? A Book of Essays*, 2nd ed., 167-96. New York: Cambridge University Press, 2015.

Cavitch, Max. "Slavery and Its Metrics." In *The Cambridge Companion to Nineteenth-Century American Poetry*, edited by Kerry Larson, 94-112. Cambridge University Press, 2014.

———. "Stephen Crane's Refrain." *ESQ: A Journal of the American Renaissance* 54 (2008): 33-53.

Chasar, Mike. *Everyday Reading: Poetry and Popular Culture in Modern America*. New York: Columbia University Press, 2012.

Cheng, Vincent J. "'The Twining Stresses, Two by Two': The Prosody of Joyce's Prose." *Modernism/Modernity* 16, no. 2 (2009): 391-99.

Clark, Suzanne. *Sentimental Modernism*. Urbana: University of Illinois Press, 2007.

Clark, T. J. "Arguments about Modernism: A Reply to Michael Fried." In *Pollock and After: The Critical Debate*, edited by Francis Frascina, 2nd ed., 102-12. London: Routledge, 2000.

Cohen, Michael. "Popular Ballads: Rhythmic Remediations in the Nineteenth Century." In *Meter Matters: Verse Cultures of the Long Nineteenth Century*, edited by Jason David Hall, 196-216. Athens: Ohio University Press, 2011.

Collecott, Diana. *H.D. and Sapphic Modernism 1910-1950*. Cambridge: Cambridge University Press, 1999.

Corbière, Tristan. *Selected Poems and Prose: The Centenary Corbière*. Translated by Val Warner. New York: Routledge, 2003.

Cornford, Frances Darwin. *Spring Morning*. London: Poetry Bookshop, 1915.

Cramer, Jeffrey S. *Robert Frost among His Poems: A Literary Companion to the Poet's Own Biographical Contexts and Associations*. Jefferson, NC: McFarland, 2007.

Crawford, Margo Natalie. "'Perhaps Buddha Is a Woman': Women's Poetry in the Harlem Renaissance." In *The Cambridge Companion to the Harlem Renaissance*, edited by George Hutchinson, 126-40. Cambridge: Cambridge University Press, 2007.

Croll, Morris W., Paull F. Baum, Raymond M. Alden, Felix E. Schelling, and F. N. Scott. "Report of the Committee on Metrical Notation Appointed at Philadelphia 1922." *PMLA* 38, no. (Appendix) (1923): lxxxvii-xciv.

Cullen, Countee, ed. *Caroling Dusk: An Anthology of Verse by Negro Poets*. Evanston, IL: Harper, 1927.

Culler, Jonathan. "Theories and Methodologies: Why Lyric?" *PMLA* 123, no. 1 (2008): 201-6.

——. *Theory of the Lyric*. Cambridge, MA: Harvard University Press, 2015.

Cunningham, J. V. "The Poetry of Wallace Stevens." *Poetry* 75, no. 3 (1949): 149-65.

Cureton, Richard. "Temporality and Poetic Form." *Journal of Literary Semantics* 31, no. 1 (2002): 37-59.

Cushman, Stephen. *Fictions of Form in American Poetry*. Princeton, NJ: Princeton University Press, 1993.

——. *William Carlos Williams and the Meanings of Measure*. New Haven, CT: Yale University Press, 1985.

Davie, Donald. "Essential Gaudiness." In *The Poet in the Imaginary Museum: Essays of Two Decades*, edited by Barry Alpert, 11-17. New York: Persea Books, 1977.

Davis, Alex, and Lee M. Jenkins. *A History of Modernist Poetry*. New York: Cambridge University Press, 2015.

Davray, Henry. "*Georgian Poetry, 1916-1917.*" *Mercure de France*, April 16, 1918, 716-18.

De Man, Paul. "Lyric and Modernity." In *Blindness and Insight*, 166-86. Minneapolis: University of Minnesota Press, 1971.

Dennis, Helen. "Pound, Women and Gender." In *The Cambridge Companion to Ezra Pound*, edited by Ira B. Nadel, 264-83. Cambridge: Cambridge University Press, 1999.

Dickinson, Emily. *The Poems of Emily Dickinson*. Edited by R. W. Franklin. Cambridge, MA: Belknap Press of Harvard University Press, 1999.

Dodd, Elizabeth. *The Veiled Mirror and the Woman Poet: H.D., Louise Bogan, Elizabeth Bishop, and Louise Glück*. Columbia: University of Missouri Press, 1992.

Donoghue, Denis. *Speaking of Beauty*. New Haven, CT: Yale University Press, 2003.

D.[oolittle], H[ilda]. *Collected Poems 1912-1944*. Edited by Louis L. Martz. Rev. ed. New York: New Directions, 1986.

———. *HERmione*. Edited by Perdita Schaffner. Rev. ed. New York: New Directions, 1981.

Dryden, John. *The Poems of John Dryden*. London: H. Frowde, 1910.

Du Bois, William Edward Burghardt. Foreword to *Bronze*, by Georgia Douglas Johnson, 7. Boston: B. J. Brimmer, 1922.

———. *The Souls of Black Folk: Essays and Sketches*. Chicago: A. C. McClurg., 1903.

Dubrow, Heather. *Genre*. London: Methuen, 1982.

Duffell, Martin J. *A New History of English Metre*. Studies in Linguistics 5. London: Legenda, 2008.

———. "Tennyson's 'Metre of Catullus': The Ambivalent Hendecasyllable." *Language and Literature* 22, no. 1 (2013): 19-31.

DuPlessis, Rachel Blau. *Blue Studios: Poetry and Its Cultural Work*. Modern and Contemporary Poetics. Tuscaloosa: University of Alabama Press, 2006.

Dyck, Carrie. "Defining the Word in Cayuga (Iroquoian)." *International Journal of American Linguistics* 75, no. 4 (October 2009): 571-605.

Easthope, Antony. *Poetry as Discourse*. London: Methuen, 1983.

Eccles, Anastasia. "Formalism and Sentimentalism: Viktor Shklovsky and Laurence Sterne." *New Literary History* 47, no. 4 (2016): 525-45, 633.

Edwards, Brent Hayes. *The Practice of Diaspora: Literature, Translation, and the Rise of Black Internationalism*. Cambridge, MA: Harvard University Press, 2003.

———. "The Seemingly Eclipsed Window of Form: James Weldon Johnson's Prefaces." In *Jazz: The Jazz Cadence of American Culture*, edited by Robert G. O'Meally, 580-601. New York: Columbia University Press, 1998.

Ehlers, Sarah. "Making It Old: The Victorian/Modern Divide in Twentieth-Century American Poetry." *Modern Language Quarterly* 73, no. 1 (March 1, 2012): 37-67.

Eliot, T. S. *Collected Poems, 1909-1962*. New York: Harcourt Brace Jovanovich, 1991.

———. *Ezra Pound: His Metric and Poetry*. New York: Alfred A. Knopf, 1917.

———. "Isolated Superiority." *Dial* 84, no. 1 (January 1928): 4-7.

———. *The Letters of T. S. Eliot*. Edited by Valerie Eliot and Hugh Haughton. Rev. ed. Vol. 1, *1898-1922*. London: Faber and Faber, 2009.

———. *The Poems of T. S. Eliot: Practical Cats and Further Verses*. Edited by Christopher Ricks and Jim McCue. Annotated ed. Baltimore: Johns Hopkins University Press, 2015.

———. "Reflections on *Vers Libre*." In *Selected Prose*, 31-36. New York: Farrar, Straus and Giroux, 1975.

———. *Selected Prose of T. S. Eliot*. London: Faber, 1975.

———. *The Use of Poetry and the Use of Criticism: Studies in the Relation of Criticism to Poetry in England*. Cambridge, MA: Harvard University Press, 1933.

———. *The Waste Land*. 1st Norton Critical Edition. New York: W. W. Norton, 2000.
———. *The Waste Land: A Facsimile and Transcript of the Original Drafts Including the Annotations of Ezra Pound*. Boston: Mariner Books, 1974.
Ellmann, Richard. *Eminent Domain: Yeats among Wilde, Joyce, Pound, Eliot and Auden*. New York: Oxford University Press, 1970.
———. *James Joyce*. New and rev. ed. New York: Oxford University Press, 1982.
Empson, William. *Seven Types of Ambiguity*. 3rd ed., rev. New York: New Directions, 1966.
England's Favourite Poems. Audio CD. The Gift of Music, 2004.
Epstein, Josh. *Sublime Noise: Musical Culture and the Modernist Writer*. Hopkins Studies in Modernism. Baltimore: Johns Hopkins University Press, 2014.
Esenwein, J. Berg, and Mary Eleanor Roberts. *The Art of Versification*. Springfield, MA: Home Correspondence School, 1913.
Evans, William R., ed. *Robert Frost and Sidney Cox: Forty Years of Friendship*. Hanover, NH: University Press of New England, 1981.
Fabb, Nigel, and Morris Halle. *Meter in Poetry: A New Theory*. Cambridge: Cambridge University Press, 2008.
Farr, Florence. *The Music of Speech*. London: Elkin Mathews, 1909.
Felski, Rita. "Introduction." *New Literary History* 33, no. 4 (2002): 607–22.
Figueroa, John. "Problems of a Writer who does not quite . . ." *Caribbean Quarterly* 49, nos. 1/2 (2003): 54.
Finch, Annie. "Dickinson and Patriarchal Meter: A Theory of Metrical Codes." *PMLA* 102, no. 2 (1987): 166–76.
———. *The Ghost of Meter: Culture and Prosody in American Free Verse*. Ann Arbor: University of Michigan Press, 1993.
Flint, F. S. "Imagisme." *Poetry* 1, no. 6 (March 1913): 198–200.
Ford, Ford Madox. *Critical Writings*. Lincoln: University of Nebraska Press, 1964.
———. "Mr. Robert Frost and *North of Boston*." *Outlook*, June 27, 1914, 879–80.
Forrest-Thomson, Veronica. "Cordelia: Or, 'A Poem Should Not Mean, but Be.'" *Kenyon Review Online*. http://www.kenyonreview.org/kr-online-issue/index-2/selections/cordelia-or-a-poem-should-not-mean-but-be/.
———. *Poetic Artifice: A Theory of Twentieth-Century Poetry*. 2nd rev. ed. Bristol: Shearsman Books, 2016.
Frank, Elizabeth. "The Pleasures of Formal Poetry." *Atlantic*, September 1998. https://www.theatlantic.com/magazine/archive/1998/09/the-pleasures-of-formal-poetry/377226/.
Frattarola, Angela. *Modernist Soundscapes: Auditory Technology and the Novel*. Gainesville: University Press of Florida, 2018.
French, Amanda Lowry. "Refrain Again: The Return of the Villanelle Periodicals." *Dissertation Abstracts International, Section A: The Humanities and Social Sciences* 65, no. 10 (2005): 3799.

Fried, Debra. "Andromeda Unbound: Gender and Genre in Millay's Sonnets." *Twentieth Century Literature: A Scholarly and Critical Journal* 32, no. 1 (1986): 1-22.
Friedman, Susan Stanford. "Gender and Genre Anxiety: Elizabeth Barrett Browning and H.D. as Epic Poets." *Tulsa Studies in Women's Literature* 5, no. 2 (1986): 203-28.
Frost, Robert. *Collected Poems, Prose, and Plays*. New York: Library of America, 1995.
———. "The Figure a Poem Makes." In *Collected Poems, Prose, and Plays*, 776-78. New York: Library of America, 1995.
———. *The Notebooks of Robert Frost*. Edited by Robert Faggen. Cambridge, MA: Belknap Press of Harvard University Press, 2009.
———. *Selected Letters of Robert Frost*. New York: Holt, Rinehart and Winston, 1964.
Frye, Northrop. *Anatomy of Criticism: Four Essays*. Princeton, NJ: Princeton University Press, 1971.
Fussell, Edwin S. *Lucifer in Harness: American Meter, Metaphor, and Diction*. Princeton, NJ: Princeton University Press, 1973.
Gaskill, Nicholas. "The Close and the Concrete: Aesthetic Formalism in Context." *New Literary History* 47, no. 4 (2016): 505-24, 633.
Gates, Rosemary L. "T. S. Eliot's Prosody and the Free Verse Tradition: Restricting Whitman's 'Free Growth of Metrical Laws.'" *Poetics Today* 11, no. 3 (1990): 547-78.
Gerber, Natalie. "Beyond Meaning: Differing Fates of Some Modernist Poets' Investments of Belief in Sounds." In *Critical Rhythm: The Poetics of a Literary Life Form*, edited by Ben Glaser and Jonathan Culler, 223-46. New York: Fordham University Press, 2019.
———. "Stevens' Prosody: Meaningful Rhythms." *Wallace Stevens Journal* 29 (2005): 178-87.
Gilbert, Sandra. "Female Female Impersonator: Millay and the Theatre of Personality." In *Critical Essays on Edna St. Vincent Millay*, edited by William B. Thesing, 293-312. New York: Hall, 1993.
Gillis, Everett. "American Prosody in the Eighteen Nineties: With Special Reference to Magazine Verse." PhD diss., University of Texas-Austin, 1948.
Gilroy, Paul. *The Black Atlantic: Modernity and Double Consciousness*. Cambridge, MA: Harvard University Press, 1993.
Gitelman, Lisa. *Scripts, Grooves, and Writing Machines: Representing Technology in the Edison Era*. Stanford, CA: Stanford University Press, 1999.
Glaser, Ben. "Autobiography as Ars Poetica: Satire and Rhythmic Exegesis in 'Saint Peter Relates an Incident.'" In *New Perspectives on James Weldon Johnson's "The Autobiography of an Ex-Colored Man,"* edited by Noelle Morrissette. Athens: University of Georgia Press, 2017.
———. "Modernist Scansion: Robert Frost's Loose Iambics." *ELH* 83, no. 2 (2016): 603-31.

———. "Polymetrical Dissonance: Tennyson, A. Mary F. Robinson, and Classical Meter." *Victorian Poetry* 49, no. 2 (2011): 199-216, 283.

Glaser, Ben, and Jonathan Culler, eds. *Critical Rhythm: The Poetics of a Literary Life Form*. New York: Fordham University Press, 2019.

Goldsby, Jacqueline. *A Spectacular Secret: Lynching in American Life and Literature*. Chicago: University of Chicago Press, 2006.

Goldstone, Andrew. *Fictions of Autonomy: Modernism from Wilde to de Man*. Modernist Literature & Culture. New York: Oxford University Press, 2013.

Golston, Michael. *Rhythm and Race in Modernist Poetry and Science*. New York: Columbia University Press, 2008.

Gordon, Lyndall. *T. S. Eliot: An Imperfect Life*. London: Vintage, 1998.

Gould, Jean. *Amy: The World of Amy Lowell and the Imagist Movement*. New York: Dodd, Mead, 1975.

Graham, T. Austin. *The Great American Songbooks: Musical Texts, Modernism, and the Value of Popular Culture*. Modernist Literature and Culture. New York: Oxford University Press, 2013.

Green, Elizabeth Lay. *The Negro in Contemporary American Literature*. Chapel Hill: University of North Carolina Press, 1928.

Grieder, Josephine. "Robert Frost on Ezra Pound, 1913: Manuscript Corrections of 'Portrait d'une Femme.'" *New England Quarterly* 44, no. 2 (June 1971): 301-5.

Gross, Harvey Seymour. *Sound and Form in Modern Poetry*. 1st ed. Ann Arbor Paperbacks. Ann Arbor: University of Michigan Press, 1964.

———. *The Structure of Verse: Modern Essays on Prosody*. Rev. ed. New York: Ecco Press, 1979.

Grossman, Allen R. *The Long Schoolroom: Lessons in the Bitter Logic of the Poetic Principle*. Ann Arbor: University of Michigan Press, 1997.

Guillory, John. *Cultural Capital: The Problem of Literary Canon Formation*. Chicago: University of Chicago Press, 1993.

———. *Poetic Authority: Spenser, Milton, and Literary History*. New York: Columbia University Press, 1983.

Gumbrecht, Hans Ulrich. "Rhythm and Meaning." In *Materialities of Communication*, edited by Hans Ulrich Gumbrecht and K. Ludwig Pfeiffer, 170-86. Stanford, CA: Stanford University Press, 1994.

Gummere, Francis Barton. *A Handbook of Poetics, for Students of English Verse*. Boston: Ginn, 1885.

Hall, Jason David. *Nineteenth-Century Verse and Technology: Machines of Meter*. Palgrave Studies in Nineteenth-Century Writing and Culture. New York: Palgrave Macmillan, 2017.

Halle, Morris, and Samuel Jay Keyser. *English Stress: Its Form, Its Growth, and Its Role in Verse*. Studies in Language. New York: Harper & Row, 1971.

Halliday, Sam. *Sonic Modernity: Representing Sound in Literature, Culture and the Arts.* Edinburgh: Edinburgh University Press, 2013.

Hammer, Langdon. *Hart Crane and Allen Tate: Janus-Faced Modernism.* Princeton, NJ: Princeton University Press, 1993.

Hanson, Kristin. "Generative Metrics: The State of the Art." In *Current Trends in Metrical Analysis,* edited by Christopher Kueper, 45-62. Frankfurt: Peter Lang, 2011.

Hardy, Thomas. *The Complete Poems of Thomas Hardy.* Edited by James Gibson. New York: Macmillan, 1976.

———. *Jude the Obscure.* Edited by Ralph Pite. 3rd ed. New York: W. W. Norton, 2016.

Harper, Michael. "An Integer Is a Whole Number." In *After Winter: The Art and Life of Sterling A. Brown,* 273-84. Oxford: Oxford University Press, 2009.

Harrington, Joseph. *Poetry and the Public: The Social Form of Modern U.S. Poetics.* Middletown, CT: Wesleyan University Press, 2002.

Hart, Matthew. *Nations of Nothing but Poetry: Modernism, Transnationalism, and Synthetic Vernacular Writing.* Oxford: Oxford University Press, 2010.

Hartman, Charles O. *Free Verse: An Essay on Prosody.* Evanston, IL: Northwestern University Press, 1996.

Hegel, G. W. F. *Aesthetics: Lectures on Fine Art Volume II.* Oxford University Press, 1998.

Henderson, Stephen. "The Heavy Blues of Sterling Brown: A Study of Craft and Tradition." In *After Winter: The Art and Life of Sterling A. Brown,* edited by John Edgar Tidwell and Steven C. Tracy, 31-57. New York: Oxford University Press, 2009.

———. *Understanding the New Black Poetry.* New York: Morrow, 1973.

Higginson, Thomas Wentworth. *Army Life in a Black Regiment.* New York: Penguin, 1997.

Holder, Alan. *Rethinking Meter: A New Approach to the Verse Line.* Lewisburg, PA: Bucknell University Press, 1995.

Holley, Margaret. "The Model Stanza: The Organic Origin of Moore's Syllabic Verse." *Twentieth Century Literature* 30, nos. 2/3 (1984): 181-91.

Holmes, Oliver Wendell. "The Physiology of Versification." In *Pages from an Old Volume of Life,* 8:315-21. *The Works of Oliver Wendell Holmes.* Boston: Houghton, Mifflin, 1892.

Hopkins, Gerard Manley. *Poems and Prose of Gerard Manley Hopkins.* Edited by W. H. Gardner. New York: Penguin Classics, 1953.

Howarth, Peter. *British Poetry in the Age of Modernism.* Cambridge: Cambridge University Press, 2005.

Hughes, Langston. *The Collected Poems of Langston Hughes.* Vintage Classics. New York: Vintage Books, 1995.

Huxley, Aldous. *Brave New World.* Repr. ed. London: Harper Perennial Modern Classics, 2006.

Huyssen, Andreas. *After the Great Divide: Modernism, Mass Culture, Postmodernism.* Bloomington: Indiana University Press, 1987.
Izenberg, Oren. *Being Numerous: Poetry and the Ground of Social Life.* Princeton, NJ: Princeton University Press, 2011.
Jackson, Thomas H. *The Early Poetry of Ezra Pound.* Cambridge, MA: Harvard University Press, 1968.
Jackson, Virginia. *Dickinson's Misery: A Theory of Lyric Reading.* Princeton, NJ: Princeton University Press, 2005.
———. "Specters of the Ballad." *Nineteenth-Century Literature* 71, no. 2 (2016): 176.
———. "'The Story of Boon'; or, The Poetess." *ESQ: A Journal of the American Renaissance* 54, nos. 1–4 (2008): 241–68.
Jackson, Virginia, and Yopie Prins, eds. *The Lyric Theory Reader: A Critical Anthology.* Baltimore: Johns Hopkins University Press, 2014.
Jaji, Tsitsi. *Africa in Stereo: Modernism, Music, and Pan-African Solidarity.* New York: Oxford University Press, 2014.
Jarrell, Randall. "Robert Frost's 'Home Burial.'" In *No Other Book: Selected Essays,* 42–66. New York: Harper Perennial, 2000.
Jarvis, Simon. "For a Poetics of Verse." *PMLA* 125, no. 4 (October 2010): 931–35.
———. "Sordello's Pristine Pulpiness." In *Critical Rhythm: The Poetics of a Literary Life Form,* edited by Ben Glaser and Jonathan Culler, 60–83. New York: Fordham University Press, 2019.
———. *Wordsworth's Philosophic Song.* New York: Cambridge University Press, 2007.
Jefferson, Thomas. "Thoughts on English Prosody." In *The Writings of Thomas Jefferson,* edited by Albert Ellery Bergh, 17:415–51. Washington, DC: Thomas Jefferson Memorial Association of the United States, 1907.
Johnson, Barbara. "Apostrophe, Animation, and Abortion." *Diacritics* 16, no. 1 (1986): 29–47.
Johnson, Georgia Douglas. *Bronze.* Boston: B. J. Brimmer, 1922.
———. *The Heart of a Woman, and Other Poems.* Boston: Cornhill, 1918.
———. "The Ordeal." In *The New Negro,* edited by Alain Locke, 146. New York: Simon and Schuster, 1925.
———. *Selected Works of Georgia Douglas Johnson.* Edited by Claudia Tate. New York: G. K. Hall, 1997.
Johnson, James Weldon. *The Autobiography of an Ex-Colored Man: Authoritative Text, Backgrounds and Sources, Criticism.* Edited by Jacqueline Denise Goldsby. A Norton Critical Edition. New York: W. W. Norton, 2015.
———, ed. *The Book of American Negro Poetry.* Rev. ed. New York: Harcourt, 1983.
———. *The Book of American Negro Spirituals.* New York: Viking Press, 1925.
———. *Writings.* New York: Literary Classics of the United States, 2004.
Jones, Ewan James. *Coleridge and the Philosophy of Poetic Form.* Cambridge: Cambridge University Press, 2014.

Joyce, James. *Ulysses*. Edited by Hans Walter Gabler. New York: Vintage, 1986.
Kane, Brian. *Sound Unseen: Acousmatic Sound in Theory and Practice*. Oxford: Oxford University Press, 2016.
Kappeler, Erin. "Constructing Walt Whitman: Literary History and Histories of Rhythm." In *Critical Rhythm: The Poetics of a Literary Life Form*, edited by Ben Glaser and Jonathan Culler, 128-52. New York: Fordham University Press, 2019.
———. "Editing America: Nationalism and the New Poetry." *Modernism/Modernity* 21, no. 4 (2014): 899-918.
———. "Shaping Free Verse: American Prosody and Poetics 1880-1920." PhD diss., Tufts University, 2014.
Kearns, Katherine. *Robert Frost and a Poetics of Appetite*. Cambridge: Cambridge University Press, 1994.
Kenner, Hugh. "Blood for the Ghosts." In *New Approaches to Ezra Pound*, edited by Eva Hesse, 331-48. Berkeley: University of California Press, 1969.
———. *A Homemade World: The American Modernist Writers*. New York: Knopf, 1974.
———. *The Poetry of Ezra Pound*. Norfolk, CT: New Directions, 1951.
Kerlin, Robert Thomas. *Negro Poets and Their Poems*. Washington, DC: Associated, 1923.
Kindley, Evan. *Poet-Critics and the Administration of Culture*. Cambridge, MA: Harvard University Press, 2017.
Kiparsky, Paul. "The Rhythmic Structure of English Verse." *Linguistic Inquiry* 8 (Spring 1977): 189-247.
Kiparsky, Paul, and Gilbert Youmans, eds. *Rhythm and Meter*. Vol. 1, *Phonetics and Phonology*. San Diego, CA: Academic Press, 1989.
Kittler, Friedrich A. *Gramophone, Film, Typewriter*. Writing Science. Stanford, CA: Stanford University Press, 1999.
Kleinzahler, August. "A Peacock Called Mirabell. Review of 'James Merrill' by Langdon Hammer." *London Review of Books*, March 2016. https://www.lrb.co.uk/the-paper/v38/n07/august-kleinzahler/a-peacock-called-mirabell.
Koestenbaum, Wayne. "*The Waste Land*: T. S. Eliot's and Ezra Pound's Collaboration on Hysteria." *Twentieth Century Literature* 34, no. 2 (1988): 113-39.
Krauss, Rosalind E. *The Originality of the Avant-Garde and Other Modernist Myths*. Cambridge, MA: MIT Press, 1985.
Kutzinski, Vera. "Unseasoned Flowers: Nature and History in Placido and Jean Toomer." *Yale Journal of Criticism* 3 (Spring 1990): 153-79.
Laity, Cassandra. *H.D. and the Victorian Fin de Siècle: Gender, Modernism, Decadence*. Cambridge: Cambridge University Press, 1996.
Lehman, Robert S. "Eliot's Last Laugh: The Dissolution of Satire in *The Waste Land*." *Journal of Modern Literature* 32, no. 2 (2009): 65-79.
———. "Formalism, Mere Form, and Judgment." *New Literary History* 48, no. 2 (2017): 245-63.

———. *Impossible Modernism: T. S. Eliot, Walter Benjamin, and the Critique of Historical Reason*. Stanford, CA: Stanford University Press, 2016.

Leighton, Angela. *On Form: Poetry, Aestheticism, and the Legacy of a Word*. New York: Oxford University Press, 2007.

Lerner, Ben. *The Hatred of Poetry*. New York: FSG Originals, 2016.

Levenson, Michael. *A Genealogy of Modernism*. Cambridge: Cambridge University Press, 1984.

Lewis, C. S. *Selected Literary Essays*. Cambridge: Cambridge University Press, 2013.

Longenbach, James. *Modernist Poetics of History: Pound, Eliot, and the Sense of the Past*. Princeton, NJ: Princeton University Press, 2014.

———. *Stone Cottage: Pound, Yeats, and Modernism*. New York: Oxford University Press, 1988. http://site.ebrary.com/lib/yale/Doc?id=10087197.

Lowell, Amy. "Editorial Comment: Vers Libre and Metrical Prose." *Poetry* 3 (March 1914): 213-20.

———. Preface to *Some Imagist Poets: An Anthology*, v-viii. Boston: Houghton Mifflin, 1915.

———. "Some Musical Analogies in Modern Poetry." *Musical Quarterly* 6, no. 1 (1920): 127-57.

Loy, Mina. *The Last Lunar Baedeker*. Highlands, NC: Jargon Society, 1982.

Lynen, John F. *The Pastoral Art of Robert Frost*. New Haven, CT: Yale University Press, 1960.

Manson, Michael Tomasek. "Sterling Brown and the 'Vestiges' of the Blues: The Role of Race in English Verse Structure." *MELUS* 21, no. 1 (1996): 21-40.

———. "Worrying the Lines: Versification in Sterling Brown's *Southern Road*." In *After Winter: The Art and Life of Sterling A. Brown*, 111-36. Oxford: Oxford University Press, 2009.

Mao, Douglas. "Modern American Literary Criticism." In *The Cambridge Companion to American Modernism*, edited by Walter B. Kalaidjian, 284-307. Cambridge: Cambridge University Press, 2005.

———. "The New Critics and the Text-Object." *ELH* 63, no. 1 (1996): 227-54.

———. *Solid Objects: Modernism and the Test of Production*. Princeton, NJ: Princeton University Press, 1998.

Markovits, Stefanie. *The Victorian Verse-Novel: Aspiring to Life*. Oxford: Oxford University Press, 2017.

Martin, Meredith. "'Imperfectly Civilized': Ballads, Nations, and Histories of Form." *ELH* 82 (2015): 345-63.

———. "Picturing Rhythm." In *Critical Rhythm: The Poetics of a Literary Life Form*, edited by Ben Glaser and Jonathan Culler, 197-222. New York: Fordham University Press, 2019.

———. *The Rise and Fall of Meter: Poetry and English National Culture, 1860-1930*. Princeton, NJ: Princeton University Press, 2012.

———. "Rupert Brooke's Ambivalent Mourning, Ezra Pound's Anticipatory Nostalgia." In *Modernism and Nostalgia: Bodies, Locations, Aesthetics*, edited by Tammy Clewell, 183-97. New York: Palgrave Macmillan, 2013.

Masters, Edgar Lee. *Spoon River Anthology*. Edited by John E. Hallwas. Urbana: University of Illinois Press, 1993.

Mayor, Joseph. *Chapters on English Metre*. London: C. J. Clay and Sons, 1886.

McDonald, Gail. *Learning to Be Modern: Pound, Eliot, and the American University*. Oxford: Clarendon Press, 1993.

McGill, Meredith. "What Is a Ballad? Reading for Genre, Format, and Medium." *Nineteenth-Century Literature* 71, no. 2 (2016): 156-75.

Menand, Louis, and Lawrence Rainey. Introduction to *The Cambridge History of Literary Criticism*, 7:1-14. Cambridge: Cambridge University Press, 2000.

Meredith, William. *Earth Walk: New and Selected Poems*. New York: Knopf, 1970.

Mill, John Stuart. "Thoughts on Poetry and Its Varieties." In *Victorians on Literature & Art*, edited by Robert L. Peters, 77-99. New York: Appleton-Century-Crofts, 1961.

Millay, Edna St Vincent. *Collected Poems*. 2nd ed. New York: Harper Perennial Modern Classics, 2011.

Mills, Mara. "Evocative Object: Auditory Inkblot." *Continent* 5, no. 1 (2016): 15-23.

Monroe, Harriet. Harriet. "Dr. Patterson on Rhythm." *Poetry* 12, no. 1 (April 1918): 30-36.

———. "Editorial Comment: Rhythms of English Verse." *Poetry* 3 (March 1914): 61-69, 100-111.

———. Introduction to *The New Poetry*, edited by Harriet Monroe and Alice Corbin Henderson, v-xiii. New York: Macmillan, 1917.

———. "Review of *Rivers to the Sea*, by Sara Teasdale." *Poetry*, December 1915, 148-50.

———. "What Next." *Poetry*, October 1919, 33-38.

Morrissette, Noelle. *James Weldon Johnson's Modern Soundscapes*. Iowa City: University of Iowa Press, 2013.

Murphet, Julian, Helen Groth, and Penelope Hone, eds. *Sounding Modernism: Rhythm and Sonic Mediation in Modern Literature and Film*. Edinburgh: Edinburgh University Press, 2017.

Murphy, James. "'A Thing so Small': The Nature of Meter in Robert Frost's 'Design.'" *Modernism/Modernity* 14 (2007): 309-28.

Napolin, Julie Beth. "The Fact of Resonance: An Acoustics of Determination in Faulkner and Benjamin." *Symploke* 24, nos. 1/2 (2016): 171-86.

Naremore, James. "The Imagists and the French 'Generation of 1900.'" *Contemporary Literature* 11, no. 3 (1970): 354-74.

Nelson, Cary. *Repression and Recovery: Modern American Poetry and the Politics of Cultural Memory, 1910-1945*. The Wisconsin Project on American Writers. Madison: University of Wisconsin Press, 1989.

Newcomb, John Timberman. *How Did Poetry Survive? The Making of Modern American Verse*. Urbana: University of Illinois Press, 2012.

———. *Would Poetry Disappear? American Verse and the Crisis of Modernity*. Columbus: Ohio State University Press, 2004.

Nicholls, David. *Conjuring the Folk*. Ann Arbor: University of Michigan Press, 2000.

Nicholls, Peter. *Modernisms: A Literary Guide*. Berkeley: University of California Press, 1995.

Niedecker, Lorine. *Collected Works*. Edited by Jenny Penberthy. Berkeley: University of California Press, 2002.

Nielsen, Aldon Lynn. *Writing between the Lines: Race and Intertextuality*. Athens: University of Georgia Press, 1994.

North, Michael. *The Dialect of Modernism: Race, Language, and Twentieth-Century Literature*. New York: Oxford University Press, 1994.

Nowlin, Michael. "Race Literature, Modernism, and Normal Literature: James Weldon Johnson's Groundwork for an African American Literary Renaissance, 1912-20." *Modernism/Modernity* 20, no. 3 (2013): 503-18.

Nurhussein, Nadia. *Rhetorics of Literacy: The Cultivation of American Dialect Poetry*. Columbus: Ohio State University Press, 2013.

Ochoa Gautier, Ana María. *Aurality: Listening and Knowledge in Nineteenth-Century Colombia*. Durham, NC: Duke University Press Books, 2014.

O'Driscoll, Dennis. *Stepping Stones: Interviews with Seamus Heaney*. New York: Faber & Faber, 2009.

Omond, T. S. *English Metrists*. Oxford: Clarendon Press, 1921.

O'Rourke, Meghan, and A. E. Stallings. "This Condensery: An Exchange by Meghan O'Rourke, A. E. Stallings." *Poetry*, January 2004.

Parrish, Stephen. "Wordsworth and Coleridge on Meter." *Journal of English and Germanic Philology* 59 (1960): 41-49.

Patmore, Coventry. *Essay on English Metrical Law*. Washington, DC: Catholic University of America Press, 1961.

Perloff, Marjorie. "A Conversation with Kenneth Goldsmith." *Jacket* 21 (February 2003). http://jacketmagazine.com/21/perl-gold-iv.html.

———. "English as a 'Second' Language: Mina Loy's 'Anglo-Mongrels and the Rose.'" *Jacket* 5 (1998). http://jacketmagazine.com/05/mina-anglo.html.

———. "Pound/Stevens: Whose Era?" In *Critical Essays on American Modernism*, edited by Michael J. Hoffman and Patrick D. Murphy, 135-44. New York: G. K. Hall, 1992.

Pinsky, Robert. *Democracy, Culture and the Voice of Poetry*. Princeton, NJ: Princeton University Press, 2002.

Poe, Edgar Allan. "The Rationale of Verse." In *The Works of the Late Edgar Allen Poe*, edited by Rufus Wilmot Griswold. New York: J. S. Redfield (reproduced by the Edgar Allan Poe Society of Baltimore), 1850. http://www.eapoe.org/works/essays/ratlvrsd.htm.

Poirier, Richard. *The Performing Self*. New York: Oxford University Press, 1971.
———. *Poetry and Pragmatism*. Cambridge, MA: Harvard University Press, 1992.
Poovey, Mary. "The Model System of Contemporary Literary Criticism." *Critical Inquiry* 27, no. 3 (April 1, 2001): 408-38.
Pound, Ezra. *The Cantos of Ezra Pound*. New York: New Directions, 1995.
———. *Collected Early Poems of Ezra Pound*. Edited by Michael King and Louis L. Martz. London: Faber and Faber, 1977.
———. *Early Writings: Poems and Prose*. Penguin, 2005.
———. *Ezra Pound and Music*. Edited by R. Murray Schafer. New York: New Directions, 1976.
———. "A Few Don'ts by an Imagiste." *Poetry* 1, no. 6 (March 1913): 200-206.
———. *The Letters of Ezra Pound to Alice Corbin Henderson*. Edited by Ira Bruce Nadel. 1st ed. Austin: University of Texas Press, 1993.
———. "A List of Books." *Little Review* 4, no. 11 (March 1918): 54-58.
———. *Lustra by Ezra Pound: With Earlier Poems*. Knopf: New York, 1917.
———. *Poems and Translations*. New York: Library of America, 2003.
———. *Pound/Williams: Selected Letters of Ezra Pound and William Carlos Williams*. Edited by Hugh Witemeyer. New York: New Directions, 1996.
———. "A Retrospect." In *Poetry in Theory: An Anthology, 1900-2000*, edited by Jon Cook, 83-90. Malden, MA: Blackwell, 2004.
———. "Review of *A Boy's Will*, by Robert Frost." *Poetry* 2 (1912): 72-74.
———. *The Selected Letters of Ezra Pound, 1907-1941*. Edited by D. D. Paige. New York: New Directions, 1971.
———. *Selected Prose 1909-1965*. New York: New Directions, 1973.
———. "Three Cantos." *Poetry* 10, no. 3 (June 1917): 113-21.
———. "Treatise on Metre." In *ABC of Reading*, 197-206. New York: New Directions, 2010.
———. "Vorticism." *Fortnightly Review* 96, no. 573 (September 1914): 461-71.
Powell, Grosvenor. "The Two Paradigms for Iambic Pentameter and Twentieth-Century Metrical Experimentation." *Modern Language Review* 91, no. 3 (July 1996): 561-77.
Preston, Carrie J. *Modernism's Mythic Pose: Gender, Genre, Solo Performance*. Modernist Literature & Culture. New York: Oxford University Press, 2011.
Prins, Yopie. *Ladies' Greek: Victorian Translations of Tragedy*. Princeton, NJ: Princeton University Press, 2017.
———. "'Lady's Greek' (with the Accents): A Metrical Translation of Euripides by A. Mary F. Robinson." *Victorian Literature and Culture* 34, no. 2 (2006): 591-618.
———. "Metrical Translation: Nineteenth-Century Homers and the Hexameter Mania." In *Nation, Language, and the Ethics of Translation*, edited by Sandra Bermann and Michael Wood, 229-56. Princeton, NJ: Princeton University Press, 2005.

———. "Victorian Meters." In *The Cambridge Companion to Victorian Poetry*, edited by Joseph Bristow, 89–113. Cambridge: Cambridge University Press, 2000.

———. *Victorian Sappho*. Princeton, NJ: Princeton University Press, 1999.

———. "'What Is Historical Poetics?'" *Modern Language Quarterly: A Journal of Literary History* 77, no. 1 (2016): 13–40.

Ramazani, Jahan. *Poetry of Mourning: The Modern Elegy from Hardy to Heaney*. Chicago: University of Chicago Press, 1994.

Ray, Man. "Object of Destruction." *This Quarter*, September 1932, 55.

Reed, Anthony. *Freedom Time: The Poetics and Politics of Black Experimental Writing*. Baltimore: Johns Hopkins University Press, 2014.

Richards, I. A. *Practical Criticism: A Study of Literary Judgement*. Edited by John Constable. Vol. 4 of *Selected Works, 1919–1938*. London: Routledge, 2001.

———. *Principles of Literary Criticism*. 5th ed. International Library of Psychology, Philosophy, and Scientific Method. New York: Harcourt, Brace, 1934.

Robinson, Edwin Arlington. *Poems*. Edited by Scott Donaldson. New York: Everyman's Library, 2007.

Roethke, Theodore. "The Poetry of Louise Bogan." *Critical Quarterly* 3 (1961): 142–50.

Rogers, Timothy, ed. *Georgian Poetry, 1911–1922: The Critical Heritage*. London: Routledge & K. Paul, 1977.

Ronda, Margaret. "'Work and Wait Unwearying': Dunbar's Georgics." *PMLA* 127, no. 4 (2012): 863–78, 1067.

Rosenblitt, J. Alison. "Pretentious Scansion, Fascist Aesthetics, and a Father-Complex for Joyce: E. E. Cummings on Sapphics and Ezra Pound." *Cambridge Classical Journal* 59 (December 2013): 178–98.

Rudy, Jason. *Electric Meters: Victorian Physiological Poetics*. Athens: Ohio University Press, 2009.

———. "Material Patmore." In *Meter Matters: Verse Cultures of the Long Nineteenth Century*, edited by Jason David Hall, 135–56. Athens: Ohio University Press, 2011.

Sanders, Mark A. *Afro-Modernist Aesthetics and the Poetry of Sterling A. Brown*. Athens: University of Georgia Press, 1999.

Schulze, Robin. *The Degenerate Muse: American Nature, Modernist Poetry, and the Problem of Cultural Hygiene*. Modernist Literature & Culture. New York: Oxford University Press, 2013.

Sergeant, Elizabeth Shepley. *Robert Frost: The Trial by Existence*. New York: Holt, Rinehart and Winston, 1960.

Sider, Justin A. *Parting Words: Victorian Poetry and Public Address*. Charlottesville: University of Virginia Press, 2018.

Silkin, Jon. *The Life of Metrical and Free Verse in Twentieth-Century Poetry*. New York: St. Martin's Press, 1997.

Simpson, John. "Ohio." *James Joyce Online Notes*. Accessed October 21, 2015. http://www.jjon.org/joyce-s-allusions/ohio-1.

Skinner, B. F. *The Shaping of a Behaviorist*. New York: Alfred A. Knopf, 1979.

———. "The Verbal Summator and a Method for the Study of Latent Speech." *Journal of Psychology* 2 (1936): 71-107.

Smethurst, James E. "Genesis and Crisis: Foundations of a Modern Black Literary Intelligentsia." *Modernism/Modernity* 18, no. 2 (2011): 449-54.

Smith, Gary. "The Literary Ballads of Sterling A. Brown." *College Language Association Journal* 32, no. 4 (June 1989): 393-409.

Steele, Timothy. *Missing Measures: Modern Poetry and the Revolt against Meter*. Fayetteville: University of Arkansas Press, 1990.

Stepto, Robert. "'When De Saint Go Ma'chin' Home': Sterling Brown's Blueprint for a New Negro Poetry." *Callaloo* 21, no. 4 (1998): 940-49.

Sterne, Jonathan. *The Audible Past: Cultural Origins of Sound Reproduction*. Durham, NC: Duke University Press, 2003.

Stewart, Susan. *Poetry and the Fate of the Senses*. Chicago: University of Chicago Press, 2002.

Stowe, David W. "Babylon Revisited: Psalm 137 as American Protest Song." *Black Music Research Journal* 32, no. 1 (2012): 95-112.

Sullivan, Hannah. "T. S. Eliot—His Poetry." tseliot.com. Accessed December 3, 2019. https://tseliot.com/editorials/his-poetry.

———. *The Work of Revision*. Cambridge, MA: Harvard University Press, 2013.

Sundquist, Eric J. *To Wake the Nations: Race in the Making of American Literature*. Cambridge, MA: Belknap Press of Harvard University Press, 1993.

Talbot, John. "Robert Frost's Hendecasyllabics and Roman Rebuttals." *International Journal of the Classical Tradition* 10, no. 1 (2004): 73-84.

Tapper, Gordon A. *The Machine That Sings: Modernism, Hart Crane and the Culture of the Body*. London: Routledge, 2014.

Tarlinskaja, Marina. "What Is 'Metricality'? English Iambic Pentameter." In *Formal Approaches to Poetry: Recent Developments in Metrics*, edited by B. Elan Dresher and Nila Friedberg, 53-75. Phonology and Phonetics 11. Berlin: Mouton de Gruyter, 2006.

Tate, Claudia. Introduction to *Selected Works of Georgia Douglas Johnson*, xvii-lxxx. New York: G. K. Hall, 1997.

Taupin, René. *The Influence of French Symbolism on Modern American Poetry*. Translated by William Pratt. AMS Press, 1985.

Taylor, Dennis. *Hardy's Metres and Victorian Prosody: With a Metrical Appendix of Hardy's Stanza Forms*. Oxford: Clarendon Press/Oxford University Press, 1988.

Teasdale, Sara. *Collected Poems*. New York: Macmillan, 1937.

Tennyson, Alfred Lord. *The Letters of Alfred Lord Tennyson*. Vol. 2, *1851-1870*. Edited by Cecil Y. Lang and Edgar F. Shannon Jr. Cambridge, MA: Belknap Press of Harvard University Press, 1987.

———. *The Poems of Tennyson*. Edited by Christopher Ricks. 2nd ed. Vol. 2. 3 vols. Berkeley: University of California Press, 1987.

Thomas, Lorenzo. *Extraordinary Measures: Afrocentric Modernism and 20th-Century American Poetry*. Tuscaloosa: University of Alabama Press, 2000.

Thurman, Wallace. *The Collected Writings of Wallace Thurman: A Harlem Renaissance Reader*. Edited by Amritjit Singh and Daniel M Scott. New Brunswick, NJ: Rutgers University Press, 2003.

———. *Infants of the Spring*. New York: Macaulay, 1932.

Tidwell, John Edgar. "Two Writers Sharing: Sterling A. Brown, Robert Frost, and 'In Divés' Dive.'" In *After Winter: The Art and Life of Sterling A. Brown*, edited by John Edgar Tidwell and Steven C Tracy, 81-93. Oxford: Oxford University Press, 2009.

Tiffany, Daniel. *My Silver Planet: A Secret History of Poetry and Kitsch*. Hopkins Studies in Modernism. Baltimore: Johns Hopkins University Press, 2014.

Toomer, Jean. *Cane*. Edited by Darwin Turner. New York: W. W. Norton, 1987.

———. *Cane*. Edited by Henry Louis Gates Jr. and Rudolph P. Byrd. 2nd ed. New York: W. W. Norton, 2011.

———. *The Letters of Jean Toomer, 1919-1924*. Edited by Mark Whalan. University of Tennessee Press, 2006.

Trager, George L., and Henry Lee Smith. *An Outline of English Structure*. Studies in Linguistics 3. Norman, OK: Battenburg Press, 1951.

Tsur, Reuven. "Metricalness and Rhythmicalness: What Our Ear Tells Our Mind." In *Frontiers in Comparative Prosody*, edited by Mihhail Lotman and Maria-Kristiina Lotman, 57-79. Bern: Peter Lang, 2011. https://arcade.stanford.edu/content/metricalness-and-rhythmicalness-what-our-ear-tells-our-mind.

Tucker, Herbert F. "Doughty's *The Dawn in Britain* and the Modernist Eclipse of the Victorian." *Romanticism and Victorianism on the Net* 47 (August 2007). http://www.erudit.org/revue/ravon/2007/v/n47/016705ar.html?vue=resume.

———. "Tactical Formalism: A Response to Caroline Levine." *Victorian Studies: An Interdisciplinary Journal of Social, Political, and Cultural Studies* 49, no. 1 (2006): 85-93.

Vendler, Helen. "Poet of Two Worlds." *New York Review of Books*, March 4, 1982. http://www.nybooks.com/articles/1982/03/04/poet-of-two-worlds/.

Wagner, Jean. *Black Poets of the United States: From Paul Laurence Dunbar to Langston Hughes*. Urbana: University of Illinois Press, 1973.

Walcott, Derek. "The Road Taken." In *Homage to Robert Frost*, 93-117. New York: Farrar, Straus and Giroux, 1997.

Walker, Cheryl. *Masks Outrageous and Austere: Culture, Psyche, and Persona in Modern Women Poets*. Bloomington: Indiana University Press, 1991.

Wesling, Donald. *The Chances of Rhyme: Device and Modernity*. Berkeley: University of California Press, 1980.

———. "The Inevitable Ear: Freedom and Necessity in Lyric Form, Wordsworth and After." In *Forms of Lyric: Selected Papers from the English Institute*, edited by Reuben Brower, 103-26. New York: Columbia University Press, 1970.

———. *The Scissors of Meter: Grammetrics and Reading*. Ann Arbor: University of Michigan Press, 1996.

Whalan, Mark. Review of *Brother Mine: The Correspondence of Jean Toomer and Waldo Frank*, Ed. Kathleen Pfeiffer. *Modernism/Modernity* 18, no. 3 (2011): 661-63.

Wheeler, Lesley. "The Formalist Modernism of Edna St. Vincent Millay, Helene Johnson, and Louise Bogan." In *The Cambridge History of American Poetry*, edited by Alfred Bendixen and Stephen Burt, 628-49. Cambridge: Cambridge University Press, 2015.

———. *Voicing American Poetry: Sound and Performance from the 1920s to the Present*. Ithaca, NY: Cornell University Press, 2008.

Whitworth, Michael H. *Reading Modernist Poetry*. Chichester, UK: John Wiley & Sons, 2010.

Williams, Carolyn. *Gilbert and Sullivan: Gender, Genre, Parody*. Gender and Culture. New York: Columbia University Press, 2011.

Williams, Francis Howard. "Browning's Form." *Poet-Lore* 2 (June 1890): 300-305.

Williams, R. John. *The Buddha in the Machine: Art, Technology, and the Meeting of East and West*. New Haven, CT: Yale University Press, 2014.

Williams, Raymond. *Marxism and Literature*. Oxford: Oxford University Press, 1977.

Williams, William Carlos. Introduction to *Illustrated Leaves of Grass by Walt Whitman*, 9-13. New York: Madison Square Press, 1971.

Wilson, Edmund. *Axel's Castle*. New York: C. Scribner's Sons, 1931.

Wiman, Christian. *Ambition and Survival: Becoming a Poet*. Port Townsend, WA: Copper Canyon Press, 2013.

Wimsatt, W. K., and Monroe C. Beardsley. "The Concept of Meter: An Exercise in Abstraction." *PMLA* 74, no. 5 (December 1959): 585-98.

Winslow, Ann, ed. *Trial Balances*. New York: Macmillan, 1935.

Winters, Yvor. *In Defense of Reason*. Edited by Kenneth Fields. Athens, OH: Swallow Press, 1987.

———. "Problems for the Modern Critic of Literature." *Hudson Review* 9, no. 3 (Autumn 1956): 325-86.

Wood, Michael. "R. P. Blackmur." In *The Cambridge History of Literary Criticism*, edited by A. Walton Litz, Louis Menand, and Lawrence Rainey, 7:235-47. Cambridge: Cambridge University Press, 2000.

Woodson, John. *Anthems, Sonnets, and Chants: Recovering the African-American Poetry of the 1930s*. Columbus: Ohio State University Press, 2011.

Woolf, Virginia. "Aurora Leigh." In *The Common Reader*, 2. New York: Harcourt, Brace, 1948.

Wordsworth, William. *The Major Works*. Edited by Stephen Gill. New ed. New York: Oxford University Press, 2008.

Work, John Wesley. *Folk Song of the American Negro*. Nashville, TN: Press of Fisk University, 1915.

Wright, John. "The New Negro Poet and the Nachal Man: Sterling Brown's Folk Odyssey." *Black American Literature Forum* 23, no. 1 (1989): 95-105.

Yeats, W. B. *The Letters of W. B. Yeats*. Edited by Allan Wade. New York: Macmillan, 1955.

Zellinger, Elissa. "Edna St. Vincent Millay and the Poetess Tradition." *Legacy* 29, no. 2 (2012): 240-62.

Ziff, Larzer. *The American 1890s: Life and Times of a Lost Generation*. New York: Viking Press, 1968.

Index

Abercrombie, Lascelles, 254n2
accentual-syllabic meter, 55, 219; in Frost's poetry, 31, 49; Harriet Monroe on, 58; in Pound's "Portrait d'une Femme," 97
Adams, Stephen J., 91, 241-42n26
African American poetics: and Anglo-American poetics, 181-82, 185-86, 191-92; Weldon Johnson on, 156. *See also* Brown, Sterling; Johnson, Georgia Douglas; Johnson, James Weldon; New Negro Renaissance poets; Toomer, Jean
African American poets, 28; reception of works by, 182-88
African Americans: as represented in works by white authors, 139
Agawu, Kofi, 28, 181
Albright, Daniel, 84
Aldington, Richard, 32, 243n2
Alexander, Elizabeth: "The Venus Hottentot," 205-6
Anderson, David, 193
Anderson, Margaret, 99
Anderson, Paul, 155
Anderson, Sherwood, 139; *Winesburg, Ohio*, 147
Antheil, George, 232n99
Art of Versification (1913), 11, 146
Attridge, Derek, 117, 236n57, 245n34
Auden, W. H., 27
audile imagination: Frost's concept of, 33-34, 42
audile technique, 17-19, 80, 81-82; and the metrical vestige, 21-22, 75, 131. *See also* meter

Baker, Houston, 115
ballad theory, 144-47, 193
Barkas, Pallister, 229n48
Barnard, Mary, 101
Bartlett, John, 34
Beardsley, Monroe, 213
Beasley, Rebecca, 226n12
Beckett, Samuel, 14
Bedient, Cal, 72-73, 240n57
Bell, Clive, 212
Beloof, Robert, 215
Benston, Kimberly, 187, 193-94, 198
Berryman, John, 27
Bérubé, Michael, 183
Beyers, Chris, 4, 231n92
Bishop, Elizabeth, 215
Blackmur, R. P., 216; "Lord Tennyson's Scissors," 213-15
blank verse, 12; Frost's use of, 32, 38; Virginia Woolf on, 9. *See also* iambic pentameter
Blanton, C. D., 152, 217, 225n3
Blount, Marcellus, 5
blues: in Sterling Brown's poetry, 22, 188, 194-95
Boas, Franz, 247n13
Bogan, Louise, 28, 107, 109, 110-11, 244n21; "Ad Castitatem," 129; "Betrothed," 124, 127; *Blue Estuaries: Poems 1923-1958*, 125; *Body of This Death*, 124, 126, 128, 129-30; "The Changed Woman," 129; *Collected Poems 1923-1953*, 125; "The Crows," 129; "Fifteenth Farewell," 127-28, 129; influences on, 131-32;

Bogan, Louise (*cont.*)
"A Letter," 129; "Medusa," 124-25; meter in works by, 124-34; and the metrical vestige, 124, 131; "My Voice Not Being Proud," 130; on poetry, 133; "The Romantic," 128-29, 130, 131; "Single Sonnet," 128; "Sonnet," 129-30; "Stanza," 130; "A Tale," 125-26, 127, 128, 130; "Women," 131-32
Bollobás, Eniko, 59
Bolton, Thaddeus, 230n58
Booth, Phillip, 53-54
Borroff, Marie, 233n13
Braddock, Jeremy, 155, 247n1
Braithwaite, William Stanley, 115, 116-17, 119, 120, 122, 190
Brathwaite, Kamau, 143, 156; on Eliot, 204-5, 254n74
Brewer, R. F.: *Orthometry: The Art of Versification*, 13, 190
Bridges, Robert, 3, 10, 20, 31, 78; *Milton's Prosody*, 12; *Spirit of Man*, 159, 160
Brinkman, Bartholomew, 19
Bromwich, David, 22
Brooke, Rupert: "The Old Vicarage, Grantchester," 13
Brooke-Rose, Christine, 222
Brooks, Cleanth, 211; *The Well Wrought Urn*, 213
Brooks, Gwendolyn, 27; "The Anniad," 203; "The Mother," 121-22
Brooks, Van Wyck, 140
Brower, Reuben, 32, 38
Brown, Sterling, 115-16, 138, 143, 156; and African American poetics, 180, 181-82; on Anglo-American poetics, 181-82, 185-86, 191-92; on black poetry and scholarship, 184-88; "Cabaret," 151; on dialect, 194; on Weldon Johnson, 170-71; meter in works of, 185, 194-201; and the metrical vestige, 182; "Mill Mountain," 27, 203; *Outline for the Study of the Poetry of American Negroes*, 182, 187-92, 195, 201; on prosody, 190; reception of poetry of, 169-70; "Slim Greer" poems, 202; *Southern Road*, 115, 193; "Southern Road," 168, 201-2, 203; on Jean Toomer, 141; "Vestiges," 22, 27, 193; "When de Saints Go Ma'ching Home," 28-29, 193-203
Browning, Elizabeth Barrett, 243n44; *Aurora Leigh*, 101, 103, 105; "The Dead Pan," 99; iambic pentameter of, 110; "A Musical Instrument," 99
Browning, Robert, 58, 82-83, 96; "My Last Duchess," 98; "The Ring and the Book," 103; *Sordello*, 85, 86, 234n32
Bryant, William Cullen, 226-27n20
Buckley, Jennifer, 20
Burke, Carolyn, 92
Burns, Robert, 146, 147, 165
Byron, George Gordon, Lord, 190
Bysshe, Edward, 229n52

Campbell, Roy, 13
Cane (Toomer), 136; "Box Seat," 142; "Carma," 142, 150; "Cotton Song," 150, 248n29; "Esther," 155; "Fern," 148-49, 151-52; folk culture as manifested in, 142-43, 144-52; "Georgia Dusk," 150; "Kabnis," 135, 143, 152-56, 180; "Karintha," 150; meter in, 137, 138-39, 150-52; and the metrical vestige, 137, 139, 150, 152; "November Cotton Flower," 150; "Reapers," 150; short stories in, 153; "Song of the Son," 135-36, 141, 149-51, 152, 153, 154, 155, 180; and spirituals, 150; as a swan song, 143, 156; and Toomer's complicated relationship with race, 141-43; women in, 142. *See also* Toomer, Jean
Carne-Ross, D. S., 242n26
Carr, Helen, 226n12
Catullus, 44, 47-48, 50
Cavell, Stanley, 67
Cavitch, Max, 2, 14
Chasar, Mike, 6
Chaucer, Geoffrey, 50, 234n26; *Canterbury Tales*, 75
Child, Francis, 144
Clark, Suzanne, 114; on Bogan, 125, 127, 130-31
Clark, T. J., 57
Cohen, Michael, 144
Coleridge, Samuel Taylor: preface to *Christabel*, 207-8, 254n2

Index

Collecott, Diana, 243n46
Conover, Roger, 108
Corbière, Tristan, 62; "Épitaphe," 96
Cornford, Frances: "The Watch," 12
Cotter, Joseph, 155
counting, 228–29n47, 229n48
Cox, Sidney, 33
Crane, Hart, 22, 31, 140, 217; "Repose of Rivers," 24–25
Crane, Stephen, 2
Crapsey, Adelaide, 15, 31
Cullen, Countee, 156, 173, 189; *Caroling Dusk*, 192; "Heritage," 151, 249–50n46; "Yet Do I Marvel," 191–92
Culler, Jonathan, 216; *Theory of the Lyric*, 209
cummings, e. e., 91
Cunard, Nancy, 68
Cunningham, J. V., 227
Cureton, Richard, 216
Cushman, Stephen, 19, 256n37

Davie, Donald, 4, 227n21
Davis, Big Boy, 194–200
Davray, Henri D., 238–39n40
Day, John, 239n43; *Parliament of Bees*, 69
"Deep River" (spiritual), 175
Dett, R. Nathaniel: "The Rubenstein Staccato Étude," 190
dialect in poetry, 14, 73, 143, 183, 251n13; Sterling Brown on, 194; Robert Burns's use of, 146, 165; Dunbar's use of, 202; Weldon Johnson on, 166–67; in Toomer's poetry, 248n29
dialect orthography, 13–14
Dickinson, Emily, 131, 132, 207, 244n21, 256–57n46
Dolmetsch, Arnold, 76
Donne, John, 37, 57, 221
Donoghue, Denis, 10, 228–29n47
Doolittle, Hilda. *See* H.D.
Doughty, Charles, 8, 226n7
Dryden, John, 50, 80, 170, 171
Du Bois, W. E. B., 118, 122, 251n11; "Of the Coming of John," 155; *The Souls of Black Folk*, 19, 147, 156, 183, 190
Duffell, Martin, 4, 75, 235n46, 256n36, 257n2

Dunbar, Paul Lawrence, 202; "The Haunted Oak," 202; "Sympathy," 116
DuPlessis, Rachel Blau, 93, 244n14

Eccles, Tasha, 107
Edwards, Brent Hayes, 169, 181–82
Ehlers, Sarah, 226n7, 229n56
Eliot, T. S., 3, 15, 20, 40, 114, 171, 213–14, 236n56; *Ash Wednesday*, 60; Brathwaite on, 204–5; "Burbank with a Baedecker," 67; "The Death of the Duchess," 62; *Ezra Pound: His Metric and Poetry*, 75–76, 78; "The Fire Sermon," 68, 73; *Four Quartets*, 70; gendering of meter in poetry of, 57–67, 69; "The Hollow Men," 75; "Hysteria," 65; "La Figlia che Piange," 66–67, 70; "The Love Song of J. Alfred Prufrock," 60–62, 66, 82–83; on meter, 12, 18, 75–76, 81, 83, 107; and meter as associated with the effeminate, 60–67; meter in works by, 5, 8–9, 28, 56–80; and the metrical vestige, 28, 56, 60, 66–67, 69, 71, 72–73, 75, 78; on Milton, 77–79, 216; *Murder in the Cathedral*, 70; on poetry, 133; "Portrait of a Lady," 62–67, 71, 72–73, 74, 88; Pound's annotations to works by, 62, 69–75; on Pound's meter, 75–76; on Pound's *Ripostes*, 97; *Prufrock and Other Observations*, 57, 66; "Reflections on Vers Libre," 77, 78; on rhythm, 78–79; "Sweeney among the Nightingales," 67, 71; "Sweeney Erect," 67; *The Waste Land*, 13, 20, 57, 58, 60, 64, 65, 67–75, 85, 125, 127, 213; "Whispers of Immortality," 56, 67, 209; women as depicted in poems of, 56–58, 60–68, 72–73
Eliot, Vivienne Haigh-Wood, 67
Elizabethan poetry: Eliot's interest in, 79; metrics of, 209
Elliot, Missy, 109
Empson, William, 53, 164, 215, 250n65
epic tradition: and folk forms, 145–46
Epstein, Josh, 2, 74, 232n99
Esenwein, J. Berg, 230n58

Fabb, Nigel, 75, 236n50
Farr, Florence Emery, 19, 93, 228n39, 238n29

Faulkner, William, 21
Felski, Rita, 110
femininity: and meter, 57-62, 107, 110. *See also* women poets
Fenollosa, Ernest, 228n33, 241n10
Figueroa, John: "Problems of a Writer," 204-5
Finch, Annie: *The Ghost of Meter*, 3
Fletcher, John Gould, 100
Flint, F. S., 1, 8, 228n38, 238n25, 239n40
folk culture: and the lyric, 192-94; as measure of authenticity, 147; in modern genres, 147-48; in Toomer's *Cane*, 142-43, 144-52
Ford, Ford Madox, 9, 32
formalism: and music theory, 76; and New Criticism, 210, 216; in tension with modernism, 5, 10, 15, 16, 216-17; and women poets, 133
Forrest-Thomson, Veronica, 54, 107; on Eliot, 109; and the metrical vestige, 109
Frank, Elizabeth, 132
Frank, Waldo, 137, 139, 140, 183, 247n2
free verse: defenses of, 9-10; Eliot on, 38, 98; Frost on, 31, 33, 36, 43, 56, 81; and H.D., 108; and Douglas Johnson, 120, 122; Weldon Johnson on, 157; and meter, 3, 18, 31, 215; Pound on, 66, 87, 98; and rhythm, 2, 7, 55
Fried, Debra, 5
Friedman, Susan Stanford, 103
Frost, Lesley, 48
Frost, Robert, 3, 4, 7, 20, 21, 24, 98, 157, 233n13; "The Aim Was Song," 44; "Birches," 37-38; blank verse in works by, 38; *A Boy's Will*, 33, 37, 42, 43, 95, 125-26; "Design," 44; "Directive," 53-54; "The Figure a Poem Makes," 33; on free verse, 31, 33, 36, 43, 56, 81, 215; "For Once, Then, Something," 44-45, 49-53; "Home Burial," 38-42; "Hyla Brook," 44; "Into My Own," 126-27; loose iambics of, 31-32, 42, 49; on meter, 33-36; meter in works by, 28, 30-55; and the metrical vestige, 24, 31, 32-34, 42, 44, 52-53, 54-55; "Mowing," 42-43, 44, 50, 51-52, 177, 213; "The Oven Bird," 31, 44; and Pound, 31, 32, 37; on Pound's "Portrait d'une Femme," 94-97; reception of poetry of, 32-33; scansion as practiced by, 30-44; "To Earthward," 43-44; "Tuft of Flowers," 42-43
Frye, Northrop, 209
Fussell, Edwin, 4, 89, 226-27n20

Gaskill, Nicholas, 216
Gates, Henry Louis, Jr., 184
Gautier, Théophile, 40, 96
Gerber, Natalie, 24, 32, 232n107
Gilbert, Sandra, 110
Gilroy, Paul, 28, 137-38, 248n28, 251n74
Gitelman, Lisa, 15-16
Goldsmith, Kenneth, 229n48
Goldstone, Andrew, 225n3
Golston, Michael, 18, 222, 230n58
Gordon, Lyndall, 57-58
Graham, Austin, 240-41n3
Green, Elizabeth Lay, 115; *The Negro in Contemporary American Literature*, 188-89, 190
Green, Fiona, 226n12
Green, Peter, 46
Gregg, Frances, 102
Gregory, Montgomery, 141
Grieder, Josephine, 94
Gross, Harvey, 3, 4, 211
Grossman, Allen, 25, 217
Guest, Edgar, 159
Guest, Edwin: *History of English Rhythm*, 219
Guillory, John, 79, 210, 255n12
Gumbrecht, Hans, 209
Gummere, Francis Barton, 144, 147, 153, 156, 166; *Handbook of Poetics*, 145-46, 230n58

Hale, Emily, 67
Hall, Jason David, 15, 18, 245n34
Halle, Morris, 75, 219, 220-21, 236n50
Hammer, Langdon, 18, 222, 232n108
Hanson, Kristin, 24, 221
Hardy, Thomas, 22-24, 25, 31, 81, 124; "The Darkling Thrush," 112, 245n22; "In a Museum," 23, 24
Harlem Renaissance. *See* New Negro Renaissance poets
Harper, Michael, 188, 193
Harrington, Joseph, 225n7
Hart, Matthew, 115

Index

Hartman, Charles O., 19, 231n92
Hayden, Robert: "Middle Passage," 203
Hayes, Roland, 186-87, 188, 189
H.D., 70, 82, 91, 126, 133, 239n47, 243n46; *HERmione*, 82, 102-5, 107; meter in works by, 108
Hegel, Georg Wilhelm Friedrich, 144, 254n2; *Aesthetics*, 146, 208
hendecasyllabics, 45-46, 235n47; in Frost's "For Once, Then, Something," 44-45, 49-53; Tennyson's parody of, 44-45, 46-49
Henderson, Alice Corbin, 82, 100-101
Henderson, Stephen, 146-47, 194
Herder, Johann Gottfried, 144
Higginson, Thomas Wentworth: *Army Life in a Black Regiment*, 144-45
Hill, Lauryn, 109
Holder, Alan, 3
Holley, Margaret, 256n36
Holmes, Oliver Wendell, 58
Hopkins, Gerard Manley, 157, 168, 171, 234n32, 236n49; and Weldon Johnson's scansion of "Spring and Fall," 159, 160-65; sprung rhythm of, 158, 161, 170
Housman, A. E., 112
Howarth, Peter, 225n6
Hughes, Langston, 115, 123, 183, 184, 187, 192-93; *Fine Clothes to the Jew*, 115; Pound on, 200-201; "Weary Blues," 251n10
Hurston, Zora Neale, 183, 251n11
Huxley, Aldous: *Brave New World*, 237n5; *Crome Yellow*, 68

iambic pentameter, 219-20; in Sterling Brown's poetry, 195; in Elizabeth Barret Browning's poetry, 110; in Eliot's poetry, 60-61; in Frost's poetry, 31-32, 36-37; in twentieth-century poetry, 32
Imagists: on rhythm, 8, 9, 86, 157
Izenberg, Oren, 217, 225n3

Jackson, T. H., 92, 93
Jackson, Virginia, 145, 147, 193, 202, 244n20, 249n39, 256-57n44
Jaji, Tsitsi, 28, 181, 248n28, 251n74
Jarrell, Randall, 40, 234n33
Jarvis, Simon, 22, 232n103, 234n32

Jespersen, Otto, 36, 234n25
Johnson, Barbara, 121
Johnson, Fenton, 190
Johnson, Georgia Douglas, 98, 110-11, 156, 189, 190; artistic environment of, 115; "Black Woman," 119, 121, 122; *Bronze*, 118-21, 139; *Heart of a Woman*, 115, 116, 122, 139; "Heart of a Woman," 116, 118, 119, 122; "I Want to Die While You Love Me," 247n1; "Love's Tendril," 118, 119; meter in works by, 115-23, 131, 182; and the metrical vestige, 119, 120, 121-22, 123; "Moods," 120; "Motherhood," 119; and the New Negro Renaissance, 114, 115, 120; "The Ordeal," 122-23; "The Passing of the Ex-Slave," 135, 151; race as theme in poetry of, 115, 119-23; reception of poetry of, 119; rhythm in poetry of, 123; Tennyson as influence on, 116-19, 120; Jean Toomer on, 139, 147, 154; "To Samuel Coleridge Taylor," 121
Johnson, James Weldon, 28, 115, 135-36, 143, 147, 181, 187, 199; on African American poetics, 156-57; *Autobiography of an Ex-Colored Man*, 136-38, 167-69; *Book of American Negro Poetry*, 182; Sterling Brown on, 170-71; and Brown's *Outline* for Johnson's book, 182, 187-92; "Creation," 169; on the double audience, 136, 137-38, 186-87; *God's Trombones*, 167, 169, 170, 175; and Hopkins's "Spring and Fall," 157, 159, 160-65, 166-67; "Lift Every Voice and Sing," 179, 185-86; meter in works by, 172-80; and the metrical vestige, 179-80; metrics and satire in, 138, 170-71; "O Black and Unknown Bards," 173; reception of poetry of, 169-70; on rhythm, 158-67; rhythm in works by, 167-80; I. A. Richards as influence on, 158; "Saint Peter Relates an Incident of the Resurrection Day," 138, 170-80, 186
Joyce, James, 14, 231n80; *Portrait of the Artist as a Young Man*, 58-59; *Ulysses*, 16-17

Kane, Brian, 20
Kappeler, Erin, 145, 225n7
Kearney, Douglas, 140

Kearns, Katherine, 51, 234n34
Keats, John, 34, 116, 191, 201; "La Belle Dame sans Merci," 99, 122, 125
Kenner, Hugh, 1, 10, 89, 133-34, 242n26
Kerlin, R. T., 146, 156, 166; *Negro Poets and Their Poems*, 193
Keyser, Samuel J., 219, 220-21
Kiparsky, Paul, 220, 221, 257n3
kitsch: and modern poetry, 14
Kittler, Friedrich, 17, 143, 202-3
Koestenbaum, Wayne, 70
Krauss, Rosalind, 40
Kutzinski, Vera, 141, 248n19

Laforgue, Jules, 58, 62, 96, 99
Laity, Cassandra, 101-2, 239n47
Lanier, Sidney, 35, 190, 229-30n58; *Science of English Verse*, 11
Lawrence, D. H.: "The Piano," 108
Leavis, F. R., 108
Lehman, Rob, 67, 216, 237n1, 238n34
Lerner, Ben, 217, 225n3, 256-57n46
Levine, Caroline, 216
Levy, Amy, 115
Lewis, C. S., 5
Lewis, David Levering, 248n19
Lindsay, Vachel, 171, 181, 196; *The Congo*, 182
Liveright, Horace, 139
Locke, Alain, 115, 156
Longfellow, Henry Wadsworth, 7, 190; *Evangeline*, 7; *Hiawatha*, 10, 52; "My Lost Youth," 127; "The Wreck of the Hesperus," 202
Lowell, Amy, 9, 20, 32, 133; Pound's critique of, 99-100; on rhythm, 208
Lowell, Robert, 27
Loy, Mina, 3, 70, 82, 130, 239n47; *Anglo-Mongrels and the Rose*, 109; "Apology for Genius," 108-9; meter in works by, 108-9; Pound on, 99, 100
Lynen, John, 233n13
lyric, 146-47, 209-10, 249n39; and folk culture, 192-94; and form, 207
Lyric Theory Reader (Jackson and Prins), 210

Macaulay, Thomas, 144
MacLeish, Archibald: "Ars Poetica," 109
Manson, Michael, 184, 192, 193

Mao, Doug, 15, 59, 212
Margetson, George Reginald, 175; "Fledgling Bard and the Poetry Society," 190-91
Markovits, Stefanie, 42
Marsden, Dora, 99
Martin, Meredith, 10, 144, 163, 168, 227n30; on Robert Bridges, 3, 10, 233n2; on Rupert Brooke, 13; on English meter, 5, 6-7, 183-84; on Pound, 82, 221-22; *The Rise and Fall of Meter*, 3
Marvell, Andrew, 239n42; "To His Coy Mistress," 69
Masefield, John, 9
Masters, Edgar Lee, 185; *Spoon River Anthology*, 12-13, 147
Mayor, Joseph, 11
McDonald, Gail, 58, 59, 84-85
McGill, Meredith, 113
McKay, Claude, 156, 173; "Harlem Dancer," 151
Meredith, William: "About Poetry, II: Iambic Feet Considered as Honorable Scars," 3-4
Merrill, James, 27, 222
meter: aesthetic significance of, 3; as audile technique, 17-18, 80, 81-82; and free verse, 18, 31; gendering of, 57-67, 69, 107, 110; as metronomic, 3, 8, 6-14, 17, 83, 110; in modern poetics, 2-3, 7, 110; parody of, 8-9; persistence of, 1, 6; as practiced by women poets, 107-11; and print culture, 19-20; and rhythm, 11, 57; as satire, 65, 66, 67; satires of, 13, 40, 107. *See also* accentual-syllabic meter; hendecasyllabics; iambic pentameter; scansion; *and names of individual poets*
metrical vestige, 1-6, 13, 14, 27, 57, 59, 107, 207; in African American poetry, 201-2, 205-6; in Bogan's poetry, 124, 131; in Sterling Brown's poetry, 182, 201-2; in Eliot's poetry, 28, 56, 60, 66-67, 69, 71, 72-73, 75, 78; in Frost's poetry, 24, 31, 32-34, 42, 44, 52-53, 54-55; in Douglas Johnson's poetry, 119, 120, 121-22; in Weldon Johnson's poetry, 179-80; as manifested in modern poetry, 21-29, 60; in Marianne Moore's poetry, 215; and the New Negro Renaissance poets, 135; Pound's perspective on, 56; in Pound's

poetry, 81-82, 84, 85, 88, 89, 96-97, 104, 106; and race, 203-4; in Teasdale's poetry, 114; in Toomer's poetry, 137, 139, 150, 152; and women poets, 109, 110, 114

Mill, John Stuart, 80

Millay, Edna St. Vincent, 5, 27, 110, 111, 124, 127, 133-34, 158, 185, 189; criticized as sentimental, 108; "First Fig," 134; Weldon Johnson on, 158-59

Milton, John, 12, 95, 96; Eliot on, 77-79, 216; "L'Allegro," 24; *Paradise Lost*, 73, 77, 78

modernist poetry: changing status of meter in, 2-3, 7, 110; female figures in, 58, 107-11; as revolt against effeminacy, 56-57. *See also names of individual poets*

Moffatt, Adelaide, 62

Monroe, Harriet, 83, 84, 99, 108, 229n56, 230n58; on meter, 9-10, 11-12, 32, 35-36, 58, 169; on Pound's *Cantos*, 7-8; on rhythm, 208-9; on Teasdale, 111, 112-13

Moody, William Vaughn, 157

Moore, Marianne, 3, 82, 214, 215; Pound on, 99

Morrisette, Noelle, 136, 169-70

Mullen, Harryette, 135, 136

Munson, Gorham, 247n2

Murphy, James, 44

music: and Sterling Brown's poetics, 190-203; and ideas of blackness, 28, 136, 166, 181, 183, 248n26; and Weldon Johnson's poetics, 169-70, 175, 179; and poetry, 1-2, 76, 93, 105, 150, 217; and scansion, 11, 35-36, 83, 214, 223, 229n58

Napolin, Julie Beth, 20-21

Native American songs, 252-53n37

Negro Caravan, The (Brown, Davis, and Lee), 183

Newcomb, John Timberman, 225n6

New Criticism: and discourse on meter, 29, 209, 210-11, 212-13, 215-16

New Negro Renaissance poets, 28, 111, 114, 115, 120; aesthetic practices in, 155; and Anglo-American poetics, 181-82, 184; and the metrical vestige, 135; prosody of, 135-38, 181. *See also* Johnson,

Georgia Douglas; Johnson, James Weldon; Toomer, Jean

Nicholls, David, 184-85

Nicholls, Peter, 61

Niedecker, Lorine, 134

Nielsen, Aldon, 138

North, Michael, 57, 183, 247n2, 251n13

Nowlin, Michael, 115, 156-57

Nurhussein, Nadia, 13-14, 143, 202, 248n29

Ochoa Gautier, Ana María, 143, 248n26

Omond, T. S., 229n52; *English Metrists*, 13

Parker, Dorothy, 124

Parrish, Steven, 254n2

passing, rhetoric of: among the New Negro Renaissance poets, 28, 135-36

Pater, Walter, 240-41n3

Patmore, Coventry, 208, 242-43n42, 254n2

Perloff, Marjorie, 4, 227n21

Picasso, Pablo, 57

Pinsky, Robert, 38

Plantation school poets, 196, 253n60

Poe, Edgar Allan, 30, 157, 190

Poirier, Richard, 32, 50, 52, 233n13, 235n43

Poovey, Mary, 209

Pope, Alexander, 58, 65, 69, 170, 171, 215, 230n67; "Epistle to Dr. Arbuthnot," 192; *The Rape of the Lock*, 68

Pound, Ezra, 2, 6, 7, 20, 31, 40, 114, 171, 181, 204, 213-14, 228n38, 241n10; "Against Form," 89; anima figures in life and poetry of, 82, 90-93, 103; "Apparuit," 91, 93; "Au Salon," 88; Canto 81, 1, 8; Canto 98, 222; Canto 116, 137; *The Cantos*, 85-87, 91, 103, 137, 221-22, 241-42n26; *Canzoni*, 88-89; and Cavalcanti, 18, 86; *A Draft of XVI Cantos*, 86; as Eliot's adviser and editor, 62, 68-77, 100; Eliot's judgment of *Ripostes*, 97; "Envoi," 84-85, 91; "Fodder," 84; on free verse, 66, 87, 98; on Frost, 32; Frost's critique of "Portrait d'une Femme," 94-97; and the gendering of meter, 58, 59-60; in H.D.'s *HERmione*, 102-5; *Hilda's Book*, 88, 89, 91, 96, 103-4; "The House of Splendour," 88-89; on Langston Hughes, 200-201; *Hugh Selwyn Mauberly*, 66, 84-85, 88; "Leviora," 89; "Medallion," 84-85, 214;

Pound, Ezra (*cont.*)
 on meter, 7, 8, 12, 82-87, 107; meter in works by, 4-5, 8, 10, 18, 28, 81-106; and the metrical vestige, 56, 81-82, 84, 85, 88, 89, 96-97, 104, 106; and modern prosodic culture, 56; Harriet Monroe on, 7-8; *The New Age*, 97; "An Object," 92; "Pan Is Dead," 98-99; *Personae*, 77; "Phasellus Ille," 92, 93; "Portrait d'une Femme," 92-98, 242n34; "Quies," 92; "Redondillas," 89-90; *Ripostes*, 88, 91, 92, 97, 98, 222; "The Seafarer," 52; "Swinburne: A Critique," 82; "Thus Ides Till," 91; "Treatise on Meter," 83; "Und Drang," 88, 89; "Ur-Cantos," 85-86, 222; and Victorian meter, 82-83, 87; "Villanelle: The Psychological Hour," 59; "A Virginal," 90, 91-92, 93; women as depicted in poetry of, 88-89, 90-98; on women poets, 99-100
Preston, Carrie, 105
Princeton Prosody Archive, 6, 10, 208, 209
Prins, Yopie, 9, 15, 19, 101, 103, 235n46; "Victorian Meters," 2-3; *Victorian Sappho*, 2-3
prosodic training, 7, 11-12, 17-19, 31-32, 87, 158, 163, 210
prosody, twentieth-century: and earlier periods, 4-6; Weldon Johnson on, 157-58; and race, 135, 190; and Victorian theories of prosody, 7, 15, 58, 76. *See also* meter; metrical vestige; rhythm; scansion; *and names of individual poets*
Psalm 137, 186-87

Rainey, Ma, 115, 194
Ramazani, Jahan, 78
Ransom, John Crowe, 211-12
Ray, Man: *Objet à détruire*, 25, 26
Reed, Anthony, 136, 140
resonance, 20
rhythm, 54-55; Eliot on, 78-79; and free verse, 2, 7; in Douglas Johnson's poetry, 123; Weldon Johnson on, 158-67; in Weldon Johnson's poetry, 167-80; modern theories of, 83-84; and poetry criticism, 207-9, 217; and race, 136-37; racialization of, 28, 146-47, 181-82, 183-84. *See also* meter

Rich, Adrienne, 134
Richards, I. A.: on Hopkins's "Spring and Fall," 159, 163-64; as influence on Weldon Johnson, 158; on meter, 212-13; *Practical Criticism*, 19-20, 158-61, 163; *Principles of Literary Criticism*, 212; on women poets, 108
Roberts, Mary Eleanor, 230n58
Robinson, E. A., 157, 225n6; "Miniver Cheevy," 12; "Oh, for a Poet," 12
Roethke, Theodore: on Bogan, 130; on women poets, 123-24
Ronda, Margaret, 202
Rossetti, D. G., 70, 239n47
Rudy, Jason, 15

Saintsbury, George, 6, 11, 20, 211, 227n30
Sandburg, Carl, 185
Sapphic stanzas, 8, 102; in Pound's poetry, 91, 100, 102, 242n26; in Teasdale's poetry, 112
Sappho, 100
satire and meter, 13, 40; in Eliot, 65, 66, 67-69; in Weldon Johnson, 138, 170-71
scansion, 257n2; of Sterling Brown's poetry, 199-200; as counting, 10, 228-29n47, 229n48; and free verse, 10, 18; Frost's practice of, 20, 30-44, 223; of Hopkins's "Spring and All," 159-65; Weldon Johnson on, 158, 169, 173; of Weldon Johnson's poetry, 174-77; mechanized, 15; and metrical notation, 8, 211, 219-23; of Pound's poetry, 85, 86, 91; of Tennyson's poetry, 117. *See also* meter
Scarry, Elaine, 14
Schaeffer, Pierre, 20
Senghor, Leopold, 169, 181
"sentence sound": in Frost's poetry, 21, 34, 36, 42
Shakespear, Dorothy, 88
Shakespear, Olivia, 88
Shakespeare, William, 96; *Macbeth*, 95; meter in works by, 35-36; *The Tempest*, 20-21
Shaw, George Bernard: *Pygmalion*, 20
Shelley, Percy Bysshe, 83
Sider, Justin, 19, 148
Silkin, Jon, 227n24
Skinner, B. F., 21, 232n101

Index

Smith, Henry, 213
Snell, Ada, 15
sonnet: political history of, 5
Sounding Modernism, 17
sound studies, 14-15
Sowards, Robin, 219
Spencer, Anne, 115
spirituals, 145, 150
Stallings, A. E., 134
Steele, Joshua, 35
Steele, Timothy: *Missing Measures*, 3
Stepto, Robert, 194, 195, 196
Sterne, Jonathan, 17
Stevens, Wallace, 4, 227n21, 232n107, 234n32
Stewart, Susan, 144, 222
Stowe, David, 185
Sullivan, Hannah, 69, 75
Swift, Jonathan, 171; "Lady's Dressing Room," 68
Swinburne, Algernon Charles, 19, 82, 83, 102, 236n56; and H.D., 105; "Itylus," 104
Symons, Arthur, 131-32, 190
Synge, J. M., 191
Syrinx, myth of: in Bogan's poetry, 129; in Pound's "Pan Is Dead," 99; in Teasdale's poetry, 112

Talbot, John, 49
Tarlinskaja, Marina, 234n26
Tate, Allen, 24, 132, 133, 232n108
Tate, Claudia, 119, 123
Taupin, René, 238n25
Taylor, Dennis, 23-24
Teasdale, Sara, 28, 100, 110-11, 124, 245n22; "The Carpenter's Son," 112; "A Castilian Song," 112; "Mary Trevor's Sampler," 113-14; meter in works by, 111-14, 131; and the metrical vestige, 114; Harriet Monroe on, 111, 112-13; reception of poetry of, 113; and revisions to her own work, 112-13; *Rivers to the Sea*, 111-12, 113; Sappho as influence on, 111-12
Tennyson, Alfred, Lord, 83, 235n46; "Break, Break, Break," 116-17; "Hendecasyllabics," 44-45, 46-49; *In Memoriam*, 77-78; and Georgia Douglas Johnson, 116-19; "Locksley Hall Sixty Years After," 90; recitation by, 9; "To Virgil," 118

Thomas, Lorenzo, 182-83
Thurman, Wallace, 187, 192-93; *Infants of the Spring*, 184
Tiffany, Daniel, 14
Tolson, Melvin, 115, 185; "Dark Symphony," 183
Toomer, Jean, 28, 115, 123, 181, 193, 248n19, 247n2; and folk songs, 139-40, 142-43, 248n28; meter in works by, 28, 137, 138-39, 150-52. See also *Cane*
Trager, George, 213
Tsur, Reuven, 221
Tucker, Herbert, 216, 226n7
Turbyfill, Mark, 111

Understanding Poetry (Brooks and Warren), 211

variable foot, 9
Vendler, Helen, 204
Victorian prosody: and modern poetics, 7, 15, 58, 76; Pound's ambivalence toward, 82-83, 87. *See also* Tennyson, Alfred, Lord
Virgil, 89, 102, 118

Walcott, Derek, 31, 204
Walker, Cheryl, 124, 134
Warren, Robert Penn, 211
Washington, Mary Helen, 5
Weaver, Harriet Shaw, 99
Webster, John, 57
Wellek, Rene, 211
Wesling, Donald, 210-11, 216, 242n41, 254n2, 256n37
Wheeler, Lesley, 131, 244n14
Whitman, Walt, 7, 9, 58, 90, 147, 208, 254n2; "When Lilacs Last in the Dooryard Bloom'd," 31
Whitworth, Michael, 226n12
Williams, Carolyn, 8, 228n37
Williams, Raymond, 1
Williams, R. John, 227-28n33, 241n10
Williams, William Carlos, 9, 10, 20, 101, 204, 231n92, 256n37; *Spring and All*, 138
Wilson, Edmund, 62, 238n25
Wiman, Christian, 81
Wimsatt, W. K., 213
Winters, Yvor, 18, 111, 216

women poets, 107; Eliot on, 243n46; meter as practiced by, 107-11; and the metrical vestige, 109, 110, 114; Pound on, 99-100; Roethke on, 123-24; stereotyping of, 110, 123-24. *See also* Bogan, Louise; Browning, Elizabeth Barrett; H.D.; Johnson, Georgia Douglas; Loy, Mina; Millay, Edna St. Vincent; Teasdale, Sara

Woods, Michael, 214

Woolf, Virginia, 9, 56, 59

Wordsworth, William, 98, 144, 190-91; *Lyrical Ballads*, 193; "Nuns fret Not," 91; Pound's critique of, 85-86; "Tintern Abbey," 242n41; "The World Is Too Much with Us," 53

Work, John Wesley, 249n45

Wylie, Elinor, 124

Yeats, William Butler, 17, 66, 93, 114, 132, 213-14, 228n39, 242n32; "An Irish Airman Foresees His Death," 22; "The Lake Isle of Innisfree," 127, 246n57; meter in works by, 22, 217; Pound on, 100; reading style of, 9; "The Second Coming," 126, 127; "To Some I Have Talked with by the Fire," 217

Youmans, Gilbert, 257n3

Zellinger, Elissa, 110

Ziff, Larzer, 10-11, 237n9

Zukofsky, Louis, 134

www.ingramcontent.com/pod-product-compliance
Lightning Source LLC
Chambersburg PA
CBHW030119240426
43673CB00041B/1330